Croner's A–Z Essential Health and

Written by a panel of Health and Safety experts and practitioners.

Consultant Editor: Alison Millward MIOSH, RSP, Health and Safety Advisor

CRONER ⓒ CCH

Croner.CCH Group Ltd
145 London Road
Kingston upon Thames
Surrey KT2 6SR
Tel: 020 8547 3333
Fax: 020 8547 2637
www.croner.cch.co.uk

Published by
Croner.CCH Group Ltd
145 London Road
Kingston upon Thames
Surrey KT2 6SR
Tel: 020 8547 3333

First published July 2000

Although great care has been taken in the compilation and preparation of this book to ensure accuracy, the publishers cannot in any circumstances accept responsibility for any errors or omissions.

Readers of this book should be aware that only Acts of Parliament and Statutory Instruments have the force of law and that only the courts can authoritatively interpret the law.

British Library cataloguing in Publication Data. A CIP Catalogue Record for this book is available from the British Library

ISBN 1 85524 609 0

Printed by Creative Print and Design, Wales

CONTRIBUTORS

Alison Millward MIOSH, RSP
Health and Safety Advisor

Geoffrey Laycock BSc, FIOSH, FRSH, MErgS, RSP
Principal Consultant, The Otter Consultancy

Jane Brown MIOSH, RSP, Lic.IPD
Personnel Health and Safety Consultants

Louisa Johnstone BSc (Hons)
Freelance Health and Safety Writer

Stephen King BSc (Eng), FIOSH, Dip SM, MIIRSM, MRSH, RSP
Director, Personnel Health and Safety Consultants Ltd

Sarah Tullett MIOSH, CBiol, MI Biol, MRSH
Health and Safety Advisor, The Children's Trust

Contents

Introduction

A

B

C

G

H

I

L

M

S

T

U

V

W

Y

Appendices

Index

Introduction

Health and Safety Law

Overview

Health and safety is of prime importance in the workplace. The consequences of inattention to health and safety measures are severe, possibly resulting in serious injury, illness or death. The essence of health and safety is to protect people who may be affected by the work that is being done, either by them, or by those around them. It is often said that ensuring safety at work is just common sense, and in many ways it is. However, we need a little more than common sense and moral guidance to maintain health and safety at work. Legislation gives us this guidance, along with sanctions to ensure that it is complied with. Legislation is drawn up, debated and agreed by our elected representatives. Therefore, in many cases, if the underlying principle of looking after people is considered it is more likely that the spirit of these laws is adhered to — and this reinforces the point that health and safety is common sense. The main issues regarding health and safety legislation will be outlined here, but each section contains the necessary information to follow the path from the general issues to the specific requirements of the relevant legislation.

Legislation

General introduction to UK law

Laws are intended to guide social conduct and provide sanctions to ensure their compliance. UK law is divided into criminal and civil law.

Criminal law deals with offences against the State, whereas civil law settles disputes between two individuals or organisations. There are different courts and procedures for criminal and civil cases. Both become involved in the field of health and safety at work.

There are two sources of law: statute law (legislation) and common law. Statute law relates to both criminal and civil proceedings and consists of Acts of Parliament and their associated Statutory Instruments (eg Regulations and Orders). The statutes specify criminal offences which are punishable by a fine and/or imprisonment. The principle of the sanctions of a criminal law case is to deter both the perpetrator from repetition and society as a whole from considering the criminal action as acceptable behaviour. Usually the burden of proof is on the prosecution (the State) who must show that the proof is beyond reasonable doubt.

Common law, rather than being laid down by Parliament, has traditionally grown up over the centuries: principles derived from judgments made in earlier cases create binding precedents, but there is scope for the courts to interpret such precedents in the light of changing circumstances. Precedents established in civil courts apply in both criminal and civil courts. The branches of civil law applicable to health and safety at work are "contract", "employment law" and "tort". A tort is a "civil wrong" whereby one party fails to fulfil a duty of care and causes harm to the person, property, reputation or economic interests of another. The torts most relevant to health and safety are "negligence" and "breach of statutory duty". Therefore, failure to comply with certain statutory requirements may be actionable under civil law as well as criminal law. However, the remedies as a result of a civil case are to restore the injured party to the situation they were at before the damage occurred, usually by financial means, and possibly with a little extra to compensate for "pain and suffering"; it is not punitive but restorative. The standard of proof in a civil case is lower than in a criminal case as it is about the resolution of a dispute and is based on the balance of probabilities.

Making law

A law is made by an Act of Parliament. Acts of Parliament are the statutes which lay down fundamental principles and enable a Government department to make more detailed Statutory Instruments (eg Regulations). The creation of new Acts involves both Houses of Parliament and is a formal procedure during which a proposal or "Bill" is carefully examined and, if necessary, amended — Bills may be introduced by either the Government or by back-benchers (Private Members' Bill).

Since the law-making process from Bill through to Act is an involved and time-intensive procedure, many Acts allow for "delegated legislation" known as Regulations. The enabling Act will lay down the general provisions and permit the relevant Secretary of State to draft and publish delegated (sometimes known as subordinate) legislation. These Regulations do not have to pass through all the processes that an Act does and are therefore quicker and easier to issue in response to changes.

Note: Law can only be enacted by Parliament and interpreted in a court of law. A common misapprehension is to wrongly attribute the power of making law to the agencies that advise on, or prepare legislation, such as the Health and Safety Commission (HSC) or the Health and Safety Executive (HSE) — only Parliament has this power. It is also worth noting that England, Scotland and Northern Ireland do not have entirely codified legal systems.

The law courts

Law is decided in the courts and only in the courts. In the instance of Statutes, Parliament is the lawgiver and the Judges cannot change them. They do, however, "interpret" what is meant by the statute in a particular circumstance.

In the instance of civil law, this is "made" by the judiciary deciding on cases presented before them. Case law is built up from precedents, ie previous decisions. The decisions of a "superior" court are binding on a lower court and similarly the decisions of a lower court can be overturned by a superior one. For civil and criminal cases the hierarchy is as follows.

Civil cases	Criminal cases
6. The European Court of Justice	6. The European Court of Justice
5. The House of Lords	5. The House of Lords
4. The Court of Appeal	4. The Court of Appeal
3. Divisional/High Court	3. Divisional/High Court
2. County Court	2. Crown Court
1. Magistrates' Court	1. Magistrates' Court

For civil cases regarding employment law, the Employment Appeal Tribunal is bound by the Court of Appeal and the House of Lords and its decisions bind Industrial Tribunals (on matters of law).

EC legislation

European Community legislation takes three forms: Regulations, which are binding on Member States; Directives, which require implementation within the laws of the Member States; and Decisions, which are made by the Council of Europe regarding compliance with EC treaties on specific matters. EC legislation usually starts with the EC Commission and proceeds to the Council of the European Community which consults with the Economic and Social Committee and the European Parliament, with the aim of achieving a common position on the proposal. The proposal is then adopted as a Regulation or Directive which places an obligation on Member States to adopt it within their legislation. It is worth noting that reference to a Directive is not useful except to indicate the direction that English law will take when it is adopted.

Legislation adopted by the Council is published in the *Official Journal (of the EC)*.

Primary Health and Safety Legislation

Prior to the early 1970s health and safety legislation was prescriptive in nature. Thus, to control a particular risk, eg injuries from spinning machines, very restrictive and exact legislation had to be drafted. This meant that every time a new process or type of machinery was developed, legislation had to be developed to control the risks. This usually only occurred after a disaster took place or an incident so incensed a large group of the population that something was done about it. As a result there was much confusing and conflicting legislation.

This was seen as such a barrier to maintaining good worker welfare and good business that a committee, chaired by Lord Robens, was set up to investigate. The result was the development of an Act of Parliament, the **Health and Safety at Work, etc Act 1974** (HSW Act). This HSW Act is an "umbrella" designed to cover all of the health and safety issues at work. The Act provides the general principles to ensure the good health, safety and welfare of those at work and the health and safety of those affected by it. It does not attempt to be specific in its requirements, but gives general duties to both employers and employees. (See the section on the *Health and Safety at Work, etc Act* later.)

As a result of the general nature of this Act, it has the provision to allow for subordinate legislation to be made under it, eg Regulations which give more detailed guidance to "flesh out" the principles of the performance requirements given by the general duties. There are a number of these Regulations, but all of them take their strength from HSW Act. However, even these Regulations have their limitations and these limitations are solved by non-legislative guidance.

Non-legislative Guidance

As has been mentioned above, the prime source of law in the UK consists of Acts of Parliament. An Act may confer on a Minister the power to make or amend additional law by means of Regulations. In many cases these Acts and Regulations set out the performance requirements, eg the general requirements of ss.2 and 3 of the HSW Act, without giving much guidance as to the method of achieving them. The purpose of this is to ensure that the Act or Regulations do not have requirements that could become obsolete, by virtue of increasing knowledge or technology, thus reducing the necessity of frequent revisions.

Various sources can be investigated to gain the required information — either clarification of the statutory requirement (or intent) or the "best practice" method for achieving that end.

The sources of information and guidance include:
* Approved Codes of Practice (ACOPs)
* British Standards
* Guidance Notes
* industry-wide codes of practice (eg those from the IEE)
* Industrial Sector Codes of Practice
* industrial "best practice" publications
* journals
* magazines
* publications such as this.

These different sources have varying status depending on their publisher. None have the legal status in a court of law that an Act or Regulation has, but any can be used to show that there is *prima facie* (at first sight) evidence of negligence through non-observance of their guidance.

Approved Codes of Practice

To provide the guidance mentioned above, Parliament has authorised a number of organisations to issue Codes of Practice. These do not have the force of law, but can be taken into consideration by the Courts and Employment Tribunals as appropriate. With respect to health and safety codes of practice, s.16 of the HSW

Act, gives the HSC the power to approve and issue codes of practice to assist in the application of the general duties sections (ss. 2–7) of this Act or any other health and safety Regulations or existing statutory provisions.

In addition, the HSC is empowered to authorise codes drawn up by other organisations, such as British Standards. The HSC must obtain the consent of the Secretary of State before it can approve a code of practice, but before the final draft is presented it must be issued for public comment, usually through professional bodies and employer associations and other Government departments. The purpose of the public comment is to ensure that the widest aspects of "best practice" are obtained, and that the guidance is actually practicable and reasonable.

Where a person (or organisation) has failed to comply with the requirements of an ACOP, this does not automatically render them liable either criminally or civilly. However, in criminal proceedings if someone is alleged to have committed an offence for which an ACOP is in force, the provisions of that code are admissible as evidence. A failure to observe the ACOP constitutes a proof of the breach of duty, or contravention of the Regulations or statutory provision, unless the accused can show that the system of work used instead to comply with the duty of care was as effective (or more so) than that given in the ACOP.

British Standards

The HSC can approve British Standards to act as ACOPs. Not all British Standards are approved, but some are, notably BS 7671: *Requirements for Electrical Installations* (also known as the IEE Wiring Regulations 16th Edition). Where a British Standard is not an ACOP, it may taken as a good indication of national "best practice" and can be used as such in court or at a tribunal.

Guidance notes

Through the HSE, the HSC issue many guidance papers to give further advice, guidance and suggestions. An example of some of the series issued are: Chemical Series (CS), Environmental Hygiene (EH), General Series (GS), Medical Series (MS), Plant and Machinery (PM), Guidance papers in numerical series (HSG).

These Guidance Notes have no legal standing but they can be used to indicate the state of current knowledge — more so than articles in journals, magazines or the popular press, even though these can also be used for this purpose. Case law shows that the Courts will regard Guidance Notes to be indications of industrial "best practice" and these have formed key aspects of prosecutions.

Industrial Codes of Practice

Many industries, professional bodies, trades unions and employer's associations issue their own codes of practice and guidance papers. Again these have no legal standing, but can be used — as with the HSE Guidance Notes — as an indication of the state of current knowledge in an industrial sector and best practice. However, in some cases, due in part to the restricted application of these papers, there is a reluctance to accept them as a general indication of best practice. Care must be taken when applying the principles in these papers, to ensure that they are directly applicable in a particular case.

Health and Safety Management

Systems

In any size of organisation, from sole trader to self-employed to a multi-national organisation, safety will form some part of the system of management. What is good to remember, and indeed forms part of the requirements of both the HSW Act and the **Management of Health and Safety at Work Regulations 1999**, is the need to more formally consider the safety management system. The larger the organisation the more important it is to have formal systems. However, in smaller organisations, the pressures of other aspects of running the business are quite likely to cause the health and safety considerations to slip from memory and be missed if there is not some system present to keep them there. The system can be as simple as a series of diary entries to remind you to do or check something, or a more formalised process for monitoring and auditing the safety performance of your organisation — however large or small.

The most basic safety system involves four aspects:
- policy
- organisation
- planning and implementation
- monitoring and review.

There is a requirement for a health and safety policy in all businesses, the only difference is that in small organisations, ie those with fewer than five employees, it does not need to be written down (although it is good practice to do so). In reality, the safety policy is just a statement of fact that the organisation will work safely. Work pressures and human nature will probably mean that the health and safety policy is sidelined unless someone is made responsible and accountable for it.

Organisation

The health and safety organisation is the means by which people within a business can determine not only what they are responsible for, but also who to contact to deal with a particular issue. To do this requires the identification of two areas: which responsibilities need to be allocated and who should be made accountable for those responsibilities.

The first will best be identified through the risk assessment process and by reference to this publication. The accountabilities will best be determined by considering the managerial structure of the organisation.

6

It is not reasonable to make someone responsible for something unless they have the authority to carry it out. All too often a senior manager will "delegate" without passing over the authority, thus making the task almost impossible. Similarly, the resources must be available to carry out the work. It is a perfectly reasonable business process to weigh up all aspects of a decision; however, if health and safety is compromised by that decision then the person responsible must be aware of the personal consequences as embodied within s.37 of the HSW Act. The two other areas of organisation that are important are the means to monitor the compliance — both with the internal policy and also with the legislative requirements — and the means of communication between those with responsibility for planning and those with responsibility for carrying out health and safety duties.

Human factors

Accidents are caused by people, not "things". The costs of incidents at work are high and frequently higher than is understood. For every £1 an incident causes industry in direct costs, for repairs, absent staff cover, etc, there can be around £11 and sometimes as much as £30 in indirect costs, such as higher insurance premiums, loss of business, etc. Because of this, if we do not address human factors, incidents and their resultant costs are likely to cause severe difficulties for businesses.

Developing a safety culture is one way to stem the leak of profits. Most people will work safely provided they have a safe system of work, adequate equipment and adequate maintenance of that equipment. If employees are made aware of the risks in their job, then they are more likely to work safely — thus reducing problems. This is one of the benefits of adequate instruction, information and training as required by the legislation. The side effect is an improvement in the profitability of the organisation.

A particular factor increasing the likelihood of accidents is lack of concentration. These days the need to make the workforce as efficient as possible can be counterproductive as it may cause overloading of the worker. The stress that this causes is fast being recognised as a serious and unacceptable work condition. Litigation relating to stress-related issues is starting to make an impact on many organisations.

As well as work-related issues, personal problems can also result in lower levels of concentration at the workplace. On the one hand the employer should not be responsible for the private life of the worker, but on the other the private life of the worker will inevitably intrude into their work. Many organisations are now starting to take an interest in the welfare of their staff both at and away from the workplace. This can greatly assist in the efficiency of the organisation; however, a reasonable balance must be struck and both the organisation and employees must be happy with the level of interest taken in their personal lives.

Planning and implementation

Good safety within an organisation does not just occur, it needs to be planned. The basis for this planning is the health and safety policy. The first step to planning good health and safety performance is to identify the needs that are required to carry out the intent of the policy.

To ensure that the intents are carried out, the best technique is to set goals or targets along with timetables for their achievement. The timetable must be reasonably achievable otherwise despondency will prevent it even being started, but it must be understood that in many cases the principle timetable is set by legislation.

Once the policy and the organisation is in place, the risks identified by the risk assessments can be prioritised and the controls put in place. Initially, due to constraints, these controls are likely to be reactive, ie putting right problems which exist. However, with developing experience and policy more proactive controls will be possible. Documentation may seem to be excessively bureaucratic, but it is important so that everyone knows what is required and how it is achieved — ie what they have to do.

Communication

The health and safety documentation, ie the policy and the means of achieving it, forms the first part of communication between employer and employee. The attitude of the workforce has the greatest impact on safety, and the attitude of the management has the greatest impact on the workforce. Thus an effective means of communication between both is probably the greatest key to effective health and safety within an organisation. One of the most effective ways of achieving this is through safety committees (see *Safety Committees* later).

As well as through direct communication, the safety attitude of an organisation may be positively promoted by regular "reminders". These take many forms, such as:

- health promotion and safety campaigns on specific issues
- information posters
- internal newsletters
- the inclusion of health and safety issues during departmental meetings
- the visible involvement of senior management in health and safety issues — particularly their compliance with health and safety rules.

None of these can work in isolation, but together they form an effective part of a health and safety awareness and attitude process which is all part of good health and safety management.

Monitoring and review

There are two main types of monitoring systems: proactive and reactive. Proactive monitoring measures the level of achievement and levels of compliance. Reactive monitoring measures the failures, ie the number of incidents. Reactive monitoring is often the most common as it is sometimes the easiest to see; however, this is not an ideal method, as it is a measure of failure, not achievement. Research has shown that there is great benefit in monitoring schemes where the workforce set their own targets as they are more likely to "buy into" the scheme.

One management technique that appears seductively easy is the use of some form of reward for good health and safety. The encouragement of a positive attitude may at first sight seem beneficial. However, any system of reward which is based on reported figures, such as the number of incidents in a department, does not encourage good health and safety as it encourages under-reporting. Reward schemes can work, but great care must be taken over the criteria used to gauge them.

No system is perfect and there will always be changes in the work. It is therefore necessary to regularly check and review the policy, to ensure that the systems and their implementation are still relevant and valid. A particularly useful tool is auditing. A health and safety audit can check:

- the components of a system
- the adequacy of these components
- the compliance of the workforce and its managers
- that the current system is achievable and does not place an unacceptable burden on managers.

The result of the audit establishes the level of compliance with the policy and highlights areas for improvement and priorities for action.

Conclusion

In this introduction the different aspects of health and safety law and management have been outlined. The best way to approach this is to remember the underlying principle that health and safety is about looking after people.

Take a mental step back from the immediate problem and think: what is it in this task or function that could cause problems to people, either the workers or those affected by the work? You do not need to be a technical expert for this as this is where the common sense angle comes in.

From this overview, you are then more likely to be in a position to identify the areas that you need to consider in more depth. From this list you can determine the sections in this publication to start you off. Each of the sections that you look at will then give you pointers to related issues. You can then follow these "chains" until you have reasonable confidence that you have covered the main aspects of the problem that you set out to solve.

Remember, good health and safety can help you and your organisation, but it does not happen on its own — it needs to be managed.

Abrasive Wheels

Summary

The use of abrasive wheels in manufacturing and construction work is extensive. Wheels that are incorrectly mounted or used can result in serious injury or even death.

Practical Guidance

Definition

An abrasive wheel is a wheel, cylinder, disc or cone which consists of abrasive particles held together by mineral, metallic or organic bonds, whether natural or artificial. It may also be a mounted point, a wheel or disc of metal, wood, cloth, felt, rubber or paper having any surface consisting wholly or partly of abrasive materials, or a wheel, disc or saw to which is attached a rim or segments consisting of diamond abrasive particles. In each case they are intended to be power driven for the purpose of grinding or cutting.

Abrasive wheels may be fitted to fixed machines operated manually or automatically, or hand held tools such as angle grinders or disc cutters.

Training

The training of any person who uses an abrasive wheel is very important to minimise the risks of injury from flying particles, from the workpiece or "wheel", disintegrating "wheels", noise, fire or vibration. Training of operators is a duty placed on employers by the **Provision and Use of Work Equipment Regulations 1998**.

Training in the correct mounting of wheels, discs, cones, or any other form of the defined "abrasive wheel" is vital, as incorrect installation can lead to failure in use, disintegration and substantial potential for injury.

Training of those selected and appointed to mount abrasive wheels should also include:

- approved advisory literature
- hazards arising from the use of abrasive wheels and precautions to be observed
- methods of marking abrasive wheels as to type and speed

- methods of storing, handling and transporting abrasive wheels
- methods of inspecting and testing abrasive wheels to check for damage
- the functions of all components used, including flanges, blotters, bushes and nuts used in mounting, and including knowledge of the correct and incorrect methods of assembling all components and correct balancing of abrasive wheels
- the proper method of dressing an abrasive wheel
- the adjustment of the rest.

Safety in use

The following are important aspects of safe use:

- "wheels" must be correctly stored as they are easily damaged or affected by moisture and humidity
- incorrect handling can result in damage which may not be immediately identifiable but which may later result in failure
- mounting of wheels must be done correctly according to the type of wheel
- during use and depending on type, the wheel will need to be dressed to maintain its trueness, balance and quality of finish
- operators must understand the dangers from use of abrasive wheels and how each can be minimised
- wheels must be guarded to the greatest extent possible, to prevent injury to the operator from contact, and also, if appropriate, to contain flying debris and/or pieces of wheel which may cause injury.

Eye protection

One of the greatest risks of injury from normal use is to the eyes. Fixed guards or screens should be used to prevent eye injuries, or suitable eye protection should be used by the operator. In some cases the use of both forms of protection may be advisable. Flying debris can also be a significant risk of eye injury to other persons working or walking nearby. Such risks should be assessed and prevented either by the use of screens to contain debris, or by the exclusion of others from the danger area.

Clothing

Loose clothing such as ties and sleeves are easily drawn into a rotating wheel and should not be worn. Rags or other waste may also become entangled and should not be used near a revolving wheel.

Noise

Grinding and cutting wheels in use can generate considerable noise, well above the second action level of 90dB(A) set in the Noise at Work Regulations 1989. Suitable hearing protection is usually necessary even for short-term use. Consideration must be given to the possible effects of the noise on other persons nearby.

Health risks

Grinding and cutting can release substantial amounts of abrasive dust and grit from the wheel, as well as dust from the surface being ground or cut. Depending on the material, this airborne dust may be highly toxic and very damaging to health. An assessment of risks to health must be carried out for operators and others who may be nearby.

Fire and explosion risks

Considerable heat will be generated by use of abrasive wheels or cutting discs and this could ignite flammable materials. Flying sparks can easily ignite flammable materials. Use in an atmosphere which is potentially flammable due to liquid spillages or vapour is very likely to result in a fire or explosion. Use in potentially flammable atmospheres must be carefully controlled by appropriate use of a permit-to-work system.

Questions and Answers

Q I am aware that the Abrasive Wheels Regulations have been revoked and are now subject to PUWER, what training is now required?

A Under regulation 9 of the Abrasive Wheels Regulations it was required that no person should mount or train on abrasive wheels unless trained in accordance with these regulations. This last remaining regulation has now been revoked by PUWER 98. This however does not mean that it is now not necessary to train those who mount or dress abrasive wheels. Regulation 9 of PUWER 98 requires work equipment to be suitable in every respect that is reasonably foreseeable that will have an effect on the health and safety of any person, and regulation 5 requires work equipment to be maintained in an efficient state. In order for an abrasive wheel to be suitable and in an efficient state those who mount and dress wheels must be trained to carry out the tasks safely. HS(G) 17 — the ACOP to the Abrasive Wheels Regulations still remains and gives guidance on the training of abrasive wheel users.

Q I have been told that I should have several posters about abrasive wheels on the wall, is this true?

A This previous legal requirement is no longer required, but the poster "Approved Cautionary Notice Form 2347" is a good source of information and you might still want to use it.

Q Can employees under the age of 18 use abrasive wheels?

A Where any person under the age of 18 is employed, you are required by the **Management of Health and Safety at Work Regulations 1999** to carry out specific assessment of risks, taking account of a number of factors such as maturity, knowledge, experience, etc. Provided proper training and supervision are given, and the individual has been considered suitable to work with such equipment (in terms of maturity of approach, physical ability, etc), there is no reason why they should not.

Access/Egress

Summary

One of the basic duties within the **Health and Safety at Work, etc Act 1974** is to provide and maintain, so far as is reasonably practicable, safe access to and egress from any place of work under the employer's control.

Practical Guidance

Definitions

Section 2 of the **Health and Safety at Work, etc Act 1974** states that "it shall be the duty of every employer to ensure, so far as is reasonably practicable, the health, safety and welfare at work of all his employees". One duty is to maintain the place of work in a condition that is safe and without risks to health, and provide and maintain means of access to and egress from it that are also safe and without such risks. Access and egress means the route through or means of entry to or exit from a workplace. It can include footpaths, corridors, doorways, ladders, steps, etc.

Workplace (Health, Safety and Welfare) Regulations 1992

These Regulations apply to almost all work situations and contain basic safety and health requirements. They do not specifically mention access to or egress from workplaces, although many of the provisions relate to the layout, construction and maintenance of the workplace fabric and the equipment or devices provided for reasons of health and safety within the workplace.

Condition of floors and traffic routes

Workplace floors and traffic route surfaces must be suitably constructed for their intended uses and, so far as is reasonably practicable, kept free from obstructions, articles or substances likely to cause slips, trips or falls ("traffic route" is defined as a route for pedestrians, vehicles or both and includes stairs, staircases, fixed ladders, doorways, gateways, loading bays and ramps). Floors must be provided with adequate drainage where necessary. In particular, floors and the surfaces of traffic routes must not be uneven or slippery, and must not have any holes or unnecessary slopes.

The Regulations require the provision of suitable and sufficient handrails or guards on staircases, except where such a handrail, etc would obstruct the traffic route. The Approved Code of Practice (ACOP) recommends every open side of a staircase should be securely fenced, and that such fencing should consist of two rails, the upper rail at a height of 900mm or higher. In addition, at least one secure and substantial handrail should be provided on every staircase and this should be increased to both sides if there is a particular risk of falling. The height of the second handrail should take into account the expected users, particularly small children.

Falls

Where persons may fall a distance, or be struck by a falling object likely to cause personal injury, suitable and effective measures must be taken, so far as is reasonably practicable, to prevent such events. Any areas where these events may occur must be clearly indicated. Where there is a risk of falling into a tank, pit or structure containing a dangerous substance, such tanks, pits and structures must be securely covered or fenced, so far as is reasonably practicable. Similarly, every traffic route over, across or within an uncovered tank, pit or structure containing a dangerous substance must be securely fenced.

The ACOP recommends that secure fencing should be provided where a fall is two metres or more, or where the fall is less than two metres if there is a particular danger, eg on to a vehicle route, etc. As a minimum, the ACOP recommends two rails with the top of the fencing at 1100mm from the surface from which the fall may occur. Falling objects may require the provision of a more substantial barrier.

Organisation, etc of traffic routes

Workplaces must be organised to allow the safe circulation of pedestrians and vehicles. Traffic routes must be suitable for their intended use, sufficient in number, suitably positioned and of sufficient size. Suitable measures must be taken to ensure that:

- the use of traffic routes does not give rise to health and safety risks to persons working nearby
- vehicle routes are separated from pedestrian routes
- doorways or gates leading on to vehicle routes should be sufficiently separated from the route
- vehicles and pedestrians using the same traffic route are sufficiently separated.

Traffic routes must be suitably indicated where necessary. The ACOP recognises the need to consider the requirements of disabled persons when deciding what is suitable.

Disabled persons

Under the **Disability Discrimination Act 1995** employers with 20 or more employees are required to treat disabled employees equally with non-disabled employees in all employment matters. They are also required to make reasonable changes to the premises, provided these do not contravene any health and safety laws, in order to accommodate the needs of the disabled employees. These changes could include means of access and egress. To fulfil their duty to ensure the health and safety of employees at work under s.2 of the HSW Act, there is an implicit obligation to take account of employees with special needs, eg disabled employees, and to ensure that those needs are met, so far as is reasonably practicable.

Duty to non-employees

The **Health and Safety at Work, etc Act 1974** applies where non-employees enter a firm's premises to carry out work or as visitors. Section 3(1) provides that employers must conduct their undertakings so that people not employed by them are not exposed to risks to their health and safety, so far as is reasonably practicable — the provision of safe access could well form part of this duty. If non-employees use non-domestic premises as a place of work, or are able to use plant or substances provided there, then s.4(2) imposes a duty on persons who are in control of the premises or of the means of access to (or egress from) the premises. They must take measures to ensure that the premises themselves and the means of access and egress are safe and without risk to health, so far as is reasonably practicable.

Other primary legal duties

A number of specific Regulations have duties relating to safe access and egress, including the following.

Lifting Operations and Lifting Equipment Regulations 1998

These require a safe means of access to and egress from (which includes the provision of adequate handholds and footholds where necessary) any work carried out on lifting appliances where the person is liable to fall further than 2m.

Construction (Health, Safety and Welfare) Regulations 1996

These Regulations require, so far as is reasonably practicable, the provision of maintained, suitable and sufficient access to and egress from every place of work and any other place used by a person at work. Suitable and sufficient steps must be taken to ensure no person has access to any place which is unsafe or a risk to health, so far as is reasonably practicable.

Electricity at Work Regulations 1989

Regulation 15 requires adequate means of access, so as to prevent danger and/or injury, to be provided for all electrical equipment. Access to every switchboard passageway should be free from danger, and access to cut-off switches must be kept clear, unobstructed and free from tripping/slipping hazards, etc.

Questions and Answers

Q Every year we try hard to clear snowfalls from the yard which employees cross to enter the factory. What happens if we have not cleared the snow and ice, or there is still some which an employee slips on?

A An important case that considered this was *Thomas v Bristol Aeroplane Co. Ltd* [1954] 2 AII ER 1 where it was said that the mere fact that the plaintiff (injured employee) was required to walk on icy surfaces which are a normal incident of winter does not of itself indicate a defective means of access. Other cases have considered what a reasonable employer should do. If you are making reasonable efforts to clear icy patches, and maintain that condition, then an accident to an employee may not be deemed by a court to be your liability.

Q Why can't we just talk about "access" — egress seems such an outdated word?

A In any legislation the use of specific words has to be looked at very carefully. Access means "entering or going to a place of work" whereas egress means "going out" or "an exit or way out". Both have different meanings and as such if only the word access is used, the legislation would apply only to entry into a place of work and not exiting the workplace.

Q How frequently should we clean steps, corridors and general areas used by employees for access?

A **The Factories Act 1961** used to contain the requirement for accumulations of dirt and refuse to be removed daily. The **Workplace (Health, Safety and Welfare) Regulations 1992** contain general requirements for maintaining workplaces in a clean condition and removing waste materials. The Approved Code of Practice to those Regulations states that floors and traffic routes should be cleaned at least once a week. In factories and other workplaces where dirt and refuse is merely likely to accumulate, any dirt and refuse which is not in suitable receptacles should be removed at least daily.

Accident Reporting

Summary

It is a legal requirement to report and/or record certain work-related accidents under both health and safety and social security laws. In addition, accident statistics compiled from accident records in the workplace are an extremely useful tool in identifying the most common causes of accidents and any associated trends.

Practical Guidance

An accident may be defined as an unplanned and uncontrolled event which may, but does not have to, result in personal injury. Accidents where no personal injury occurs are often referred to as "near miss" incidents. There are well-recognised accident ratios and although the figures vary between studies the principles are the same, eg for every 1 serious or disabling injury accident there are 10 minor injury accidents, 30 damage accidents and 600 near miss incidents. When diagramatically represented (see below), these figures form a pyramid, known as the "accident triangle". This shows that there are many more near-misses than major injuries, but the difference between them is merely a matter of chance. If employees can be encouraged to work in a safe manner, this should reduce the number of near misses that occur. This will in turn mean that the number of minor accidents and serious or disabling accidents will be reduced.

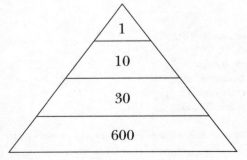

1	Serious or disabling injuries
10	Minor injuries
30	Damage accidents
600	Accidents with no injury or damage - the near miss accidents

Accident statistics

In addition to the legal obligations to record and report work accidents, employers will find it very useful to use these statistics as a measure of their health and safety performance. Although it is a "reactive" tool, ie it monitors something that has already happened, accident statistics are an important part of the employer's risk assessments as they should identify types and causes of accidents, locations, and times, etc which will help to decide control measure priorities.

The legal requirements covering the recording and reporting of work-related accidents are contained in social security and health and safety legislation respectively.

Accident book

Under the **Social Security (Claims and Payments) Regulations 1979,** factory employers, or any employer who employs 10 or more people, must keep a record of all accidents at work (normally in the form of an accident book), regardless of how minor the injuries appear. The accident book should be kept at a central location in the workplace, and may be inspected by enforcing officers. *Accident books* (BI 510) may be obtained from The Stationery Office (tel: 0870 600 5522).

The following information should be recorded:

- name, address and occupation of the injured person (or the person making the report if not the injured person)
- date and time of accident
- location details of where the accident happened
- the cause and nature of any injuries.

The accident book or records must be kept for a period of three years from the date of the last entry.

Reportable accidents

The **Reporting of Injuries, Diseases and Dangerous Occurrences Regulations 1995** (RIDDOR) require certain specified accidents and dangerous occurrences to be reported to the enforcing officer for the premises.

For reporting purposes, work-related accidents are accidents that arise from, or are in connected with:

- the way the work is conducted
- the use of any substances or equipment at work
- the condition of the work premises
- acts of physical violence against employees
- suicides associated with specified transport systems.

The following accidents and occurrences must be reported:

- any fatality (to employees and non-employees)
- major injuries to employees
- major injuries to non-employees which require the person to be taken directly to hospital for treatment

- specified dangerous occurrences
- accidents causing more than three consecutive days' incapacity for work (the day of the accident is excluded from the calculation, although days off, including weekends, should be included, even if these are not usually worked)
- certain specified diseases
- certain events associated with the safe supply of gas.

The case of *Woking Borough Council v BHS plc* (1994) confirms that RIDDOR applies to accidents involving non-employees, ie members of the public if they have suffered an injury or condition which is reportable.

Reporting procedure

All reportable accidents must be reported by the quickest means, ie the telephone, and followed up with the written notification on form F2508 as appropriate within 10 days. Over-three-day accidents and diseases should be reported on form F2508 as soon as possible after they are known.

Record keeping

A record of any accident reported to the enforcing authority must be kept at the workplace to which it relates for a period of three years from the date on which it was made. A photocopy of form F2508 is sufficient.

Questions and Answers

Q   Who is responsible for reporting accidents under RIDDOR?
A   In a large majority of workplaces it is the responsibility of the employer to report any "reportable" accidents or occurrences. Other designated people are responsible for accident reporting in mines, quarries and offshore installations. Where the accident involved is related to an injury of a self-employed person, the responsibility for reporting it lies with the occupier of the premises on which it occurred.
Q   Do reportable accidents to trainees have to be reported?
A   Yes, where the **Health and Safety (Training for Employment) Regulations 1990** apply, trainees on an employer's premises are considered to be employees under health and safety law.
Q   Why do these accidents have to be reported?
A   Accidents reported to the enforcing authorities allow the inspectors to determine whether more serious accidents warrant further detailed investigation and whether there has been, or is, a likely breakdown of health and safety control. The figures also make up the annual accident statistics published by the Health and Safety Executive (HSE) which act as a type of benchmark across different industries — there is currently significant under-reporting.

Accident Reporting

Q If there is an accident book on the premises, do RIDDOR accidents still have to be reported?

A Yes. The accident book and the reporting of injuries, etc under RIDDOR are totally separate requirements. The accident book contains details of any injury suffered at work in case there is a future claim made for social security benefit, when the original details may need to be referred back to. Accidents reported under RIDDOR are for the information and use of the enforcing authorities in determining appropriate inspection systems, etc. Not all accidents recorded in the accident book would necessarily need to be reported under RIDDOR.

Q When calculating over-three-day injuries, what days are actually included in the calculation?

A The calculation does not include the day of the accident but would include any rest days, eg the weekend, even if these are not usually worked.

Administration and Enforcement

Summary

Like criminal law, the **Health and Safety at Work, etc Act 1974** (HSW Act) and all the other relevant Acts and Regulations are subject to a system of administration and enforcement. The Health and Safety Executive (HSE) or local authority Environmental Health Officers (EHOs) are responsible for that enforcement. The HSW Act details several offences, each with an associated penalty.

Practical Guidance

Administration

The main use of the work premises determines which body is responsible for enforcement. The enforcing inspectors will either be Health and Safety Executive (HSE) inspectors who are responsible for enforcement in industrial premises, or local authority Environmental Health Officers (EHOs) who are responsible for enforcement in non-industrial premises. There is no self-enforcement so HSE premises are enforced by EHOs and vice versa.

Powers of inspectors

Fire authority inspectors are responsible for enforcing fire legislation.

Enforcing inspectors may:
- enter workplaces at any reasonable time, or at any time if there is a serious risk
- undertake examinations or investigations
- take photographs, copies of relevant documents and samples as necessary
- interview staff
- require workplaces, equipment, etc to be left undisturbed during an investigation
- remove or render harmless equipment or substances in cases of imminent danger.

Enforcement notices

There are two types of enforcement notice:
- improvement notices
- prohibition notices.

Improvement notices are served when there has been a contravention of a legal duty. They must state what the contravention is and give a time period for corrective action — this time period must not be less than 21 days. A two-week period for

23

representations from the employer against whom the notice is served is required before the improvement notice can finally be served. Appeals against an improvement notice will suspend the notice until a final decision is reached by the tribunal. Appeals must be made within 21 days of the notice being served.

Prohibition notices are served when there is, or is likely to be, a serious risk of personal injury. They may be *immediate*, ie the activity or equipment must be stopped immediately, or *deferred*, ie stop the activity or equipment, etc at a later specified date. Appeals against prohibition notices do not cause the notice to be suspended — the notice will remain in effect until the tribunal confirms otherwise.

In a case heard at Preston Magistrates' Court in December 1995, a commercial laundry was fined for deliberately failing to comply with prohibition notices placed on their spin dryers on two separate occasions on the same day. The spin dryers all had defective interlocks which meant they would still operate with the doors open.

Offences

Offences may be *summary*, ie tried in a Magistrates'/Sheriff Court, or *triable either way*, ie tried in a Magistrates'/Sheriff Court or in the Crown Court or High Court. More serious cases tend to be referred up from Magistrates' Courts to the Crown Court or High Court. Offences include:

- failing to fulfil a duty under ss.2 to 6 of the HSW Act (duties on employers, premises controllers and manufacturers or suppliers)
- failing to comply with s.7 (duty on employees)
- misusing anything provided in the interests of health and safety
- levying charges for anything required to be provided in the interests of health and safety
- failing to comply with any other health and safety related legislation, eg regulations
- obstructing inspectors or other authorised persons from performing their duties
- failing to comply with enforcement notices or court orders
- providing false information.

Crown/High Courts may impose unlimited fines and two year prison sentences where custodial sentences are specified.

Fire legislation

As fire legislation is not under the control of the Health and Safety Commission (HSC) or HSE it does not come under their remit for inspection or enforcement. Instead, the local fire authority is responsible for enforcing fire safety law, although in practice HSE and EHO inspectors may request that a fire officer accompanies them on visits where fire safety is likely to be, or known to be, an issue.

EU law

British and UK law is becoming increasingly influenced by law emanating from the European Union (EU). Generally, there are three levels of EU requirements, each with its own status. The European Court of Justice provides interpretations on European law — its decisions are passed back to the Member State involved for compliance.

EU Regulations

These are immediately effective in all EU Member States and override any relevant existing national legislation; they do not require implementing laws and cannot be altered or adjusted in any way.

EU Directives

These are less strict and although they have to be implemented by appropriate laws in the Member States they can be adjusted to suit individual legislative and enforcement differences between states — they represent minimum standards that have to be achieved.

EU recommendations

These are the least strict and do not have to be implemented in Member States — they represent good practice although they may be taken into account in court cases where problems with national interpretation arise.

European Health and Safety Agency

The objectives of this Agency are to promote improvements in occupational health and safety by raising awareness and improving the availability of health and safety, and other relevant or associated information. The Agency is based in Bilbao, Spain.

Questions and Answers

Q   Can individual employees be prosecuted for breaching health and safety laws?
A   Yes, s.7 of the **Health and Safety at Work, etc Act 1974** places a specific duty on employees to ensure their own health and safety at work, and to make sure that they do not endanger anyone else. An employee who deliberately fails to comply with this duty is breaking the law and can be taken to court.
Q   Is it true that enforcing officers can enter a work premises at any time?
A   Yes, although for routine inspections the visit will usually be made at a reasonable time, ie when the premises is normally operational. If premises are used continually over 24 hour shifts the visit could be considered reasonable at any time. Where there is thought to be a serious and/or imminent danger inspectors may enter at any time.
Q   What determines whether the enforcing authority is the HSE or the local authority EHOs?

Administration and Enforcement

A The HSE is responsible for enforcement in premises where the main use is industrial, eg factories, construction sites, hospitals, schools, etc. EHOs are responsible for enforcement in premises where the primary use is non-industrial, eg offices, shops, residential care homes, animal care establishments, etc. The deciding factor is the main use of the premises, so an office which is part of a large factory will be inspected by the HSE.

Q How is uniformity of enforcement achieved between the different enforcing bodies?

A There is a local authority unit (LAU) within the HSE which prepares guidance for EHOs. There is also an HSE/LA enforcement liaison committee (HELA), which provides a forum for informal discussions and dissemination of information between the HSE and EHOs. Finally, each HSE area office has a liaison officer who is responsible for maintaining links with the local EHOs in the area.

AIDS/HIV

Summary

With the exception of those employed in healthcare professions and emergency services, infection with Human Immunodeficiency Virus (HIV) and the development of Acquired Immune Deficiency Syndrome (AIDS) during normal work activity is very unlikely.

Practical Guidance

How HIV is transmitted

HIV is transmitted when infected blood and body fluids are passed from one individual to another. Sexual contact (both homosexual and heterosexual), and the sharing of needles by drug abusers are the most common causes. This means that in most work situations transmission of the virus is extremely unlikely to occur.

There is substantial evidence to confirm that HIV is not transmitted via insects, food, water, urine, sweat, tears, sneezing, coughing, sharing toilet facilities, cups, cutlery, towels, etc. All evidence points to the virus being fragile, and unable to survive outside the human body for any significant length of time.

At risk professions

In some circumstances, such as the healthcare professions and emergency services, the residual risk of infection is likely to be due to exposure to blood spillages or contaminated syringes. Similar risks may arise for those engaged in the collection of refuse from areas frequented by drug abusers.

There is no specific legislation relating to AIDS, but the **Health and Safety at Work, etc Act 1974** requires employers to provide a safe place of work without risks to health. For example, the employer must take suitable precautions to ensure that the risk of any type of infection from blood spillage in the event of an accident is minimised, and any used syringes or contaminated wastes are handled and disposed of safely.

Discrimination

The majority of persons who are HIV-positive are not aware of their status, and can live and work normally for many years without problem. Some people will have become aware that they are HIV-positive through blood tests, and may disclose this to an employer.

HIV-positive status classifies someone as disabled under the **Disability Discrimination Act 1995**. It is important that the employer ensures that employees who are known to be HIV-positive, or who have developed AIDS, will not be discriminated against in the provision of services or employment. Employees who develop AIDS should be treated in the same manner as any other employee with a potentially progressive illness.

Where the residual risk of infection is higher, eg in some healthcare functions, arrangements for protection against HIV should be included in the organisation's safety policy and a safe system of work established.

The employer must maintain medical confidentiality and know how and when to seek additional assistance, for example by using the Employment Medical Advisory Service.

Permission must be obtained from the person who is HIV-positive before a third party is informed of their HIV status. There is no statutory requirement for HIV-infected employees to inform any person of their condition.

Writing a policy

Where the risk of infection is low in the workplace, the following points should be included in a policy.

1. The company will encourage employees who have been diagnosed as HIV-positive to obtain counselling advice and support.
2. Management will treat disclosure of such information in the utmost confidence and employment rights will not be affected.
3. Employees will not discriminate against fellow workers who have or may have HIV. Any employee who refuses to work beside such a person will be subjected to disciplinary procedures.
4. Employees who develop AIDS will be treated in the same manner as any other employee with a potentially progressive illness. This may include:
   (a) modifying the job design and content
   (b) offering flexible hours of work
   (c) modifying the work environment
   (d) redeployment to more suitable work
   (e) providing time off for treatment.
5. The employer will protect against the minimal risk of contamination by HIV at work by:
   (a) providing all employees with up-to-date information about HIV and AIDS, to enable them to recognise and protect against the very low transmission risks associated with normal work activities
   (b) ensuring as far as possible that equipment used in the workplace does not present a risk of cutting, abrasions or puncture wounds
   (c) informing all staff that if they sustain an injury which may bleed, the wound must be dressed
   (d) ensuring that first aiders are trained in, provided with and use the

necessary equipment for preventing contact with body fluids when administering first aid or disposing of clinical waste

(e) ensuring that any spillages of blood or body fluids are cleared by a responsible and authorised person (normally the first aider)

(f) ensuring that those engaged in the collection of refuse are provided with gloves and any other appropriate personal protective equipment.

6. Where an employee legitimately needs to use a syringe at work because of a medical condition, the employer should co-ordinate the arrangements for safe storage and disposal of used needles without infringing upon personal liberty.

7. All employees will receive training on:
   (a) how the virus is transmitted
   (b) how to deal with blood spillages
   (c) the importance of covering wounds
   (d) the low risk of transmission during artificial respiration
   (e) why it is normally quite acceptable for an infected person to continue with work activities.

8. First aiders will be trained in, and provided with the necessary equipment for, preventing contact with bodily fluids when administering first aid or disposing of clinical waste.

9. Where there is a higher risk of infection, eg health sector personnel, a risk assessment should be carried out and a safe system of work agreed, implemented and monitored.

10. The risks of infection with HIV should be covered with other bloodborne diseases in an assessment under the **Control of Substances Hazardous to Health Regulations 1999**. This will assess the health risks created by work activities and define what steps should be taken to prevent or adequately control exposure.

Questions and Answers

Q Are first aiders at risk from someone who is HIV positive?

A There is no recorded case of a first aider having been infected during treatment; however, protective equipment such as disposable gloves should be used where practicable. This is good practice because there are also other bloodborne infections that are easier to transmit than HIV, such as hepatitis. In reality an HIV-positive person is more at risk from the first aider, due to their reduced ability to fight infections.

Q How long does it take for HIV to develop into AIDS?

A On average, a period of 8–10 years elapses before the development of AIDS.

Q Will someone with HIV be able to carry on working effectively?

A Individuals generally feel quite well and many do not experience any physical signs or symptoms of the disease. They may, however, be more likely to contract other infections.

Alcohol

Summary

The effects of alcohol can lead to accidents at work. Even slight intoxication can lead to loss of concentration and affect judgment and physical co-ordination. This can result in serious injury if machinery or vehicles are operated. Also, if driving is part of an employee's work, the employer is vicariously liable for the actions of the employee. Thus if an employee is convicted of drunk driving, the employer may be sued under civil law for damages caused, irrespective of the driver's insurance.

Practical Guidance

Alcohol and health and safety law

Two pieces of legislation relate specifically to the consumption of alcohol at work.

1. The **Transport and Works Act 1992** makes it an offence for certain workers to be unfit through drink while working on railways, tramways and other guided transport systems. The operators of the transport system would also be guilty of an offence unless they can show that they have done everything reasonably practicable to prevent such an offence being committed.

2. The **Work in Compressed Air Regulations 1996** state that no-one who is under the influence of drink which impairs their ability to carry out their work will be allowed to work in compressed air. Workers in compressed air are prohibited from consuming or having in their possession any alcoholic drink. It is the responsibility of the compressed air contractor to ensure that workers comply with this requirement.

Both of these pieces of legislation relate to specific work situations, but there are also implied duties under the **Health and Safety at Work, etc Act 1974** (HSW Act) which apply to all workplaces.

Sections 2 and 3 of the HSW Act state that the employer must ensure that employees are not put at risk by work activities. This does impose an obligation on the employer to do what is reasonably practicable to identify alcoholism and to ensure no employee under the influence of alcohol is allowed to be at work and thus endanger themselves or others.

Employees who are under the influence of alcohol at work may similarly be in breach of s.7 of the HSW Act, which requires them to take care of themselves and others whilst at work.

The effects of drinking on productivity and safety

The consumption of alcohol may result in loss of productivity and poor work performance. Alcohol is estimated to cause between 3–5% of all absences from work. This equates to approximately 8–14 million lost working days in the UK each year. This in turn may damage customer relations. Also, there may be resentment among employees who have to cover for colleagues whose work declines because of their drinking. It may also lead to bad behaviour or poor discipline.

There are no exact figures on accidents where alcohol is thought to be the cause, but it is a known fact that alcohol affects judgment and physical co-ordination. Drinking even a small amount of alcohol before or while carrying out a medium to high-risk job will increase the chance of the operator having or causing an accident.

For many people drinking alcohol does not cause any problems, but drinking too much at the wrong time can be harmful; medical opinion suggests four units a day for men and three units a day for women as a safe limit for alcohol consumption. There are risks in particular before or during driving or before using machinery, electrical equipment or ladders.

There are many reasons why someone may develop a drinking problem. Working conditions may cause stress, excessive work pressure, unsociable hours or monotony, any of which may be a factor in increases drinking, as can the opportunity to drink at work (eg when entertaining customers/clients).

Developing a policy

All organisations will benefit from having an agreed policy on alcohol which is clearly communicated to all employees. This is best achieved by consultation with management, staff and trade union representatives and employees. In larger companies, the policy should take into account the issue of alcohol as it affects the business.

When developing a policy the following steps should be taken.

1. The aims of the policy should be stated and could be as follows:
   (a) to ensure the health and safety of employees by minimising the risk of accidents/incidents occurring because of employees suffering from the effects of alcohol
   (b) to identify those employees who may have an alcohol problem at the earliest possible stage
   (c) to offer employees who are known to have a alcohol problem which is affecting their work referral to an appropriate source.
2. The name and job title of the person who is responsible overall for implementing the policy should be stated.
3. Arrangements for implementing the policy should be listed. For example, the employer will, in consultation with workers and their representatives:
   (a) provide all existing and new employees with information relating to the risks to health as a result of the effects of alcohol consumption

   (b) provide supervisors and managers with information and training to enable them to recognise a potential problem relating to alcohol and know who to refer it to

   (c) encourage any employee who may have an alcohol problem which affects their work to take advantage of the company referral procedure for diagnosis and treatment

   (d) agree upon a programme of treatment where it is confirmed that an individual's work if affected by the misuse of alcohol, in consultation with the appointed medical advisor or GP and the employee.

4. The rules relating to alcohol should be stated and could be as follows:

   (a) employees will ensure that their alcohol consumption is below the level that would have a detrimental effect on their work

   (b) no employee shall attend work whilst under the influence of alcohol

   (c) no alcohol shall be brought on to the company premises

   (d) never drive or operate machinery whilst under the influence of alcohol

   (e) ask for help if you feel you have a problem.

5. It should be stated that any employee with a drink problem should have the same rights to confidentiality and support as those who have a medical or psychological condition.

6. A description of the help and support available to employees who have a drink problem should be included.

7. A description of the circumstances under which disciplinary action will be taken should be stated.

Note: Disciplinary action should be the last resort. If an employee is dismissed, a court may find the dismissal unfair if the employer has made no attempt to help an employee whose work problems are related to alcohol.

Training

Training for employees should include:

- the effects of alcohol on the body
- the dangers and problems linked to misuse
- the company policy and rules.

Training for managers and supervisors should cover the above points plus the following:

- an awareness that alcoholism is a recognised disease
- the importance of maintaining medical confidentiality
- how to recognise a potential problem and who to refer it to.

The emphasis in the policy statement should be to help those who may have a problem. It may be very difficult for someone to acknowledge or admit they have a problem. They need to be sure that admission will not be seen as an immediate cause for dismissal or disciplinary action. Also, colleagues may be reticent to report suspected drinking problems to management.

Questions and Answers

Q Do I have to ban the consumption of alcohol on the premises?

A This is not necessary in most organisations, but there should be a policy that clearly defines the occasions on which it will be acceptable.

Q Can I discipline someone who is found unfit to work due to alcohol consumption?

A Yes, providing you can show that the employee was fully aware of the company policy on alcohol at work, and that everything reasonably practicable had been done to encourage the employee to seek help.

Q Can I introduce alcohol testing at work?

A Yes, but it is essential to gain the agreement of the workforce, and it must be clearly used to prevent risks to others. Agreement must be incorporated into each employee's contract of employment.

Asbestos

Summary

Asbestos is a general term covering a number of fibrous minerals which cause well-known adverse health effects such as asbestosis, various cancers of the respiratory tract and mesothelioma when the fibres are released as dusts and inhaled. Strict controls are in place for asbestos encountered in work situations.

Practical Guidance

Duties

Employers have a duty under the **Control of Asbestos at Work Regulations 1987** (as amended) to protect any person from exposure to asbestos, whether those people are at work or not, although the provisions relating to information, instruction, training and health records do not apply to non-employees. The case of *Bryce v Swan Hunter Group* confirms that asbestos-related ill-health was recognised from around 1947 and that employers since then had a duty to protect their employees against such exposure.

Identification and assessment

Prior to the start of any asbestos work employers must make an assessment of any possible exposure, including the type of asbestos involved (it is acceptable to assume the worse case scenario, ie exposure is to the most hazardous form of asbestos), the nature and degree of any exposure, and the necessary control measures. Assessments should be reviewed regularly, and certainly when there are any changes in the original circumstances, and they should be revised as necessary. The cases of *Nurse v Morganite Crucible Ltd* and *Edgson v Vickers plc* both confirmed that any work with asbestos should be included in the definition of a "process" under the **Factories Act 1961** and the **Asbestos Regulations 1969** (the latter was revoked and replaced by the **Control of Asbestos at Work Regulations 1987** (as amended)).

Plan of work

Plans of work must be drawn up by employers before any work involving asbestos removal and these should be retained for the period of the work. The plan of work should include details of the:

- location address
- nature of the work
- expected duration

- intended asbestos handling methods
- characteristics of employee protection and decontamination equipment
- protection equipment for others who may be affected by the work.

Notification

Enforcing authorities must be notified of any asbestos work to which the 1987 Regulations apply at least 14 days prior to the start of the work — a lesser period may be agreed by mutual consent.

The following work does not have to be notified:
- work undertaken in accordance with the **Asbestos (Licensing) Regulations 1983** (as amended)
- work where the level of exposure to asbestos is not likely to exceed the "action level".

Information, instruction and training

Employers must provide employees exposed to asbestos with information, instruction and training to enable them to carry out their work effectively, and to understand the associated risks and necessary precautions.

Prevention or reduction of exposure

Exposure to asbestos must be prevented where reasonably practicable, or where this is not possible it must be reduced to the lowest reasonably practicable level. Control of exposure should be achieved by substitution for safer alternatives; engineering means, such as exhaust ventilation; or as a last resort, if no other measures are reasonable, by providing suitable personal protective equipment (PPE), including respiratory protective equipment (RPE).

Control limits and control measures

Where exposure levels to asbestos exceed relevant "control limits" owing to an unexpected release, only authorised people with suitable personal protective equipment and clothing may enter the affected area. Anyone who may have been affected by the escape must be informed immediately.

Control measures provided must be properly used, cleaned, maintained and, where necessary, disposed of safely. Defects must be reported and all records of work carried out and any control measures must be retained for five years. The efficiency and effectiveness of control measures must be monitored and suitable records maintained — 40 years for health records, 5 years for other records.

Cleanliness

Areas where asbestos work is carried out and any equipment used must allow for thorough cleansing and must be kept clean.

Designated areas

Areas in which the "action levels" are likely to be exceeded must be designated as "asbestos areas". Similarly, areas where the "control limits" are likely to be exceeded must be designated "respirator zones". In both cases the areas must be clearly marked and entry restricted to permitted persons only. Employees may not eat, drink or smoke in these areas.

Health records

Health records must be kept for 40 years in relation to any employees exposed to asbestos above the "action levels", and such employees must also undergo medical surveillance programmes. Medical examinations must be provided prior to employment and at intervals of not more than two years thereafter — appropriate facilities must be made available by employers.

Washing and changing facilities

Suitable washing and changing facilities, including storage for personal clothing and personal protective equipment, must be provided for employees exposed to asbestos at work.

Storage and labelling

Raw asbestos and asbestos waste must be stored and transported in sealed, properly labelled containers. Similarly, products containing asbestos intended for use at work must be properly labelled.

Licensing

Work with asbestos insulation or coatings, ie their removal, repair or disturbance, must be licensed by the Health and Safety Executive (HSE), under the **Asbestos (Licensing) Regulations 1983** (as amended). Exemptions include such work where:
- less than one hour in any period of seven consecutive days is spent in contact with asbestos by any person and the total time spent by all workers is less than two hours
- the work is carried out on the premises of which the employer is the occupier and the enforcing authority has been notified 14 days in advance.

Prohibitions

The importation, supply, use and spraying of specified types of asbestos are prohibited under the **Asbestos (Prohibition) Regulations 1992**. The disposal of such asbestos is exempt.

The importation, supply and use of chrysotile (white) asbestos is prohibited within Great Britain under the **Asbestos (Prohibitions)(Amendment) Regulations 1999**, except for use in a very restricted number of fields such as research, etc. Products containing chrysotile that were in use prior to 24.11.99 may continue to be used until they reach the end of their service life.

These Regulations also prohibit the supply and use of second-hand asbestos cement products and of boards, tiles and panels which have been painted or covered with paints or plasters containing asbestos.

Questions and Answers

Q What are the main types of asbestos and which ones are the most hazardous?

A The **Control of Asbestos at Work Regulations 1987** (as amended) define asbestos as including crocidolite, amosite, chrysotile, fibrous anthophyllite, fibrous actinolite, fibrous tremolite and any mixture of these. Crocidolite (blue asbestos) and amosite (brown asbestos) are considered to be the forms most hazardous to health.

Q Is there any difference between the terms "control limits" used in the **Control of Asbestos at Work Regulations 1987** (as amended) and "maximum exposure limits" used in the **Control of Substances Hazardous to Health Regulations 1999** (COSHH)?

A No, the terms control limits and maximum exposure limits are equivalent to each other, although maximum exposure limits is the term currently used.

Asthma, Occupational

Summary

Occupational asthma is a disorder of the respiratory system caused by exposure and sensitisation to certain chemicals while at work. This means that if someone who has occupational asthma breathes in a chemical to which he or she is sensitised, he or she may suffer decreased respiratory function or an asthma attack.

Practical Guidance

Agents which cause asthma

On the following list are agents which are known to cause occupational asthma. However, this list is not exhaustive.

1. Isocyanates.
2. Platinum salts.
3. Fumes and dusts arising from the manufacture, transport or use of hardening agents based on phthalic anhydride, tetrachlorophthalic anhydride, trimellitic anhydride or triethylenetetramine.
4. Fumes arising from the use of rosin (colophony) as a soldering flux.
5. Proteolytic enzymes.
6. Animals or insects and their larval forms used for the purposes of research or education or in laboratories.
7. Dusts arising from the sewing, cultivation, harvesting, drying, handling, milling, transport or storage of barley, oats, rye, wheat or maize, or handling, milling, transport or storage of meal or flour made from these cereals.
8. Antibiotics.
9. Cimetidine.
10. Wood dust.
11. Ispaghula.
12. Caster bean dust.
13. Ipecacuanha.
14. Azodicarbonamide.
15. Animals and insects or other arthropods and their larval forms used for pest control or fruit cultivation purposes.
16. Glutaraldehyde.
17. Persulphate salts or henna.
18. Crustaceans, fish or their products arising from their use in the food industry.
19. Reactive dyes.

20. Soya bean.
21. Tea dust.
22. Green coffee bean dust.
23. Fumes from stainless steel welding.
24. Any chemical bearing the warning "may cause sensitisation by inhalation".

Controlling exposure

Under the **Control of Substances Hazardous to Health Regulations 1999** (COSHH), employers must assess the risk of exposure to agents in their workplace which may cause occupational asthma. If there is a risk that workers may develop occupational asthma, suitable control measures must be put in place, used and maintained. Workers must receive suitable information, instruction and training.

Where there is exposure to agents that may cause occupational asthma, employers should provide their employees with suitable health surveillance (regulation 11).

If workers develop occupational asthma in the workplace, the work should be changed so that they are no longer exposed to the agent to which they have developed sensitisation.

Reporting occurrences

Under the **Reporting of Injuries, Diseases and Dangerous Occurrences Regulations 1995** (RIDDOR), all cases of occupational asthma must be reported to the enforcing authority, if they are caused by exposure to any of the agents listed under Agents which cause asthma above.

Relevant cases of occupational asthma must be reported on form F2508A, available from HSE Books, tel: 01787 881165.

Social security payments

The **Social Security (Industrial Injuries) (Prescribed Diseases) Regulations 1985** allow people suffering from occupational asthma to claim benefit for a prescribed disease, so long as they can show that their illness was caused by exposure to one of the agents listed under Agents which cause asthma above, or any other sensitising agent.

Chemical labelling

The **Chemical (Hazard Information and Packaging for Supply) Regulations 1994** (CHIP) require suppliers of chemicals to label the containers of any hazardous substances that they supply. If the substance has been classified as one that may cause occupational asthma, the label must tell the user that it "may cause sensitisation by inhalation".

Symptoms

If someone who has been exposed to a material, particularly an organic material, develops a wheeze or a persistent dry cough, he or she may be sensitised to that material, and this is associated with occupational asthma. These symptoms may develop only after the employee returns home after work. Quite often, if someone is sensitised to an agent they will develop the symptoms of occupational asthma immediately after being exposed to that agent for the first time after they have been away from it for a while.

Questions and Answers

Q What is the difference between asthma and occupational asthma?

A Asthma is a disorder of the respiratory system, often caused by an allergic reaction, that many people develop, either as children or adults. It causes attacks of wheezing and shortness of breath. Very severe attacks may sometimes prove fatal if the correct medication is not immediately available to the sufferer. Occupational asthma is the same disease, but caused specifically by exposure to certain agents at work.

Q Who might develop occupational asthma?

A Anyone might develop the condition when exposed to certain agents, even if they have never had an allergic reaction to anything before. However, certain people may be more susceptible to occupational asthma, such as those who are already known to be asthmatic or heavy smokers.

Q How do I know if a chemical in my workplace might cause occupational asthma?

A First, check the list given under Agents which cause asthma above. This list contains many of the agents known to cause occupational asthma. If the chemical being used is not on the list, check the label of the container that it was supplied in. If it is known to cause occupational asthma, the label must contain the words "may cause sensitisation by inhalation". If there is any doubt, check with the supplier.

Q What is a respiratory sensitiser?

A A respiratory sensitiser is a chemical or agent, such as isocyanates or dust from animal enclosures, to which someone may react when he or she inhales it, eg by persistent dry coughing or an asthma attack. If that person becomes sensitised to the agent, the reaction will occur even if they breathe in very small amounts of the agent.

Audits and Inspections

Summary

The setting of standards and the establishment of safe systems of work and procedures are vital but so is the establishment of effective systems of auditing or monitoring, including inspections, to ensure that the standards which have been set are being complied with everywhere throughout the organisation concerned.

Practical Guidance

Safety audit

No system is perfect and they all require checking to ensure that they are: as comprehensive as possible, suitable for the purpose, sufficient for the purpose, being used properly and are up to date.

Health and safety is no exception. For example it would be no defence in court to state that all required risk assessments had been undertaken if no check was made of them. Auditing helps give this proof. Auditing also helps to indicate that there is suitable and sufficient compliance with an organisation's health and safety policies and procedures. A great benefit of audits is as a technique for quantifying health and safety effectiveness. This is because auditing is a positive measure, ie it measures achievement rather than the more common negative measures such as incident and injury statistics — which only measure failure. The aims of health and safety audits are similar to the aims of financial audits; they are:

- to check progress in specific areas (eg in a particular department or completion of all risk assessments)
- to ensure consistency and accuracy of application across an organisation
- to provide feedback on implementation of the health and safety policies and procedures of an organisation.

There are two main types of audit: comprehensive and specific. Both have their role at different times and for different purposes.

Comprehensive

This is a large scale systematic audit of the performance of a whole organisation. In a multi-divisional organisation where each division is in reality a large organisation in its own right, it can be used separately as well, but should be repeated centrally to give the overall picture. This type of audit is very time consuming and is likely to involve a large number of auditors and amount of managerial time to undertake it properly. It is not unknown to use an external consultancy for this. However it is not always useful since the local knowledge of in-house auditors can play a large part in a successful audit. However, the auditor does need a high level of health and safety training and experience if the audit is to properly achieve its aims.

Specific

This type of audit is designed to monitor one process or activity and is usually undertaken with a much greater frequency than the comprehensive type. It may be: site based, process based, task based or based on the requirements of a particular statutory aspect (eg COSHH compliance). It can involve auditors who do not have a great deal of health and safety training. However there are some areas of the audit which, while restricted in scope, require a certain technical skill or qualification, eg testing the adequacy and function of local exhaust ventilation.

Safety inspections

These are not as in-depth as audits and tend to concentrate on identifying hazards in the area being inspected. They are a positive way to improve health and safety standards and form part of an overall programme of risk assessment. They should be carried out at regular intervals, depending on the type of business, a report produced and actions monitored.

Questions and Answers

Q Is there a specific legal requirement to carry out safety inspections?

A No. However various legal duties placed on employers are difficult to satisfy unless some form of inspection or other monitoring of standards is carried out.

Q Can we carry out audits ourselves or should we use a consultant?

A Audits are generally recognised as best being done by someone who has the knowledge and experience, who is impartial and who is respected by the people being audited. Consultants can satisfy these and other criteria but equally there may be people with the desirable attributes within the organisation.

Q How many different forms of workplace audits or inspections are there?

A Safety audits or inspections can take many forms. Every time a manager walks around the area they are responsible for should be a form of inspection as they should be on the lookout for hazards, unsafe practices, etc. At the other end of the scale, perhaps every three months, a manager, with people from the work area, should use some form of checklist to carry out a more structured inspection. There are various ways of carrying out inspections in between. What is important is to use a variety of techniques developed through experience to achieve good safety standards in your own business. A good audit system will enable the auditor to obtain all the necessary information without excessive decisions being needed at the workplace. Many commercial systems exist, either computer based or paper based, which provide an off the shelf solution. Most of these can be tailored to suit the individual requirements of a particular audit. The expense of these systems must be balanced against the very real time and cost burden of designing a system in-house. It is important to remember that the record of the audit may be needed to prove compliance with the requirements of the **Management of Health and Safety at Work Regulations 1999**, and thus must, of itself, be adequate and credible.

B

Biological Hazards

Summary

Biological hazards are caused by agents which are living micro-organisms capable of causing disease or harming the environment. These agents include viruses, bacteria, protozoa, parasites and fungi.

Various occupations may involve contact with biological hazards, for instance healthcare work, working with animals, research, sewage work, and work outdoors which involves contact with soil, eg construction and gardening.

Practical Guidance

Classification

Biological agents are classified into four groups. These are detailed in the following table.

Group number	Type of agents
Group 1	Agents that are unlikely to cause human disease.
Group 2	Agents that can cause human disease and may be hazardous to employees. However, they are unlikely to spread into the community, and there is usually an effective prophylaxis or treatment available.
Group 3	Agents that can cause serious human disease and may be seriously hazardous to employees. They may spread into the community, but there is usually an effective prophylaxis or treatment available.
Group 4	Agents that can cause serious human disease and may be seriously hazardous to employees. They may spread into the community, and there is usually no effective prophylaxis or treatment available.

The Health and Safety Commission (HSC) has classified a wide range of biological agents, and publishes these classifications in "Classification of biological agents according to hazard and categories of containment". If a micro-organism is not on this list, it is up to employers to classify it.

Controlling risk

Under the **Control of Substances Hazardous to Health Regulations 1999** (COSHH), an assessment of the risk of exposure to biological agents must be made. Where there is a risk from biological agents to the health of employees, or other people, this risk must be controlled.

The preferable method of control is to eliminate the risk altogether, by removing the harmful micro-organism from the work activity, using a less hazardous one, or treating it in some way so that it is no longer harmful. If this is not reasonably practicable, control measures should be set up to prevent or reduce the risk of infection, such as safe systems of work and engineering controls. A "biohazard" sign must be displayed to warn of the presence of biological agents which give rise to a hazard to human health.

It is up to employers to make sure that all control measures are used properly, well maintained, and regularly cleaned. COSHH requires local exhaust ventilation to be thoroughly examined at least once every 14 months.

Personal protective equipment

Personal protective equipment (PPE) should only be provided as a last resort, where the other measures will not adequately control exposure. Work with biological agents classified as group 2, 3 or 4 will require protective clothing to be worn. All PPE should be removed when the worker leaves the contaminated area, stored in facilities that will prevent cross-contamination of personal clothes, etc and must be regularly cleaned, checked and maintained.

Containment

Work with biological agents in groups 2, 3 or 4 must include suitable containment measures, eg separate workrooms with restricted access, disinfection procedures, ventilation systems, pest control, etc. Schedule 9 to COSHH gives tables of containment measures that must be taken:

(a) in veterinary and health care facilities, laboratories and animal rooms

(b) for industrial processes.

Employees

Employees have a legal duty under COSHH to properly use all control measures (including PPE), and to report any defects they find to their employer. They must also report any accidental releases of a biological agent which is capable of causing serious health effects.

They must be given suitable information, instruction and training, including the risks of working with biological agents, personal hygiene, how to carry out their work safely and use control measures, reporting defects and accidental releases, emergency procedures for dealing with accidents, spills, etc, health surveillance procedures and how to dispose of biological agents safely.

Monitoring

In some situations, it may be appropriate to monitor employees' exposure to biological agents. If this is the case, a suitable method should be used and records should be made and kept for at least five years.

Health surveillance

Employees must be provided with suitable health surveillance if the agent is associated with an identifiable disease, there are valid techniques for identifying the disease and there is a reasonable likelihood that the disease may result from the work activity. Suitable health surveillance procedures may include:
- immunisation where appropriate
- provision of contact cards
- health questionnaires
- medical examination
- tests for immune status or evidence of infection.

Health records must be made and kept for at least 40 years.

List of exposed employees

A list must be kept of any employees who have been exposed to group 3 or 4 biological agents, and it must include the following details:
- the employees' names
- the work activity
- the biological agent
- exposure, accidents and incidents.

The list must be kept for at least 10 years, or at least 40 years for certain biological agents specified by COSHH.

Notifying the authorities

The Health and Safety Executive (HSE) must be notified in writing at least 30 days before:
- a group 2, 3 or 4 biological agent is first stored or used by an employer
- subsequent listed micro-organisms (see below) or a group 3 agent without an approved classification, is first stored or used by an employer
- listed micro-organisms (see below) are consigned.

The listed micro-organisms are all group 4 agents: rabies virus, simian herpes B virus, Venezuelan equine encephalitis virus, tick-borne encephalitis viruses in group 3, monkey pox virus, and mopeia virus.

The HSE must also be notified in writing of any substantial changes that will affect the original notification.

Genetically modified organisms

The **Genetically Modified Organisms (Contained Use) Regulations 2000** apply to work activities where any organism is modified using one of the artificial techniques listed in the Regulations. This does not include modification of humans or human embryos. The Regulations specify requirements for the following.

1. A risk assessment must be carried out, recorded and reviewed.
2. The HSE must be notified before the commencement of any work involving genetically modified organisms (GMOs). There is a fee for notification, and the HSE will keep a public register of all activities notified.
3. A genetic modification safety committee must be set up to provide advice.
4. Certain standards of safety must be followed.
5. An emergency plan must be drawn up and kept up-to-date. The plan must be made available to the public, with the help of the local authority.

Questions and Answers

Q What is the legal definition of a biological agent?

A The COSHH Regulations define a biological agent as "any micro-organism, cell culture, or human endoparasite, including any which have been genetically modified, which may cause any infection, allergy, toxicity, or otherwise create a hazard to human health".

Q What is a biohazard?

A The term "biohazard" is not defined by the COSHH Regulations, although they do depict the official biohazard sign. This sign must displayed where the presence of a biological agent gives rise to a hazard to human health.

Q I work for a vet. Should I be worried about biological agents?

A Yes. A variety of diseases may be passed from animals to humans, and measures must be taken to protect you from coming into contact with harmful micro-organisms. You should make sure that you are up to date with any vaccinations needed, such as tetanus.

For pregnant workers (or those who may be pregnant) toxoplasmosis is especially of concern. It may be contracted by coming into contact with cat faeces. Although the symptoms in adult humans are usually fairly mild, it is very damaging to the unborn baby, especially in the first three months of pregnancy. Workers who are, or may be, pregnant should avoid cleaning out cat litter. If this is not possible, they must exercise extremely high standards of personal hygiene, and clean their hands and their fingernails thoroughly immediately after working with animal waste.

Q I collect samples of river water for environmental reasons for my company. What biological agents should I be concerned about?

A   A variety of water-borne micro-organisms can cause ill-health if they are accidentally ingested. These include salmonellosis, hepatitis A, leptospirosis and shigellosis. You should use the protective measures and equipment provided by your employer, eg protective gloves, good personal hygiene, putting lids on to sample containers. Your employer should also tell you what symptoms to look out for, and who to tell if you suspect that you may have contracted one of the diseases.

Chemical Safety

Summary

Chemicals are substances or preparations (ie mixtures of substances) which may be present in the workplace in a variety of forms, ie gases, liquids, vapours, fumes, solids and powders. Many chemicals may be harmful to human health, or may present other hazards, such as causing fire or explosions.

Practical Guidance

Classification and labelling of chemicals
Under the **Chemicals (Hazard Information and Packaging for Supply) Regulations 1994** (as amended), all chemicals which are dangerous for supply must be classified into one or more of the following categories.
1. Physico-chemical properties: explosive, oxidising, extremely flammable, highly flammable and flammable.
2. Health effects: very toxic, toxic, harmful, corrosive, irritant, sensitising, sensitising by inhalation, sensitising by skin contact, carcinogenic (three categories), mutagenic (three categories) and toxic for reproduction (three categories).
3. Dangerous for the environment. The supplier of the chemical must put certain information on the container it is supplied in to provide the user with details of how to handle, store and dispose of the chemical safely.

Controlling health risks
Under the **Control of Substances Hazardous to Health Regulations 1999** (COSHH), an assessment of possible exposure to chemicals in the workplace must be carried out to determine:
- the nature and effects of the chemicals
- the possible routes of exposure, eg inhalation, absorption, ingestion
- how the chemical is used
- how employees engaged in the work activity may be exposed, and possible exposure of other people in, or near, the area

- how the chemical may react with other chemicals present, and their combined effect on health
- any maximum exposure limits or occupational exposure standards that have been set for the chemical (these are listed in Health and Safety Executive (HSE) guidance note EH40 (see *Further Information*).

The assessment should take into account existing control measures, such as engineering controls, and should look at what controls may be needed to prevent or reduce exposure to the chemical.

Controlling fire and explosion risks

The **Highly Flammable Liquids and Liquefied Petroleum Gases Regulations 1972** cover the safe use, handling, storage and fire and emergency arrangements for highly flammable liquids. The Regulations apply to premises where liquids are present which have a flashpoint of less than 32°C and which support combustion.

The Regulations require that all highly flammable liquids must be stored safely in fixed storage tanks or closed vessels. The storage tanks and closed vessels must be:

- in a safe position
- provided with containment for any spills or leakages, or otherwise treated to make them safe
- with all openings kept closed.

Closed vessels must be in the open air, protected against sunlight if necessary, or suitably closed in a fire-resistant storeroom. Every storeroom or vessel used for storing highly flammable liquids must be marked with an appropriate sign, such as "Highly Flammable". If a highly flammable liquid is likely to leak or be spilt during an operation, all reasonably practicable steps must be taken to contain it.

Sources of ignition, such as naked flames or cigarettes, must be removed if there is a likelihood that a dangerous concentration of vapour may build up. Materials such as cotton waste or other material contaminated with highly flammable liquid must be removed to a safe place or put in a closed metal container. Smoking is prohibited where highly flammable liquid is present, and "No Smoking" signs must be displayed in any place where there is a risk of fire.

Under the **Control of Explosives Regulations 1991**, anyone who acquires or keeps explosives must have an explosives certificate issued by the chief officer of police. Occupiers of licensed factories and magazines must appoint someone to be responsible for security of explosives. Anyone who acquires or keeps explosives must make, and maintain, up-to-date records containing specified information.

Elimination

COSHH requires that, where reasonably practicable, the risks from hazardous substances must be prevented by eliminating the chemical, for example by using an alternative, less hazardous substance, eg replacing solvent-based paints with water-based paints.

Control measures

If it is not possible to eliminate the hazardous substance, COSHH requires that the risks must be prevented or controlled. Control measures include:

- enclosing the process that gives rise to a risk
- methods of suppressing or containing dusts, fumes, vapours, spills, leaks, etc produced by work activities, including engineering controls such as ventilation
- reducing to a minimum the number of people exposed to the chemicals
- introducing systems of work which reduce the likelihood of ingesting chemicals, ie prohibiting eating, drinking and smoking in contaminated areas, and providing washing facilities
- regular cleaning of work areas to remove chemical residues
- restricting access to contaminated areas, and putting up signs to warn people of the risks
- keeping chemicals in suitable, properly labelled containers and in suitable storage areas.

All engineering controls must be well maintained in good working order, and records of tests must be kept for at least five years.

Personal protective equipment

COSHH only allows personal protective equipment (PPE) to be provided as a control measure if the other control measures the employer provides do not offer adequate protection. Any PPE provided to control exposure to hazardous substances must be suitable for its purpose, regularly cleaned, and maintained in good working order.

Notification of sites

Under the **Notification of Installations Handling Hazardous Substances Regulations 1984**, the HSE must be notified of premises where any of the substances listed in the Regulations may be present in the quantities listed.

Under the **Dangerous Substances (Notification and Marking of Sites) Regulations 1990**, the fire brigade and the enforcing authority (HSE or local authority) must be notified if 25 tonnes or more of any dangerous substance is present on the premises.

Under the **Control of Major Accident Hazards Regulations 1999** (COMAH), a number of industrial processes are identified as presenting a major risk to the surrounding area. Applications of COMAH will be triggered by the presence of specific quantities of dangerous substances, and all sites must have a Major Accident Prevention Policy (MAPP).

Procedures for handling chemicals

Procedures for handling chemicals include the following instructions.
1. Use the least hazardous chemicals possible for the job.
2. Use any enclosures, eg fume hoods, provided for handling chemicals.

3. Do not eat, drink or smoke in any area where chemicals are used or stored.
4. Keep the amount of chemical used to a minimum.
5. Always read the label on the bottle and safety data sheet provided by the supplier, and follow any safety instructions given.
6. Wear any PPE provided for work with chemicals, and report any defects to the supervisor.

Chemical storage

Chemicals should be stored in suitable storage areas, which may need to be kept locked. Incompatible chemicals should not be stored together, and:

- flammable or toxic substances must not be stored with any other type of hazardous substance, except those classified only as harmful or irritant
- oxidising substances must not be stored with any other type of hazardous substance, except those classified only as harmful or irritant, and then only if special precautions are taken
- explosive or radioactive substances must not be stored with any other type of hazardous substance.

Disposal of chemicals

Waste and spilled chemicals must be disposed of properly and safely. There is an environmental duty of care on all employers who produce waste. Check the supply label to find out how to dispose of any chemical waste and empty chemical containers. If in doubt, ask the supplier or a specialist waste disposal contractor for advice.

Note: Never pour waste chemicals down the drain unless you are absolutely sure that it is legal for you to do so.

Questions and Answers

Q   I manage a small office. Is chemical safety relevant to me?
A   Chemicals are found in practically every workplace, even small offices. You probably have correction fluids, ozone from photocopiers, organic dust from paper, solvents in paints and thinners, chemical cleaning products such as bleaches and detergents, and so on. You will need to assess the chemicals used in your office, but it will be much less complicated than it is for an industrial process.
Q   Do I need to keep my chemical storeroom locked?
A   It depends on how hazardous the chemicals are, and who is likely to have access. If it is possible that people who are not trained to handle the chemicals, especially children, may help themselves to the products in your storeroom, you will need to keep it locked. If you do lock your storeroom, it is sensible to provide the responsible people, who are allowed access, with a key.

Q Are there any Regulations relating to chemical safety that specifically require employees to be given instruction, information and training?

A Within the following list of Regulations the requirement for instruction, information and training is explicit:

- **Control of Substances Hazardous to Health Regulations 1999**
- **Personal Protective Equipment at Work Regulations 1992**
- **Control of Asbestos at Work Regulations 1987**
- **Control of Pesticides Regulations 1986.**

Q Is correction fluid really hazardous?

A Correction fluids contain substances which are hazardous. However, in the normal small bottle that it is supplied in, the quantities are unlikely to be particularly harmful to health. Users should avoid inhaling the fumes, and should keep the lid on the bottle when they are not using it.

Classification, Packaging, Carriage and Storage of Dangerous Goods

Summary

Dangerous goods, ie substances and articles, have to be classified, labelled and packaged according to a range of statutory requirements before they can be transported, or used in a workplace. The detailed statutory requirements are contained in a series of Regulations.

Practical Guidance

Classification

No dangerous substance or preparation may be supplied or carried unless it has been classified under the appropriate Regulations. The "Approved Supply and Carriage Lists", which are regularly revised, contain classifications for many chemicals. For supply purposes, where a substance does not appear in that list then it must be classified under one of the following categories:

- physico-chemical properties: explosive, oxidising, extremely flammable, highly flammable and flammable
- health effects: very toxic, toxic, harmful, irritant, sensitising, carcinogenic, mutagenic, toxic for reproduction
- environmental effects: dangerous for the environment.

Preparations for supply need only be classified under the first two classification groups.

All dangerous goods must be provided with a safety data sheet which contains detailed information on the substance or preparation, including any associated hazards, first aid information, etc.

Dangerous goods intended for carriage must be classified according to the danger they represent — the "Approved Carriage List" and Schedules 1 and 2 of the **Carriage of Dangerous Goods (Classification, Packaging and Labelling) and Use of Transportable Pressure Receptacles Regulations 1996** contain the relevant information.

Packaging

The packaging of dangerous goods intended for supply must be suitable, must safely contain the goods during normal handling, must not cause any adverse effects with the goods they contain or are likely to come into contact with, and have closures which allow repeated opening and closing without leaking. The packaging must also prevent access by children and must display tactile warnings.

There are similar requirements for the packaging of dangerous goods intended for carriage, although they must also be certified to prove that they are of an approved and tested design type. They must also bear an approved international road or rail carriage mark.

Labelling

All containers must display a label which can be clearly seen and read at all times, and which contains information specified in the **Carriage of Dangerous Goods (Classification, Packaging and Labelling) and Use of Transportable Pressure Receptacles Regulations 1996**. The information should be indelible, in English (usually) and must meet specified size requirements. The labelling requirements are similar for both the supply and carriage of dangerous goods. In a case heard at Scunthorpe Magistrates' Court in August 1996, a cleaning equipment supplier was fined £2000 after a worker was seriously burnt by a highly caustic detergent which had no warning label. The supplier had initially received the detergent in bulk but had not transferred the relevant warning information after decanting it into smaller containers.

Carriage

The Health and Safety Commission (HSC) has published various "approved documents" which detail standards for vehicle design and construction, tank filling, testing and certification, and for the classification, packaging and labelling of dangerous goods.

There are several different Regulations depending on the mode of carriage, ie road or rail, and on the goods being carried, eg explosives, radioactive materials and other dangerous goods, etc.

Certain information from consignors and operators must be provided, eg information on the classification, designation, UN (United Nations) number, transport category, control measures, and quantities. Relevant transport documentation must also be provided.

Containers, tanks and vehicles must display information specified in their respective Regulations. There are also requirements covering the loading and unloading of dangerous goods, and emergency and parking procedures.

Drivers of dangerous goods must hold vocational training certificates from an approved training course.

With effect from 31 December 1999 employers who are involved in the transport of dangerous goods by road or rail must appoint vocationally qualified safety advisors. The legislation lays down the specific duties of such advisors, who must hold the appropriate vocational training certificate.

Storage

The appropriate criteria for storing dangerous goods and substances are totally dependent on their specific nature and associated hazards. Generally, all dangerous items should be stored securely with authorised and limited access to them. There should be procedures in place for containing and dealing with liquid spillages. Flammable goods should be kept in fire-resistant structures and smoking and the presence of naked lights or other ignition sources should be prohibited from the area — appropriate means for fighting any fires should be provided. Poisonous goods should be kept away from food items — certain poisons specified in the Poisons Rules 1982 are subject to detailed storage requirements.

Containers and stock should generally be regularly checked to ensure against leaks and goods becoming out of date, etc. Stock quantities held in any location should be the minimum that is feasible. Substances and goods with different hazard classifications should generally be stored separately to each other.

Premises where certain specified dangerous substances are held must meet various notification and marking requirements.

The fire brigade should be made aware of the type, quantities and location of dangerous goods on work premises.

Questions and Answers

Q   Is the "dangerous goods" legislation the same as the COSHH Regulations?

A   No. The "dangerous goods" legislation applies standards for classifying, labelling and packaging substances and preparations which are known to be dangerous for supply, ie use at work, and for carriage, ie transportation. This legislation is not concerned about the actual use of, or exposure to, the substances, etc, which are generally covered by the **Control of Substances Hazardous to Health Regulations 1999** (COSHH) (with the exception of explosives and radioactive material which are covered by other legislation). However, the "dangerous goods" legislation does define the "hazardous" classifications used in the COSHH Regulations.

Q   What are "dangerous goods"?

A   "Dangerous goods" may generally be accepted to be articles or substances which are explosive, radioactive, individually listed in the "Approved Carriage List" or "Approved Supply List" (unless they are so dilute that they are no longer hazardous) or that have one or more hazardous properties.

Q   Who enforces the "dangerous goods" legislation?

A Generally, the Health and Safety Executive (HSE) is responsible for enforcement, although the police are responsible for ensuring compliance with road traffic laws and for certain provisions concerning explosives.

Q What is a substance and is it different to a preparation?

A A substance is any individual chemical, whereas a preparation is a mixture (solids) or solution (liquids) of two or more substances.

Cleanliness

Summary

Without regular cleaning of the workplace, waste materials will build up and present a hazard. Waste may be hazardous for a number of reasons, including increasing the risk of tripping and slipping, spread of disease (especially in toilet facilities), attracting pests, increasing the risk of fire, and increasing the risk of adverse health effects if the waste is a hazardous substance.

Practical Guidance

Maintenance of workplaces

The **Health and Safety at Work, etc Act 1974** requires workplaces to be maintained in a condition that does not present a risk to health. This duty includes cleaning the workplace.

Construction of surfaces

Under the **Workplace (Health, Safety and Welfare) Regulations 1992** (Workplace Regulations), the floors, walls and ceilings in workplaces must be capable of being cleaned. This includes making sure that they are maintained in a condition that allows them to be cleaned, eg repairing or replacing scratched surfaces and cracked tiles and repainting chipped paint.

Cleanability

All surfaces, equipment, furniture, etc must be capable of being easily cleaned. Machinery must be designed and made so that it is capable of being cleaned safely. Always make sure that any new machinery, equipment or furniture purchased is easy to clean — if in doubt, ask the supplier.

Smooth surfaces that do not absorb liquids are the easiest to clean, such as smooth tiles, sealed wooden floors and vinyl floor or work surfaces. For areas where hygiene is important, such as toilets, washrooms and kitchens, only smooth, easy-to-clean surfaces should be used. In areas where dirt and waste accumulates, such as factory floors, machine rooms and workshop areas, the floors should be easy to sweep and clean regularly, eg concrete. In office areas, carpets may be used, but these should be relatively flat and short-fibred, rather than thick and long-fibred, for ease of cleaning.

Cleaning

The Workplace Regulations require all workplaces to be kept clean, including furniture, furnishings and fittings. The standard of cleanliness required will depend on the type of workplace, the activities carried out and the materials involved. For example, an office would be expected to have a higher standard of cleanliness than a motor vehicle repair workshop.

Under the Workplace Regulations, waste materials must not be allowed to accumulate in the workplace. This usually involves bins being provided for waste, regular emptying of these bins and removal of waste from the premises. Special bins may need to be provided for particular types of waste, such as clinical waste or waste oils.

Toilets and washrooms

The Workplace Regulations require sanitary conveniences and washing facilities to be kept clean. This includes suitable means of disposal of sanitary dressings, which must be emptied regularly.

First aid rooms

Where compliance with the **Health and Safety (First Aid) Regulations 1981** requires the provision of a first aid room, it must be easy to clean and must be cleaned daily. Of course, all first aid equipment must be kept clean and dressings, etc must be sterile.

Engineering controls and PPE

The following Regulations require engineering controls and personal protective equipment (PPE) to be kept clean:
- **Control of Substances Hazardous to Health Regulations 1999**
- **Personal Protective Equipment at Work Regulations 1992**
- **Control of Lead at Work Regulations 1998**
- **Control of Asbestos at Work Regulations 1987.**

Asbestos

Under the **Control of Asbestos at Work Regulations 1987**, all areas where asbestos work is carried out, and any plant or equipment used in connection with that work, must be:
- capable of being cleaned thoroughly
- kept in a clean state.

When work which produces asbestos dust is being planned, the considerations should include ways of designing and constructing the building to make cleaning easier.

Lead

Adequate steps must be taken to keep the workplace, premises, plant and protective equipment clean under the **Control of Lead at Work Regulations 1998**. The washing and eating facilities must be kept clean. Cleaning should be frequent enough to ensure cleanliness, in order to remove lead deposits which may be ingested or inhaled.

Construction

Under the **Construction (Health, Safety and Welfare) Regulations 1996**, construction sites must be kept in good order and in a reasonable state of cleanliness.

Food handling

The **Food Safety (General Food Hygiene) Regulations 1995** place duties on food proprietors to provide food preparation facilities, equipment, etc which are easily cleansable, and which are kept clean. There should be separate facilities for the washing of utensils and for hand-washing in the food preparation area.

Machinery and other work equipment

Manufacturers, designers, importers and suppliers must make sure that the machinery that they make or supply is capable of being cleaned without presenting a safety risk to the person cleaning it, as required by the **Consumer Protection Act 1987**.

Safety signs

Under the **Health and Safety (Safety Signs and Signals) Regulations 1996**, any safety signs provided must be maintained. This would include regular cleaning to make sure they remain easy to see.

Housekeeping

Housekeeping means keeping the workplace in a clean, tidy and organised condition. It takes effort, discipline and organisation on the part of the workers and management. Workers should be instructed on what standard of housekeeping is expected of them, and supervisors should look out for obstructions, disorder and untidiness on a daily basis. In order to check that the systems for housekeeping are operating efficiently, the person responsible for managing health and safety in the workplace should carry out regular housekeeping inspections. The following checklist may be of assistance.

- Are all corridors, passageways, exit routes and walkways clear of objects and obstructions?

- Are there any cables or cords trailing across any area where people walk? (Wherever possible, trailing cables should be avoided, or if this is not possible, covered and secured.)
- Are all items kept in the correct storage place while not in use?
- Are employees keeping their workstations tidy?
- Are rubbish bins emptied regularly?
- Are all drawers closed when not in use?
- Are there any items left on floors which could prevent a trip hazard?
- Are there any items left on work surfaces which are in a position to fall off easily?
- Are all fire extinguishers in their correct position?

Window cleaning

Windows must be designed and constructed to allow them to be cleaned safely. Window cleaning is a hazardous activity, and a safe system of work must be in place. If outside contractors are brought in to clean windows, the client employer should make sure that they carry out their job safely. If they do not, another contractor should be found.

Safe systems of cleaning windows include:
- windows that turn sideways, so that both sides can be cleaned from inside
- the use of suspended cradles or travelling ladders that have safety harness attachments, and are used properly
- mobile access platforms that have safety harness attachments, and are used properly
- if normal ladders are used, anchor points for safety harnesses should be fitted at appropriate locations so that the cleaner always has somewhere to anchor to, the safety harness must be worn and anchored to the points whenever the cleaner is working at height.

Questions and Answers

Q How often should work areas be cleaned?

A The Workplace Regulations put the onus on employers to decide how often they need to clean different items and areas. However, the following table gives a few suggestions for cleaning frequency.

Item/Area	Frequency of Cleaning
Rubbish bins	Empty daily
Toilet areas	Clean daily, check stocks of toilet paper
Washing areas	Clean daily, mop floors, check stores of soap, clean/disposable towels, check cleanliness of nail-brushes

Kitchens	Clean daily, mop floors, check stocks of detergent and clean towels
Office carpets	Vacuum weekly
Factory floors	Sweep whenever waste accumulates, and at least daily
Staircases	Sweep or vacuum weekly
Windows	Clean monthly
Walls and ceilings	Wash yearly, repaint every seven years
Workstations, desks, computers	Dust weekly

Q What arrangements do I need to make with contract cleaners?

A Contract cleaners are used by many companies for routine cleaning operations. The contractor, as an employer, is responsible for the health and safety of their employees. They will supply the cleaning materials and equipment, and must train their staff in how to use them safely and the procedures for cleaning operations. There must be a good system of communication between the client employer and the contractor, to make sure your activities do not present a risk to the cleaners, and the cleaners' activities do not present a risk to your employees.

Before selecting a contract cleaner, ask questions about their safety procedures and ask them for a copy of their safety policy. When drawing up the contract, make sure you include a definition of what operations they are responsible for carrying out, and a statement that they must comply with your company's safety procedures (give them a copy of the procedures that apply to them, eg keeping cleaning products locked when not in use). Make arrangements to ensure that your staff do not use, or come into contact with, any of the contractor's cleaning products or equipment — lockable cleaning cupboards are usually provided by the client. Make sure the contractor understands the hazards of your workplace, and passes this information on to their staff.

Q How often should our bins be emptied?

A In most cases, rubbish bins in work areas will need to be emptied daily. The waste should be stored in a safe place, eg a covered skip in the car park, and collected regularly (eg weekly) by a waste disposal contractor. These frequencies may not be enough. Check whether bins are becoming too full, and if they are, provide extra bins or larger bins, or empty them more often.

Q What is a suitable disposal method for sanitary dressings?

A If you only have a few women using each toilet and you are confident that blockages will not occur, it is possible for them to be flushed. However, many plumbing systems combined with frequent use of the toilets cannot cope with the number of sanitary dressings flushed. In this case, separate bins should be provided. These bins must be suitable for disposal of clinical waste, should reduce odour to the lowest possible level and must be emptied regularly by a specially trained person. It is not suitable to dispose of sanitary dressings as part of your normal waste disposal system, eg that used for office waste.

There is a choice of specialist disposal contractors which provide bins and emptying services. Bear in mind that sanitary dressings are clinical waste, which is classified under environmental legislation as special waste. Clinical waste should be incinerated at a licensed facility.

Clothing, Changing and Storage

Summary

Some jobs require the use of overalls or other special work clothing, to protect against physical or chemical hazards or to protect the worker's personal clothes from dirt, paint, etc. Workplaces must have suitable storage facilities both for work clothes and for personal clothes that are not worn at work.

Practical Guidance

Suitable accommodation for the clothing storage

Suitable accommodation for the storage of clothing is required by the **Workplace (Health, Safety and Welfare) Regulations 1992**. Such accommodation is needed:

- for special work clothing provided which is not taken home by the workers
- workers' personal clothing which is not worn while at work.

Storage accommodation for clothing should be located in a suitable area. Facilities for work clothing and personal clothing should be separate if there is a risk of contamination from the work clothes, eg if they are worn for working with hazardous substances. Storage areas for personal clothes should be secure, to prevent theft or damage of the workers' own clothes. Where necessary, a means of drying wet clothes should be provided.

In order to be considered suitable, storage facilities for clothing should be:

- separate from any eating facilities provided
- connected to any shower or bath areas provided
- provided with adequate seating, ie chairs or benches
- large enough for the number of people who are likely to be using them at any one time.

If special clothing is worn at work, suitable facilities for changing clothes must be provided. Arrangements must be in place for men and women to change separately.

Personal protective equipment

Under the **Personal Protective Equipment at Work Regulations 1992**, suitable accommodation must be provided for storing personal protective equipment (PPE) while not in use. This would include protective clothing provided for the purposes of health and safety, eg protective gloves, safety boots, hard hats and high-visibility clothing. Storage facilities for PPE should be designed to prevent damage to the clothing and equipment.

Construction

Under the **Construction (Health, Safety and Welfare) Regulations 1996**, facilities for changing clothes and for storing them must be provided. There should be means for drying wet clothes.

Asbestos

Employees who are exposed to asbestos at work must be provided with suitable clothes changing facilities, as required by the **Control of Asbestos at Work Regulations 1987**. These facilities must include somewhere suitable to store protective and personal clothes separately, to avoid the risk of contamination.

Lead

Where protective clothing and/or respiratory protective equipment (RPE) is provided for work with lead, the **Control of Lead at Work Regulations 1998** require suitable clothes changing and storage facilities to be provided. As with asbestos and other hazardous substances, the storage arrangements must separate protective and personal clothing to avoid the risk of contamination.

Radiation

Under the **Ionising Radiations Regulations 1999**, suitable facilities must be provided for changing clothes and storing protective equipment and clothing. These facilities must be positioned at a place where the workers enter or leave an area where work with ionising radiations is carried out.

Food safety

Under the **Food Safety (General Food Hygiene) Regulations 1995**, suitable changing facilities should be provided for food handlers. These changing facilities should include accommodation for storing clothes.

Overclothes

In some workplaces, the only storage accommodation needed is for overclothes, such as coats, scarves, boots, etc. A cupboard with coat-hangers or sufficient numbers of hatstands may be all that is needed. However, if there is a risk of theft of clothes, there should be some means of security, such as providing lockable cupboards or putting hatstands in an area where there are always workers around to keep an eye on them.

Uniforms and overalls

Some companies require their workers to wear uniforms. Many types of worker, such as painters, maintenance workers and mechanics, require overalls to prevent personal clothing from becoming dirty. If it is necessary for workers to take off more than overclothes, a changing area will be required for reasons of propriety. The changing area should:

- contain benches or chairs
- be large enough to allow enough space for the maximum number of people using it at any one time
- be in a convenient location, considering where the work will be carried out
- be at a suitable temperature
- be kept clean and tidy
- be adequately lit and ventilated
- allow men and women to change separately.

It may not be necessary to provide separate changing rooms for men and women, so long as arrangements are in place to allow them to change separately. For example, there could be allocated times when each sex is allowed into the changing rooms. Alternatively, cubicles with doors or curtains which completely obscure the view into the cubicle could be provided.

Lockers, shelves, pigeon-holes or some other place to store personal clothes while the employees are at work should be provided in the changing rooms.

Protective clothing

Where work clothes are provided to protect workers from hazardous substances, there is a risk of dirty clothes contaminating other items of clothing. Contaminated protective clothing must be cleaned regularly. The storage facilities should allow it to be kept separately from personal clothes.

Drying facilities

It may be necessary to provide a means of drying wet clothes. These means may vary from providing clothes-horses to hang wet clothes on, to supplying tumble dryers. When making a decision on what drying facilities to provide, the following should be considered:

- how quickly do the clothes need to be dried?
- what factors will affect the speed of drying, eg humid conditions?
- how likely is it that work clothes will become wet?
- what volume of wet clothing is likely to be produced?
- is spare, dry clothing available to replace wet clothing?
- what resources are available to be spent on drying facilities?

Valuable items

Storage of personal clothing must be secure to prevent theft and damage. However, normal storage areas for coats, etc, may not be secure enough for certain valuable items. Some items of protective clothing and equipment are very expensive, and it would be cost effective for employers to have systems in place to prevent them being stolen, lost, damaged or inadvertently removed from the workplace. For example, protective equipment and clothing may be issued personally, and each individual has a responsibility to look after it, store it in lockers, etc.

It may be necessary for workers to remove valuable personal items while they work, eg jewellery should be removed when working with certain machinery. Personal items which are valuable to the owner, either due to their monetary value or sentimental value, should be kept in a very secure place, such as a safe. There should be a system of administration and identification in place to prevent workers taking one anothers' property.

Questions and Answers

Q Are toilet cubicles suitable as changing facilities?

A If employees have to remove anything more than overclothes to put on work clothes, the answer is likely to be no. There is unlikely to be enough space in a toilet cubicle to change, and it is not suitable for hygiene reasons, for example if clothes are dropped on the floor. It may be possible to extend your toilet areas to include changing facilities, for example by designating an area as a changing area with benches, lockers, etc. However, the toilet areas in many premises are unlikely to provide adequate space to incorporate changing facilities.

If changing into work clothes is not a requirement of the job, you may find that some employees still choose to change at work, eg if they cycle into work or go out socially straight from work. As these changes of clothes are voluntary and optional, there is nothing in law to require employers to provide changing facilities or to prevent employees from choosing to use toilet cubicles.

Q Do we have to provide lockers for storing clothes?

A The law requires that personal clothing which is not worn while at work must be in a secure storage area. Lockers allocated to individual workers is one way of meeting this requirement. It depends on the likelihood of theft, which depends on the workplace. If members of the public or other visitors are commonly on-site, it is likely that lockers or lockable storage areas will be needed. However, if site security is generally high, it may only be necessary to store clothes in a place where there is always people around. It is a good idea to position coat-hangers where the people using them can see them from their workstation.

Q How can we make sure workers do not contaminate their personal clothing by storing it with their protective work clothes?

Clothing, Changing and Storage

A   Communication is the key to this. All new workers should be told about the arrangements for storing contaminated clothing separately from personal clothing — explain why it is so important that they follow the rules. Clear signs should be put up showing which areas are provided for work clothes and which are for personal clothes. It may be useful to have different types of storage facilities in different areas, for example lockers for personal clothes at one end of the room, and pigeon-holes and a laundry bin for contaminated work clothes at the other end of the room. Supervisors should check regularly that the system is being followed, and remind workers where necessary.

Compressed Air

Summary

Work in compressed air means work in pressures which exceed 0.15 bar above atmospheric pressure which, for completeness in this publication, includes diving work. Such work is subject to very strict controls due to the very serious associated risks of illness and injury (decompression and recompression are particularly relevant).

Practical Guidance

The **Work in Compressed Air Regulations 1996** apply to work in compressed air which forms part of a construction project, and place specific duties on "compressed air contractors" (appointed by the project "principal contractor"), employers, employees and self-employed persons.

Safe systems, equipment and emergencies

Written notification of work in compressed air, and its cessation, must be given to the Health and Safety Executive (HSE) and any hospital with facilities for dealing with the medical conditions associated with compressed air work. Local emergency services and any other establishment with an operational medical air lock should also be notified. The notice period to the HSE is 14 days prior to the start of the work, although shorter periods may be accepted in emergencies.

Safe systems of work, including means of entering and leaving the work areas, must be established and followed by all compressed air workers. Supervision of compressed air work is required at all times, and where the work involved pressures at 0.7 bar, supervision is also required for the 24-hour period immediately afterwards.

Equipment must be suitable, safe and undergo appropriate testing, examination and maintenance. The risk of fire must be minimised. Suitable and sufficient welfare facilities, including toilets, washing facilities, drinking water, rest and changing facilities must be provided. Adequate information, instruction and training on the risks associated with compressed air work, and the necessary precautions must be given to compressed air workers.

Employees' duties

Workers may not work in compressed air if they are under the influence of alcohol or drugs. Additionally, such workers may not consume or have on them any alcoholic drinks, or smoke or carry smoking materials during compressed air work.

Health aspects

Controls are generally based on well-defined fitness to work criteria, appropriate supervision and access to special medical facilities, assistance and surveillance.

Given the potentially serious health/medical conditions associated with compressed air work a "contract medical advisor" must be appointed for all such projects. In addition, all compressed air workers must be fit for such work, be on an appropriate medical surveillance programme and undergo regular medical examinations (at least annually) — suitable facilities for conducting such examinations must be provided. Medical surveillance may extend beyond the actual compressed air work if this is considered necessary.

A designated employment medical advisor or appointed doctor may also prohibit or impose certain other conditions on workers undertaking compressed air work. These prohibitions or conditions must be entered on the worker's health record and must be obeyed by the worker's employer, until such time as they are cancelled by the employment medical advisor or appointed doctor.

Where the work involves compressed air at 0.7 bar or more pressure, a medical airlock and a competent airlock operator and medical advisor must be provided.

Compression and decompression

There must be HSE-approved procedures in place for the compression or decompression of workers, and no worker may be exposed to pressures greater than 3.5 bar, except in emergencies.

The procedure of "decanting" workers, ie their rapid decompression to atmospheric pressure in an air lock, followed by rapid compression in another air lock and a second decompression to atmospheric pressure, must be avoided except in emergencies. Records of pressure exposures and times must be maintained for 40 years from date of last entry, as must records of individual exposure pressures (including maximum pressures exposed to), times and dates — workers should be given the relevant information from these records on completion of their compressed air work. Decompression sickness is reportable under the **Reporting of Injuries, Diseases and Dangerous Occurrences Regulations 1995** (RIDDOR).

Where workers have been exposed to pressures at or greater than 0.7 bar they must wear a badge, label or other device which contains approved particulars and which is intended to inform other people if the worker becomes ill after leaving work. The badge must be worn for the 24-hour period after such work.

Diving

Generally, the controls on diving work are broadly similar to those in compressed air work and include notification of the work, the appointment of competent persons to oversee and supervise the work, the certification of fitness and appropriate training for divers to dive, the maintainance of specified records and the provision of suitable and sufficient equipment, including a means of communication, a means of supplying a breathing mixture and a lifeline, etc.

Questions and Answers

Q What are the "bends"?

A The "bends" is the commonest form of decompression sickness and occurs when dissolved nitrogen is released from, and forms bubbles in, the blood on reduction of atmospheric pressure. The symptoms include severe pains in the joints, dental cavities and abdomen, or in more serious cases in severe neurological conditions if the bubbles form in the brain.

Q Are there any more physiological effects of work in compressed air?

A Yes, there are known degenerative conditions of the bones in people who habitually work in compressed air, while lesser conditions include ear infections and blocked Eustachian tubes which may affect hearing and/or balance.

Q How long do medical and health records have to be kept for?

A Medical and health records must be kept for 40 years.

Confined Spaces

Summary

A confined space is any work area where there is restricted access, a lack of a free-flowing supply of breathable air, or a presence of dangerous gases, vapours or fumes. The **Confined Spaces Regulations 1997** define a confined space as any chamber, tank, vat, silo, pit, trench, pipe, sewer, flue, well or other similar space which presents a foreseeable specified risk by virtue of its enclosed nature.

Practical Guidance

Definition of a confined space

Some confined spaces, such as closed tanks and silos, are easily definable. However, some are less obvious, but may be equally dangerous. For example, maintenance and inspection pits are included within the definition of a confined space because, although they are open at the top, there is no air circulation. Some hazardous vapours are heavier than air, and would not escape from the open top. Therefore there can be a build-up of flammable or toxic gases, or a reduction in oxygen.

The two defining features of a confined space are:
- a place which is substantially, though not always entirely, enclosed
- there is a reasonably foreseeable risk of serious injury from hazardous substances or conditions within the space or nearby.

It should be noted that some work areas may only fall into the category of confined space owing to the type of work being undertaken, eg a workshop during paint spraying.

General legal duties

Under the **Health and Safety at Work, etc Act 1974** an employer must provide and maintain safe plant and systems of work, and information, instruction, training and supervision to ensure that all work is carried out safely and without risk to health.

Employees must co-operate with their employer and take reasonable care of themselves and others who may be affected by their actions.

Self-employed persons are responsible for conducting their work in such a way so as not to endanger themselves or anyone else who may be affected by their work.

Specific legal duties

The **Confined Spaces Regulations 1997** consolidate the general requirements in the Factories Act 1961 regarding confined spaces, and extend these to all work premises. They require the employer to eliminate work in confined spaces where reasonably practicable. If this is not possible, the employer or self-employed person must assess the risk to those entering or working in the space.

A risk assessment must be carried out by a competent person, ie someone with sufficient experience of, and familiarity with, the relevant processes, plant and equipment to understand the risks involved and who can devise necessary precautions to meet the requirements of the **Confined Spaces Regulations 1997**.

Where it is not possible to avoid entering a confined space to undertake work, the employer or self-employed person is responsible for ensuring that a safe system of work is used. When designing the safe system, the precautions should include the following.

1. The space should be isolated where possible to prevent the ingress of substances or any danger from mechanical or electrical equipment.
2. There should be adequate supervision and the workers required to work in confined spaces must be competent.
3. There should be a means of communicating with workers in confined spaces and for raising the alarm in the event of an emergency.
4. Where there is a risk of the atmosphere being contaminated, there should be a procedure for testing and monitoring the air supply. This should be undertaken by a competent person and preferably from outside the confined space.
5. If there are flammable or toxic gases or vapours present these should be purged from the confined space with either air or inert gas.
6. Personal protective equipment (PPE) and respiratory protective equipment (RPE) should be provided where necessary.
7. Smoking should be prohibited.
8. If there is a risk of flammable or potentially explosive atmospheres, precautions should be taken to eliminate the risk by cleaning, ventilation and control of sources of ignition.
9. Where the use of PPE/RPE cannot be avoided, there should be adequate ventilation to prevent the build-up of harmful gas and enable safe operation.
10. Gas equipment should be checked for leaks before entry into the confined space.
11. Static discharges can often occur from equipment, material and clothing. All conducting items such as steel trunking should be bonded and effectively earthed, and anti-static clothing and footwear considered.
12. There should be adequate lighting including emergency lighting.
13. There should be safe access and egress.
14. Arrangements should be made in the event of an emergency or rescue and these procedures communicated to workers.

15. There may need to be a limit of the working time in the confined space. Employers and self-employed persons must comply or ensure compliance with the Regulations. They are also responsible for compliance in work undertaken by others where they have control over the work area or systems of work.

Employers and self-employed persons must consider the steps necessary, in the event of an emergency, to safely rescue people working in confined spaces. The risks to the rescuers must be minimised. If it is likely that resuscitation will be needed, suitable equipment must be available and maintained.

If the risks to the health and safety of a person working in a confined space are sufficiently small, the Health and Safety Executive may grant an exemption from the need to comply with these Regulations.

The hazards

The most likely hazards present in a confined space are as follows.

Flammable substances and oxygen enrichment

Fire or an explosion may arise from the presence of flammable substances, from an excess of oxygen in the atmosphere, or from leaks from adjoining plant or processes that have not been isolated properly.

Toxic gas, fume or vapour

Fumes may remain as a result of a previous process or previous storage, or may arise from sludge or other deposits disturbed. Fumes may also enter the space from adjoining plant that has not been effectively isolated. Work inside the confined space, eg welding, or outside it may also produce fumes and vapours.

Oxygen deficiency

This may result from purging the confined space with an inert gas, from naturally occurring biological processes which consume oxygen, or as a result of fermentation.

The process of rust formation and burning operations such as welding also consume oxygen and may lead to a deficiency.

The ingress or presence of liquids or solid materials

Liquids flowing into a confined space may drown or seriously injure a person. Free-flowing solids, eg grains, granules or powders, may submerge a person thereby preventing breathing.

Presence of excessive heat

Excessive heat can lead to increased body temperature which may cause heatstroke, dehydration and unconsciousness. If the person is wearing personal protective equipment (PPE) the weight of the clothing or equipment may add to the increase in body heat.

Use of a permit-to-work procedure

Where there is a risk of serious injury a permit-to-work system should be introduced. This is a formal written system which should include:

- the hazards involved in the work
- the identity, nature and extent of the work to be carried out
- a formal check confirming that the elements of a safe system of work are in place
- authorisation to commence work by more than one person and time-limit on entry.

Emergencies and rescue

Arrangements will depend on the nature of the confined space, the risks identified and the likely nature of emergency rescue. However, they should take into account arrangements for:

- rescue and resuscitation
- equipment raising the alarm and rescue
- safeguarding the rescuers
- fire safety
- control of plant
- first aid
- public emergency services
- training.

Questions and Answers

Q Does a crowded office count as a "confined space"?

A No, as this issue is dealt with under the space requirements of the **Workplace (Health, Safety and Welfare) Regulations 1992**.

Q What is the definition of a confined space?

A A confined space has two defining features. First, it is a place which is mainly, though not always completely, enclosed. Second, there is a reasonably foreseeable risk of serious injury from hazardous substances or conditions within the space or nearby.

Q If someone is trapped in a confined space, such as an underground tank, should we go in to help them?

A Your emergency procedures should include contingency plans for how to assist people trapped in confined spaces. It is important that the rescuers are properly protected themselves, or they may just become additional victims. Multiple fatalities have occurred where rescuers have been overcome by the same fumes, etc that have affected the victim in the first place.

Construction

Summary

Construction work, including demolition, is one of the most hazardous types of work and accounts for many accidents and deaths each year. By its nature it involves heavy and dangerous work equipment, falling objects, hazardous substances, work at height, manual handling, excavations and the use of contractors/subcontractors.

Practical Guidance

Construction work is highly dangerous and accounts for many workplace accidents each year. In addition to the heavy equipment and the various substances used in construction work, the management of health and safety is made more complicated by the widespread use of contractors, subcontractors and casual labour. The duty of care owed to this latter category of worker is confirmed by the case of *Galek's Curator Bonis v Thomson* where a casual worker was injured falling from some scaffolding which had been altered by two other contractors. He claimed damages from the contractors. In this case the casual worker was deemed to be employed and, therefore, owed a duty of care.

The Construction (Design and Management) Regulations 1994 (as amended)

Clients and clients' agents
Clients' agents must make a written declaration to the Health and Safety Executive (HSE) stating they are the clients for a particular construction project (contact details must be provided). The clients, ie the people or organisation requiring the construction work, must ensure that the agent and other designated personnel receive relevant information and are competent. They must also appoint a planning supervisor and principal contractor, and ensure they allocate adequate resources for health and safety.

Notification
Planning supervisors must submit written notification of the construction work to the HSE. The details required to be notified include the construction site address, contact details of designated people, start date, duration and the maximum number of workers.

Designers
Designers should ensure that health and safety is taken into account in their designs with regard to the actual construction and subsequent maintenance, and should also ensure that risks are minimised. The duty extends to the provision of information in relation to any hazardous structures or substances encountered.

Planning supervisors
Planning supervisors must ensure that designers fulfil their duties, that different designers on the same project co-operate with each other, advise on the competency of designers and contractors, ensure that appropriate resources are allocated for health and safety, prepare the first part of the health and safety plan, and ensure the health and safety file is completed throughout the project and handed to the client.

Health and safety file
This contains all the health and safety information relevant to the construction project, including subsequent maintenance. The file is completed by the planning supervisor and handed to the client at the end of the work. The client must retain the file and ensure it is available for inspection (the file must be passed on to subsequent owners of property, etc when the original client disposes of their interest in the property).

Health and safety plan
This provides the focus for health and safety in the project and is started by the planning supervisor and passed on to the principal contractor for completion at the construction phase.

Principal contractors
Principal contractors must co-ordinate all contractors on site and ensure they are competent, have allocated appropriate resources for health and safety, follow the health and safety plan and are provided with all necessary information and training.

Contractors
Contractors must comply with their legal duties, and co-operate with other contractors and the principal contractor, including providing relevant information and risk assessments of their work.

In the case of *Kealy v Heard* [1983] 1 All ER 973 HC, a contractor was injured when scaffolding erected by another contractor collapsed. The injured man claimed damages against the property owner on the basis that the owner was a contractor. The judge held that a contractor was a person who actually undertook building operations — it did not cover owners who hired independent contractors. However, the owner did still have a duty of care to the contractors and was negligent in not ensuring proper care and control over appliances, eg scaffolding, on his property.

Conversely, plant hire operators who hire out equipment and operators are considered contractors even though they are not directly involved in the work (see *Williams v West Wales Plant Hire Co and Others* [1984] 3 All ER 353).

Lifting Operations and Lifting Equipment Regulations 1998

These comprehensive Regulations cover lifting appliances, eg chains, ropes and lifting gear, and hoists, the carriage of people and the secureness of loads. There are detailed examination, testing and record-keeping requirements. Generally, all lifting equipment must be of good construction, sound material and adequate strength and must be properly maintained and free from patent defect. Stability of such equipment, safe working zones and safe working load indications are also important.

Construction (Health, Safety and Welfare) Regulations 1996

Safe places of work

Every workplace must be safe and without risks to health, including means of entry and exit.

Falls and falling objects

Measures must be taken to prevent people falling from their place of work, or through fragile materials. This may include the provision of guard-rails, toe-boards, personal suspension equipment, fall-arrest harnesses, etc.

In the case of *Astell v London Transport Board* [1996] 2 All ER 748, CA, a construction worker fell under a single guard-rail after bending down in order to manoeuvre some scaffolding poles around a corner. The judge held that a guard-rail could not be considered suitable unless it created a physical barrier against falling, and therefore what is suitable will depend on the circumstances of each individual situation — in this case a single guard-rail was not suitable in the circumstances.

Measures must also be taken to prevent objects falling on to people below. In a case heard at Isleworth Crown Court in April 1997, a construction company was fined a total of £19,800 when a member of the public was paralysed after a roll of asphalt fell 12 storeys on to him. The company had taken insufficient precautions to prevent the roll of asphalt from falling off of the platform.

Excavations

Measures should be taken to ensure excavations do not collapse, ie that they are adequately supported and are not endangered by the proximity of vehicles above.

Inspections

Inspections required for	Frequency
Work platforms (including scaffolds) and personal suspension equipment	(a) prior to first use (b) weekly thereafter (c) after repairs, modifications, alterations, additions, dismantling — where these could affect the integral strength and stability
Excavations — where side and/or roof supports are present	(a) prior to the start of each shift (b) after any event which could affect their strength and stability (c) after any rock, earth or other material falls
Caissons and cofferdams	(a) prior to the start of each shift (b) after any event which could affect their strength and stability

Traffic routes
There should be adequate organisation to allow vehicular and pedestrian traffic to move around safely, and the routes themselves should not create additional risks. Appropriate signing may be necessary.

Emergency procedures
People must be able to reach a place of safety quickly and safely in any emergency. Such routes must be of sufficient number, clearly signed and kept free of obstructions, and they must be familiar to the workers.

Welfare facilities
Suitable and sufficient toilets, washing facilities, rest and changing areas, facilities for preparing and eating meals and boiling water, and a supply of drinking water must be provided.

Equipment
Equipment must be safe, suitable, of good construction and well maintained. Other provisions cover the stability of structures; demolition, use of explosives; cofferdams/caissons; prevention of drowning; safety of doors and gates; prevention, detection and means of fighting fire; temperature; protection from adverse weather; lighting; maintenance; and training.

In a case heard at Lewes Crown Court in July 1996, a construction company was fined £20,000 plus costs after an employee was drowned when the dumper truck he was driving came off the road and fell into the sea — the company had not taken any precautions to prevent the truck coming off the road.

Construction (Head Protection) Regulations 1989

Head protection must be suitable, must fit securely and comfortably and be provided where there is a foreseeable risk of injury from falling objects. Damaged head protection must be replaced. Workers must wear any head protection provided, store it in appropriate accommodation provided and report any losses, defects or damage.

Questions and Answers

Q Are Sikhs exempt from the **Construction (Head Protection) Regulations 1989**?

A Yes, Sikhs who wear turbans as part of the integral tradition of their religion do not have to wear hard hats on construction sites.

Q What is meant by construction work?

A Construction work means building, civil engineering or engineering construction work and includes:

- construction
- alteration
- conversions
- fitting out
- commissioning and decommissioning
- renovations
- repairs
- maintenance (including high-pressure cleaning)
- redecoration
- demolition/dismantling
- site clearance prior to and at the end of construction work
- assembly/dismantling of prefabricated units
- installation, maintenance and removal of services associated with a structure.

Q What is meant by the term "structure"?

A Structure means any buildings, steel or reinforced concrete structures that are not buildings, tunnels, shafts, underground works, bridges, viaducts, aqueducts, waterworks, reservoirs, cables, pipes, pipelines (regardless of contents), sewers, sewerage works, drainage, gasholders, tanks, roads, river works, lagoons, dams, earthworks, walls, caissons, towers, pylons, masts, earth-retaining structures, scaffolds, formwork, falsework, other supporting or access structures and fixed plant where there is a risk of someone falling two or more metres.

Q What work do the **Construction, Design and Management Regulations 1994** apply to?

A The **Construction, Design and Management Regulations 1994** (CDM Regulations) apply to:

- demolition work — regardless of the duration or number of workers involved
- non-notifiable work where there are five or more people on-site at any one time

- notifiable work, ie where the work lasts more than 30 days or involves more than 500 person days of work
- design work, regardless of duration or number of people involved.

Domestic premises are exempt unless they are used for business purposes.

Contractors

Summary

The evolution of the UK economy has resulted in a culture where each organisation tends to concentrate on its core business, drawing on external resources for a wide variety of tasks. The use of contractors ranges from occasional work such as window cleaning to regular work such as providing a security or catering service. In addition, there are one-off requirements such as construction and maintenance projects. Most contracts run effectively and efficiently. However, several accidents/incidents have occurred as a result of inadequate communication between the client and the contractor, and a lack of understanding of their respective legal responsibilities.

Practical Guidance

When employing contractors to carry out work activities, both the client and the contractor have legal responsibilities.

Both parties are normally employers, and therefore have general responsibilities under the **Health and Safety at Work, etc Act 1974** (HSW Act) to safeguard, so far as is reasonably practicable, the health, safety and welfare of their employees and others who may be affected by work activities. In particular, they should provide and maintain:

- safe plant and safe systems of work
- safe handling, storage, maintenance and transport of articles and substances
- necessary information, instruction, training and supervision
- a safe place of work, with safe access and egress
- a safe working environment with adequate welfare facilities.

There is, therefore, a shared responsibility of a duty of care between the site occupier and the contractor (as both are employers) to ensure that all reasonably practicable precautions are taken to safeguard their own employers, other persons on site and the general public.

Those contractors who are self-employed carry the same responsibility as any other employer to make proper provisions for health, safety and welfare during their activities. Persons who control premises that are used by people at work, but who are not their employees, need to ensure so far as is reasonably practicable that the premises, access to them, and the plant and substances used on them are safe and free from risk to health.

Under the **Occupiers' Liability Act 1957** and the **Occupiers' Liability Act 1984**, occupiers of premises have a duty to take reasonable care to see that their visitors are safe. An occupier cannot be prosecuted for a breach of this duty, but if a visitor is injured the occupier may be liable to pay compensation.

Specific legislation

The **Management of Health and Safety at Work Regulations 1999** are relevant to occupiers of premises in terms of co-operation and co-ordination. Where the activities of different employers and self-employed people interact, they may need to co-operate with each other to ensure that each employer's general duty of care is met.

Where employees or self-employed persons, eg contractors, carry out work in the premises of another employer under a service contract, or engage employees in temporary employment, they must be provided with comprehensible information. The information provided must include the risks highlighted in the risk assessment and the measures in place to control/reduce the risks. The contractors must also be made aware of emergency procedures in place and any persons nominated to help with emergency evacuation.

The contractor may well be a specialist who is better informed than the host employer of the particular risks associated with their work. The contractor should then inform the host employer of such risks and make available their risk assessment. The host employer's instructions should be concerned with the risks which are particular to the activity or premises.

Construction work

Where contractors are carrying out construction work for an employer or occupier, specific duties are placed on each party under the **Construction (Design and Management) Regulations 1994** (as amended) (CDM Regulations). Construction work is defined as such work which will last for more than 30 days, or will involve more than 500 person-days of work, or more than five people on site at one time. The CDM Regulations also apply to any demolition work.

The person for whom a project is carried out must ensure that the contractor is competent for the work and is able to provide adequate resources for health and safety. They will also be responsible for the "client" duties which relate to:

- the appointment of a competent planning supervisor and principal contractors, who will allocate adequate resources for health and safety
- ensuring work does not commence until the contractor has prepared a satisfactory health and safety plan
- providing information relevant to health and safety on the project
- ensuring that the health and safety file is available for inspection after the project is completed.

Contractors

The principal contractor has to take over and develop the health and safety plan and co-ordinate the activities of all contractors so that they comply with health and safety law. Their key duties are to:

- develop and implement the health and safety plan
- ensure the co-ordination and co-operation of contractors
- obtain from contractors the main findings of their risk assessments and details of how they intend to carry out high-risk operations
- ensure that all concerned have information about risks and are adequately trained
- ensure contractors comply with any site rules which may have been set out in the health and safety plan
- monitor health and safety performance
- ensure that only authorised people are allowed on to the site
- pass information to the planning supervisor for the health and safety file.

Selection of suitable contractors

When an employer selects a contractor, it should be done on the basis of their good reputation (including high standards of health and safety) and competency to carry out the work, as opposed to lowest price for the job.

The following points should be considered when selecting a potential contractor:

- where the contractor has five or more employees, availability of an up-to-date written health and safety policy signed by a director which includes:
  - the organisation and arrangements for its implementation
  - a clear statement of duties and responsibilities for identifying hazards, assessing risks and controlling them
  - identification of responsibilities on staff to follow health and safety instructions and report dangers
  - procedure for dealing with emergencies
- ability to identify senior managers who are responsible for health and safety management, and can visibly demonstrate this
- arrangements for health and safety training of the contractor's employees
- are the contractor's staff properly trained and competent?
- does the contractor carry adequate insurances?
- availability of health and safety advice within the contractor's organisation
- existence of safe systems of work, eg procedures, permits-to-work, evidence of method statements from previous contracts
- references from other customers for similar work
- evidence of risk assessments from previous contracts
- evidence that the company maintains accident and ill-health records, and investigation reports
- evidence of a work inspection system
- details of any claims or prosecutions relevant to health and safety.

Having selected competent contractors to carry out the work, the client must appoint a competent planning supervisor whose duties are to:
- co-ordinate the health and safety aspects of the project design and initial planning
- prepare a health and safety plan which will include a general description of the work, details of timings, details of risks to workers so far as possible at that stage
- provide advice to the designers and contractors
- notify the project to the HSE (where applicable)
- prepare the health and safety file which is a record of information for the client/end user detailing the risks that have to be managed during maintenance, repair or renovation.

Questions and Answers

Q Am I expected to provide equipment and facilities for the use of contractors?

A Generally, contractors would be expected to provide all their own tools, plant, equipment and materials. Facilities such as use of staff canteens, first aid equipment, etc are a matter for agreement prior to the start of the contract.

Q What information do I need to give contractors about fire procedures?

A All contractor's employees should be made aware of the fire warning systems operating in the premises and given instructions on action to be taken in the event of a fire. Fire-fighting equipment should also be made known to the contractor.

Q If one of my employees trips over something that a contractor has left in the corridor, is it me or the contractor that is liable?

A You have a duty towards your employees to provide contractors who will not put them at risk. If a claim was to result, in the first instance your employee would claim against your employer's liability insurance. The contractor could be joined in the action. It would be for you to demonstrate that you were not negligent, ie that you had appointed competent contractors to do the work and had put an effective monitoring system in place.

Control of Substances Hazardous to Health

Summary

A hazardous substance is most simply defined as any substance capable of causing an adverse health effect, and may include chemicals, biological agents (eg bacteria/viruses) and even substantial quantities of any dust. Control is based on risk assessment and the introduction of appropriate control measures.

Practical Guidance

Exposure to hazardous substances is generally covered by the **Control of Substances Hazardous to Health Regulations 1999** (COSHH) — there are separate specific Regulations for lead, asbestos and ionising radiations, which are consequently excluded from COSHH.

Definition of substances hazardous to health

COSHH contains specific definitions of hazardous substances including any chemical classified and labelled (under the **Chemicals (Hazards Information and Packaging for Supply) Regulations 1994** (as amended)) as being:

- harmful or irritant — warning label is a St Andrew's cross
- corrosive — warning label is two horizontal dripping test tubes over a hand and workbench
- toxic or very toxic — warning label is a skull and crossbones.

Note: All the warning labels are an orange square with an appropriate black symbol, and will be clearly displayed on chemical containers.

Substances allocated a maximum exposure limit (MEL) under COSHH, or an occupational exposure standard (OES) as listed in the HSE publication EH40 *Occupational Exposure Limits* (revised annually) are also included, as are substantial quantities of dust and any other substances capable of causing adverse health effects. Biological agents, eg bacteria and viruses, are included in the latter category.

Application of COSHH

COSHH applies to all the substances defined above where exposure could lead to an adverse effect on health, ie cause illness. Substances which represent a danger to safety, ie which can cause injury as opposed to illness, as a result of their flammability or explosivity, etc are excluded from COSHH, as are lead, asbestos and ionising agents which have their own legislation and which are dealt with separately in this publication.

Assessment and control of hazardous substances

The risks associated with hazardous substances must be assessed and reduced as far as possible. Any control measures provided must be properly used, and maintained in efficient working order — certain mechanical ventilation controls have specified examination periods and record keeping requirements which must be adhered to. Faulty and defective equipment must be reported, removed and repaired/ replaced. All control measures must be monitored to ensure that exposure levels are maintained within safe limits and any failures can be quickly identified and addressed.

It is a good idea to draw up a complete inventory of every hazardous substance to which employees are likely to be exposed during the work activities, ie chemical and biological agents and dusts, etc. It is relatively straightforward to identify (from container labels, safety data sheets, etc) any hazardous substances, including ones with statutory control limits, from this inventory and to determine existing and necessary control measures. Biological agents do not come conveniently labelled so any contact with biological agents, eg body fluids, must not be forgotten.

By-products of processes must also be considered and assessed.

Failure to assess and control the risks associated with hazardous substances may lead to prosecution as in a case heard at Enfield Magistrates' Court in May 1996 where a metal reclamation company was fined £6000 plus costs when an employee became unconscious after inhaling hydrogen sulphide released during an aluminium removal process. The release of hydrogen sulphide and the health hazards associated with this process were well known in the industry — the company had simply not taken adequate precautions. Failure to determine associated hazards may also lead to prosecution as in the case of *Ogden v Airedale Health Authority* where a company was found to be negligent and in breach of COSHH when an employee suffered occupational asthma on exposure to film-developing chemicals. The company should have known that the chemicals in question were irritant and therefore controlled exposure to them.

In a case held at Thetford Magistrates' Court in June 1996, a company was prosecuted for failing to prevent or adequately control the exposure of a young person to sand particles released during sandblasting. The protective helmet provided was inadequate, old, defective and unsuitable.

Health surveillance

COSHH specifies several particular instances when health surveillance is considered appropriate, including when an identifiable disease or adverse health effect is associated with exposure to a hazardous substance, and this is reasonably likely to occur under the normal working conditions. There must also be valid techniques for detecting the resultant health condition. A health record must be made and retained for 40 years. Employment medical advisors (EMAs) or appointed doctors may prohibit or suspend employees from work involving exposure to hazardous substances, where this is considered necessary to safeguard the employees' health.

The **Management of Health and Safety at Work Regulations 1999** also require employers to undertake health surveillance of employees where this is identified as necessary by the risk assessment — health surveillance already being addressed under COSHH does not have to be repeated.

Information, instruction and training

Employees must be given information on any risks associated with hazardous substances they may be exposed to at work along with the necessary control measures, and the results of any monitoring carried out (except where this includes personal health-related information which is confidential). They must also be instructed and trained in the use and limitations of any control measures provided. Where a MEL has been exceeded, employees must be informed.

Employees' duties

Employees must use any protective equipment or other control measures fully and properly and attend health or medical surveillance programmes if identified as being necessary.

Questions and Answers

Q In what circumstances would employees be exposed to biological agents?

A Obvious examples would be in laboratories and hospitals where work with bacteria and viruses is carried out. However, there are many more work examples such as contact with clinical waste, blood and other body fluids/excretions as encountered in care services and laundries, contact with animals and animal products, and contact with soil as in gardening and agriculture. Exposure to Legionella bacteria (which cause legionnaires' disease) through contact with contaminated water systems in buildings is also covered by COSHH.

Q What information are substance manufacturers and suppliers, etc obliged to provide?

A   Chemical container labels display a lot of relevant information about the product and should always be referred to. Under s.6 of the **Health and Safety at Work, etc Act 1974**, manufacturers and suppliers are obliged to provide safety data sheets for all substances which are classified as dangerous. The safety data sheets provide detailed information about the chemical, including handling, storing, first aid and relevant supplier or manufacturer contact details, etc. This information must be provided when the chemicals are initially supplied, and every attempt made to ensure consumers receive any revisions made at a later date.

Retail suppliers are not obliged to provide such information but may do so if they are informed that the chemicals are intended for work — if this information is not readily available the manufacturer or supplier should be contacted directly. It is good practice to keep a central record of all the safety data sheets.

Q   If flammable and explosive substances are excluded from COSHH what legislation are they covered by?

A   Any hazardous or dangerous substance not covered by COSHH must still be assessed and controlled if it is identified as representing a risk, under the requirements of the **Management of Health and Safety at Work Regulations 1999** and other relevant legislation such as the **Highly Flammable Liquids and Liquefied Petroleum Gases Regulations 1972**, the **Petroleum Spirit (Consolidation) Act 1928**, and the **Control of Explosives Regulations 1991**.

Q   What is the difference between "hazard" and "risk"?

A   Hazard is the potential of something to cause harm, while risk is the realisation of that harm actually occurring, ie the likelihood and severity of the outcome. For example, a closed bottle of bleach in a cupboard is a hazard — it has the potential to cause harm, but lidded and in a cupboard there is no exposure to that hazard. Once the bottle is removed from the cupboard, opened and the contents poured out, it is a risk as there is exposure to the hazard. How great the risk is will depend on the effectiveness of any control measures provided.

Dermatitis

Summary

Dermatitis is a skin condition which is usually caused by contact with certain chemicals or agents. The skin becomes dry, cracked and itchy. The likelihood of contracting dermatitis varies widely from person to person. Sensitisation to a particular chemical may cause dermatitis on exposure to relatively small amounts. Dermatitis is a major cause of occupational ill health in the UK. It is rarely contagious.

Practical Guidance

Causes of dermatitis

Certain chemicals, agents and activities are known to increase the risk of susceptible people contracting dermatitis. These include the following (although the list is not exhaustive):

- exposure to cement
- exposure to chromates
- exposure to solvents
- exposure to detergents
- exposure to irritant dusts
- exposure to nickel
- exposure to some foods, eg citrus fruit, sugar, flour, fish and seafood, chillies, etc
- working in warm, dry environments
- wearing impervious gloves, which trap sweat and make the hands hot
- x-rays
- frequent wetting and drying of hands.

Chemical labelling

The **Chemicals (Hazard Information and Packaging for Supply) Regulations 1994** (CHIP Regulations) (as amended) require suppliers of chemicals to label the containers of any hazardous substances that they supply. If the substance has been classified as one that may cause dermatitis, the label must tell the user that it is "by skin contact".

Preventing dermatitis

Under the **Control of Substances Hazardous to Health Regulations 1999** (COSHH), employers must assess the risk of exposure to substances in their workplace which may cause dermatitis. The risk assessment should identify any chemicals that may cause dermatitis. To start with, check whether any of the chemicals listed under Causes of dermatitis are used, and check the label on any chemicals used to see if they are classified as "sensitising on skin contact", "irritant" or "corrosive".

If an agent is found which may cause dermatitis, the likelihood of someone contracting the condition should be assessed. Look at the following:

- how exposure occurs
- how much of the agent the workers are exposed to
- medical histories of the people who may be exposed to see if they have become sensitised to chemicals in the past.

If there is a risk that workers may develop this skin condition, suitable control measures must be put in place, used and maintained.

Records must be kept of any maintenance of engineering controls or personal protective equipment.

Washing facilities

The **Workplace (Health, Safety and Welfare) Regulations 1992** require adequate washing facilities to be provided. These facilities must have hot and cold (or warm) running water, soap, nail-brushes and a means of drying, ie towels or an electrical hand dryer. It is vital that anyone who is exposed to an agent which may cause dermatitis washes thoroughly after finishing work. Soap itself may cause dermatitis, so it should be rinsed off with clean water after washing. Frequent hand-washing with detergent is also a known cause of dermatitis, so a balance should be reached.

Health surveillance

Health surveillance is required by COSHH, but only where appropriate. In the case of dermatitis, there are methods of checking for development of the condition, and action which should be taken if it is found. Appropriate health surveillance for dermatitis would include workers checking their skin for symptoms on a regular, eg daily, basis. The symptoms they should look out for include:

- red skin
- small blisters
- itching
- cracked skin, particularly between the fingers.

Anyone who thinks they may have symptoms should report them to a responsible person as soon as possible, and be referred to a doctor for confirmation and treatment. In order to make sure health surveillance is carried out, it is a good idea for supervisors to be responsible for inspecting their staff's hands for symptoms regularly, although this is likely to be done less frequently than self-examination.

Reporting requirements

Under the **Reporting of Injuries, Diseases and Dangerous Occurrences Regulations 1995** (RIDDOR), cases of occupational dermatitis must be reported to the enforcing authority. Dermatitis resulting from work involving exposure to any of the agents listed below must be reported:

- acrylates and methacrylates
- antibiotics and other pharmaceuticals and therapeutic agents
- biocides, anti-bacterials, preservatives or disinfectants
- cement, plaster or concrete
- chromate (hexavalent and derived from trivalent chromium)
- colophony (rosin) and its modified products
- epoxy resin systems
- fish, shellfish or meat
- formaldehyde and its resins
- glutaraldehyde
- hairdressing products, particularly dyes, shampoos, bleaches and permanent waving solutions
- mercaptobenzothiazole, thiurams, substituted paraphenyl-diamines and related rubber-processing chemicals
- metalworking fluids
- organic solvents
- plants and plant-derived materials, particularly daffodil, tulip and chrysanthemum families, the parsley family (carrots, parsnips, parsley and celery), garlic, onion, hardwoods and the pine family
- soaps and detergents
- strong acids, strong alkalis, strong solutions, oxidising agents (eg bleach) and reducing agents
- sugar or flour
- any other known irritant or sensitising agent, particularly any chemical labelled "may cause sensitisation by skin contact".

The report must be made using form F2508A, available from HSE Books (tel: 01787 881165).

Social security benefits

The **Social Security (Industrial Injuries) (Prescribed Diseases) Regulations 1985** allow people suffering from occupational dermatitis to claim benefit for a prescribed disease, so long as they can show that they have non-infective dermatitis of external origin resulting from exposure to dust, liquid or vapour, or any other external agent capable of irritating the skin. This includes friction and radiant heat, but excludes ionising and electromagnetic radiation.

Types of dermatitis

There are two main types of dermatitis.

Dermatitis

1. Contact dermatitis, which is caused by repeated contact with certain agents. This contact removes the skin's natural protective oils, causing drying and cracking. The skin then becomes more susceptible to other agents, making the condition worse.
2. Allergic dermatitis, which is usually less common but more serious than contact dermatitis. It is sensitisation of the skin to particular chemicals, such as cement. Once the skin becomes sensitised, future exposure to the chemical will cause a reaction. Sometimes the reaction is so severe that the sufferer can no longer work with that chemical.

Medical screening

Before employing a new worker, many employers carry out medical screening to find out if they have any pre-existing conditions that may affect their ability to do the job. This screening should include enquiries about any history of skin sensitisation to the chemicals which the worker is likely to encounter, should they be given the job.

Protective equipment

Providing protective gloves or other protective clothing to protect workers against chemicals which cause dermatitis should only be used as a last resort. Wearing gloves may make the tasks more difficult, and increase the risk of other hazards, such as dropping tools from a height or losing grip on machinery controls. Gloves may sometimes cause dermatitis, due to lining powders and build up of sweat inside the glove. They require maintenance and replacement, and are ineffective as a control measure if the worker is not wearing them.

Barrier cream

Barrier cream is sometimes provided to control exposure to agents that cause dermatitis. Although it may be useful as part of a safe system of work, its effectiveness is limited. Some people claim that its main use is that it encourages workers to wash their hands after finishing work. Considerations when using barrier creams include the following:

- it must be used in conjunction with good occupational hygiene practices, such as thoroughly washing hands
- it must be suitable for protection against the chemicals being handled
- it must cover the whole hand, and care must be taken to make sure it has been applied under fingernails and in between the fingers
- it must be replaced every two or three hours, and every time the hands are washed
- it does not provide effective protection for allergic dermatitis, as even tiny amounts of the chemical may cause a reaction.

Treatment

If employees develop dermatitis they should be treated by a qualified doctor. The employer should take the following action:

- change their work so that they are no longer exposed to the agent to which they have developed sensitisation
- record their case of occupational dermatitis in the company's accident book, so that they can claim social security benefit if they need to
- report the case to the local enforcing authority on form F2508A (within ten days of finding out)
- keep case details in employees' personal health records.

For contact dermatitis, a reduction in exposure is often effective in controlling the condition. However, if allergic dermatitis is contracted, exposure to even small amounts of the agent may cause a reaction. The severity of the reaction and the level of exposure that causes it will vary depending on the individual.

Questions and Answers

Q How common is dermatitis?

A Dermatitis is the most common occupational skin disease in the UK. In fact, it is one of the major causes of occupational ill-health. Statistics show that occupational dermatitis makes up almost two thirds of compensation claims under the scheme for social security for prescribed industrial diseases.

Q Is it only the hands that are affected by dermatitis?

A No, skin elsewhere on the body may be affected by dermatitis. However, it is usually found in the hands, as these are the parts of the body that come into contact with chemicals most of the time. Some instances of facial dermatitis have been associated with low humidity and also with the use of visual display units (VDUs) (as discovered by the NRPB in a report on the hazards of ionising and non-ionising radiation in VDU users), although cases are rare and the causes have not been proven.

Q Who is likely to be susceptible to dermatitis?

A It is usually impossible to predict who will develop dermatitis. In the case of contact dermatitis, caused by the removal of natural oils, anyone may be susceptible. High standards of personal hygiene are important, so workers who fail to wash their hands after working with solvents, etc may be more likely to develop the condition.

In the case of allergic dermatitis, anyone may develop sensitisation, even if they have never had an allergic reaction in their life. However, some doctors believe that people who are more prone to allergic reactions, such as those with existing cases of eczema, may be more susceptible to occupational dermatitis. High levels of stress are known to increase the severity of eczema and so this is also likely to be a trigger to allergic dermatitis in someone who has not previously suffered.

Disabled Persons

Summary

The needs of disabled employees should be addressed in work situations. The measures required to accommodate the needs of disabled people will be dependent on the type and extent of their disabilities as well as the actual work premises and activities.

Practical Guidance

Legal duties

Health and Safety at Work, etc Act 1974

Employers have a duty to ensure the health and safety of employees at work, so far as is reasonably practicable. This duty is owed to employees individually and not collectively, which means that any employee with special needs, such as a disability, is owed a greater duty of care. In these cases employers may need to take additional control or protective measures to ensure the health and safety of these employees. The case of *Paris v Stepney Borough Council* illustrates this. Mr Paris who was blinded in one eye during the war, subsequently suffered an injury to his good eye while at work, which left him totally blind. He claimed that his employer owed him a greater duty of care because the consequences of losing his only good eye were of much greater significance than to a normally sighted employee. The House of Lords agreed that a greater duty of care is owed in such cases.

Similar consideration should be given to the needs of any disabled visitors to the work premises.

Disability Discrimination Act 1995

This Act is designed to ensure that disabled people are not unnecessarily discriminated against in employment matters, and in the service they receive from service providers. It provides a comprehensive definition of disability and requires employers to address certain factors which may unfairly discriminate against a disabled person. Measures which employers may need to consider include widening access routes for wheelchair access, rearranging workplace layouts, altering hours of work, etc.

This Act applies to employers with 15 or more employees, although employers with fewer than 15 employees are encouraged to follow good practices in this respect.

Definition of disability

The most comprehensive definition of "disability" is contained in the **Disability Discrimination Act 1995** and includes any physical, mental or sensory impairment that affects the ability of a disabled person to perform normal day-to-day activities. The disability must be substantial, ie have a significant long-term effect — that is the effects must last, or be expected to last, at least 12 months, or be recurring. The definition also includes severe disfigurements, and progressive conditions such as AIDS, muscular dystrophy and multiple sclerosis, etc where the effects are likely to become substantial even if they are not so at first. The beneficial effects of artificial aids or medication on a disability are not taken into consideration when assessing the effects of an impairment.

Employment

Employers may not discriminate against disabled people in their recruitment, promotion, training, development or dismissal procedures, ie disabled people may not be treated less fairly than non-disabled people solely because of their disability. Where discrimination does occur it must be totally justifiable after considering all reasonable alternatives and changes. Employers are not, however, expected to contravene health and safety laws in accommodating the needs of disabled people.

Addressing special needs

Employers are required to make any reasonable changes in order to accommodate the needs of a disabled person. Such changes may be structural ones such as widening doorways, installing disabled lift access, providing Braille directional signs or fitting visual flashing lights as warning signs, eg to supplement fire alarms. They may also be procedural ones such as revising emergency procedures so as to ensure disabled colleagues are not put at greater risk in emergencies. Colleagues may need to be enlisted to assist the disabled person in emergency evacuations, etc. The changes may also be operational ones such as redesigning work areas to allow easy access routes, and revising hours of work with regard to both the duration and timing of a work shift. Additional time off may also need to be given to allow the disabled person to attend clinics and medicals.

Dismissals

In order for the dismissal of a disabled person to be held as fair, the employer must take into account all reasonable alternatives and means of accommodating the disabled person. In the case of *Cannon v Scandecor*, a disabled employee was employed on the understanding that her productivity would be lower than that of her colleagues. She then suffered a series of illnesses and a car accident which subsequently reduced her productivity still further on her return to work. She was dismissed, although her dismissal was deemed to be unfair as the employer had not allowed sufficient time for her to make a full recovery.

In *Milk Marketing Board v Grimes*, Grimes was a milk float driver who was deaf and who could only communicate by means of written questions and answers. On examining him, the employer's occupational health advisor deemed him unfit to continue driving and felt that a hearing aid would not sufficiently restore Grimes' hearing to the desired level for driving. Grimes was dismissed. The Industrial Tribunal held that he had been unfairly dismissed, because he produced a consultant's report which stated that a hearing aid would restore his hearing to a safe level for driving, and evidence that he had driven for 34 years without an accident. Before dismissing him the employers had not given him the opportunity to deal with his disability, ie use a hearing aid.

In *McCall v Post Office*, McCall was employed as a cleaner, and had failed to inform his employer that he suffered from epilepsy. After he had suffered several minor fits his employers took medical advice, and on the strength of that, dismissed him as no suitable alternative safe work was available in a "no risk" area, as had been recommended. Because no safe alternative work was available and McCall had to be moved in the interests of his own and his colleagues' health and safety, the dismissal was held to be fair.

Questions and Answers

Q What is the relationship between health and safety and disability discrimination law?

A The **Disability Discrimination Act 1995** basically aims to ensure that disabled people are not unnecessarily discriminated against in a work and/or service receiver situation. However, it would be deemed fair to discriminate against disabled people if accommodating their specific needs caused a contravention of any health and safety laws, or their own health and safety or that of someone else was compromised. In these cases, health and safety law would override disability discrimination law, but such actions must be fully justifiable.

Q In the definition of disability what does "normal day-to-day activities" mean?

A These are activities which are carried out by a majority of people on a regular basis and which generally involve mobility, manual dexterity, physical co-ordination, continence, use of the main senses, ie sight, hearing, speech, and mental dexterity, ie memory, concentration, comprehension, perception of danger, etc.

Q What redress is available for people who become disabled through a work-related accident or disease?

A There are several factors to be considered. First, there could be compensation from successful civil actions taken against employers for personal injuries suffered by employees at work. Second, the **Congenital Disabilities (Civil Liability) Act 1976** allows children born disabled through the direct fault of an identifiable party, to claim civil damages against that party. Finally, disability benefit is available for people suffering specified conditions provided that certain defined criteria relating to the type and extent of the disability are met — further information is available from local DSS offices.

Q Do employers still have to employ a specific quota of disabled people in their workforce?

A No, the previous registration and quota requirements have been removed by the **Disability Discrimination Act 1995.**

Display Screen Equipment

Summary

With certain exceptions, display screen equipment includes screens which display numbers, letters and/or graphics. The use of such equipment is widespread throughout all workplaces and is most commonly associated with problems such as upper limb disorders (and the controversial term "repetitive strain injury") which are caused by poor posture and repetitive finger movements on the keys.

Practical Guidance

Workstations

The display screen equipment workstations of both users and operators must meet the minimum requirements detailed in the Schedule to the **Health and Safety (Display Screen Equipment) Regulations 1992** (DSE Regulations). In addition, they must be assessed and reviewed as necessary, and any risks eliminated or reduced to the lowest reasonably practicable level.

Work breaks

Regular breaks from display screen work should be taken — the guidance suggests a 5–10 minute break every hour of such work. The breaks cannot be "saved" in lieu of a shorter day, and should not involve activities which require eye focal distances similar to those associated with screen work, or which require repetitive movements of the arms, hands or fingers.

Eyesight tests

Free eye and eyesight tests must be provided for "users" on their request or where there is visual difficulty in carrying out display screen work — the tests must be repeated at appropriate intervals, ie every two years or as advised by an optician. Where glasses or other corrective appliances are necessary the employer must provide those free of charge, but only to the extent of the cost of basic frames and the lens prescription necessary to do display screen work.

Information and training

Adequate information and training must be provided on any risks associated with the workstation and the necessary control measures. Users should be made aware of the provisions relating to work breaks and eyesight tests.

Health effects

The common health effects associated with display screen work include:

- upper limb disorders (including repetitive strain injury) through continuous prolonged repetitive use of the keyboard and poor posture
- temporary eye and eyesight effects such as visual fatigue, headaches, dry/sore eyes through continuous prolonged use, poor posture, deep concentration, poor legibility of the screen or input documents, poor lighting, screen flicker
- fatigue and stress through poor job design, poor posture or lack of control over work or imposed work rates.

In the controversial case of *Mughal v Reuters*, the judge refused to accept the term "repetitive strain injury" as it had no pathology or clinical symptoms and therefore could not exist as a medical condition.

Questions and Answers

Q What determines whether a worker is classified as a user (employee) or an operator (self-employed)?

A The DSE Regulations define a "user" as someone who habitually uses a display screen for a significant part of his or her daily work and who is an employee of the employer, regardless of whether the workstation is used at the employer's workplace, or at the employee's home. In situations where the workstation belongs to another employer, then both the employee's employer and the employer providing the workstation have specified duties.

An "operator" is defined as someone who is self-employed, ie not under a contract of employment, but who habitually uses display screen equipment for a significant part of his or her day and who uses a workstation provided by the client employer.

Q What determines whether a worker is covered by the DSE Regulations?

A Basically, the duration and frequency of display screen work are the main determining factors, regardless of whether the worker is an operator or user.

The following criteria can be applied:

- the display screen equipment is essential for the work being performed
- training and certain skills are required in the use of the display screen equipment
- the display screen equipment is used regularly for one or more hours daily
- rapid information transfer between the worker and display screen is necessary for the job
- serious concentration is required for the duration of the display screen work, eg air traffic controllers.

Q Are users and operators owed the same duties under the DSE Regulations?

A No, employers are not under a duty to ensure that operators take regular breaks away from display screen work or to provide eyesight tests or training. They must provide information on identified risks associated with the workstation and any necessary control measures.

Q Can display screen equipment cause epileptic seizures?

A The majority of users of display screen equipment who suffer from epilepsy are unaffected. However small numbers of people who suffer from the rare photosensitive form of epilepsy may be affected by screen flicker in some circumstances. However even they can often work successfully with display screen equipment without problem. As a precaution, the Health and Safety Executive's Employment Medical Advisory Service should be contacted if there any concerns about epilepsy in these situations.

Q Is there a danger of radiation from display screen equipment and are pregnant women at particular risk?

A The levels of radiation emitted from display screen equipment are minimal and well below any levels known to cause adverse health effects. Pregnant women are not at any greater risk than other workers although their concerns may cause them to suffer from stress if ignored. Information, instruction and training to increase awareness are important factors.

Q Do the DSE Regulations apply to "laptop" computers?

A Since the introduction of the DSE Regulations the use of portable or "laptop" computers has become far more widespread. The DSE Regulations state that "portable display screen equipment (DSE) (such as laptop computers) is exempt from the Regulations if it is not in prolonged use." However portable equipment that is habitually used by a DSE "user" as a significant part of his or her normal work should be regarded as covered by the Regulations, in the same way as most other forms of DSE. Additionally, in July 1997 the HSE advised that "employers should ensure that users have sufficient training to enable them to recognise and avoid risk factors when using portable DSE." It is important that an employer recognises that a laptop should not be used when there is any realistic alternative, and that for those who use a laptop whilst away from the main work location, the logical step is to provide a "docking station" or at least a full-sized screen for use whenever the individual is at that location. Wherever possible a separate mouse should be used, rather than the ball-type devise, or other integral devices found on many laptops.

Doors, Gates and Windows

Summary

Employers must provide a safe place of work, without risk to health. This includes providing and maintaining safe means of access to and egress from places of work. There are specific requirements relating to doors, gates and windows.

Practical Guidance

The **Workplace (Health, Safety and Welfare) Regulations 1992** expand upon the duty in the **Health and Safety at Work, etc Act 1974** to provide and maintain safe access to and egress from any place of work. The Regulations specify particular requirements relating to doors, gates and windows.

Construction material

Transparent or translucent surfaces in doors, gates and windows should be constructed of a safety material or otherwise adequately protected against breakage in the following cases:

- where any part of the transparent or translucent surface of a door or gate, or their side panels, is at or below shoulder level
- where any part of the transparent or translucent surface or window is at or below waist level, except in glasshouses where people are likely to be aware of the presence of glazing and will automatically avoid contact.

Safety materials are defined as:

- materials which are inherently robust, eg polycarbonates or glass blocks
- glass which, if it breaks, breaks safely
- ordinary annealed glass which meets the thickness criteria in the following table.

Nominal thickness	Maximum size
8mm	1.10m × 1.10m
10mm	2.25m × 2.25m
12mm	3.00m × 4.50m
15mm	Any size

As an alternative, transparent or translucent surfaces may be protected against breakage by means of a screen or barrier which will prevent a person coming into contact with the glass by falling against it. Where the risk is that a person may fall from height on to the glass, the screen or barrier must be difficult to climb.

Where there is a risk of people walking into doors, windows or gates, they should be conspicuously marked and at an appropriate height. The risk of this happening is greater where there is a large uninterrupted surface, eg glass doors, and the floor level is the same on both sides.

Windows

It should be possible to safely reach and operate the control to open any window. Controls should be placed so that people are not likely to fall through or out of a window. Additional devices should be provided to prevent anyone falling from a open window at height.

An open window should not project into an area where persons are likely to collide with it. The bottom edge should normally be 800mm above floor level.

All windows in a workplace must be designed and constructed so that they may cleaned safely.

Doors and gates

Doors and gates which swing in both directions and are on a main corridor or gangway should have a transparent panel to enable someone to see if there is anyone or anything on the other side, unless they are low enough to see over. Panels should be positioned to enable a person in a wheelchair to be seen from the other side.

Sliding doors should have a stop or other means of preventing the door coming off the end of the track. They should also have a retaining rail to prevent the door falling if the rollers leave the track, or the suspension system fails.

Upward-opening doors should be fitted with an effective device to prevent them falling back down and causing injury.

Power-operated doors and gates should be fitted with safety features to prevent people being struck or trapped. Where necessary, power-operated doors or gates should have a readily identifiable and accessible control switch or device so they can be stopped in an emergency. The normal on/off control may be sufficient for this purpose.

If the doors do not open automatically in the event of a power failure, the tools necessary to open them manually should be readily available at all times.

Fire doors and fire exit doors

Smoke doors are provided in premises to prevent the spread of heat and smoke and to protect escape routes. The location of these doors will be indicated on the plans attached to the fire certificate. All fire doors should be fitted with a self-closing device and marked on both sides with the words "Fire Door — Keep Closed" by means of an approved sign.

Fire exit doors should be kept unobstructed and should open in the direction of travel. If fastened for security reasons, they must be easy to open from within. Where there are large numbers of occupants doors should only be secured by panic bolts and marked "Push Bar to Open". Exit doors which are not normally used should be marked "Fire Exit" with an approved sign. Fire exit doors should have a minimum width of 750mm unless they are only ever to be used by less than 5 people.

Construction sites

The **Construction (Health, Safety and Welfare) Regulations 1996** make specific reference to doors and gates provided on construction sites. These are similar to the requirements under the **Workplace (Health, Safety and Welfare) Regulations 1992**:

- suitable safety devices must be fitted to doors, gates and hatches where there is risk of injury
- sliding doors must be fitted with a device that prevents the door leaving its track during use
- upward-opening doors must be fitted with devices to prevent them falling down and trapping someone
- powered doors must be fitted with devices to prevent them trapping people, and must be capable of manual operation in the event of a power failure, unless the doors open automatically.

Doors and gates which are part of mobile equipment are excluded from the above Regulations.

Questions and Answers

Q Do doors have to have a glass panel in them?

A Doors and gates which swing in both directions must have a transparent panel in them. The exception to this is when the door or gate is low enough to see over. Doors on main traffic routes which are conventionally hinged should also include transparent panels. Remember that the panels should be positioned carefully so that they enable any wheelchair-bound employees or visitors to be seen from the other side.

Q What safety requirements should be taken into account for a glass-fronted office building?

A The glass front should ideally be constructed from a safety material. These are materials which are inherently robust (eg glass blocks or polycarbonates), glass which breaks safely if it is broken, or ordinary annealed glass which meets the criteria contained in the table in Practical Guidance above.

The glass should also be marked in an appropriate fashion, eg with stickers or posters, or incorporate other features which make the glass apparent.

Drivers' Hours and Records

Summary

Whereas many work activities have no such controls, there are strict controls on the hours worked by commercial drivers. In addition, there are also statutory rest periods laid down between driving shifts.

Practical Guidance

Health and safety considerations

Legal restrictions on hours of work and appropriate record keeping are provided by road traffic, as opposed to health and safety laws, in certain cases. However, employers of employees who drive as part of their work still have a duty to ensure the employees' health and safety under the **Health and Safety at Work, etc Act 1974** (HSW Act). This duty is extended by the **Management of Health and Safety at Work Regulations 1999**, particularly the requirement to undertake a risk assessment of work-related risks.

Where the risk assessment identifies long driving hours as a risk, appropriate control measures must be implemented. Employees should be trained to recognise the dangers of tiredness while driving and to take breaks whenever necessary. Productivity targets and diary appointments should not offer significant incentives to continue working. Consideration should also be given to the fitness to continue driving of pregnant women and others with special needs and the risks that long hours could involve.

Well targeted, positive driver training can also raise awareness and minimise the risk of accidents.

Road traffic considerations

Daily driving

Drivers of goods (and certain passenger) vehicles exceeding 3.5 tonnes gross plated weight (including the weight of any trailers) engaged in commercial operations may not drive for more than nine hours in any day, and may not drive for more than 4.5 hours without taking a break of 45 minutes. This 45 minutes may be broken down into 15 minute (minimum) periods provided that when added together over the driving period of 4.5 hours, the total break time is at least 45 minutes.

Daily rest period

Drivers must take a rest period of 11 consecutive hours in each period of 24 hours. Again this can be reduced to nine consecutive hours on three days a week providing the reductions are fully compensated for by the end of the following week. Alternatively, drivers may split down the daily rest period into 2 or 3 separate periods (minimum of 1 hour) providing there is one rest period of at least 8 consecutive hours — however, if this system is adopted the minimum rest period is increased from 11 hours to 12 hours.

Weekly driving

Drivers may not drive for more than 56 hours in any week.

Weekly rest period

Drivers must take a weekly rest period of 45 consecutive hours (although certain reductions are allowed) at the latest after 56 hours' driving, ie 6 daily driving periods. Where the rest period is taken at the end of the sixth day, the total time spent driving must not exceed the maximum corresponding six daily driving periods. A weekly rest period which starts in one week and ends in the next may be attached to either week.

Case law

In the case of *Kelly v Shulman*, a driver was found not guilty of breaking various rest period requirements, although the case did legally define the accepted meaning of "day", which is taken to mean any successive period of 24 hours beginning with the moment the driver resumes work after the weekly rest period.

Fortnightly driving

This must not exceed 90 hours.

British limitations

Drivers of vehicles exempt from the European requirements above must comply with the following limitations under the **Transport Act 1968**.

Daily driving	10 hours maximum
Daily duty	11 hours maximum

Records

Drivers of vehicles must maintain records of their work and rest hours. This is achieved through the tachograph equipment which should be installed in all the vehicles. The tachograph equipment automatically records the distance travelled, the speed of the vehicle, the driving time, the periods of non-driving work, and rest breaks.

Questions and Answers

Q   Do limitations on drivers' hours apply throughout Europe or just in the UK?

A   The limitations on drivers' hours apply throughout Europe, as well as in the UK.

Q   Which drivers and/or vehicles are covered by the **Drivers' Hours (Goods Vehicles) (Keeping of Records) Regulations 1987**?

A   The Regulations apply to drivers of goods (and certain passenger) vehicles exceeding 3.5 tonnes gross plated weight (including the weight of any trailers) engaged in commercial operations.

Q   Are there recognised definitions of "day" and "week"?

A   There is no given definition of day in the legislation, although a week is defined as the period between 00.00 hours Monday and 24.00 Sunday. However, the case of *Kelly v Shulman* did define day as any successive period of 24 hours beginning with the moment the driver resumes work after the weekly rest period.

Drugs

Summary

Taking medicines (on prescription or otherwise) can affect people's ability to work safely. For example many prescribed and over-the-counter drugs for easing the symptoms of hay fever can cause drowsiness. A significant number of people who abuse drugs are in employment. Drug abuse can harm the abuser both mentally and physically, and can also increase the risk of accidents at work.

Practical Guidance

Legal requirements

There are two pieces of legislation which specifically ban the use of drugs:

- the **Work in Compressed Air Regulations 1996** state that no one who is under the influence of drugs which impairs their ability to carry out their work will be allowed to work in compressed air — it is the responsibility of the compressed air contractor to ensure that workers comply with this requirement
- the **Transport and Works Act 1992** makes it an offence for certain workers to be unfit to work due to the use of drugs while working on railways, tramways and other guided transport systems — the operators of the transport system would also be guilty of an offence unless they can show that they have done everything reasonably practicable to prevent such an offence being committed.

However, the main legislation for controlling drug use and preventing abuse is the **Misuse of Drugs Act 1971**. It deals with nearly all drugs with potential for abuse and/or dependence. The Act lays down specific requirements for drugs to be prescribed, safe custody and record keeping. It also defines the offences relating to their production, cultivation, supply and possession.

As far as the employer is concerned, the Act applies to them in that if they knowingly permit the production, supply or use of any controlled drugs to take place on their premises, they will have committed an offence.

The Act classifies drugs into three categories according to how harmful they are when abused:

- Class A — includes, cocaine, heroin, LSD
- Class B — includes oral amphetamines, barbiturates, codeine
- Class C — includes most sleeping pills, tranquillisers and less harmful amphetamines.

Sections 2 and 3 of the **Health and Safety at Work, etc Act 1974** (HSW Act) state that the employer must ensure that employees are not put at risk by work activities. This does therefore impose an obligation on the employer to do what is reasonably practicable to identify the effects of drugs, and cases of drug abuse, and to ensure that no employees under the influence of drugs are allowed to be at work and thus endanger themselves or others.

Employees who are under the influence of drugs at work may similarly be in breach of s.7 of the HSW Act, to take care of themselves and others whilst at work.

It is possible that in certain circumstances charges may be brought against an employer or an employee under both of the above Acts. An employer who knowingly allows a drug abuser to continue working without doing anything either to help the abuser or to protect the rest of the workforce may be liable to charges.

The effects of drugs

Drugs are taken for various reasons and can affect the body and mind in a number of ways. For examples of this, see the table below.

The Effects of Drugs	
Depressants — drugs that depress the nervous system	
Name	**Harmful effects**
Opiates, eg heroin, morphine, codeine, co-proxamol.	Physical and psychological dependence, impotence. Following abstinence, risk of overdose due to loss of tolerance.
Barbiturates ("downers").	Risk of dependence and overdose, especially if mixed with alcohol. Clumsiness, loss of co-ordination.
Tranquillisers, eg valium, librium, ativan.	Risk of overdose if mixed with alcohol. Risk of dependence.
Cannabis ("marijuana", "grass", "hash").	Respiratory problems including lung cancer, risk of dependence, hallucinations. Slowed reaction time may impair work performance.
Stimulants — drugs that stimulate the central nervous system	
Name	**Harmful effects**
Amphetamines ("speed", "uppers" or "blues").	Increased pulse rate. Distorted hearing and vision. Anxiety, panic and paranoid delusions. Risk of dependence.

Cocaine ("crack" or "coke").	Psychosis. Paranoid delusions likely with repeated doses. Dependence. Distress following initial elation.

Hallucinogens — drugs that alter mood and perception	
Name	**Harmful effects**
LSD ("acid").	Anxiety and panic. Perceptual distortions causing confusion or reckless behaviour, which has resulted in death.
"Magic mushrooms".	Similar to LSD, risk of poisoning by eating wrong type of fungi.
Hallucinogenic amphetamines, eg "ecstasy" ("E"), "fantasy", designer drugs.	Panic, insomnia, flashbacks, anxiety, visual and auditory hallucinations, confusion. Deaths have occurred from perceptual distortions causing reckless behaviour or confusion.
Phencyclidine (ie "PCP", "angel dust", "crystal".	Breathing failure. Intoxication, hallucinations, convulsions and coma. Disturbance of speed and vision. Violence, suicide and bizarre paranoid behaviour.

Solvents — alter perception and mood	
Name	**Harmful effects**
Volatile substances, eg lighter fuel, aerosols.	Extreme intoxication. Risk of heart and brain damage. Perception disorientation. Asphyxiation. Death from choking on inhaled vomit.

Given the information above, it is clear that the potential for injury and accidents at work is high when individuals are abusing such drugs, and that there is potential risk when individuals have been prescribed such drugs.

Signs of drug abuse

The employer should be aware that some of the signs associated with drug abuse may be caused by other factors such as stress:

- sudden change in behaviour pattern
- a tendency to become confused
- irritability and possibly violence
- abnormal fluctuations in mood and energy
- impaired job performance
- poor time-keeping
- increase in short-term sickness absence

- deterioration in relationships with other people.

Due to the cost of obtaining illegal drugs, other problems such as theft can occur.

The workplace may well provide the opportunity for detection of drug abuse. The provision of help for such individuals will benefit both the employer and employees, as well as ensuring that employers comply with their legal responsibilities.

Questions and Answers

Q   Where can I obtain further information on drug abuse?

A   The Health Education Authority or your local Employment Medical Advisory Service (contact your HSE Area Office for more details).

Q   How should I deal with employees who are legitimately taking drugs which may affect their work performance?

A   It should be made clear to employees that the policy applies to drug abuse, rather than to those taking drugs legitimately. Employees should be encouraged to inform their managers if they are taking any drugs which may affect their performance at work, in order that action can be taken to minimise the risk of injury or accidents occurring.

Dusts

Summary

Dusts vary in size, properties and effects, depending on the source of the dust. The main hazards associated with dusts are their effects on the respiratory system, potential for skin and eye irritation, and potential for causing fire and explosions.

Practical Guidance

Respiratory effects

Dust particles are often airborne, and so may be breathed in by workers. The effects of inhaling dusts may be short-term, eg coughing and tightness of the worker's chest, or long-term (see below). The effects depend on the size of the dust particles and the properties of the material producing dust.

Dust particles which are smaller than 0.2 microns are generally not retained by the lungs, whilst those greater than 5 microns do not reach the alveoli in the lungs. The size of dust particle which is likely to cause the most problems in the lungs is 1–2 microns.

Inhaling dust may lead to occupational asthma, chronic bronchitis, fibrosis (scarring of the lung tissue) and emphysema. Moulds or fungi inhaled with the dust may also lead to diseases, such as Farmer's Lung. Certain dusts are associated with particular lung conditions, for example:

- asbestos dust is associated with asbestosis (a form of lung fibrosis), mesothelioma (cancer of the pleura or peritoneum) and bronchial cancer
- cotton and flax dust is associated with byssinosis
- dust from dried sugar cane is associated with bagassosis
- cork dust is associated with suberosis.

Skin and eye irritation

If eyes are exposed to dust, it may cause irritation, pain, redness, watering and inflammation. Some eye irritation may be due to an allergic reaction to the dust.

Dust can also be irritating to the skin, and allergic reactions to particular dusts may lead to the development of eczema or dermatitis.

Controlling health effects

Under the **Control of Substances Hazardous to Health Regulations 1999** (COSHH), a risk assessment must be carried out for exposure to all hazardous substances, including dusts. The assessment should consider:

- the hazardous effects of the dust
- the likely level of exposure
- the routes of exposure, ie inhalation, eye and skin contact
- who is likely to be exposed, including any individual susceptibility.

Once exposure has been assessed, measures to prevent or control exposure to dust must be put into place. These control measures include:

- elimination of dust from the workplace, eg by using chemicals in a liquid rather than powdered form
- substituting a hazardous product which produces dust with a less hazardous one
- using methods which suppress dusts, eg wet methods
- restricting access to areas where dust is produced
- reducing the number of people exposed to dust
- setting up good hygiene practices, eg washing after handling dusts using ventilation to remove dust from the workplace
- providing workers with personal protective equipment (PPE), but only as a last resort.

All control measures must be used properly and be well maintained. Local exhaust ventilation and respiratory protective equipment (RPE) must be thoroughly examined at intervals prescribed by COSHH.

Occupational exposure standards

COSHH sets a maximum exposure limit of 0.4 mg/m^3 (8 hour time-weighted average (TWA)) for crystalline silica (respirable dust). The Health and Safety Executive (HSE) has set occupational exposure standards (published in EH40: *Occupational Exposure Limits*) of 10mg/m^3 (total inhalable dust) and 5mg/m^3 for respirable dust (8 hour TWA). These limits must be observed regardless of the composition of the dust, except where more specific occupational limits have been assigned.

Personal protective equipment

PPE must only be used to control exposure to dust as a last resort, when other control measures would not provide adequate protection. The standards of RPE are covered by COSHH. Provision of other types of PPE, including protective gloves and eye protection, is covered by the **Personal Protective Equipment at Work Regulations 1992**.

Monitoring

COSHH requires air samples to be taken, where appropriate. It will be necessary to monitor air for dust concentrations where exposure may be approaching or exceeding an occupational exposure standard.

Health surveillance

COSHH requires health surveillance to be provided to workers exposed to hazardous dusts, where appropriate. Health surveillance may be appropriate for certain activities involving contact with dust known to cause occupational asthma, dermatitis, etc.

Under the **Control of Asbestos at Work Regulations 1987**, workers who are exposed to certain levels of asbestos dust must be given medical surveillance before they start work and then at least every two years.

Reportable diseases

Byssinosis (a respiratory disease found in flax and cotton workers, usually after at least five years' exposure to the dust) is a reportable disease under the **Reporting of Injuries, Diseases and Dangerous Occurrences Regulations 1995**.

Dust explosions

High concentrations of flammable dusts, such as those of vegetable origin, present a risk of fire and explosion. A dust explosion within a building can cause extensive damage, injury and fire. Some dusts are so easily ignited that the use of totally enclosed plant and inert atmospheres is essential. This applies to magnesium, zirconium, aluminium, sulphur and metallic hydrides, for instance.

Under s.31 of the **Factories Act 1961**, if any process, such as grinding or sieving, produces dust liable to explode on ignition, all reasonably practicable steps must be taken to enclose the plant carrying out the process and other measures taken to prevent or remove accumulations of dust that may escape into the atmosphere.

Questions and Answers

Q   What activities produce dust?
A   There are many activities that may produce dust, and it is impossible to list them all here. However, the following are some examples:
- crushing and grinding of materials, eg stone or metal
- sieving powders
- opening and unloading sacks containing powders and other dry materials
- keeping animals
- handling powdered substances and materials, eg cement
- cutting large amounts of paper, cardboard, etc
- sanding or cutting wood.

Q   How should an accumulation of dust be cleared up?
A   Use a method that will not cause the dust to become airborne. Spraying the accumulation with a water jet is not suitable, and neither is sweeping. A vacuum cleaner could be used to suck up the dust. A wet cloth may be used to mop up small accumulations.

Q   How should I choose RPE for use with dust?

Dusts

A RPE must be suitable for its purpose, so you should choose a respirator that is designed to protect the wearer against the particular type of dust encountered. Check that the RPE complies with any manufacturing standards set, and bear in mind maintenance requirements, comfort of wearing and how severe the effects will be if the equipment fails. BS 4275: *Recommendations for the Selection, Maintenance and Use of Respiratory Protective Equipment* is a useful reference source.

Electricity

Summary

The **Electricity at Work Regulations 1989** require employers to assess and prevent all foreseeable dangers arising from work involving, or being carried out in the vicinity of, electricity. The Regulations apply to portable electrical equipment and building wiring systems in all workplaces.

Practical Guidance

Electricity at Work Regulations 1989

Work involving or near electricity must be safe so as not to create a risk of injury or danger, ie fire or explosion. Electrical systems must be properly constructed and maintained so as to be safe and must have a readily accessible means of isolating the electrical supply. Work activities involving, or in the vicinity of, electricity must be planned, and protective equipment, etc provided as necessary. The specified strength of any given electrical equipment must not be exceeded, and any reasonably foreseeable risks associated with the use of electrical equipment in adverse weather must be eliminated or adequately controlled. Other provisions cover insulation; protection; siting and earthing electrical conductors; live work, and the provision of adequate space, lighting and means of access.

Overhead and underground electrical cables

Apart from the risks directly associated with the use of electrical equipment, there are also significant risks of electrocution and electric shocks associated with overhead and underground electrical cables. Care must be taken to prevent inadvertent contact with these cables, either through carrying long ladders or through raised fork-lift truck arms, etc or through cutting through a buried cable during construction work. To prevent the latter, plans should be consulted where they exist and special detector apparatus used, in order to determine where buried cables are located. Careful transportation and siting of tall equipment is necessary to prevent contact with overhead cables.

Low voltage equipment

The **Electrical Equipment (Safety) Regulations 1994** apply to electrical equipment which operates within the range of 50 to 1000 volts for alternating current and 75 to 1500 volts for direct current. Such equipment must be safe (ie not represent a danger to humans and domestic animals, or damage property), comply with European Union (EU) harmonised standards, be constructed in accordance with good engineering practice, and carry the CE mark. It is also necessary to protect against hazards arising from the use of the equipment and/or any external influences.

Explosive atmospheres

Equipment provided for use in potentially explosive atmospheres must meet certain safety requirements as defined in the **Equipment and Protective Systems Intended for Use in Potentially Explosive Atmospheres Regulations 1996**. Electrical equipment is included as it has integral ignition sources, ie sparks generated during switching on and off, and heat build-up during operation, which are capable of causing an explosion in such atmospheres. Equipment safe to use in potentially explosive atmospheres must meet EU conformity criteria and be CE marked accordingly.

The safety requirements cover:
- design and construction
- maintenance
- work environment
- marking
- instructions
- overloading
- flame proofing
- possible ignition sources, eg static electricity, electrical current leakage and overheating
- control measures and systems
- power failures.

Questions and Answers

Q What conditions must be met in order for work to be carried out on live electrical equipment?

A Work on "live" electrical equipment may only be carried out when three criteria conditions are met, ie it is unreasonable for the work to be carried out on "dead" equipment; it is reasonable for the work to be carried out "live", and all necessary precautions have been taken to prevent danger. These conditions are specified in the **Electricity at Work Regulations 1989**.

Q What factors should be considered when deciding whether electrical equipment is suitable?

A The three important factors to consider are:
- what the equipment is required to do — is heavy duty, as opposed to domestic standard, equipment more appropriate, or is the equipment required to come into contact with water, eg water vacuum cleaners
- where it is to be used — is the equipment intended for external use, etc
- who is to use it — is any special training or supervision, etc required, or are there any particular risks, eg to young people.

Careful thought and consideration before purchase will ensure the best equipment for the tasks and operators is purchased, and thus reduce unnecessary problems later on.

Q Is there a legal requirement for microwave ovens to be checked for microwave leakage?

A No, there is no legal requirement for such checks, although microwave leakage is a recognised hazard, particularly with heavily used and/or older equipment. It is therefore a sensible precaution to include annual microwave leakage tests in any planned preventative maintenance programmes for microwave ovens.

Emergency Procedures

Summary

Every organisation must ensure that procedures are in place to deal with all foreseeable emergencies. Such emergencies will usually include fire, bomb threats, and loss of power or lighting. Any site-specific hazards will also require emergency procedures, eg where there is a risk of a chemical spillage, or the area is prone to natural disasters such as floods.

Practical Guidance

An emergency such as any of those identified above could have serious consequences to individuals, and also to the business. Therefore it is important to have adequate and suitable emergency procedures in place to ensure injury and damage limitation and containment of the hazard, in the event of such an emergency occurring.

There are a number of statutory provisions relating to emergency procedures. The main requirements are set out below.

General duty

Under s.2 of the **Health and Safety at Work, etc Act 1974**, the employer must provide suitable information, instruction, training and supervision. This includes training in emergency procedures at the workplace.

The employer must also provide and maintain a safe working environment and ensure that employees and other persons who are not employees are not put at risk by any work activities. An employer would obviously be in breach of this legislation if it did not have adequate emergency procedures in place.

The **Management of Health and Safety at Work Regulations 1999** require the employer to put procedures in place to be followed in the event of serious and imminent danger to those at work, and to inform employees of the nature of the hazard and the steps to be taken to avoid it. They also require the employer to nominate a sufficient number of competent persons to implement the procedures, in relation to the evacuation of the premises. Managers and supervisors must be provided with additional training in legal requirements, procedures for disabled employees and visitors, the importance of employee co-operation, and actions to be taken if they do not co-operate. It is also worth considering appointing, and training, a person to deal with the public relations issues that may arise as a result of an emergency. The employer is also required to make any necessary contacts with external services, particularly with regard to rescue work, emergency medical care and first aid.

Risk assessment

When employers carry out their risk assessments, they should identify the foreseeable emergencies which may occur, and those who these emergencies may affect, and procedures should be written to cover these. For many employers the only foreseeable risks will be fire and possibly bomb threats. However, some workplaces or activities may pose other risks, eg chemical spillage, which must be subject to a particular procedure.

Responsibilities

It may be necessary for the procedure to define the responsibilities of specific employees, or groups of employees, who may be required to perform specific tasks in the event of emergencies. An example would be a requirement to shut down a particular plant that may otherwise compound the danger. There may be some employees who need to be trained to bring an emergency situation under control. The conditions under which these people stop work and move to a place of safety may well be different from the rules applying to other employees, and this should be defined in the procedure.

The procedure should set out the roles and responsibilities of the competent persons nominated to implement the detailed actions required. All employees must be aware of who the competent persons are, and their roles.

When and how the procedure is activated

Emergency events can occur and develop rapidly, and by their nature there is little advance warning. This usually requires employees to respond quickly and without waiting for further guidance. The procedures should specify when and how a situation is to be regarded as an emergency to enable employees to proceed in good time to a place of safety. As an example, if a chemical process is in danger of running out of control, it may be necessary to commence evacuation whilst attempts are still being made to control the situation. In these circumstances, evacuation is as a precaution in case it is not possible to control the process.

Emergency procedures should be written down, and should clearly set out the limits of actions to be taken by employees. Information on the procedures should be made available to all employees, and any other workers who may be in the workplace, eg contractors. Emergency procedures should be covered in induction training, and it would be advisable to carry out exercises to familiarise employees with those procedures. A common example is to ensure that the sound of the fire alarm and the way that evacuation drills should be carried out are known.

All reasonable steps should be taken to ensure that non-employees are given sufficient information to enable them to recognise nominated persons for the purposes of emergency evacuation. This is essential as the authority vested in those nominated persons under emergency conditions may be different than the authority under normal conditions. For example, an evacuation marshal may have authority to instruct people from a different department to leave the building in an emergency, but may have no jurisdiction over those staff in other circumstances.

Recommencement of work

Work should not recommence after an emergency if serious danger remains. If there are any doubts, expert assistance should be sought from the emergency services. There may be exceptional circumstances where re-entry is deemed necessary, eg by the emergency services themselves, where human life is a risk.

Depending on why the emergency has arisen, there may be a need for a review of the risk assessment.

Co-operation and co-ordination

Where different employers (or self-employed persons) share a workplace, their separate emergency procedures should take account of others in the workplace. As far as is appropriate, their emergency plans should be co-ordinated.

Fire procedures

A significant factor in fires where there are multiple fatalities is the incorrect response of building occupants. Therefore, there must be a well-planned and rehearsed fire procedure which should take into account the findings of the employer's fire risk assessment for the particular premises. Such a procedure will need to be approved by the fire authority before a fire certificate is issued under the **Fire Precautions Act 1971**.

The requirements for emergency procedures in non-certificated premises are reinforced by the **Fire Precautions (Workplace) Regulations 1997**. These require the employer to include fire precautions in their general risk assessment, and to give adequate instruction and information for staff. Where necessary, there must be procedures to ensure co-operation and co-ordination with other employers in shared premises.

Specific legislation which requires emergency procedures

There are specific requirements for emergency procedures under various Regulations, including:

- **Diving at Work Regulations 1997**
- **Construction (Health, Safety and Welfare) Regulations 1996**
- **Carriage of Dangerous Goods by Road Regulations 1996**
- **Gas Safety (Management) Regulations 1996**
- **Control of Major Accident Hazard Regulations 1999**
- **Pressure Systems Safety Regulations 2000**
- **Highly Flammable Liquids and Liquefied Petroleum Gases Regulations 1972.**

Questions and Answers

Q What information do I need to give visitors with regard to emergency procedures?

A This is dependent on circumstances and duration of the visit. Visitors who will be accompanied at all times need only be made aware of what an alarm means and how and where to evacuate to. This could usefully be relayed on the back of a printed visitor's pass.

Q How often should I rehearse evacuation?

A Fire drills are recommended to take place at least once a year, and preferably every six months. If a fire certificate is in force, this will specify the frequency. It would be good practice to adopt the same recommendation for other emergency procedures.

Q If the workplace is open to the public, how can I ensure the evacuation will be carried out successfully?

A Members of staff should be nominated to be responsible for directing people via the evacuation route in the event of an emergency. If possible these members of staff should be clearly identifiable.

Employees, Duties of

Summary

Although the majority of statutory duties are placed firmly on the employer, there are many instances of specific duties placed on employees (some examples are given below) which can result in prosecution with resultant substantial fines, and possible custodial sentences in some instances.

Practical Guidance

The employer's role

As with any law, ignorance is not an excuse for failing to comply with it. However, it has to be realised that the majority of employees will be unaware of legal duties placed on them unless they are brought to their attention. A responsible employer should do this, not as a threat, but to ensure employees are fully aware of the part they must play in ensuring satisfactory standards of health and safety, the consequences of not playing that part and that they comply with the information, instruction and training requirements of the **Management of Health and Safety at Work Regulations 1999**.

The primary duties are those within the **Health and Safety at Work, etc Act 1974** (HSW Act) added to by numerous others within Regulations. The following are examples.

Duties of every employee

Section 7 of the HSW Act applies to all employees at all levels, including managers, and states that it is the duty of every employee while at work:

- to take reasonable care of the health and safety of himself or herself and of other persons who may be affected by his or her acts or omissions at work
- as regards any duty or requirement imposed on his or her employer or any other person by or under any of the relevant statutory provisions, to co-operate with him or her so far as is necessary to enable that duty or requirement to be performed or complied with.

Duties of every person

Section 8 of the HSW Act states that no one may intentionally or recklessly interfere with or misuse anything provided in the interests of health, safety or welfare in pursuance of any of the relevant statutory provisions.

Electricity at Work Regulations 1989

Regulation 3 places duties on the employer and the self-employed, but additionally employees are required:

- to co-operate with their employer so far as is necessary to enable any duty placed on that employer by the Regulations to be complied with
- to comply with the provisions of the Regulations in so far as they relate to matters within their control.

Noise at Work Regulations 1989

Regulation 10 requires employees:

- so far as is practicable, to make full and proper use of personal ear protectors when they are provided to comply with the requirements relating to the second action level in the Regulations, and of any other protective measures provided
- to report any defects.

Management of Health and Safety at Work Regulations 1999

Regulation 14 effectively expands the duties under s.7 of the HSW Act by requiring employees:

- to use any machinery, equipment, dangerous substances, transport equipment, means of production or safety devices in accordance with any training and instructions provided by the employer
- to inform the employer of any serious and imminent dangers to health and safety
- to inform the employer of any shortcomings in the employer's protection arrangements for health and safety.

Personal Protective Equipment at Work Regulations 1992

Regulations 10 and 11 apply specifically to any work situation where personal protective equipment has been provided by the employer. Similar duties are placed on the self-employed. Employees are required to:

- use any personal protective equipment provided in accordance with both any training in its use and instructions provided as a requirement of regulation 9
- take all reasonable steps to ensure the personal protective equipment is returned to the accommodation provided for it after use
- report any loss or obvious defect in the personal protective equipment to the employer.

Manual Handling Operations Regulations 1992

Regulation 5 supplements the duties on employees in s.7 of the HSW Act and regulation 14 of the **Management of Health and Safety at Work Regulations 1999** by requiring employees to follow appropriate systems of work laid down by the employer to promote safety during manual handling operations. It specifically requires employees to make full and proper use of any system of work provided for their use whilst at work by the employer in compliance with regulation 4. Regulation 4(1)(b)(ii) requires the risk of injury to be reduced to the lowest level reasonably practicable.

Control of Substances Hazardous to Health Regulations 1999

Regulation 8 relates to control measures, personal protective equipment (PPE), etc provided by the employer, who has to take all reasonable steps to ensure that it is properly used. Employees are required:

- to make full and proper use of any control measure, PPE or other thing or facility provided
- to take all reasonable steps to ensure that PPE, etc is returned after use to any accommodation provided for it
- to report any defects they discover forthwith.

Questions and Answers

Q Can employees be prosecuted for not complying with safety laws?

A Yes, depending on the actual statutory provision they fail to comply with they could be prosecuted in a Magistrates' Court with the maximum penalty a fine of £5000, or the Crown Court with the penalty an unlimited fine.

Q Our managing director does not use the personal protective equipment I have attempted to provide him with for use in an area where there is a serious risk of eye injury. Could he be prosecuted?

A Yes, under regulation 10 of the **Personal Protective Equipment at Work Regulations 1992** and s.7 of the **Health and Safety at Work, etc Act 1974**. He could also be considered to be guilty of an offence under s.37 by virtue of his position as a director of a company which has committed an offence in failing to comply with relevant statutory provisions.

Q If employees are found guilty of an offence because they failed to comply with one of the legal duties specifically placed on them, could the company still be prosecuted?

A Yes, depending on the circumstances. Section 36 of the HSW Act would apply and there would be consideration of how much effort the employer had put into getting the employee to comply. There is existing case law on this, such as how much effort must be put into ensuring an employee wears personal protective equipment.

Q If employees are injured at work, and subsequently found to have failed to comply with a legal requirement, would they still get compensation if they made a claim?

A There is no simple answer to this question as many facts would be taken into account, along with many examples of previous case law regarding interpretation.

Employer, Duties of

Summary

In addition to their general duty of care in common law, employers have general and specific statutory duties under numerous Acts and Regulations. Extensive case law interprets both.

Practical Guidance

Extent of duties

Acts of Parliament and Regulations place extensive duties on employers and the self-employed. The more generally applicable are outlined below, but reference must be made to those specifically applying to the business. An example of recent legislation placing very specific duties on an employer is the **Confined Spaces Regulations 1997**.

General statutory duty

Section 2(1) of the **Health and Safety at Work, etc Act 1974** (HSW Act) states "It shall be the duty of every employer to ensure, so far as is reasonably practicable, the health, safety and welfare at work of all employees". Section 2(2) gives more detail of what this includes, qualified by the phrase, "so far as is reasonably practicable":

- the provision and maintenance of plant and systems of work that are safe and without risks to health
- arrangements for ensuring safety and absence of risks to health in connection with the use, handling, storage and transport of articles and substances
- the provision of such information, instruction, training and supervision as is necessary to ensure the health and safety at work of the employees
- the maintenance of any place of work under the employer's control in a condition that is safe and without risks to health and the provision and maintenance of means of access to and egress from it that are safe and without such risks
- the provision and maintenance of a working environment for the employees that is safe, without risks to health and adequate as regards facilities and arrangements for their welfare at work.

Section 37(1) of the HSW Act provides that "where an offence committed by a body corporate is proved to have been committed with the consent or connivance of, or to have been attributable to any neglect on the part of, any director, manager, secretary or other similar officer of the body corporate...he, as well as the body corporate, shall be guilty of that offence and shall be liable to be proceeded against and punished accordingly".

Managing health and safety

This general duty on employers is expanded by the **Management of Health and Safety at Work Regulations 1999**. These Regulations cover, amongst other things:

- carrying out risk assessments
- health and safety arrangements
- health surveillance
- health and safety assistance
- procedures for serious and imminent dangers
- provision of information and training
- co-operation and co-ordination with other employers
- employees' duties
- temporary workers.

Safety policy

Every employer must prepare, and revise as and when appropriate, a written statement (where there are five or more employees) of the company's general policy on health and safety. This should include details of the organisation and arrangements currently in force for carrying out that policy and the employer must bring the document and any revisions to it to the notice of all employees.

Consultation

Under the **Safety Representatives and Safety Committees Regulations 1977**, it is the duty of every employer to consult any recognised trades union-appointed safety representatives with a view to making and maintaining arrangements enabling effective co-operation in promoting and developing measures to ensure the health and safety of employees at work. The employer's duty is extended to all employees, whether union members or not, by the **Health and Safety (Consultation with Employees) Regulations 1996**.

Duty to other persons

Section 3 of the HSW Act imposes a duty on every employer (and every self-employed person) to conduct their business in such a way as to ensure that people not in their employment are also not exposed to risks to their health and safety whilst on the employer's premises. An employer or self-employed person who fails to take reasonably practicable steps to protect persons not in their employment (such as customers in a shop, salespersons, delivery drivers, post office employees, contractors, factory inspectors, etc) from harm, is guilty of an offence.

Control of premises

The HSW Act continues the duty of care to non-employees in s.4, which places responsibility for ensuring health and safety on the person in control of certain premises. The Act makes no specific mention of an occupier as having duties. However, s.4 does impose duties on a controller of premises in relation to those who use non-domestic premises made available to them as a place of work where they may use plant or substances provided for their use there but who are not the controller's employees. It is the duty of each person who has control, to any extent, of such premises to take reasonable measures to ensure that the premises are safe and without risks to health.

Occupiers' liability

The occupier is, in effect, the person who runs the premises in question, and who regulates and controls the work that is done there (ie the employer, in most cases). That person may be a limited company, an individual manager, a senior partner, the owner or, in some cases, a receiver. Many Acts and their subordinate Regulations impose duties and obligations on occupiers.

Under the **Occupiers' Liability Act 1957**, an occupier owes a "common duty of care" to all visitors, ie a duty to take such care as is reasonable (given the circumstances) to see that visitors will be reasonably safe in using the premises for the purposes for which they are invited or permitted to be there. An employer (or occupier) cannot be prosecuted for a breach of their duties under the 1957 Act, but if a visitor is injured the occupier may be liable to pay compensation for the injury.

The **Occupiers' Liability Act 1984** defines the circumstances under which a duty is owed. In particular, occupiers owe a duty if:

- they are aware of a danger
- they know (or should know) that a person may put themselves at risk
- the risk is one which the occupier might reasonably be expected to do something about.

The occupier must take such care as is reasonable in the circumstances of the case to see that the other person does not suffer injury; the duty may be discharged by one of the following means:

- giving warning of the danger
- discouraging people from putting themselves at risk in the first place, eg by making it more difficult for trespassers, etc to enter the premises.

Vicarious liability

An employer may be held civilly or criminally liable for the negligent or unlawful acts of an employee, even though the employee can be shown to have wilfully disobeyed the express instructions of the employer. This is known as the doctrine of vicarious liability, whereby under certain circumstances one party becomes liable for the actions of another. If employers are party to the negligent or unlawful act, or aid and abet the unlawful activities of another, they assume personal liability along with that other person.

Insurance

The **Employers' Liability (Compulsory Insurance) Regulations 1998** requires all employers to insure against liability for bodily injury or disease sustained by employees whilst at work. Insurance must be for a minimum £5 million in respect of claims arising from any one occurrence but there is now a maximum "cap" of £10 million per occurrence. A valid certificate of insurance must be displayed in a position that is easy to see and read. Although employers are required in law to insure against contingent civil liabilities for bodily injury or disease sustained by employees in the course of their employment, they are under no similar legal obligation to insure against public liability.

Questions and Answers

Q I have heard duties described as civil and criminal, are they the same?

A Civil law and criminal law are not the same. You are most likely to come across a civil action should an employee be injured or develop illness related to work, when a claim for compensation may happen. Criminal law is when you have a legal duty to do something, or not to do something, and fail in that duty. The result can be prosecution with subsequent fines and/or imprisonment.

Q Am I totally responsible for employees' safety when they are at work?

A Not totally, many duties are qualified with the phrase, "so far as is reasonably practicable", which means there is a calculation to be made between how large the risks are and how much effort needs to be made to remove or reduce those risks. There is considerable case law which interprets many past cases and defines when employers are responsible for ensuring employee's safety, and when they are not.

Q There seem to be numerous examples of very old Regulations where only bits and pieces are still in existence. Are they still in force and can I still be prosecuted for not complying with them?

A Yes; the replacement of old laws is a slow process but 1996 and 1997 saw much old legislation replaced, and more will be removed in the immediate future.

Ergonomics

Summary

Ergonomics is a broad subject which assists employers in taking account of the way that employees, the work environment and work equipment interact with each other to improve efficiency and quality, and minimise the risks of injury and ill-health.

Practical Guidance

Definition

A simple definition of ergonomics is "the application of scientific information concerning human beings to the design of objects, systems and environments for human use" or, put another way, the science of fitting the task to the person. Work can be used in a broad sense and ergonomics covers the industrial situation, military applications, "work" at home, leisure and hobby activities. As a subject it uses knowledge of anatomy, physiology, anthropometry, biomechanics and psychology.

Postural analysis

The body can be a highly flexible structure but as such it is also prone to abuse. Poor posture is easily adopted and can cause rapid symptoms of muscle fatigue and strain, or longer term strains, damage and deformations. These effects have been known about for over 200 years but still workstations are inadequately designed and frequently provide insufficient space, and are responsible for incorrect postures, over-reaching, bending, twisting and other motions that may result in acute or chronic injury.

Physiology of work

Human beings need energy for the body to function. The harder the body is expected to work, the greater the demand on the available energy. Strenuous jobs require more energy than sedentary jobs. As the level of work effort increases a greater degree of interest should be taken in the energy demands on the employees. This may also require an investigation of the working environmental conditions as both increased and decreased temperature create additional difficulties.

Repetitive strains

The body can carry out many repetitions of the same action and is often expected to do so. Any machine expected to carry out repetitious motions would be regularly maintained and would require the replacement of parts as they wear out. We do not do this with humans, but the end result can be the same — complete breakdown. Any activity involving high numbers of repetitions should be looked at carefully and redesigned to avoid this as far as possible.

Work design and a systems approach

The overall investigation and design of work tasks should result in a close match between the human involved and the tasks to be carried out. The resulting combination is often referred to as the "man–machine interface" (MMI). A simple MMI would consist of a machine, which may have displays (possibly involving sight, sound, vibration), and a "man", who receives the information from the displays and processes the information, makes decisions, then operates "controls" to change the operation of the machine. This process carries on as necessary to ensure the task proceeds as intended. Driving a car, typing and controlling an aeroplane are all MMIs. The display and control elements between the "machine" and the "man" are usually referred to as the interface.

Getting elements of the MMI wrong can have serious consequences. In an aircraft, if the pilot cannot see various displays, or wrongly interprets them, this could result in a crash. At a different level, having lighting levels inadequate to allow a seamstress to see what she is sewing could result in poor quality of the finished garment.

One further concept used when considering task design is FPJ–FJP, "Fit the Person to the Job — Fit the Job to the Person". FJP involves designing equipment, the environment and elements of the task itself so that humans can function correctly. FPJ includes selection and training: ensuring the right person is selected and given the "tools" to be able to do the job required of them. The aim is for the task, environment and equipment to be designed properly, and the operators involved to be well-selected and adequately trained.

Stress, fatigue, shiftwork, work environment

Adequate consideration of the MMI involves more than just physical design. The way employees cope with stress, how they make decisions, the effects of physical and mental effort causing fatigue, changes to work patterns that cause changes in the circadian rhythms (daily body rhythms such as temperature fluctuations) and the possible short-term and long-term effects all need to be included.

Human error

In any situation, people must make decisions based on two main sources of information: that which they have received, interpreted and stored previously as part of their learning or experience process, and that presented to them at the time of making the decision. They do not always make the best decision, for many reasons. Incorrect data or difficulties in interpreting it through poor interface design may mean the decision is based on wrong facts. Lack of training or previous experience may mean that correctly supplied data is acted on inappropriately. Also, people can make deliberate wrong decisions through interpretation of the presented information, for example most people have knowingly driven at speed in excess of the prevailing speed limit. The subject of human error or human reliability is complex but the possible consequences should be included in the assessment of any new tasks.

Work with computers

Work-related upper limb disorders have been recognised for several hundred years, but a significant increase in awareness of them is probably attributable to the rapid development of computer use in business. Many problems related to their use are due to poor posture, poor equipment or adjustment of it, inadequate software design or workload/rest breaks. Application of good ergonomic principles can remove or reduce most likely problems.

Hand tools

This is another well-researched area and much is known about the problems of design and use of hand tools. Hand tools frequently involve repetitious movements, can cause undesirable postures for long periods and may generate vibration with direct effects on the hand/arm tissues. Care in the selection and maintenance of hand tools is required and the task should be carefully examined.

Questions and Answers

Q   We are designing assembly workstations but have a mixture of male and female employees, of all different sizes. We are going to use an average value for their stature to decide on the height of the bench. Is this the best way?

A   No, for those of short stature the bench would be too high and for the tallest, too low. Accommodating different sizes of people is one of the most common problems. The best solution is to look carefully at the assembly job and each task involved. Frequently, it is not just bench height that can be important. Adjustable height benches, design of the surrounding area and provision of suitable adjustable seating should be considered, followed by the education of the employees in the possible problems and how to avoid them by correct posture, adjustment of equipment, etc.

Q   The variability of human beings is so great that it cannot possibly be catered for in any design — my employees are wonderfully adaptable anyway so it doesn't matter, does it?

A   This is one of the great problems. Set a robot machine up to do a task and it will do it, provided nothing changes. Use a human being and they continually adapt to changing work pace, dimensions, object placement, speed and much more.

Unfortunately, taking posture as an example, humans will put themselves into postures that allow them to work, but will also do harm. This is a problem that has been known of for many years — a document about postural problems was written as early as 1713. You should do as much as is reasonably practicable to provide a well-designed workplace and workstations.

Q I have heard the term "human factors", is this the same as ergonomics?

A Not quite. In the US the term "human factors" broadly equates with ergonomics, but we tend to use it as a narrower topic area. We consider human factors to concentrate on the psychological aspects of work — the employees' attitudes, knowledge, etc, the mental aspects of the work carried out, and the influence of the organisation. Motivation, risk-taking behaviour and avoidance of errors are examples of human factors.

Escalators

Summary

Escalators and moving walkways are becoming more common in many workplaces, particularly retail areas. The main safety hazards related to escalators and their use are those of people falling or becoming trapped in the mechanism of the escalator.

Practical Guidance

Hazards associated with escalators

It is generally either the very young or the elderly who fall whilst using escalators. The causes may include inadequate or incorrect lighting, overcrowding or poor judgment at entry and exit points. The other main hazard is the likelihood of feet, fingers or loose clothing becoming trapped in the working parts of an escalator.

General duty

All employers are required to ensure, so far as reasonably practicable, the health, safety and welfare at work of all of their employees. In particular they should provide and maintain safe plant, safe means of access and egress, safe systems of work, the provision of suitable information, instruction, training and supervision.

As in any workplace, employers in the retail industry will have to consider the health and safety of visitors to their premises, eg customers, delivery personnel, etc.

Controllers of premises have a duty to ensure, so far as is reasonably practicable, that there are no risks to persons using the premises.

The **Management of Health and Safety at Work Regulations 1999** place a duty on employers to assess the risks associated with their work activities. This would include the risks associated with escalators and their use by members of staff and, where applicable, members of the general public. Some consideration should also be given to those people who may be more vulnerable to the hazards present, such as children (who may not perceive dangers), and persons with any physical or mental disability.

Specific duty

There are specific requirements relating to escalators under the **Workplace (Health, Safety and Welfare) Regulations 1992**.

Escalators and moving walkways shall:
- function safely
- be equipped with any necessary safety devices

- be fitted with one or more emergency stop controls which are easily identifiable and readily accessible.

Escalators must also be maintained in an efficient state, efficient working order and in good repair. "Efficient" in this context relates to health and safety not productivity or economy.

In order to comply with the legal requirements relating to escalators, organisations must ensure that escalators are safe for use at all times. The Health and Safety Executive (HSE) recommends that periodic (ie at least once every six months) thorough examination of escalators is carried out by a competent person.

There is also a legal requirement to maintain records of tests and examinations carried out by competent persons. The employer or occupier of a building should be in possession of a certificate of testing and thorough examination of the escalator prior to it first being put in to use. This should be available until such times as the escalator is taken out of use or undergoes major alteration and a new certificate is issued. The details recorded on the certificate include the:

- description, date of manufacture, identification mark and location of the equipment referred to
- safe working load
- date and details of the test and thorough examination carried out
- declaration that the information is correct and is found free from any defect likely to affect safety
- owner of the equipment
- name and address of person carrying out the test and thorough examination.

Questions and Answers

Q   How frequently should escalators be maintained?

A   This will depend of the likelihood of defects developing and the foreseeable consequences; it would be prudent to take advice from the manufacturer of the escalator, or specialists.

Q   Is it acceptable to allow people to use an escalator when it is stationary?

A   If there are other means of access and egress, these should normally be used.

Q   What steps can I take to minimise the risk of clothing, etc becoming trapped in the escalator?

A   Various deflector devices which can be fitted to existing escalators are available. If it is impractical to do this, yellow lines at least 50mm wide should be painted at the extreme edges of each step tread.

Eye and Eyesight Testing

Summary

There is a duty under the **Health and Safety (Display Screen Equipment) Regulations 1992** to provide any "users" who request it with an appropriate eye and eyesight test. The entitlement includes a test of vision and an examination of the eye. It may be necessary to check the general visual capability of other staff, eg lift truck drivers, and the colour vision of those involved in certain safety-critical tasks.

Practical Guidance

Health risks

The possible effects of the continual use of display screen equipment upon eyes and eyesight often raises questions from employees. However, after extensive research there are no indications that visual display units (VDUs) can cause disease or permanent damage to eyes. However, the fact the some tasks involve intensive and repeated use of screens may well enable an employee to identify an unknown but previously existing eye problem.

Employees who use display screen equipment (DSE) may complain of symptoms of eyestrain, ie tiredness, irritation or soreness. The most common causes of eye fatigue are a fault in the focusing of the eye, poor eye co-ordination, incorrect position of the equipment and documents, inappropriate lighting, poorly designed work areas and lack of adequate screen maintenance.

Uncorrected visual defects can make any work activity more tiring or stressful than it should be. Correcting defective vision or defective equipment can improve comfort, job satisfaction and performance.

About 8 in 100 men have defective colour vision, while only 1 in 200 women are colour blind.

Safety risks

Those who operate equipment and machinery may put themselves or others at risk if they work with uncorrected visual defects. For example, lift truck drivers with poor peripheral vision may respond slower to the presence of other workers or other vehicles. Employees engaged in certain types of work, eg civil aviation or electrical contracting, may put themselves or others at risk if they cannot distinguish subtle colour variations.

Requirement for eye and eyesight testing

Regulation 5 of the **Health and Safety (Display Screen Equipment) Regulations 1992** requires employers to provide any "user" who requests it with an appropriate eye and eyesight test as defined in the **Opticians Act 1989**. This test must be conducted by a qualified practitioner, ie an optometrist (optician) or doctor.

A user is an employee who "habitually uses" display screen equipment for the purposes of an employer's undertaking as a significant part of their normal work.

The employee is also entitled to repeat testing at regular intervals (ie as recommended by the practitioner who conducted the previous), or at any time if they are experiencing visual problems which they reasonably believe to be related to VDU work.

If available, an employee may elect to forego the entitlement to a full eye test and opt for a less comprehensive test, eg in-house vision screening by an occupational health nurse. The results of an eye and eyesight test can only be disclosed to the employer with the consent of the employee (**Access to Medical Reports Act 1988**).

Lift truck operators

The Health and Safety Executive guidance (HSG6: *Safety in Working with Lift Trucks*) states that lift truck operators should have visual acuity of 6/12 with both eyes, achieved by glasses if necessary. They should have health screening, including a vision test, at least every five years.

Eyesight testing for a trainee lift truck driver should ensure that the operative has binocular vision. Experienced operatives who become monocular should not be automatically barred from continuing employment.

Any lift truck driver with serious vision defects, eg persistent diplopia (double vision) and binocular field defects (difficulty judging distances), must be prevented from operating a lift truck.

Corrective appliances

Where corrective appliances (normally spectacles) are prescribed specifically for work with DSE, the employer must provide these regardless of where the user is working, ie even if for use at another employer's premises. The employer has to pay only the basic cost of suitable lenses and frames. Any additional costs must be met by the employee.

It is worth noting that experience has shown that in most working populations less than 10% of users will need special corrective appliances for DSE work.

Employers do not have to pay for corrective appliances for lift truck drivers, nor any other occupation except DSE users. There is an exception to this rule if safety glasses with prescription lenses are required.

Developing a policy

Where applicable, a policy statement on DSE should be drawn up, and the following points on eye and eyesight testing included:

- those employees who are identified as users of DSE will be entitled, on request, to eye and eyesight tests upon employment as a user, at regular intervals (as defined by the optometrist) and where a visual problem is experienced
- testing will also be available on request where an employee transfers to a job where they will be classified as a user, or where their work changes and involves a significant amount of DSE use
- the costs of these tests will be met by the employer, provided that testing has been arranged through the employer
- where spectacles are prescribed specifically for work with DSE, the employer will pay for the cost of a basic type and quality adequate for its function
- if the employee wishes to choose a more costly design, then they will be obliged to pay the difference between the actual cost and the price of a basic pair.

Questions and Answers

Q Do DSE users have to have an eyesight test?

A No, it is at their own request, although it should be encouraged, particularly if any visual problems are being experienced and the workstation setup has been checked. Often poor posture may be a cause of headaches.

Q Should employees go to their own opticians, or can we ask them to see a practitioner of our choosing?

A In practice, employees should be allowed to use their own opticians. However, as the employer is paying for the test, the employer can choose who conducts the test.

Q Are all my employees entitled to free eye and eyesight tests?

A No, only those defined as "users" under the **Health and Safety (Display Screen Equipment) Regulations 1992**.

Q Can I employ a lift truck driver who wears glasses?

A Yes, although you should make sure the glasses result in visual acuity of at least 6/12 with both eyes.

Q Can I restrict the amount of money spent on a pair of spectacles purchased for DSE work?

A Yes, you are only responsible for the cost of the basic frames and lenses.

Q Should I only recruit people with perfect colour vision?

A No, the majority of tasks can be performed perfectly adequately by those with defective colour vision.

Fire

Summary

Fire is an important aspect of health and safety in workplaces, accounting for many millions of pounds lost to industry through insurance claims, property damage, lost productivity, etc. More importantly, there are also human losses and injuries, which can be minimised through good fire safety management systems and effective prevention/precaution procedures.

Practical Guidance

Causes of fire
Some of the common causes of fire are as follows:
- faulty/misused electrical equipment
- smoking, discarded cigarette ends
- accumulation of refuse
- portable heaters
- fat fryers
- gas
- flammable materials and substances
- arson.

Fire spread
In order to burn, fires need:
- something that will burn (fuel)
- oxygen from the air
- heat/ignition source.

Removal of any one of these three factors will extinguish the fire.

Once burning a fire will spread around a building by:
- hot air currents (convection)
- transfer of heat between touching surfaces (conduction)
- heat waves (electromagnetic radiation, eg as from the heat bar of an electric fire).

The most common cause of fire spread is radiation. This is why fire doors — which essentially form physical barriers to divide buildings up into smaller, separate compartments — are so important in reducing the amount of fire spread, thus allowing adequate time for the evacuation of any occupants. Unless fire doors are fitted with automatic magnets which release the doors when the fire alarm is activated, they must be kept shut at all times.

Smoke will travel ahead of the fire.

Types of fire

The different types of fire are classified according to the combustible material being burnt. The four classes are:

- Class A — fires involving solid materials, eg paper, wood, fabrics, etc
- Class B — fires involving liquids or liquefiable solids, eg fats, oils, petrol
- Class C — fires involving gases
- Class D — fires involving metals
- Class F — fires involving cooking oils and fats.

There is no such thing as an electrical fire: the fire will be one of the above classes which includes electrical equipment.

Fire risk assessment

Employers must carry out fire risk assessments for their premises, and then use the findings from these assessments to provide appropriate fire-fighting measures, emergency procedures, staff training, etc.

Fire detection and warning

All workplaces should have a means of detecting and giving warning of fires. Different types of fire detectors will detect:

- smoke (most common type)
- heat (this type is often used in kitchens)
- flames.

In more sophisticated systems the detectors are automatically linked to the fire alarms which will ring when a detector is activated. In more basic systems, eg domestic smoke detectors, the detector will notify the presence of a fire but an additional action will be required to activate the general fire alarm.

The correct choice of detector and the correct siting are very important.

Care should be taken to ensure that disabled employees, eg deaf people, are made aware of an alarm signal by using flashing lights, etc in addition to an audible alarm.

Fire certificates

The following premises must have a fire certificate:

- hotels or boarding houses which provide sleeping accommodation for more than six people, or where the sleeping accommodation is above the first floor or below the ground floor
- offices, shops, railway premises and factories where more than 20 people are employed at any one time, more than 10 people are employed at any one time other than on the ground floor, the premises are part of a larger building which meets either of the conditions above or explosives or highly flammable materials are used or stored.

Fire certificates are issued by the local fire authority (except in "special premises" where the certificates are issued by the HSE), who will examine the application and if necessary request plans of the building.

A fire certificate will specify:

- the use of the premises (changes to the premises or use must be notified)
- the means of escape, including fire doors, emergency lighting, signs
- extinguishers
- means of detecting and warning of fire
- special conditions for explosives, etc
- other conditions, ie training, evacuation drills, record keeping.

Means of escape and emergency lighting

All means of escape should be clearly marked, at high level if signs at a lower level will be obstructed, with signs which comply with the **Health and Safety (Safety Signs and Signals) Regulations 1996**. Escape routes must be kept unobstructed at all times, including the exit points to the outside of the building. All staff should know the escape routes for their workplaces and any other area where they may be present, including the "Fire Assembly Points". Fire Exits must open in the direction of travel and be operated by a "one-action" mechanism, eg push bar systems — they should not be locked. Independently powered emergency lighting should be provided in areas where a total mains power failure would prevent people being able to find their way along escape routes.

Fire extinguishers

There are several different types of fire extinguishers available (see table below) and they all work by removing one or more of the three essential factors needed for fires to burn.

Extinguisher Type	Colour of the Identifying Patch	Fire Type
Water	Red	Class A
Foam	Cream	Class B
Dry Power	Blue	Class B (can be used on all types)

Carbon dioxide (CO_2)	Black	Class B, Class C (fires involving electricity)
Halon (being replaced by environmentally safer alternatives)	Green	All fires
Wet chemical	Yellow	Class F

The different types of extinguishers are used on different types of fire, and portable extinguishers can be colour coded in order to show which extinguishing medium they contain. Historically, the whole body of the fire extinguisher was coloured; however, a new European Standard (EN 3) now requires the body of every extinguisher to be red, although a small coloured area is permitted to show what the extinguishing medium is — the colours are as in the table.

Some buildings also have automatic fixed fire extinguisher systems, eg water sprinklers which are linked to the detection and alarm systems. Specialised areas such as computer rooms or electrical stations may have automatic carbon dioxide or other gas flooding systems.

Staff training

Staff must know:

- the fire hazards in their workplace and how fire can be prevented
- what the alarm signal is, ie bell, siren, flashing lights, etc
- where the fire assembly points are for their workplaces
- where the manual call points are in their workplaces
- the fire escape routes and exits
- their responsibilities, and the evacuation procedures to follow in an emergency
- the different types of fire extinguishers and when they should be used (refresher training may be necessary when the new "all red" extinguishers are introduced)
- how to call the fire brigade.

Questions and Answers

Q Do existing whole-body coloured extinguishers have to be replaced immediately?

A No. Existing extinguishers may continue in use until the end of their useful life. However, as the new extinguishers are introduced there will be a "dual" system in place and it is recommended that where possible all the new extinguishers be located in the same work area, with the old extinguishers being relocated, rather than having both types mixed together.

Q Does the European Standard have any legal status?

A   No. British or European Standards do not have any legal status, although their existence could be taken into account in formal proceedings. However, extinguisher manufacturers will comply with the new standards in order to maintain European markets, and the manufacture of whole-body colour extinguishers is unlikely to be continued.

Q   Do fire hazards have to be formally assessed?

A   Yes. The **Fire Precautions (Workplace) Regulations 1997** require all employers, whether their premises are fire certificated or not, to assess fire hazards in their workplace. Appropriate controls must be implemented to eliminate, or adequately control, those risks.

First Aid

Summary

First aid is the immediate treatment of injuries or illnesses prior to the arrival of proper medical assistance; it is intended to save lives, reduce the effects of injuries and speed recovery. Adequate and appropriate first aid equipment and facilities must be provided under the **Health and Safety (First Aid) Regulations 1981.**

Practical Guidance

Employees should have ready access to first aid equipment and facilities at all times when they are at work, even if employees work on their own, eg travelling sales representatives, farm workers, etc. In the latter cases, a small travelling first aid kit may be appropriate.

Risk assessment

In order to determine what first aid equipment and facilities are "adequate and appropriate" employers must undertake a risk assessment of their workplace to identify likely first aid needs. The assessment should take into account:
- the nature of the work activities
- the number of employees present at any one time, including trainees
- shift work
- the geographical spread of the work premises and units
- the accessibility of external accident and emergency services
- accident statistics for the workplace
- arrangements between employers in shared premises or where contractors are working on-site
- arrangements for covering the temporary absence of trained first aiders.

Facilities and equipment

Depending on the risks associated with the work activities, first aid boxes, first aid kits and/or first aid rooms may need to be provided. More guidance on the suggested contents of a first aid box is specified in L74: *First Aid at Work. The Health and Safety (First Aid) Regulations 1981. Approved Code of Practice and Guidance* (updated in 1997). First aid boxes should not contain tablets, medication or pharmaceutical preparations. In all cases, employees must be informed of their location and they must be clearly identified in accordance with the **Health and Safety (Safety Signs and Signals) Regulations 1996**, ie green background with a white St George's cross.

First aiders and appointed persons

First aid treatments may only be administered by people who have completed an approved training course — this is usually a four-day course approved by the Health and Safety Executive (HSE) — and, where relevant, have attended necessary refresher training, ie every three years. First aiders should be available at all times that employees are at work, including shifts, and alternative arrangements should be made for first aiders taking holidays or long-term sick leave. Employees chosen, or who volunteer, to become designated first aiders should meet a few basic suitability criteria, ie they should be:

- able to leave their work immediately when required
- calm, especially in pressured situations
- reliable and able to communicate
- able to cope with any injuries or ill-health likely to occur in their workplace.

All first aiders should be provided with a formal system for recording incidents.

The only exceptions to having a trained first aider are in very low-risk workplaces, in which case there should be an "appointed person" responsible for calling medical assistance, and if he or she has been trained to do so, to administer emergency first aid. Although the number of employees is not the only factor to take into account when determining the number of first aiders required, the Approved Code of Practice suggests that in low-risk premises there should be 1 first aider for every 50 employees, with an additional first aider for every 100 people employed. In high-risk premises 1 trained first aider should be provided for 5 or more employees, with an additional first aider for every 50 people employed.

Questions and Answers

Q Do employers have to provide first aid to non-employees?

A No, although employers with businesses that involve members of the public or caring for clients, pupils, etc may extend the first aid provisions to them.

Q Why can't headache pills be kept in first aid boxes?

A Headache pills and similar products are classified as medicines and may only be administered under medical supervision. First aiders are not medically trained and are therefore not qualified to administer such items. There is also a question of liability should such products be given by unsuitably qualified people and cause an adverse reaction in the recipient.

Q Where identified as necessary, can first aiders administer antidotes or other specialist treatments if this is over and above the basic course syllabus?

A   Yes; part of the assessment should identify whether any of the work activities represent special risks. Where these are identified, first aiders should be given the appropriate additional training to deal with those risks within the boundaries of first aid rather than medical assistance. For example, in work where there is a possible exposure to certain hazardous chemicals, first aiders should be specially trained to administer the appropriate antidotes.

Q   Can employees with certain recognised qualifications other than an HSE-approved first aid course be designated first aiders?

A   Yes; provided the HSE is approached and accepts the qualifications in question. Qualified medical doctors who are registered with the General Medical Council and nurses who are registered in Part 1, 2, 10 or 11 of the Single Professional Register as maintained by the UK Central Council for Nursing, Midwifery and Health Visiting are qualified to administer first aid.

Q   Are trained first aiders covered by employers' liability insurance when acting as a designated first aider at work?

A   Yes, provided the first aider has been appropriately and suitably trained on an approved course, and has followed the correct procedures in the particular circumstances. Outside of work there is the possibility of personal liability against a first aider should anything go wrong with the treatment given.

Q   Do employers have a responsibility to provide first aid cover to their employees who are working on another employer's premises?

A   Yes, the duty to provide first aid cover extends to all employees regardless of where they work. However, in practice, it is usual to sort out arrangements for providing first aid cover by utilising the arrangements already in place in the host employer's workplace, rather than setting up a totally separate system. Whatever the arrangements that are agreed, they should be written down and signed by both employers, and communicated to the respective employees, including the host employer's first aiders.

Floors

Summary

Floors are an important part of the workplace as they are the main surface that people walk and work on. If they are in poor condition, cluttered, slippery or wet, then slip and trip hazards are created.

Practical Guidance

Floor surface

The **Workplace (Health, Safety and Welfare) Regulations 1992** (Workplace Regulations) require floors to be of suitable construction for their purpose. Floor surfaces must not give risk to a health and safety risk due to:

- holes or other defects
- slopes
- unevenness
- slipperiness.

Floors should be made of non-slippery materials, and should be regularly maintained to ensure they remain in a safe state. Floor surfaces must be:

- strong enough to support any loads likely to be present
- of sound construction, ie smooth but not slippery, free of holes, etc
- provided with adequate drainage
- well maintained, ie cleaned regularly; coatings, treads, matting, etc repaired or replaced as necessary; spills cleared as soon as possible
- protected against risks arising from foreseeable environmental conditions, eg rain, humidity, ice.

Cleanliness

Floors must be made of a material that is easy to clean, as required by the Workplace Regulations. They must be cleaned regularly, eg by mopping, sweeping or vacuuming. Floor cleaning operations should not give rise to a health and safety risk, eg due to wet floors or trailing cables. Floor areas which are slippery while wet should be cordoned off during cleaning, and portable warning signs used.

Obstructions

Under the Workplace Regulations, floors must be kept free of obstructions, articles and substances that may cause people to slip, trip or fall. This necessitates high standards of housekeeping.

Guarding and rails

The Workplace Regulations provide for holes to be adequately guarded, and for steep slopes to be fitted with handrails where necessary. If a slope has a drop at either side, a rail should be fitted to prevent people from falling.

Risk assessment

Under the **Management of Health and Safety at Work Regulations 1999**, general risk assessments must be carried out. Such assessments should include consideration of the safety of floors, and ways of keeping them clear and safe. So long as holes are adequately guarded and slopes have any necessary handrails, they may be considered to be safe. The person carrying out the assessment should nevertheless consider whether the guarding around the hole is adequate (eg is it high enough?) and whether the surface of the slope provides sufficient grip.

Manual handling

Under the **Manual Handling Operations Regulations 1992**, all manual handling tasks that have to be carried out must be assessed to determine the risks to health and safety. A number of factors influence the safety of manual handling, including floors. The assessment should take the following into consideration:

- slippery floors, eg due to wetness or polished surfaces, will increase the risk that a person carrying a load will slip and be injured
- uneven floors may be difficult to negotiate by someone who is carrying a load, causing a trip hazard
- unstable floors may not give a person carrying a load enough support, resulting in a risk of them falling or having to walk so slowly that they become fatigued
- carrying loads over different levels of floor may make the manual handling task more difficult and tiring.

Accident reporting

Under the **Reporting of Injuries, Diseases and Dangerous Occurrences Regulations 1995**, the unintentional collapse of a floor is a reportable dangerous occurrence. If a floor accidentally collapses, including mezzanine floors, the responsible person must telephone the enforcing authority as soon as it is safe to do so, and follow up with a written report on form F2508 (available from HSE Books, tel: 01787 881165) within 10 days.

Fire resistance

Under the **Building Regulations 1991** (Part B), floors must be of fire-resisting construction. These Regulations apply to standards of construction of new buildings, or extensive renovations of existing ones. Fire-resisting floors can resist fire for a minimum period of time, slowing down the spread of a fire. For floors, a fire resistance of at least two hours is normally required.

Maintenance

Floors must be well maintained. Drainage should be regularly checked and blockages cleared. Any uneven surfaces, eg holes, should be guarded or repaired, broken, loose or protruding tiles, lino or other floor coverings should be repaired or replaced as soon as possible. Equipment is available which measures how slippery a floor surface is.

Housekeeping

In maintaining high standards of housekeeping, responsibilities should be allocated, for example:
- workers should be told what is expected of them and should be responsible for keeping the floors clear or reporting spills
- supervisors should check that floors are kept clear on a daily basis and should make sure that spills are cleaned up
- the health and safety manager should carry out regular inspections of housekeeping.

All spillages must be cleared immediately, and warning signs put up to show areas of slipperiness until the floor has dried.

Noise retention

In some industrial premises, noise and vibration transmitted through floors may be a problem. There are a number of possible solutions, including:
- vibrating machinery and equipment should be installed on anti-vibration mounts
- floors should be made of heavy, solid material where possible
- if floors are not substantial enough, a suspended floor above or suspended ceiling below may be fitted, using heavy material, eg plasterboard, and insulation, eg glass wool.

Questions and Answers

Q How often should floors be cleaned?

A It is up to the employer to devise an appropriate cleaning schedule for floors. As a baseline, sweeping or vacuum cleaning floors once a week is suitable for many workplaces. In areas where waste or substances accumulate on the floor, they may need to be cleaned daily. The floors of food preparation areas should be mopped at least once a day.

Q How much floor space should be allowed per person?

A The Workplace Regulations require employers to provide adequate working space. The Approved Code of Practice to these Regulations gives a minimum floor space of $11m^3$ per person. When calculating working space, rooms over 3m in height should have their space calculated based on a ceiling of 3m. The calculation would not need to take into account space taken up by furniture.

However, regardless of whether the minimum figure for floor space is met, the responsible person must make a judgment about whether there is enough space, taking into account the furniture and fittings.

Q   What materials are suitable for floor surfaces?

A   When choosing a material for floor surfaces, there are a number of considerations. For one thing, the floor should be suitable for its purpose. Carpeting may be fine for an office, where it will provide comfort for the workers, but would be unsuitable for machinery workshops, where it would be subject to a good deal of wear and tear, as well as spilt oil, etc.

The material should be smooth enough to be easy to clean, but not so smooth and polished so that it is slippery. If the surface of an existing floor is so slippery that it gives rise to a risk to peoples' safety, it can be made less slippery by being covered in matting or a non-slip coating.

Finally, it is prudent to choose a floor surface material that is durable, both in terms of safety and economics. A good quality surface that wears well will need replacing less often, and is less likely to curl, peel or become uneven.

Food Safety

Summary

The definition of food includes any food ingredients, animals eaten alive, drinks, dietary aids and supplements, and water used in food processes or drawn from a tap in the course of a food business. Food safety law aims to protect the consumer of food products. It applies to anyone who runs a food business.

Practical Guidance

General provisions

The **Food Safety Act 1990** lays down general provisions governing food safety, and covers:

- provision of food for human consumption that is safe to eat
- accurate presentation of food
- enforcement of food safety law, including the issue of enforcement notices.

Food premises

Under the **Food Safety (General Food Hygiene) Regulations 1995**, food preparation, manufacturing, processing, packaging, storing, transporting, distributing, handling and sale must be carried out in a hygienic manner. In order to meet this requirement, food premises must:

- be easy to clean
- be designed, constructed, laid out and large enough to allow good hygiene practices
- be kept clean and in a good condition
- contain stocked hand washing facilities
- contain ventilated flush toilets
- contain changing facilities
- be adequately lit
- have an adequate drainage system
- contain facilities for cleaning and disinfecting equipment
- contain facilities for washing food
- be supplied with drinking water
- contain closed containers for food waste
- have equipment which is in such a position to allow the surrounding areas to be cleaned.

Food handlers

Under the **Food Safety (General Food Hygiene) Regulations 1995,** food handlers must practice meticulous personal hygiene to protect the health of their customers. Where possible, supervisors should check that high standards of personal hygiene are being followed. Hygiene practices that food handlers should follow include:

- wash hands using soap, water and a nail-brush before preparing any food
- do not touch the face, including nose blowing, while preparing food; if it is necessary to do this, wash hands thoroughly before returning to the task
- always wash hands thoroughly after using the toilet
- if a cut is sustained while preparing food, stop immediately, clean the cut in a basin designated only for hand washing (not food washing), apply a dressing (preferably blue), wash hands thoroughly and make sure there is no risk of contamination before returning to the task (any food contaminated when the cut was made should be discarded)
- do not eat, drink, smoke, chew fingernails, apply cosmetics, etc while preparing food
- put on a clean apron each day before starting work with food, and remove the apron if leaving the kitchen for other areas, eg during breaks
- wear a hairnet or other hair covering while preparing food; handlers with long hair should keep it tied back at all times while at work
- remove all wrist and hand jewellery while working with food (simple wedding bands may be allowed)
- do not handle food if suffering from any illness, such as upset stomach, skin infection, colds or flu, and report the illness to the supervisor.

Training and instruction

Under the **Food Safety (General Food Hygiene) Regulations 1995** food handlers must be given suitable information, instruction and training. There are three levels of training: basic, intermediate and advanced, and the level of training required will vary depending on the job. However, all food handlers should be given instruction when they start a new job, which would include:

- which tasks they are responsible for
- how to carry them out
- which tasks must be carried out by other staff (ie that they must not attempt unsupervised), eg carving meat, using dangerous machines, restocking the chiller
- general food hygiene practices
- rules that apply to the particular food business
- safety in the kitchen
- emergency procedures.

Food storage

The **Food Safety (General Food Hygiene) Regulations 1995** state that food premises must not accept any food ingredients if they may be contaminated or unfit for human consumption. Food must be stored so that it is protected from deterioration or contamination, eg by pests.

Hazard analysis

The **Food Safety (General Food Hygiene) Regulations 1995** require a hazard analysis to be carried out to identify:
- hazards which may affect the business and the stages at which they may occur
- the points which may be critical to ensuring food safety
- the ways in which the hazards should be controlled.

The Department of Health has devised a system called *Assured Safe Catering: A Management System for Hazard Analysis* to assist catering businesses. It is available from The Stationery Office. Tel: 020 7873 8372.

Temperature controls

The **Food Safety (Temperature Controls) Regulations 1995** specify the temperatures at which food must be kept:
- food which must be kept cold to prevent the growth of pathogenic bacteria or the formation of toxins, eg meat, fish and dairy products, must be kept at, or below, 8°C
- food which is cooked or reheated for service or sale which must be kept hot to prevent the growth of pathogenic bacteria or formation of toxins must be kept at or above 63°C.

If the manufacturer's instructions specify storage temperatures which are below 8°C or above 63°C, the manufacturer's temperature instructions must be followed.

Registration

Under the **Food Premises (Registration) Regulations 1991**, all food premises which are used for a food business must be registered with the local authority environmental health department.

Staff canteens

Where a company provides a canteen for staff, the following points should be taken into consideration:
- the food business must be registered with the local environmental health department
- the catering facilities have to reach a particular standard
- a hazard analysis must be carried out, looking at each critical step in food production and serving

- food handlers must be trained and must not be allowed to handle food if they may have a food transmitted disease
- food must be stored safely and subject to temperature controls.

Vending machines

Many companies provide vending machines for their staff to obtain hot or cold drinks, and snacks. A number of points should be considered when providing drinks machines:

- they must be installed by a competent person
- they must be cleaned at least daily, or in accordance with the manufacturer's instructions
- spills and leaks caused by the machine should be cleaned up as soon as possible
- clear pipes and tanks which are exposed to the light may allow algal growth
- there may be problems with build up of scale from hard water supplies; softened water contains high levels of sodium, which may cause problems for some people
- maintenance records should be kept.

When providing snack machines, there are a number of considerations, including:

- machines containing perishable food, eg sandwiches, must be temperature controlled
- the machines should be regularly cleaned, both internally and externally
- there should be a system of stock rotation, to prevent food exceeding the "use by" dates (food should be removed from the machine and discarded once this date is reached)
- some snacks are intended to be eaten hot, so a microwave or conventional oven may be required
- there should be clear procedures in place if someone loses their money in the machine, or if the product gets stuck during dispensing.

Catering contractors

If catering contractors are employed on the premises, or if they bring in food for sale that was prepared elsewhere, an individual in the host company should be given responsibility for dealing with them. The responsible person should check that they comply with food safety legislation before agreeing to the contract, perhaps by asking to see evidence of their registration as a food business and visiting their kitchen to check the levels of cleanliness and hygiene.

Once the contract is signed, the responsible person should continue to monitor the standards of the contractor on a regular basis. They may choose to check the local papers and/or with the local environmental health department to find out if the contractor has breached any food safety requirement. If it appears that the standards are unacceptable, the responsible person should terminate the contract and find another caterer.

Questions and Answers

Q To whom does food safety law apply?

A Basically, anyone who sells or provides food must comply with the legislation. It applies to anyone involved in the production, processing, storage, distribution and sale of food, including food sold at fund-raising events. Food prepared at home for consumption at home is not included. Certain food activities are exempt from the requirement to register, eg bed and breakfast businesses in domestic premises with three or fewer letting rooms, and light refreshments served in a non-food business, eg coffee served to clients during business meetings. In addition, as previously outlined, all food premises that are used for a food business must be registered with the local authority environmental health department.

Q We have a few vending machines in our company, and a contractor who visits each day to sell sandwiches. Do we have to register as a food business?

A Vending machines are exempt from the requirement for registration, so you will not have to register, so long as there are no other activities carried on that would bring you into the category of a food business. However, food safety law still applies to vending machines, in terms of cleanliness, hygiene, selling food fit for human consumption, etc.

Concerning the sandwich sellers, as they are the ones who prepare and sell the food and you only provide the venue for sale, they are responsible for complying with food safety law and registering as a food business. However, you should make sure that their standards are high and that they meet the legal requirements before you allow them to sell food to your staff on your premises.

Q We provide our staff with a kitchen to prepare their own food. Does this make us a food business?

A If your staff are responsible for preparing food for their own consumption, you are not a food business. However, you should meet certain standards of safety, such as providing facilities which are easy to clean, providing closed bins for food waste, making sure any equipment you supply is safe (eg microwaves, refrigerators, kettles, etc) and making sure that staff are instructed in how to use the kitchen equipment safely. Arrangements must be made to keep the food preparation area clean at all times, and spills should be cleared as soon as possible.

Q What is HACCP?

A HACCP stands for "hazard analysis critical control points". It is a system for assessing the hazards of a food business in relation to food safety, and examines critical points in the stages of food production, distribution, etc where risks may arise. The analysis should lead to the necessary controls being identified and implemented. The Department of Health has devised a HACCP system for the catering industry, *Assured Safe Catering: A Management System for Hazard Analysis*, which is available from The Stationery Office.

Fork-lift Trucks

Summary

Fork-lift trucks require a high level of operator skill, control and competence. Consideration should be given to the inherent dangers of the equipment itself, including the rechargeable batteries, and to ensuring that fork-lift trucks can move around the workplace safely without creating or increasing risks to pedestrians or other vehicles.

Practical Guidance

Operators

Unless operators are selected, trained and authorised to drive fork-lift trucks, they must be under competent supervision. Although no definite criteria are provided for fork-lift truck operators, generally they should be physically and mentally fit, intelligent, reliable and mature. Medical screening is advisable prior to employment as a fork-lift truck driver, after sickness or injury, and at five-year intervals during middle age.

Training

Training is broken down into three stages (see below) and should ensure that the driver has achieved the levels of skill necessary to operate the fork-lift truck safely. The three stages of training are:
• basic skills and knowledge required for safe operation
• specific job training for the particular needs of the employer
• familiarisation training under supervision at the actual workplace.

Traffic

Fork-lift truck traffic routes should be separate from pedestrian routes where possible, and where routes have to be shared warnings should be displayed.

Operation and control

Supervisors and operators must be aware of and understand the basic characteristics of the fork-lift truck, particularly its limitations.

Maintenance

The manufacturers' guidelines on recommended maintenance systems should be followed, although tyres, batteries and brakes should be checked at the start of each shift. Weekly maintenance should be carried out after 50 hours of running time, and all working parts thoroughly examined at least every six months.

A company was prosecuted at Reedley magistrates' court under s.3(1) of the **Health and Safety at Work, etc Act 1974** (HSW Act) after a faulty fork-lift truck crushed a visitor to the premises. The fork-lift truck had a faulty door lock which had been removed for repair. The fork-lift truck was allowed to remain in service and when it was used the door flew open in a gust of wind. The steering mechanism was situated in the door and the driver lost control, crushing the visitor against the wall. The visitor suffered a severed leg and a smashed pelvis.

Questions and Answers

Q Are there any proposals to extend the Approved Code of Practice (ACOP) to additional lift trucks other than the four types currently covered?

A Yes. The HSC has published a consultative document to extend the current limited remit of the ACOP to other types of lift trucks. The proposals aim to clarify certain ambiguities and include: extending the definition beyond the four designated types of lift truck currently covered; clarifying refresher training, competences of instructors and the status of the basic training certificates; and providing advice on responsibilities to non-employees, which has been included to reflect changing employment patterns.

Q What physical characteristics should fork-lift truck drivers ideally have?

A Generally, fork-lift truck drivers should be considered on their own merits although the following points are useful guidelines:
- full movement of the body, neck, arms and legs
- normal agility
- stable disposition
- good effective vision in both eyes (able to read a car number plate at approximately 25m)
- good hearing
- freedom from epilepsy (eligibility for ordinary driving licence is acceptable).

Q What information should be displayed on fork-lift trucks?

A The following information should be displayed on the lift truck:
- manufacturer's name
- type of lift truck
- serial number
- unladen weight
- lifting capacity
- load centre distance
- maximum lift height.

G

Gas Safety

Summary

Gas is commonly used in industry and commerce as an energy source for heating and production. When stored, transported and used correctly it is a clean and safe fuel; incorrectly handled it can result in fires, explosions or gassing incidents.

Practical Guidance

Responsibility

The responsibility for gas user safety was transferred by administrative arrangement from the Department of Energy to the Health and Safety Executive (HSE) on 1 February 1984. This brought within the scope of the HSE the task of the protection of the public within the two principal areas of concern; namely explosions and fires caused by leaks of gas, and carbon monoxide poisoning caused by poor combustion of gas in faulty installations. The gas industry was privatised by the **Gas Act 1986** and, as other industries, became subject to Regulations made under the **Health and Safety at Work, etc Act 1974** (HSW Act).

Gas safety legal duties

The legislation surrounding gas safety is complex and extensive. The following are key elements.

Gas Safety (Installation and Use) Regulations 1998

The **Gas Safety (Installation and Use) Regulations 1998** deal with the safe installation, use and maintenance of gas systems. This includes gas appliances, gas fittings and flues, and applies to both commercial and domestic premises. The Regulations replace the **Gas Safety (Installation and Use) Regulations 1994** and the subsequent amendments. The Regulations generally apply to any "gas" as defined by the **Gas Act 1986**, except any gas consisting mainly of hydrogen when used in non-domestic premises. Most of the legislation therefore applies to both natural gas and liquefied petroleum gas.

The Regulations place responsibilities on a wide range of people including:

- those installing gas appliances and fittings
- those servicing, repairing or maintaining gas appliance and fittings
- suppliers and users of gas, including certain landlords.

The Regulations require:

- work on any gas fittings and pipework to be carried out only by competent persons, who are registered with the Council for Registered Gas Installers (CORGI); those employing others in this field are required to ensure the competence of their employees
- any employer or self-employed person instructing such work, or in control of such work (eg a contractor), to ensure that the work is carried out by an organisation registered with CORGI, and that any gas appliance or installation at a workplace under their control is maintained in a safe condition
- the individual or organisation carrying out the work to ensure the suitability of the equipment being installed and the location of the equipment, and to ensure that work is carried out to appropriate standards and without danger, and that it is safe for use on completion of the work
- measures to be taken to protect the safety of those carrying out the work, and give requirements for testing the integrity of the installation on completion of the work
- gas fittings to be protected from damage
- emergency controls to be fitted where a new gas supply is being provided to a premises
- certain measures to be taken in respect of the siting and installation of new gas meters
- certain measures to be taken in respect of the siting and installation of pipework, to ensure that it is sited in appropriate areas of any premises
- certain measures to be taken in respect of primary and secondary meters
- any pipework in areas accessible for inspection, except in a domestic dwelling, to be marked (eg colour-coded to indicate that it is carrying gas)
- manufacturer's instructions to be provided for use by the owner or occupier of the particular premises
- the person responsible for the premises (eg the owner or landlord) not to have any unsafe appliances available for use; any person carrying out work on equipment is required to report any appliance they suspect to be dangerous
- landlords to ensure safe maintenance of all installations and appliances and to provide annual safety checks and maintain records of such checks.

The Regulations also prohibit:

- any alterations to premises and equipment that cause gas fittings or storage vessels to no longer comply with the regulations
- the installation of certain gas appliances in specified rooms unless the appliance is room-sealed; in some other locations certain appliances must be room-sealed or fitted with specific safety devices. Instantaneous water heaters are prohibited in general unless they are room sealed or fitted with the appropriate safety device

- installation of suspended appliances unless the appliance is designed for this type of use and the pipework is capable of supporting the appliance.

In addition there are certain requirements where service pipework exceeding specified feed sizes feeds certain buildings or floor areas, and certain requirements pertaining to flues.

The Regulations also give information about action to be taken by gas suppliers and other responsible persons in the event of a gas escape.

Miscellaneous provisions and landlords

The miscellaneous provisions impose duties on employers and self-employed persons to ensure that any gas appliances and associated pipework installed in any workplace are maintained in a safe condition.

The **Gas Safety (Installation and Use) Regulations 1998** introduce specific duties, with regard to gas fittings, on landlords who allow their premises to be occupied for residential purposes. In particular, such gas fittings and associated flues, etc must be maintained in a safe condition and safety-checked every 12 months — appropriate records must be kept of these checks and must be made available to the occupier on request. The landlord must also ensure that only HSE-approved gas fitters carry out any work on gas fittings in their premises.

Gas Safety (Management) Regulations 1996

The **Gas Safety (Management) Regulations 1996** are designed to ensure that the supply of gas through pipelines is properly controlled when the gas market becomes fully competitive. Gas transporters must prepare and submit "safety cases" to the HSE for its acceptance. Gas transporters must also provide 24 hour emergency cover for dealing with gas leaks and British Gas will set up a national freephone telephone number for the reporting of gas leaks and carbon dioxide emissions. In addition, gas transporters must appoint network emergency co-ordinators (NECs) who will co-ordinate emergency actions in situations where there is a total or partial supply failure. NECs must also prepare and submit a safety case to the HSE for their acceptance. The Regulations also require all other persons in the gas market to co-operate with the gas transporters and NECs so the safety cases are effective in practice.

Gas Appliances (Safety) Regulations 1995

These Regulations implement European Directive 90/396/EEC, intended to harmonise laws in Member States relating to appliances burning gaseous fuels. They do not apply to products supplied for the first time before 1 January 1992, or to those intended for use outside the EC. The supply of second-hand goods is also excluded from the provisions. Gas appliances and fittings must comply with certain criteria specified within Schedule 3 of the Regulations.

Offences relating to domestic animals and property It is a specific offence to put at risk the health and safety of domestic animals or property by contravention of these Regulations (regulation 27).

Enforcement Except for regulation 27, the Regulations are enforced under the provisions of the **Consumer Protection Act 1987**. They may be enforced by Weights and Measures Authorities in Great Britain and by district councils in Northern Ireland. The HSE may enforce the Regulations under the HSW Act where the appliance or fitting is supplied for use at work.

Building Regulations

Building Regulations (including those applying in Scotland) cover heat producing appliances including gas appliances.

Reporting of Injuries, Diseases and Dangerous Occurrences Regulations 1995

The **Reporting of Injuries, Diseases and Dangerous Occurrences Regulations 1995** (RIDDOR) cover the reporting of certain incidents, including those involving gas. Regulation 6 imposes notification and reporting duties in relation to deaths, and major injuries arising out of, or in connection with, the supply of gas (including liquefied petroleum gas in containers, the accidental leakage of gas, inadequate gas combustion, or the inadequate removal of the gas combustion products).

Questions and Answers

Q My engineer wants to install a new gas-fired boiler for heating. Is he able to do this himself?

A Only a CORGI-registered individual or a competent person working for such an employer can install these appliances. If your engineer satisfies the criteria he may be eligible to become CORGI-registered.

Q Does gas smell naturally?

A The natural gas supplied through the national distribution network has a smell added to aid detection of leaks.

Q What general procedures should exist for dealing with a gas leak?

A Guidance on gas escapes can be found in regulation 7 of the **Gas Safety (Management) Regulations 1996**. This covers establishing the precise location of the emergency and determining whether the leak is controllable or uncontrollable. Ventilation should be provided by opening doors and windows, electrical appliances should not be used in any way, smoking should be prohibited immediately and any other sources of potential ignition should not be used.

   Where the escape is from fumes (ie escape of carbon monoxide into the room), all appliances should be turned off and should not be used again until they have been checked by the emergency service provider.

The **Gas Safety (Installation and Use) Regulations 1998** state that the responsible person for a premises should have arrangements in place so that the supply can be immediately shut off, the supplier's emergency service can be immediately notified (check the notice by the meter or emergency gas control which gives the name and telephone number) and the supply is not reopened.

Health and Safety at Work, etc Act

Summary

The **Health and Safety at Work, etc Act 1974** (HSW Act) is the primary piece of health and safety law, and it lays down broad principles for managing health and safety in all workplaces, with the exception of servants in domestic premises. The HSW Act falls under criminal law and offences are punishable in the courts by way of fines and/or prison sentences.

Practical Guidance

Introduction

The HSW Act places duties on defined individuals to ensure minimum health and safety standards at work. The basic principles of the Act are implicitly dependent on employers identifying and controlling the risks associated with their business, ie undertaking a risk assessment. The duties under the HSW Act are also owed to employees on an individual basis, not only to groups of employees collectively. This means that any employees with special needs, or requiring additional control measures, are owed a greater duty of care — it is not sufficient to implement measures that are effective for a majority of employees but which leave more vulnerable employees inadequately protected.

The term "health and safety" includes physical and mental well-being, and the provision of appropriate welfare facilities.

Section 2

This is the one of the key sections of the HSW Act. It requires employers to ensure the health and safety of employees at work, so far as is reasonably practicable. In complying with their duty under s.2 employers should consider:
- identifying and providing safe systems of work
- providing safe materials and substances
- providing a safe place of work and a safe working environment
- providing information, instruction, training and supervision as necessary.

The majority of health and safety prosecutions are brought under this section.

The case of *Bolton Metropolitan Borough Council v Malrod Insulations Ltd* confirmed that employers have a duty to ensure the health and safety of employees by providing safe equipment even if that equipment is not actually in use. It is sufficient to constitute a breach of duty that the employees are exposed to risk through a defective piece of equipment.

Safety policies

Where five or more employees are employed, employers must have a written "health and safety policy" for their workplace. This policy should contain:

- a statement of intent, ie the organisation's commitment to health and safety and its intention to comply with relevant laws
- defined responsibilities for health and safety for every person and/or rank within the organisation
- recognised safe systems of work for dealing with every hazard likely to be encountered at work.

Section 3

This is the duty on employers to ensure that non-employees are not injured or otherwise harmed by the employer's work activities, so far as is reasonably practicable. Non-employees would include delivery people, members of the public, external trainers, contractors, etc. In certain circumstances, the risks to trespassers should also be considered as they are owed a duty of care, even if they are on the premises illegally (**Occupiers' Liability Act 1984**).

In the case of *R v Swan Hunter Shipbuilders Ltd and Telemeter Installations Ltd*, Swan Hunter were prosecuted for failing to provide contractors, ie employees of another employer, with relevant safety information, which resulted in the death of eight Swan Hunter employees. The Swan Hunter employees were informed of the dangers and procedures associated with oxygen-rich atmospheres but this information had not been given to the contractor's employees working alongside the Swan Hunter employees.

In the case of *R v Mara*, a contract cleaner was prosecuted for failing to ensure the health and safety of non-employees even though there were no contract cleaners on site at the time. As a suitable time for the contract cleaners to clean the loading bay area could not be agreed, the employer's employees undertook this task using the contract cleaner's scrubbing machine, which was left at the premises for that purpose. The machine had a faulty cable, which was taped up in four different places, and was used in a very wet area — the operator was electrocuted.

Self-employed people must ensure their own health and safety, and ensure that their work does not endanger anyone else.

Section 4

This section places a duty on people, other than employers, in control of premises provided for work purposes, to ensure that those premises and any substances or equipment also provided are safe and without risks to health.

The case of *Westminster City Council v Select Management Ltd* confirmed that common parts of blocks of flats, such as the lifts and foyers, were non-domestic premises and therefore subject to the HSW Act, where any employees, other than employees of the premises owner or occupier, had to go there during the course of their work.

Section 6

Manufacturers, suppliers, importers and designers must ensure that any articles or substances provided for use at work are safe and without risks to health. This includes testing, research and examination of the products, and providing relevant safety information, including revisions, when the product is intended for use at work. Retailers are not obliged to provide safety sheets for their products, even if they are intended to be used at work, although many will do so on request.

Section 7

Employees must ensure their own health and safety at work, and ensure that they do not endanger anyone else. They must also co-operate with their employer in ensuring compliance with any relevant legal requirements.

In the case of *Skinner v HM Advocate*, a supervisor responsible for the site where a new gas main was being laid was convicted of failing to ensure the health and safety of others as he had not given warning of known dangers associated with the roadworks to motorists, or ensured that someone else had put up the proper warning signs.

Sections 8 and 9

No person may interfere with any item or measure provided in the interests of health and safety. Employers may not charge employees for any protective measures or equipment identified as necessary to protect their health and safety.

Miscellaneous

Other sections of the HSW Act cover the roles of the Health and Safety Commission (HSC) and Health and Safety Executive (HSE), enforcement notices, making regulations, offences, interpretation of terms, etc.

Questions and Answers

Q   What are "relevant statutory provisions"?
A   "Relevant statutory provisions" are pieces of legislation which existed prior to the HSW Act, and all new health and safety Regulations, etc that have an association with, or are relevant to, the subject of health and safety. Schedule 1 to the HSW Act lists all the Acts which were in existence prior to the HSW Act and which are classed as "relevant statutory provisions".
Q   Do previous Acts and Regulations made before the HSW Act still apply?

A Yes. All pre-HSW Act health and safety related legislation is continued under the HSW Act. However, there is a current systematic repeal and revocation of older health and safety legislation which tended to be very prescriptive, ie comprising lists of "dos" and "don'ts". Very few functional requirements of the 1961 and 1963 Factories Acts actually remain in force.

Q Is there any difference in the terms "shall" and "shall not", "practicable", and "reasonably practicable"?

A Yes, all of those terms mean something different and have varying standards of strictness. "Shall" and "shall not" are "absolute" terms, ie they require something to be done or not done — there is no compromise. The terms "effective" and "efficient" have also been held by the courts to impose an absolute duty. The term "practicable" is less strict and requires something to be done as far as is possible in the light of current knowledge, understanding and technological development. The term "so far as is reasonably practicable" is the least strict and means that the degree of risk can be weighed against the costs, in money, time and staff, etc, of controlling that risk to acceptable standards. Thus employers who identify a high risk in their workplace will be expected to allocate more resources in controlling that risk, if necessary.

Q Does European Union legislation affect the HSW Act or any Regulations under it?

A EU legislation and Directives may amend existing UK health and safety law, including the HSW Act, or require new laws to be made. It has not, however, affected the broad-principled and self-regulatory approach to health and safety adopted in the UK, although EU laws do tend to be more prescriptive than UK laws.

Health and Safety Commission/ Health and Safety Executive

Summary

The Health and Safety Commission (HSC) has overall responsibility for ensuring health and safety at work by drafting policies and/or new legislation, identifying research programmes, and ensuring widespread consultation on new proposals. The Health and Safety Executive (HSE) is responsible for active enforcement of health and safety legislation in its designated workplaces, and for investigating major accidents at work.

Practical Guidance

The **Health and Safety at Work, etc Act 1974** (HSW Act) provided for the setting up of two controlling bodies with regard to health and safety at work, ie the HSC and the HSE.

Health and Safety Commission

The HSC comprises a chairperson and between six and nine members taken from:
- employers' organisations, eg Confederation of British Industry (CBI) (up to three members)
- employees' organisations, eg Trades Union Congress (TUC) (up to three members)
- other professional or local authority bodies (up to three members).

Duties of the Health and Safety Commission
The HSC has general responsibility for ensuring that the aims detailed in s.1 of the HSW Act are achieved. It is supported by a number of specialist advisory committees or groups who provide advice on their particular subjects, eg dangerous/toxic substances, occupational health, etc.

Health and Safety Executive

This is the operational body responsible for practical enforcement of health and safety law (within certain premises). The HSE is controlled by a Director General and two other members — all appointed by the HSC.

The HSE's Field Operations Directorate (FOD) is responsible for enforcement and has seven operational regions, with local area offices within each region. The FOD comprises factory, agricultural and quarry inspectors, and the Employment Medical Advisory Service (EMAS).

The HSE is are supported by several policy and technical units, and has access to industry-specific advice through National Interest Groups (NIGs) which are allocated to each region.

The HSE is also responsible for the Railways and Offshore Inspectorates.

Questions and Answers

Q Where can details of new proposals for legislation be obtained?

A The proposals are usually issued as "consultative documents" and their details are given in the various "health and safety" publications available, or through HSE Books.

Q Is anyone entitled to request and comment on proposals for new legislation and guidance, etc?

A Yes, the HSC has a duty to consult as widely as possible to all interested parties, and is obliged to take account of, but not necessary incorporate, any comments it receives on the proposals.

Q Where are the various addresses for the HSE area offices listed?

A The addresses for HSE area offices are listed in local telephone directories under "Health and Safety Executive". For premises where the HSE is the health and safety enforcing authority, the local HSE office for the premises should be written on the *Health and Safety Law — What You Should Know* poster which is legally required to be displayed in all workplaces.

Q What is the Employment Medical Advisory Service?

A EMAS is the medical branch of the HSE; it provides advice on medical and health matters to the HSE and any other persons, including employers and employees. EMAS comprises Employment Medical Advisors and Employment Nursing Advisors, as well as specialist advisors in toxicology, respiratory problems, etc. An Employment Medical Advisor is based at each HSE area office.

Health Surveillance

Summary

Work-related diseases should be prevented by the control of exposure to health hazards in the workplace. Occasionally this needs to be supplemented by surveillance of the people who are potentially exposed to physical, chemical or biological health risks at work to identify, at the earliest stage, any adverse effects on employees' health due to work-related causes.

Practical Guidance

General duty

Health surveillance seeks to protect the health of employees and should be used only when it is likely to benefit those at risk by identifying, at the earliest possible stage, any adverse effects on their health which are related to work activities. There is a general duty under the **Health and Safety at Work, etc Act 1974** for all employers to ensure the health of their employees, so far as is reasonably practicable. Carrying out health surveillance where required will fulfil one aspect of this duty.

Specific duty

The **Management of Health and Safety at Work Regulations 1999** make specific reference to the responsibility of employers to ensure that their employees are provided with such health surveillance as is appropriate with regard to the risks to their health and safety. Risk assessment will identify circumstances in which health surveillance is required by specific health and safety regulations, for example:

- **Work in Compressed Air Regulations 1996**
- **Control of Substances Hazardous to Health Regulations 1999** (COSHH)
- **Control of Asbestos at Work Regulations 1987**
- **Ionising Radiations Regulations 1999**
- **Control of Lead at Work Regulations 1998**.

In addition to the circumstances where these specific Regulations apply, there may be other work activities that give rise to adverse health conditions or to identifiable diseases.

Risk assesssment and health surveillance

Surveillance should be provided where the risk assessment shows that the following criteria apply.

1. There is an identifiable disease or adverse health condition related to the work concerned.
2. Valid techniques are available to detect indications of the disease or condition.
3. There is a reasonable likelihood that the disease or condition may occur under the particular conditions of work.
4. Surveillance is likely to assist in the protection of the health of the employees who may be exposed.

Surveillance may also be undertaken where it is necessary to ensure that a worker remains in a fit condition to carry out a particular task without risk to him or herself or others. An example would be lift truck drivers, who should be screened for fitness at five-yearly intervals from the age of 40. The health criteria are listed in guidance note HSG6 *Safety in Working with Lift Trucks*.

The primary benefit, and therefore the objective, of health surveillance is to detect adverse conditions as early as possible, so as to enable steps to be taken to prevent further harm or risk of harm.

In addition, the results of health surveillance can be used to:

• check the effectiveness of control measures
• provide feedback on the accuracy of the risk assessment
• identify individuals at increased risk, and thereby enable them to be better protected.

Where it is decided that health surveillance is appropriate, it should be maintained throughout the employee's period of employment unless the risk to which the worker is exposed and the associated ill-health effects are short term.

Where health surveillance is carried out under a statutory provision, the minimum requirement is to keep an individual health record. This may form part of an existing health or personnel record. Where appropriate, health surveillance procedures may include:

• inspection of readily detectable conditions by a responsible person acting within the limits of his or her training and experience
• enquiries about symptoms, eg coughs and wheezes, and inspection and examination by a qualified person, such as an occupational health nurse
• medical surveillance, which may include clinical examination and measurements of physiological or psychological effects by an appropriately qualified practitioner
• biological effect monitoring, eg the measurement and assessment of early biological effects such as diminished lung function in exposed workers
• biological monitoring, ie the measurement and assessment of workplace agents or their metabolites either in tissue, secreta, excreta, expired air or any combination of these in exposed workers, eg the monitoring of blood lead levels in workers exposed to lead.

The frequency of the use of such procedures should be determined either on the basis of suitable general guidance or on the advice of a qualified practitioner. However, the employees should be given the opportunity to comment on the proposed frequency.

Employees should also have access to an appropriately qualified practitioner for advice prior to surveillance, and to discuss the findings of the surveillance. However, where hazards are low there may be no need for a system of regular health checks, although it is suggested that the basic records listed below are kept for all employees.

Records

The Health and Safety Executive (HSE) recommends that basic personnel records should be kept for all employees no matter how low the hazards are.

These records should include an employee's:

- name
- address
- place and date of birth
- gender
- National Insurance number
- National Health Service number
- historical record of jobs, classified by job category.

Detailed records should be kept of employees:

- who are exposed to toxic substances, biological hazards or harmful physical agents
- whose work subjects them to particular physical or mental stress
- whose work could affect the safety of the public or other workers.

Some legislation stipulates the length of time that records should be kept for and this is summarised in the table below.

Note: The **Access to Medical Reports Act 1988** governs the procedures under which personal medical information can be passed to the employer. The **Data Protection Act 1998** gives employees the right to see information relating to themselves and held in the files of a medical practitioner.

Pre-employment health screening

Although this may be beneficial, excluding someone from employment for minor or irrelevant health problems should be avoided. Refusal of employment should only be taken on the basis of criteria which are carefully defined and relate specifically to the job concerned. In most instances employers should use questionnaires upon which further investigations can be based if it seems necessary from the information given.

It should be noted that the **Disability Discrimination Act 1995** does not allow the employer to discriminate against a prospective employee as a direct consequence of a disability, and where the particular physical or mental disadvantage could be overcome by the employer taking reasonable compensatory measures.

Questions and Answers

Q Where can I seek competent advice?

A By contacting an occupational health physician or nurse, or through the local office of the Employment Medical Advisory Service.

Q Must my employees take part in health surveillance?

A Yes, if it is a statutory requirement (such as under COSHH) or has been clearly stated in a contract of employment.

Q Is there any legislation which states how long records should be kept?

A The legislation listed in the following table stipulates what sort of records, including health surveillance, should be kept and for how long.

Legislation		Record	Period record must be kept
Control of Substances Hazardous to Health Regulations 1999 (COSHH)	reg 7(10)	List of employees exposed to group 3 and 4 biological agents	10 years after last exposure
	Schedule 9	Where exposure may lead to a disease many years later	40 years after last exposure
	reg 9	Examination and testing of control equipment and repairs carried out as a result	5 years
	reg 10	Exposure at the workplace: (i) general exposure (ii) personal exposure of indentifiable employee	5 years 40 years
	reg 11	Health surveillance	40 years from date of last entry
Reporting of Injuries, Diseases and Dangerous Occurrences Regulations 1995 (RIDDOR)		Reportable injuries, diseases and dangerous occurrences	3 years
Social Security (Claims and Payments) Regulations 1979		Accident book (Form BI 510)	3 years from date of last entry
The Ionising Radiations Regulations 1999		(i) Health records (ii) Examination of respiratory protection equipment	50 years from date of last entry 2 years

Homeworkers

Summary

Recent changes in employment patterns have seen a large increase in the number of people who now work from home, ie homeworkers. Traditionally, homework most commonly involved sewing, various forms of assembly, painting, gluing, machining, knitting, repairing, cutting and packing. More modern types of work such as telesales and computer work may now also be included in this list.

Practical Guidance

Employees working at home are owed the same duty of care as employees performing the same work in a workplace. This means that any control measures necessary at work will also be necessary in the home. Some Regulations such as the **Health and Safety (Display Screen Equipment) Regulations 1992** contain specific provisions covering people who work at home on display screen equipment, and these must be complied with. In other cases, the legal control rests on the general duties owed to employees and non-employees under the **Health and Safety at Work, etc Act 1974**.

Good communications between the workplace and the home are very important, not only in disseminating and receiving information, but also in including homeworkers in the business operation. Employers should ensure that health and safety audits include the work areas used by homeworkers, and that any concerns are addressed. Well-targeted training of homeworkers, especially in their increased responsibilities for ensuring their own health and safety at work, should be provided.

Enforcement

Enforcement of health and safety in homeworking environments by the employer and by enforcing authorities is difficult, not least because by definition homework is carried out in private homes. However, enforcement officers do have a legal right to visit the home.

Questions and Answers

Q Can enforcing authority inspectors insist on entering a home where homeworking is undertaken?

A Yes, enforcing inspectors have the right to visit the home where the residence is a domestic property. Employers may consider writing into any homeworking contract that access may be requested in order to undertake health and safety audits.

Q Are homeworkers employees?

A This will depend on the initial agreement and/or contract between the homeworker and the employer. In any case where homeworkers are carrying out work at home they are entitled to the same standards of care as if their were performing the work at the employer's workplace — the employer will have a duty to them under the **Health and Safety at Work, etc Act 1974**, either as employees or as non-employees.

Q Does health and safety law apply to homeworkers?

A Essentially yes, although there are a few exceptions, eg where the workers are members of the same family as the "employer".

Hours of Work

Summary

Hours of work, for most employees, are covered by the **Working Time Regulations 1998** (as amended), further details of which are given below. There is also a general duty on employers to ensure the health and safety of employees under s.2 of the **Health and Safety at Work etc Act 1974**.

Practical Guidance

Hours of work

Any excessive and/or unsociable hours which cause adverse health effects are covered here. Several factors need to be considered in addition to the actual amount of time worked. For example shift work, especially night or rotating day/night shifts, may cause health problems, as may insufficient rest periods between and during work shifts, eg "on-call" work.

The obvious effect of long work hours is fatigue, which may reduce physical and mental abilities and therefore increase health and safety risks. If left uncontrolled, excessively long hours may lead to physical exhaustion and stress. Control is made more difficult by the fact that every employee is different and will be able to undertake varying hours of work safely, depending on fitness, age, existing health conditions, etc. Controls should therefore take into account the needs of the most vulnerable person. However there are limits placed on the maximum average hours that can be worked, as given in **The Working Time Regulations 1998** (as amended).

It is important that adequate rest breaks are allowed during the shift, and again what is adequate will depend on the work and working conditions. For example, kitchens are usually very hot and humid, so regular rest breaks are needed in order for employees to be able to get drinks as well as rest.

If the work involves on-call duties, the additional hours worked by the person on call should be taken into account and adequate time off given as soon as possible after the extra hours are worked. The need for frequent or continuous overtime should be taken to indicate a staffing level problem which will need to be reviewed and addressed.

In the case of *Johnstone v Bloomsbury Health Authority*, a junior house doctor was required by his employment contract to work a basic 40 hours a week, with an additional 48 hours on-call time. His case was based on the fact that such excessive hours were intolerable and adversely affected his health and (potentially) his professional judgment. He requested a declaration making it unlawful to employ him for so many additional hours that it would foreseeably injure his health. The Court of Appeal decided that there was an implied duty of care on the employer to ensure that such excessive working hours did not damage the employee's health.

The Working Time Regulations 1998, as amended

The regulations came into force on 1 October 1998, and were subject to an amendment in 1999. They provide the following basic rights for workers:
- four weeks paid annual leave after an initial qualifying period of 13 weeks
- for adults, 11 consecutive rest hours in any 24-hour period
- for adolescents (ie those over the minimum school leaving age but under 18), 12 consecutive rest hours in any 24-hour period
- a limit of an average of 48 hours work per week, averaged over a 17-week period
- a limit of an average of eight hours work in any 24 hours for night workers, averaged over 17 weeks.

The regulations apply to all workers over the minimum school leaving age, except for those workers in a very limited number of areas including civil protection, transport and work at sea.

The definition of "worker" includes all those with a contract of employment, as well as those who undertake work under other forms of contract, such as agency staff, freelance workers etc. The regulations do not cover the self-employed.

In addition to the main points above, there are various other requirements as follows.

Limits on weekly working hours

Although the Regulations set a limit of an average of 48 hours work per week, averaged over a 17-week period, this can be extended to a 26-week period where the workers are covered by specific derogations (see below), or up to 52 weeks by an agreement between workers and employers. Individuals are also entitled to work hours in excess of 48 per week where this is done voluntarily; if this is the case the employer should seek written confirmation from each individual, and these records should be kept up to date.

Night time working

Although the Regulations set a limit of an average eight hours in any 24 hours, averaged over a 17-week period, again this can be extended by specific derogations (see below) or by an agreement between workers and employers.

Those night workers whose work involves special hazards, or heavy physical or mental strain, are restricted to a maximum of eight hours work in each 24-hour period (ie the averaging out facility and the use of agreements do not apply).

The definition of "night time" has been defined as the period 11pm–6am, unless an alternative 7-hour period (such as midnight–5am) has been agreed. A night worker has been defined as someone whose normal working time includes at least three hours of night-time working.

Night workers are entitled to a free health assessment before commencing night work, and subsequently at appropriate intervals. Staff should be transferred to day work if night work causes problems.

Rest periods

Adult workers are entitled to one day off per week, and adolescents to two days off. Both may be subject to specific derogations (see below).

Adult workers are entitled to 11 consecutive hours of rest per day, and adolescents to 12 hours. Both may be subject to specific derogations (see below).

Adult workers are entitled to a minimum 20-minute rest break per day, if their working day is longer than six hours. Adolescents are entitled to a minimum 30-minute rest break per day, if their working day is longer than 4.5 hours. Both may be subject to specific derogations (see below).

Specific derogations

There are a number of instances of specific derogations under the Working Time Regulations, as follows.

Unmeasured working time

It is accepted that there are many workers whose working time cannot effectively be measured or pre-determined, or who themselves have the flexibility to determine their own working time, eg managers and family workers. Effectively the only provision in the new Regulations that will have any effect for this category of worker is the entitlement to paid annual leave. If, however, only part of the worker's working time is unmeasured, then the provisions relating to weekly working time, night working etc will only apply to the part of the worker's work which is measured or predetermined.

Specified circumstances

In certain circumstances it is acknowledged that work which exceeds the limits specified above may be required, eg hospital services, agriculture, utilities etc. In these situations some flexibility is allowed, provided that the workers receive compensatory rest.

Flexibility is also allowed in circumstances where there are unexpected and unforeseeable occurrences that are beyond the control of the employer.

Employer/worker agreements

Collective agreements can be made with independent trade unions. Where there is no recognised trade union, a "workforce agreement" can be made.

Shift work

People work to a cyclical pattern of activity and rest — usually this is activity during the day and rest at night. In practice, many workplaces follow this pattern by operating during the day. However, there are also many workplaces, such as hospitals, residential homes, power stations, etc, which require 24-hour cover. In these situations, shift work to cover the 24-hour period will be necessary. The basic shift patterns usually worked are:

- night shifts
- early morning shifts
- early afternoon shifts
- rotating shifts, ie day and nights alternatively
- split shifts, ie where a non-work period is sandwiched between two work shifts; many hotel kitchens operate split shifts.

With regard to health and safety, the most potentially harmful shifts are night shifts and rotating shifts as they cause the most disruption to the natural body cycles, although employees on permanent night shifts do usually adapt and can work normally.

Common effects of shift work include reduced and disturbed sleep, and unusual eating patterns which may result in insufficient food being eaten.

Full and proper consultations with employees must be carried out when shift work is proposed and/or changed.

New and expectant mothers

A new or expectant mother may be suspended from night work if she submits to her employer a certificate signed by a registered midwife or doctor, stating that the night work is prejudicial to the woman's health. Employers must also alter the hours of work of new or expectant mothers if this would eliminate, or at least adequately control, any hazards and risks identified in the risk assessment.

Disabled persons

The **Disability Discrimination Act 1995** requires employers to alter hours of work for disabled persons, where this is necessary and reasonable to ensure equal employment opportunities for them.

Questions and Answers

Q   What exactly is the free health check that we have to give night workers under the **Working Time Regulations 1998**?

A   The Regulations themselves do not state specifically what constitutes a health check. However, the DTI/HSE joint guidance states that the purpose of the assessment is to determine whether a worker is fit to carry out the night work to which they are assigned. Of particular concern are conditions which could potentially be made worse by night work, such as diabetes, heart and circulatory disorders and stomach and intestinal disorders. Conditions affecting sleep, chronic chest disorders and conditions requiring regular medication are also of relevance. In some cases it may be sufficient to ask employees to complete a screening questionnaire, compiled with the assistance of a suitably qualified medical practitioner, and then only refer those individuals where doubts are raised by the questionnaire for a full health assessment. Suitable health assessments are normally available through GPs or private medical organisations, or through an in-house occupational health facility where appropriate.

Q If an employee wishes to take additional pay in lieu of some or all of his four weeks' annual leave, is this acceptable?

A No, employees must receive the four weeks' leave annually.

Industrial Injuries

Summary

If employees suffer an accident arising out of or in the course of their employment, and are incapable of work, they will qualify for certain benefits, whether or not they have paid National Insurance contributions. Employees suffering a prescribed industrial disease whilst in prescribed occupations may also qualify for benefits.

Practical Guidance

Statutory sick pay

Under the **Social Security Contributions and Benefits Act 1992**, employers are responsible for paying statutory sick pay (SSP) to their employees for the first 28 weeks of sickness absence in every period of incapacity for work. An employee who suffers an industrial injury and who is eligible for SSP will receive a payment at the prescribed rate from the employer under this scheme.

Employees who are excluded from receiving SSP, or have exhausted their entitlement, and suffer an industrial injury will receive a State benefit. There are three types of State benefit, as follows:

- sickness benefit — payable for a specified length of time and for which there are no contribution conditions when it is claimed in relation to an industrial injury
- disablement benefit — payable if the employee has suffered a loss of mental or physical faculty assessed at 1% or more
- in the event of death, a death benefit is sometimes payable to the widow of the deceased (or, in certain circumstances only, the widower) for life or until she remarries (industrial death benefit for deaths occurring on or after 11.4.88 has been abolished, but widows from industrial deaths may be entitled to claim National Insurance widows' benefits).

Qualifying circumstances

Employees will qualify for benefit if the accident occurred on or after 5.7.48 and they were gainfully employed under a contract of service, or as an office holder, eg a company director, with emoluments chargeable to income tax under Schedule E. The accident must also have happened in Great Britain.

Types of accident covered

For benefit purposes, an accident means any unexpected happening or incident at work. Benefit is paid if such an accident results in personal injury, whether immediate or delayed. An accident which happens when an employee is at work is treated as having occurred out of and in the course of employment, unless there is evidence to the contrary. Thus, if employees are injured whilst travelling to or from the place of work they will be treated as having been at work at the time, provided they were travelling in transport provided by the employer.

Benefits are also payable if an employee is injured whilst doing something expressly prohibited by the employer or in contravention of any of the relevant statutory provisions, provided that what the employee was doing at the time:

- was for the purpose of the employer's business
- was within the scope of the employee's job
- would have occurred in spite of the employer's instructions to the contrary (or without the express permission of the employer) or the existence of statutory and other regulations.

An employee who is injured whilst going to the assistance of another person who has been injured or is in danger of being injured, or whilst seeking to avert or minimise serious damage to property, will also qualify to be paid benefit.

Finally, an employee who is injured through another person's misconduct, skylarking or negligence, or by the behaviour or presence of an animal (including a bird, fish or insect), or by being struck by lightning or any object, will be entitled to receive benefit, provided the injuries were sustained in the course of the employment and that the employee did not directly or indirectly induce or contribute to the happening of the accident.

Prescribed industrial diseases

Under the **Social Security (Industrial Injuries) (Prescribed Diseases) Regulations 1985** as variously amended, there are prescribed occupational conditions or diseases which, if they occurred or developed whilst claimants were in prescribed occupations, will qualify claimants to receive benefits. The prescribed diseases or conditions will be presumed to have resulted from those prescribed occupations, unless there is evidence to the contrary, provided an individual claimant has been employed in a particular occupation for a minimum period (ranging from 1 month in most cases to 10 years, in the case of occupational deafness).

If an industrial disease or injury is not on the prescribed list, or is on the list but claimants cannot meet the occupational qualification (that is, they have not contracted the disease whilst carrying out the associated occupation), they will not be entitled to a cash benefit under the scheme.

The following shows the extent of prescribed industrial diseases; note that in many examples there are subcategories of diseases.

Conditions due to physical agents
There are 12 conditions due to physical agents. An example is carpel tunnel syndrome as a result of using hand-held vibrating tools.

Conditions due to biological agents
There are 13 conditions due to biological agents. An example is hydatidosis as a result of an occupation which included contact with dogs.

Conditions due to chemical agents
There are 29 conditions due to chemical agents. An example is poisoning by lead or a compound of lead as a result of any occupation involving the use or handling of, or exposure to the fumes, dust or vapour of, lead or a compound of lead, or a substance containing lead.

Miscellaneous conditions
There are 12 miscellaneous conditions. For example byssinosis as a result of working in any room where any process (involving spinning or manipulation of raw or waste cotton or flax or the wearing of cotton or flax) up to and including the weaving process is performed.

Reporting of accidents, etc

Under regulation 24 of the **Social Security (Claims and Payments) Regulations 1979**, an employee who suffers personal injury through an accident at work must inform the employer immediately (either orally or in writing) or as soon as possible after the accident occurred. Employers must, under regulation 25, take reasonable steps to investigate the circumstances of every accident notified to them and, if any discrepancy is discovered between their findings and the information provided by the employee, they must record that discrepancy for possible future reference.

An employer who occupies a factory or who employs 10 or more employees on the premises must maintain an accident book (Form BI 510, available from the Stationery Office, tel: 020 7873 9090) in which the appropriate particulars of any accident causing personal injury to one of the employees can be recorded by the employee or someone on their behalf. The accident book must be kept, when filled, for at least three years after the date of the last entry in the book. It must also be surrendered for examination on demand by an accredited officer of the Department of Social Security. This obligation to maintain an accident book does not relieve an employer of the similar but unrelated duty to report certain injuries and diseases to the health and safety authorities under the **Reporting of Injuries, Disease and Dangerous Occurrences Regulations 1995** (RIDDOR).

Claims procedure

If employees are incapable of work as a result of an accident which happened in the course of their employment, they must comply with the employer's requirements for claiming SSP. If the employee is excluded from receiving SSP the employer must provide a change-over form SSP 1 (this has replaced form SSP 1 (E)), which should then be forwarded to the local social security office. Where an employee submits a claim for benefit in the case of an industrial injury, the local social security office may write to the employer for further information and may ask for the relevant extract from the accident book.

Benefits — incapacity benefit

From 13.4.95 the former sickness and invalidity benefits were replaced by the "incapacity" benefit. Under this new benefit the contribution conditions remain as for the previous sickness benefit although a new medical test has been introduced to determine eligibility.

Questions and Answers

Q One of our employees has been diagnosed as having asthma and works with wood dust in a machine shop. Is this a prescribed disease?

A If it is shown that wood dust has caused the asthma, then yes it is. Asthma due to exposure to wood dust is a miscellaneous condition, number 7(j).

Q Are prescribed diseases under the Social Security (Industrial Injuries) (Prescribed Diseases) Regulations the same as the reportable diseases contained in RIDDOR?

A No, some are duplicated but the lists are not identical and some of the related occupations are slightly different.

Q We keep a copy of the accident book (BI510) locked in the first aid room and a manager makes an entry if someone is injured. Is this correct procedure?

A No. The duty on employers is to maintain an accident book in which particulars of an accident causing personal injury to an employee can be recorded by that employee or someone on his or her behalf. That person acting on his or her behalf could be a manager but the details entered are intended to be those supplied by the injured person. Should there be a discrepancy between the facts stated by the employee and those found during the investigation (which should be carried out by the employer) the discrepancy should be recorded.

Insurance and Civil Law

Summary

In addition to the many pieces of statutory (criminal) law associated with health and safety, most noticeably the **Health and Safety at Work, etc Act 1974** and its subsidiary Regulations, there is an equally important civil law aspect, which itself ties in with the role of insurance.

Practical Guidance

Insurance

Most civil cases against employers are taken for "breach of a statutory duty" or "negligence". The damages awarded in these cases are insurable under the "employers' liability insurance". Civil cases are heard in civil, not criminal, courts. Financially speaking, the damages awarded in civil proceedings are usually considerably higher than fines imposed in criminal proceedings.

Employers may not legally operate their businesses without employers' liability insurance. This insurance is designed to ensure that if employees who are injured or made ill at work make a civil claim against their employer, there is sufficient insurance cover to pay any damages awarded. A copy of the insurance certificate must be posted in the workplace.

The **Employers' Liability (Compulsory Insurance) Regulations 1998** are enforced by the Health and Safety Executive and companies may be fined for every day they do not comply. The failure of an employer to take out employers' liability insurance against personal injury sustained by an employee is a criminal not a civil offence, as illustrated by the case of *Richardson v Pitt-Stanley and Others*.

Breach of statutory duty

In order to win a case for "breach of statutory duty" several criteria have to be met. The employee must prove that:

- they were personally covered by the statutory duty
- their injury or ill-health was of a kind that the statutory duty was intended to prevent
- the statutory duty was breached by the employer
- that breach caused their injury or ill-health.

Civil damages claims against an employer for breach of a statutory duty will only succeed if the injured employee can prove there was a statutory duty of which the employer was in breach, and that the injury occurred as a result of that breach.

However, the breach need not be the sole or primary cause of the injury — it is sufficient if it made a significant contribution to it (see the case of *Bonnington Castings v Wardlaw*).

A breach of statutory duty may be taken in both criminal and civil courts although only one set of damages will be awarded if both cases are successful. Once the employee has proved that there was a breach of duty, it is up to the employer to prove that the breach did not cause the injury or ill-health, or that the injury, etc was entirely the fault of the employee.

Negligence

Negligence is based on a breach of the common law of the land, ie the duty of care that each person owes to everyone else, and is now the most usual way for employees to claim damages for personal injury, etc against their employers. Again there are certain criteria which have to be met. These are:

- that a general duty of care to prevent foreseeable injuries existed
- that the duty of care was broken by negligence
- that the breach of duty of care caused the injury, etc.

In negligence cases it is up to the employee to prove that the employer was negligent — the negligence may be through the employer's failings, through managers' failings or through the failings of employees (vicarious liability). Contributory negligence is awarded in cases where the injured employee contributed to their own injury, ie by not following safe systems of work — damages will be reduced accordingly depending on the extent of the employee's contribution.

The negligence case recognised as providing the origin of current rules relating to an employer's common law duty to take reasonable care to ensure the health and safety of their employees is the case of *Donoghue v Stevenson*. Although not strictly a health and safety case, it sets the criteria upon which negligence cases are now judged. Donoghue suffered an injury when she unknowingly drank the remains of a decomposed snail in a drink contained in a dark, opaque glass bottle. The manufacturers were held to be liable for failing to take reasonable care that their product was free from defects which were liable to cause injury to health in a situation where the defect could not be discovered prior to consumption.

The duty of care is not "absolute", ie employers do not have to guarantee a complete absence of risks, only to control risks that are foreseeable to acceptable levels. The duty of care is also owed to employees individually so a greater duty of care is owed to people at greater risk, ie young persons, new and expectant mothers, disabled employees, etc.

Questions and Answers

Q Can fines and costs imposed for successful prosecutions under any health and safety legislation be insured against?

A No, there is no insurance cover for fines imposed under criminal law.

Q Is there a minimum and maximum cover for employers' liability insurance?

A There are minimum and maximum covers for individual claims, although there are no restrictions on the number of separate claims that can be made. For any individual claim the minimum amount of cover is £5 million and the maximum £10 million.

Q Can insurance companies refuse to offer employers' liability insurance?

A In theory they could refuse cover, which would mean that the business could not continue to operate. For insurance to be refused, the circumstances would have to be so exceptional that the insurance companies could not feasibly insure against the risk. However, there could be situations where continuous poor health and safety management standards led to repeated civil claims, in which case the insurance companies may consider such dramatic action.

Q Can all health and safety legislation be used in civil "breach of statutory duty" or "negligence" cases?

A No. Sections 2–8 of the **Health and Safety at Work, etc Act 1974** and the **Management of Health and Safety at Work Regulations 1999** (except the provisions relating to the risk assessments of new and expectant mothers and young persons) are specifically exempt from civil actions.

Labelling of Dangerous Substances

Summary

Many substances have properties which make them dangerous during transport, handling, storage, cleaning spillages and so on. It is essential that the hazards of chemicals are communicated to everyone who comes into contact with them, and manufacturers, importers and suppliers of dangerous substances have legal obligations to do so.

Practical Guidance

CHIP and COSHH

The **Chemicals (Hazard Information and Packaging for Supply) Regulations 1994** (as amended) (CHIP) aim to ensure that purchasers, users, etc of chemicals are given enough information on the hazards to protect their health and safety. This extends the requirements of s.6 of the **Health and Safety at Work, etc Act 1974** for manufacturers, suppliers, designers and importers to ensure that articles and substances that they supply are safe for use at work and to provide adequate information on the hazards to allow the article or substances to be handled safely.

CHIP therefore governs the information that must be provided when hazardous chemicals are supplied. The **Control of Substances Hazardous to Health Regulations 1999** (COSHH) cover how the employer receiving the hazardous chemicals uses this information to provide a safe system of work.

Dangerous for supply

Under CHIP, a chemical is dangerous for supply if it falls under one or more of the following categories:
- explosive
- oxidising
- extremely flammable
- highly flammable
- flammable
- very toxic
- toxic

- harmful
- corrosive
- irritant
- sensitising
- sensitising by inhalation
- sensitising by skin contact
- carcinogenic (three categories)
- mutagenic (three categories)
- toxic for reproduction (three categories)
- dangerous for the environment.

The Health and Safety Executive (HSE) has categorised over 2000 common industrial chemicals. These are listed in L76: *Approved Supply List*. This list only contains substances, and not preparations (mixtures of substances). If a chemical is not on the list, this does not mean that it is not dangerous. The manufacturer, importer or supplier must carry out certain tests in order to classify the chemical themselves.

Contents of labels

CHIP requires that containers used to supply hazardous chemicals must bear a firmly attached label giving the following information:

- name and address of the supplier
- name of the substance
- for preparations, the names of the substances that make it hazardous
- indication of danger, eg "toxic" and the relevant hazard warning symbol, eg the skull and crossbones
- relevant risk and safety phrases, eg "harmful by ingestion", "keep out of reach of children"
- the EC number allocated to substances
- certain information for pesticides
- the nominal quantity (mass or volume) for preparations for sale to the public
- the words "caution: this preparation contains a substance not yet fully tested" for certain preparations.

Format of labels

Under CHIP, labels must be fixed securely to the container, and must be readable horizontally when the container is put down. CHIP gives a minimum size for labels, depending on the size of the container. The print must be clear and indelible. For substances supplied in the UK, the label must be in English.

The hazard warning symbol, eg the skull and crossbones for "very toxic", a flame for "extremely flammable", a cross ("X") for "harmful", must stand out and must have a black symbol on an orange background.

Packaging

CHIP contains various specifications relating to packaging. These include the requirement for containers of dangerous substances to meet certain standards in relation to being child-resistant and having a tactile warning of danger. A tactile warning of danger is basically a raised warning symbol which allows visually impaired people to identify the hazard of the chemical.

Safety data sheets

Under CHIP, suppliers of dangerous substances must provide safety data sheets which contain the following information:

- name of the substance or preparation
- name and address of the supplier
- composition of, and information on, the ingredients
- identification of the hazards
- first aid measures
- fire-fighting measures
- accidental release measures
- handling and storage
- exposure controls and personal protection
- physical and chemical properties
- stability and reactivity
- toxicological information
- ecological information
- disposal considerations
- transport information
- regulatory information.

Details of the information to be provided under each heading of the safety data sheet are given in L62: *Safety Data Sheets for Substances and Preparations Dangerous for Supply.*

Safety data sheets must be provided free of charge when the product is first supplied. The sheet must clearly show the date that it was published or revised.

Revisions

Under CHIP, suppliers of dangerous substances must review the safety data sheets and update them as necessary. If there are any changes, they must provide the revised safety data sheets free of charge to anyone they supplied the product to in the preceding year. The changes must be highlighted.

Retail products

CHIP allows a dangerous substance or preparation to be supplied without a safety data sheet if it is for retail sale to the public, so long as:

- sufficient information is provided to allow the user to take appropriate safety measures

- a safety data sheet is provided free on request to someone intending to use the product at work.

Pressure systems

Under the **Pressure Systems Safety Regulations 2000**, manufacturers, designers, importers and suppliers of pressure systems must provide sufficient written information, including information on:

- design
- construction
- examination
- operation
- maintenance.

Pressure vessels must be visibly, legibly and indelibly marked by the manufacturer with the following:

- name of the manufacturer
- serial number
- date of manufacture
- standard to which the vessel was built
- maximum and minimum design pressures
- design temperature.

Asbestos

Under the **Control of Asbestos at Work Regulations 1987,** raw asbestos and asbestos waste must always be stored and transported in properly labelled, sealed containers. Suppliers of asbestos products for use at work must label the containers in accordance with the Regulations.

The **Asbestos Products (Safety) Regulations 1985** set out labelling requirements for products containing crocidolite, amosite, crysotile, fibrous anthophyllite, fibrous actinolite or fibrous tremolite asbestos.

Questions and Answers

Q What is an EC number?

A All chemicals which are known to be available in Europe are either listed in the European Inventory of Existing Commercial Chemical Substances (EINECS) or the European List of Notified Chemical Substances (ELINCS). Each chemical in these lists is given a number, ie the EC number.

Q Does CHIP apply to all dangerous substances?

A There are certain substances which are currently excluded from CHIP. These include:

- animal feed
- cosmetics
- medicinal products

- controlled drugs
- pesticides
- food
- waste
- radioactive substances.

In most cases, dangerous substances which are not covered by CHIP are covered by different legislation which relates to labelling and providing hazard information.

Q What should I do if I do not receive a safety data sheet when I purchase a chemical?

A If the chemical is a dangerous substance, the supplier is legally obliged to provide you with a free safety data sheet. If you do not receive one for a substance you intend to use at work, contact the supplier as soon as possible. It may be that the chemical does not come under any of the categories of dangerous substances, in which case a safety data sheet is not required. However, if it does, ask the supplier to give you a safety data sheet by a certain date. If they still fail to provide a safety data sheet, you should return the chemical and your money should be refunded. Do not open or use the chemical until you have the safety information that you need. The HSE are responsible for enforcing CHIP, so if in doubt consult your local HSE area office.

Ladders

Summary

Ladders and steps are commonly used for access to higher workplaces. Manufactured from a variety of materials including wood, aluminium, and glass fibre, ladders have two stiles (the long sections) with rungs to stand on, and steps are in the form of an "A" with rectangular steps contained in one side, possibly with a top platform.

Practical Guidance

Definitions

A number of different types of ladder may be used:

- standing ladders are single ladders up to six metres in length
- pole ladders are often found on construction sites and are so called because their stiles are formed by splitting a long whitewood pole down its length (maximum length 10 metres)
- roof ladders are adapted for access on to sloping roofs
- extension ladders consist of 2, 3 or even 4 sections which slide over each other; three-section ladders may extend to 16 metres
- step ladders have two sections forming an "A", one or both sides being fitted with flat rectangular treads
- fixed ladders may be found in a number of situations such as access to lift rooms, to crane control cabs or plant access platforms — they can be vertical or at an angle.

Accidents

Accidents include falls from the ladder or steps from losing balance or slipping, falling for some other reason such as receiving an electric shock, the ladder or steps slipping, breaking or being displaced for some reason, and carrying or handling the ladder or steps. The history of ladder accidents is such that specific legislation exists to regulate their use in construction and demolition activities under the **Construction (Health, Safety and Welfare) Regulations 1996.**

Risk assessment

Many accidents happen through inappropriate use of ladders or steps for work where a scaffold, mobile tower or powered access platform should be used. Ladders should only be used for access to, or egress from, a workplace if it is reasonable to do so having regard for the work to be carried out and its duration. They should only be used for light work, such as painting or maintenance, that is of short duration.

Selection and inspection

Correct selection of equipment is essential and ladders and steps come within three classes (see Questions and Answers). The correct choice should be a result of activity analysis, risk analysis and employee consultation.

Once equipment has been selected it must be maintained in a safe to use condition. This is achieved through a system of inspection on a regular basis. The period between inspections is determined by:

- the type of ladder
- what it is to be used for
- where it is to be used
- its age and previous history of damage and repair.

All ladders should be given a unique mark for identification to allow records of inspection to be kept. Inspection of ladders should include:

- damage or wear to stiles, particularly at the head or foot of the ladder
- worn, broken, missing or loose rungs or steps
- movement in the rungs or stiles
- insecure tie rods
- warping or distortion which may affect the ability of the ladder to stand firmly
- decay to timber, cracks or corrosion of metal fittings
- damage or wear to any ropes, pulleys and other fittings
- security of hinges, top platforms, and retaining straps or ropes of steps.

Training

Any person who uses or is likely to use ladders or steps should receive appropriate training. This should include:

- the type of ladder for different jobs
- knowledge of the marking and record system for inspection to understand when ladders are in/out of the inspection period
- recognising defects that may render the ladder unsafe
- how to carry the ladder
- how to erect and lower the ladder
- maximum heights of use, maximum climb heights for steps (usually the knee should not extend beyond the top of the steps unless designed with a suitable handhold)

- factors that affect stability such as floor surfaces, uneven ground, incorrect opening of steps
- when and how to secure ladders
- the rules for work on the ladder or steps.

Questions and Answers

Q Our corporate colour is blue and we want to paint all our timber ladders to match, is this safe to do?

A No, timber ladders or steps should not be painted as this can hide cracks or other defects that may render them unsafe. A light coat of clear varnish or other treatment which will not obscure defects is acceptable.

Q We occasionally need to use a ladder as a horizontal bridge across the gap between two flat roofs, are there any special rules we should follow?

A This should NEVER be done. Ladders are intended for use in a position between vertical and approximately 15 degrees from the vertical (75 degrees from the horizontal base) and can be damaged or fail completely if used as you describe.

Q We mostly use ladders under three metres long for light work such as painting. Do they always need to be lashed?

A Ladders under 3m long need not be fixed or footed if they have been securely placed in position in a way to prevent them slipping and if they are not being used for access. It is always advisable to lash near the top or, if that is not possible, near to the bottom to prevent slipping, where possible.

Q We have been told that the steps we use, marked "Class 3: Domestic" are not suitable and should be "Class 1: Industrial". They are only used about once per day to gain access to storage racking where we have small cardboard boxes weighing about 5kg. Do we really need to change them?

A Not necessarily. Although there are three classes covered by the British Standards, the most important thing to do is assess the work then select the most suitable. For heavy duty use such as on a construction site you should always select Class 1. For infrequent and light duty use as you describe the Class 3 should be sufficient. Whatever the class rating you must undertake regular inspection and maintenance to ensure continuing safety.

Lead

Summary

Lead has long been recognised as a significant work hazard resulting in women and/or young persons being prohibited from work with it. The **Control of Lead at Work Regulations 1998** require an assessment of work involving lead to be carried out, in order to determine the degree and nature of the exposure and the necessary controls.

Practical Guidance

The employer and self-employed person has a general duty under the **Control of Lead at Work Regulations 1998** to ensure that the exposure of his or her employees and any other persons is either prevented or, where this is not reasonably practicable, is adequately controlled.

Exposure

The Control of Lead at Work Regulations 1998 apply where employees are exposed to lead (including lead alkyls, lead alloys, any compounds of lead and lead as a constituent of any substance or material) which is liable to be inhaled, ingested or otherwise absorbed by persons except where it is given off from the exhaust system of a vehicle on the road.

Consideration must also be given to employees who are particularly susceptible, eg women of reproductive capacity, young people and non-employees, such as contract cleaners, who may be exposed to lead during the course of their work.

In the case of *Hewett v Alf Brown's Transport Ltd*, the wife of a lorry driver who carried lead oxide waste developed a lead poisoning related illness contracted through washing her husband's contaminated clothing. Although it was agreed that the illness was directly attributable to washing the contaminated overalls, her case for negligence/breach of a statutory duty against her husband's employer failed as his exposure had been assessed as being below the lowest level on the scales contained in the relevant code of practice. No duty of care was therefore owed to either Mr or Mrs Hewett. The case does illustrate, however, the possibility of the duty of care being extended to non-employees who suffer illness through secondary exposure to such contamination although the issue of cleaning of protective clothing is now dealt with explicitly in regulation 8.

Employees' duties

Employees must present themselves for appropriate biological monitoring and medical surveillance programmes. In addition, employees must return any personal protective equipment or clothing to the designated storage areas, and may not eat, drink or smoke in any place which is, or is likely to be, contaminated by lead. They also have a duty to make full and proper use of any control measures provided by the employer and to report any defects immediately.

Assessment and controls

The assessment should determine whether the exposure of any employees to lead is liable to be significant, so that appropriate controls can be implemented. It should be undertaken before the lead work begins and be reviewed and revised if there are any changes to the initial information. Control measures should not include personal protective equipment (PPE) or clothing, except as a last resort where adequate standards cannot be achieved by other means. However, respiratory protective equipment (RPE) must be provided where there is exposure to airborne lead and other measures cannot satisfactorily control the level of exposure. All control measures, including PPE, must be well maintained, tested at suitable intervals, kept in working order and be used properly. Defects must be reported immediately.

Monitoring

Employers must implement adequate procedures for measuring and monitoring the levels of airborne lead in all cases where the lead exposure is significant.

Medical surveillance

Where lead exposure is significant and an employment medical advisor or an appointed doctor requires it, then employees exposed to lead at work must be under a medical surveillance programme. The medical certificate may prohibit the worker from lead work, or certain types of lead work, or set other conditions — all of which must be complied with by the employer.

Information, instruction and training

Adequate information, instructions and training must be provided to employees working with lead, and also those carrying out assessments, cleaning or maintenance operations, on the risks of exposure to lead and the necessary controls.

Records

Records should be kept of:
- assessments
- maintenance work

- air monitoring
- medical surveillance
- biological tests.

Health records are usually required to be retained for 40 years after the last entry, while other records should be kept for two years.

Processes where employers must not employ women of reproductive capacity or young persons (Schedule 1)

Process	Material	Activities
Lead smelting and refining	Ores or materials containing not less than 5% lead	Handling Treatment Sintering Smelting Refining Cleaning where any of above processes are carried out
Lead-acid battery manufacture	Lead oxides	Manipulation Mixing Pasting
	Metallic lead	Melting or casting
	Pasted plates	Trimming Abrading Cutting
	All of above	Cleaning where any of above processes are carried out

Welfare provisions

Adequate washing, changing and clothing storage facilities must be provided. In addition, eating, smoking and drinking are prohibited in lead areas so alternative arrangements should be made. Lead work areas must be kept clean and all possible steps should be taken by employers and employees, etc to prevent contamination from lead. Employers must ensure that workplaces, process equipment and personal protective equipment are kept clean.

Questions and Answers

Q How does lead enter the body and what are the biological monitoring standards for blood?

Lead

A   The main route of lead entry into the body is the inhalation of lead dusts and fumes into the lungs, although a small amount can be absorbed through the gut. Workers exposed to lead processes should undertake biological monitoring programmes to ensure there are no excessive levels of lead in the body. There are two critical blood lead concentrations, the action level and the suspension level, which require the employer to take steps. There are different values for the two levels for each of the following categories: women of reproductive capacity; young persons; and any other employees. If an action level is exceeded the employer is required to determine the reason for the high concentration and to take measures to reduce the concentration of the employee below the appropriate action level. The action levels are 25µg/100ml blood for women of reproductive capacity, 40µg/100ml blood for young persons and 50µg/100ml blood for any other employees. If the suspension level is exceeded the employee should be suspended from lead work. The suspension levels are 30µg/100ml blood for women of reproductive capacity, 50µg/100ml blood for young persons and 60µg/100ml blood for any other employee.

Q   Can lead be passed on to breast feeding babies after maternal exposure?

A   Yes. Lead is known to enter the mother's milk and thus be passed onto the baby during breast feeding — it can also pass across the placenta to the developing foetus in the uterus. Lead exposure is known to affect the nervous system of young children, as well as causing spontaneous abortion, stillbirths and infertility.

Q   Do the **Control of Lead at Work Regulations 1998** apply to all work involving lead?

A   No, there is a requirement to undertake a suitable and sufficient assessment of whether the exposure to lead is liable to be significant. There are certain occupations which involve exposure to lead at such minimal levels that there are not considered to be any associated health risks. Examples of such work include low temperature lead melting as in plumbing and soldering operations, and work with: low solubility paints; materials which contain 1% or less lead; lead emulsions or pastes where lead dust or fumes cannot be given off; and clean metallic lead, eg ingots, pipes, etc. Even though these are not considered significant exposures, it is good practice to refer to the accompanying approved code of practice.

Legionnaires' Disease

Summary

Legionnaires' disease (legionellosis) is caused by a species of bacteria called *legionellae* (usually *Legionnella pneumophila*). The disease was first recognised in 1976, and is contracted by inhaling the bacteria in water droplets. It may be treated by using antibiotics, although fatalities have resulted from exposure to *legionellae*.

Practical Guidance

Installations which present a risk

Legionellae are naturally occurring, widespread bacteria, which are found in lakes, rivers, water systems, etc. Usually, the concentrations of the bacteria are too low to present a risk to health. However, if conditions favour proliferation of the bacteria, outbreaks of the diseases they cause, such as legionnaire's disease, may occur. Between 100 and 200 cases of legionnaires' disease are reported voluntarily to the Communicable Diseases Surveillance Centre each year.

Certain installations present a risk of legionnaires' disease due to a number of factors which allow the rapid growth and spread of *legionellae*, including:

- areas of still water
- presence of sludge, scale, rust or algae, which provide nutrients for the bacteria
- a temperature in the range of 20°C and 45°C (the optimal temperature is 37°C, ie body temperature)
- the formation and dispersal of fine water droplets or spray.

Examples of installations which present a risk of legionnaires' disease include the following:

- air conditioning systems
- industrial cooling systems
- spa baths and whirlpools
- fire sprinkler systems
- hot and cold water systems
- showers.

Risk assessment

An assessment of risk of potential exposure to micro-organisms, including *legionellae*, must be carried out under the **Control of Substances Hazardous to Health Regulations 1999** (COSHH). The assessment should take into account any existing control measures, such as system disinfection. The assessment should consider:

- the effects of exposure to *legionellae* and how severe they are, eg legionnaires' disease, which may produce severe, short-term illness (which can result in permanent health effects) and may cause death (the fatality rate for sporadic cases is around 10%)
- the likelihood of exposure to sufficient levels of the bacteria to cause disease, which will depend on whether the factors outlined under Installations which present a risk above, eg an installation which has pools of still, untreated water at 37°C, sufficient algal growth and widespread dispersal of fine water droplets (*legionellae* may be dispersed up to 150m) would be a high-risk installation
- the routes of exposure, ie inhalation
- who is likely to be exposed, bearing in mind that people both on and off the premises may be exposed, and some people are more susceptible, eg the elderly, people who are already ill (such as those in hospitals), and people who smoke.

Control measures

If the assessment shows that there is a significant risk from *legionellae*, COSHH requires control measures to be devised and implemented. The person responsible should prepare a scheme for the prevention of legionnaires' disease (and other diseases caused by *legionellae*), and make sure this scheme is implemented. Possible control measures are outlined below, and are also given in much more detail in HSE guidance HSG70: *Control of Legionellosis, Including Legionnaires' Disease.*

The following checks are suggested for making sure the measures for controlling *legionellae* are effective.

Frequency	Action
Weekly	Check water quality
Monthly	Test water quality, eg by a water treatment specialist
Monthly	Check the temperature at the nearest and furthest tap from the calorifier after running the water for one minute
Every six months	Disinfect the system
Annually	Check the temperature at all taps after running the water for one minute

Annually	Check the insides of water tanks and calorifiers for rust, scale, sludge, etc
Annually	Check the condition of the pipework
Annually	Check and replace filters and softeners at the frequency specified by the manufacturer

Notification

Under the **Notification of Cooling Towers and Evaporative Condensers Regulations 1992**, people in control of non-domestic premises must give their local authority notification of any "notifiable devices" on their premises, ie cooling towers and evaporative condensers such as air conditioning systems. The notification must be made on an HSE approved form containing the following information:

- address of the premises
- name, address and telephone number of the person in control
- location of the notifiable devices on the premises.

Reporting legionellosis

Cases of legionellosis, such as legionnaires' disease, must be reported to the relevant enforcing authority under the **Reporting of Injuries, Diseases and Dangerous Occurrences Regulations 1995**. Form F2508A, which is available from HSE Books, must be used for reporting occupational diseases such as legionellosis.

Questions and Answers

Q What is legionellosis?

A Legionellosis is the name given to a group of diseases caused by the *legionellae* bacteria. It includes legionnaires' disease, pontiac fever and humidifier fever.

Q How can hot and cold water systems present a risk of legionnaires' disease?

A The conditions of water in hot and cold water systems may be suitable for the excessive growth of *legionellae*. Although the systems do not generate fine water droplets as part of their operation as air conditioning systems do, water spray is formed when the water from the tap hits the basin. People standing near the basin while the tap is running may inhale the water droplets, and be exposed to the bacteria in this way.

Q The water from our drinks machine does not seem very hot. Is there a risk of catching legionnaires' disease by drinking this water?

A Legionnaires' disease is spread by inhaling fine water droplets. There has been no evidence that it can be contracted by ingestion or from contact between people, so drinking water should be safe, even if it contains the bacteria.

Q What should I consider when selecting hot or cold water systems?

A There are a number of factors which should affect your decision, such as:

- the distribution systems should be enclosed
- water tanks should be covered
- it should be easy to remove scale and sludge, etc which has built up in calorifiers or tanks
- the design should avoid "dead legs" where water stands undisturbed
- parts of the system which are used infrequently should be fitted with isolating valves
- hot water pipes should not be sited so close to cold water pipes that the cold water becomes warm.

Remember that designers, manufacturers and suppliers should supply systems which will prevent the build up of legionella, or at least reduce it to the lowest level reasonably practicable. They must also provide you with written information on the safe use of the system, including maintenance requirements.

Lifting Equipment and Lifting Operations

Summary

Cranes, hoists, lifts, chains, ropes and lifting tackle are an essential part of many businesses and must be maintained and operated correctly. These terms include every item from the largest static or mobile crane down to the smallest lifting attachment such as an eyebolt.

Practical Guidance

General duties

Existing legislation relating to cranes, hoists and lifting gear was old and inconsistent. The **Lifting Operations and Lifting Equipment Regulations 1998** now apply to all work situations and provide a uniform and simplified approach.

The general duties imposed by s.2 of the **Health and Safety at Work, etc Act 1974** apply, in particular the duty to provide safe plant and systems of work, as well as appropriate training and instruction.

Lifting equipment means work equipment for lifting and lowering loads and includes its attachments used for anchoring, fixing and supporting it. This means anything from the simplest lifting sling to the largest tower crane. Lifting operations means any operation concerned with the lifting or lowering of a load using lifting equipment. Lifting or lowering of loads manually would be subject to the **Manual Handling Operations Regulations 1992** but if any sling or similar piece of lifting equipment was used, these may be subject to these Regulations.

Regulation 8 contains straightforward but vital duties to ensure safe lifting operations (the lifting or lowering of a load). Each must be properly planned by a competent person, be appropriately supervised, and carried out in a safe manner.

A major addition to any previous provisions is that on lifting equipment for lifting persons. Although this was probably drafted primarily with equipment like fork-lift trucks fitted with access platforms, man-riding cranes, etc in mind, it will also apply to the type of hoist used for patients in health care premises.

Requirements under the Lifting Operations and Lifting Equipment Regulations 1998

The **Lifting Operations and Lifting Equipment Regulations 1998** (LOLER) replaced most of the existing sectoral law relating to the use of lifting equipment, and also apply to areas such as agriculture where there has never been specific legislation relating to lifting equipment. LOLER requires the risks from lifting operations and lifting equipment to be safely managed, and contains requirements relating to:

- equipment strength and stability
- positioning and installation
- marking
- thorough examination and testing
- record keeping.

The Regulations apply to any relevant equipment provided for use at work, and also to the self-employed and to managers and supervisors responsible for lifting operations.

The main requirements of the Regulations are as follows:

Lifting equipment must be of adequate strength and stability for the particular load, and every part of the load and anything attached to it for lifting must be of adequate strength.

Any piece of equipment for lifting individuals can be used safely without risk to those in the carrier, and has devices to prevent the carrier falling and to facilitate the safe rescue of anyone trapped in the carrier.

The employer must ensure that the equipment is installed and positioned so as to reduce the risk, as far as reasonably practicable, of the equipment or any load striking a person, or from any load drifting, falling freely or being unintentionally released. There should also be appropriate devices to prevent any person from falling down a shaft or hoistway.

Machinery and accessories for lifting loads should be marked to indicate their safe working loads, and accessories should also be marked with any other information required pertaining to their characteristics, to ensure their safe use. Where the particular configuration of machinery or components affects its safe use, the equipment should be appropriately marked, or alternatively relevant information must be kept with the equipment. Any equipment intended for lifting individuals should be clearly marked as being for this purpose, and any equipment which should not be used for lifting individuals, but which might be mistaken for such equipment, should also be clearly marked.

Any lifting or lowering operation involving lifting equipment must be:

- properly planned by a competent person
- appropriately supervised
- carried out in a safe manner.

A thorough examination should be carried out before any lifting equipment is first used except where the equipment is new or where appropriate documentation of such an examination is obtained with the equipment. Where the safety of lifting equipment is dependent upon its installation conditions it must be thoroughly examined after installation but before its first use, and similarly whenever it is moved to a different location. Any equipment which is exposed to conditions where deterioration may occur, and where such deterioration may give rise to danger, should be thoroughly examined in accordance with an examination scheme as follows:

- every six months for equipment for lifting individuals
- every six months for lifting accessories
- every 12 months for other lifting equipment
- after any incident or circumstances which may have affected the safety or integrity of the equipment.

Where appropriate, equipment should also be examined at suitable intervals between these inspections by a competent person. An employer should ensure that no lifting equipment leaves his undertaking, or is used in his undertaking, without written evidence of such examinations.

The requirements for a thorough examination are given in Schedule 1 to the Regulations.

Any person carrying out a thorough examination on behalf of an employer is required to:

- notify the employer immediately of any defect which affects the safety of the equipment
- where there is an existing or imminent risk of serious injury to send a copy of the report as soon as is practicable to the relevant enforcing authority
- maintain a signed record of the thorough examination to the employer and to any organisation from which the equipment has been hired or leased.

The employer must then ensure that the equipment is not used until the defect(s) specified in such a report have been rectified.

The employer must keep:

- any EC declarations of conformity relating to the equipment
- all records of thorough examinations for specified periods of time.

Additional requirements for construction, docks and shipyards

- Most jib cranes (with fixed or derricking jibs) must be fitted with an approved automatic safe working load indicator.
- Hooks must be specially shaped "safety" hooks or be fitted with a safety catch.
- Drivers and banksmen should be 18 or over, and must be competent (trainee drivers/banksmen may be under 18 but must be under the direct supervision of a competent person).
- Crane drivers must be competent and authorised by the employer before operating any lifting devices.

Annealing chains

Annealing of chains and certain lifting gear was required by the Factories Act and the Regulations but these requirements were brought into place when low-grade steel and wrought iron were in widespread use for manufacture of lifting tackle. These materials can work-harden in use and annealing to relieve this is required every 6 months (chains/slings of 13mm bar or less, or chains used for handling molten metal or slag) or 14 months (for other chains and tackle) as appropriate. Equipment not in regular use should be annealed as necessary. Most modern lifting tackle is manufactured from high-grade steel and is usually exempt from the requirement.

Banksman signals

Confusion between crane drivers and other persons guiding them when the load cannot be seen has resulted in many serious accidents. Only clear, agreed signals must be used and the standard ones are specified in Schedule 1 of the **Health and Safety (Safety Signs and Signals) Regulations 1996**.

The banksman must be clearly visible and identifiable to the driver, who must only accept visual signals from that identified person.

Reporting incidents

All relevant persons must be aware of the reporting requirements for dangerous occurences involving cranes, etc. Under the **Reporting of Injuries, Diseases and Dangerous Occurrences Regulations 1995**, the collapse, overturning or failure of any load bearing part of the following is a notifiable dangerous occurrence whether or not anyone is injured:

- lift or hoist
- crane or derrick
- mobile powered access platform
- access cradle or window cleaning cradle
- excavator
- pile-driving frame or rig having an overall height, when operating, of more than 7m
- fork-lift truck.

Questions and Answers

Q I operate an overhead crane in a factory. Does the driver have to go on a special course and pass a test to operate it?

A No, there are no requirements for a specific test but you are expected to ensure that anyone who operates the overhead crane is competent to do so. This may be satisfied by sending your crane driver on a course organised by the manufacturer, having the manufacturer send someone to carry out training, assessment of the driver's existing skills and knowledge, etc.

Q Where can I find the standard signals to be used by our crane banksman?

A The **Health and Safety (Safety Signs and Signals) Regulations 1996** specify signals such as this. Refer to the Schedule 1 of the guidance to the Regulations (L64: *The Health and Safety (Safety Signs and Signals) Regulations 1996: Guidance on Regulations*).

Lighting

Summary

Lighting is concerned with provision of light, whether natural or artificial, as a basic need for people at work; it can affect safety, health, comfort, quality of work and visibility of hazards.

Practical Guidance

Definitions

Lighting installations comprise lamps, light fittings and control systems:

- there is a huge range of lamps, of different types and with different characteristics; this may be important for safety or quality reasons as colour rendering (ability to show a true colour) can vary
- light fittings support and protect the lamp; again the range is enormous and care must be taken in selection to ensure suitability with the task and the environment
- control systems range from a single switch to the sophisticated automatic energy saving systems.

There are three broad forms of lighting used at work:

- general lighting — provides a fairly uniform level of illumination over the entire working area
- localised lighting — provides different levels of illumination in different parts of the workplace to match the tasks being undertaken
- local lighting — normally takes the form of a low level of background lighting with specific light fittings close to the actual work area or task.

Designing lighting installations

When designing a new installation or assessing an existing one, the following should be taken account of:

- the purpose of the lighting — is it for general illumination of pedestrian walkways or for detailed precision work?
- the conditions in which it will operate — is it in a corrosive or potentially explosive atmosphere, is it outdoors and subject to adverse weather, or is it likely to be washed with hoses?
- potential problems with the workplace, such as high racking restricting placement of fittings or difficulty mounting fittings on a machine for local lighting.

This may involve several stages beginning with looking at the overall business and then at individual jobs or tasks. Employees should also be consulted about what they need for the job. In a warehouse two main areas may be identified for consideration. The storage areas would not require particularly high levels of illumination but the distribution of light units may be seriously influenced by the racking or other storage fittings. General guidance may be sought from documents such as those produced by the Chartered Institution of Building Services Engineers (CIBSE). The proposed design should be checked to ensure that it complies with the **Workplace (Health, Safety and Welfare) Regulations 1992** and any other relevant legislation.

There may be further specialist tasks for which lighting may need to be designed accordingly. A repacking and wrapping area/palletising area may require higher levels of lighting than the main storage area and it may need to be of different type — low-pressure sodium lamps may confuse colours and lead to mistakes.

Glare, discomfort and contrast

Anyone who has driven at night will have experienced glare from the headlights of an oncoming vehicle. "Discomfort glare", as the name suggests, causes discomfort but may not interfere completely with the task. "Disability glare" causes serious problems and may prevent the individual being able to see anything other than the bright light source. Both have obvious implications for safety and should be avoided where possible. Glare on display screens of computers is a common cause of poor posture, eye strain, headaches and general discomfort of the users.

Enough illumination must be provided to allow recognition between different surfaces whilst avoiding excessive contrast. An example of the effect of too much contrast would be looking inside a building doorway where there is bright sunshine, and not being able to see anything inside as the light level outside was so much greater than inside.

Maintaining lighting installations

Lighting must always be designed with ease of maintenance in mind. Lighting maintenance should be planned, but it can take several forms ranging from the replacement of individual lamps when necessary to regular 100% lamp replacement. The level and frequency of lamp replacement will depend on the criticality of the lighting and the atmosphere in which it operates.

The Approved Code of Practice to the **Workplace (Health, Safety and Welfare) Regulations 1992** (Workplace Regulations) requires lights to be replaced, repaired or cleaned as necessary, before the level of lighting becomes insufficient.

Emergency lighting

Although this is often thought of only in the context of the evacuation of premises in the event of a fire, emergency lighting may also be needed because of the design of the building and its interior fittings, or the type of work carried out. Should a failure of normal artificial lighting result in a risk of injury then additional emergency lighting might be necessary. Exposure to the risk of falls or working with machinery which is not fully guarded and depends on operator skill and observation to work safely would be examples.

Emergency lighting should be powered by an independent source to that of the normal lighting.

Lighting for construction work

Most temporary electrical lighting on a building site will be 110 volt with supply through a centre-tapped-to-earth transformer. This limits the potential shock voltage to 55 volts to earth. In some circumstances, like work inside a wet steel structure, this can still be sufficient to cause death and 25 volt or 12 volt DC lighting may be required.

Lamp disposal

Because of the variety of lamp types, methods of disposal must be chosen carefully. Broken lamps can carry a serious risk of injury and the contents of some can be toxic, either as dusts or vapour. Some can explode or ignite if broken and in contact with water.

Lamp crushing machines are available and should be considered if lighting installation maintenance is carried out in-house. Crushing and disposal within normal waste may be acceptable but this must be checked with the Local Authority responsible for waste collection and disposal. Depending on lamp type, there may be a return scheme to the supplier for those units replaced. Whatever method is used, those employees involved should be aware of the hazards, the correct procedures to follow, the use of personal protective equipment and appropriate first aid should they sustain an injury or be exposed to toxic contents.

Questions and Answers

Q I have been told by an Environmental Health Officer (EHO) that I must provide emergency lighting in my warehouse, but I thought fire precautions were the responsibility of the local Fire Authority (FA)?

A Yes, fire precautions are dealt with by the FA, but the EHO is probably concerned that you should provide emergency lighting to comply with the Workplace Regulations. Regulation 8 requires emergency lighting to be provided where employees would be exposed to danger in the event of failure of artificial lighting.

Q We have very good artificial lighting; do I still need to clean windows?

A Yes, regulation 8 of the Workplace Regulations requires suitable and sufficient lighting to be provided, so far as reasonably practicable, by natural light. The Approved Code of Practice (ACOP) to the Regulations states that windows and skylights should be cleaned regularly where possible.

Q   No one can tell me what standard of lighting to have in different areas. Where is this information?

A   There are many sources but the ones quoted in the ACOP (see above) are the guides published by the Chartered Institute of Building Services Engineers, Delta House, 222 Balham High Road, London SW12 9BS.

Loading Bays

Summary

Loading bays are areas where vans, trucks and other large vehicles stop to load and unload goods, post, etc. The combination of pedestrians and large vehicles in one, relatively small area can lead to accidents, so a safe system of work must be in place.

Practical Guidance

Traffic routes

Loading bays come under the definition of "traffic route" in the **Workplace (Health, Safety and Welfare) Regulations 1992** (Workplace Regulations). The Workplace Regulations require traffic routes to be organised so that pedestrians and vehicles circulate safely. Traffic routes must be:

- suited for their intended purpose, eg as a loading bay
- large enough, eg to allow large vehicles to enter the loading bay safely
- in a suitable position, eg loading bays should be sited as close as possible to the area where the items to be loaded or unloaded are stored
- sufficient in number, eg there should be enough loading bays to ensure health and safety so that, for example, trucks and vans are not backed up on to the road while waiting to load/unload because the bay is in constant use.

Employers must take measures to make sure that:

- traffic routes do not give rise to risks to the health and safety of people working nearby
- vehicle routes are separated from pedestrian routes
- where vehicles and pedestrians have to use the same routes, they are sufficiently separated
- doors and gates which open on to a vehicle route are sufficiently separated.

Condition of loading bays

The Workplace Regulations require that the surface of traffic routes, including loading bays, must be:

- suitable for their intended purpose, eg loading bay floors must be strong enough to bear the weight of large vehicles loaded with heavy goods
- kept free of obstructions, articles or substances which are likely to cause slips, trips or falls, eg loading bays should be kept clear of items at all times, and anything which is being loaded or unloaded should be left where it will not create a trip hazard.

Construction

Under the **Construction (Health, Safety and Welfare) Regulations 1996**, traffic routes, including loading bays, must:

- not create a risk to the health and safety of people working nearby
- separate pedestrians and vehicles sufficiently
- have any pedestrian doors or gates which lead on to them fitted so that pedestrians can see approaching traffic from a safe place
- have adequate means of warning where there is a risk of people being crushed or trapped by vehicles.

The 1996 Regulations specifically require loading bays to have at least one exit point which is designated for pedestrians only. If a gate intended for vehicles cannot be safely used by pedestrians, there must be a clearly marked pedestrian door in the immediate vicinity. All pedestrian doors must be kept clear of obstructions.

In relation to loading bays and other traffic routes, the 1996 Regulations also require the following:

- vehicles may only be used on traffic routes if they are free from obstruction and have sufficient clearance
- if it is not reasonably practicable for the route to be free from obstruction and have sufficient clearance, vehicle drivers must be given adequate warning of this.

Risk assessment

Under the **Management of Health and Safety at Work Regulations 1999**, a suitable and sufficient assessment of risk must be carried out for all work activities. This would include a risk assessment for loading bays. Once the risks have been identified they must be controlled, and employees must be given adequate information, instruction and training.

Manual handling

The **Manual Handling Operations Regulations 1992** will apply to the activities carried out in loading bays. The loading and unloading of articles will involve lifting and carrying. Where possible, manual handling should be eliminated, eg by the use of mechanical lifting devices. However, in many situations found in loading bays, manual handling is necessary. Under the 1992 Regulations, these tasks must be assessed, based on the task, the load, the environment and the individual.

Once the activity has been assessed, control measures must be put into place to prevent or reduce the risks from manual handling tasks. For a loading bay, these may include:

- using mechanical means for moving loads, such as barrows, pallet trucks or fork-lift trucks
- restricting loading and unloading activities to designated people, who have been shown by the assessment to be at a low risk of injury due to their personal capability

- locating the storage area for articles which are loaded or unloaded close to the loading bay, so that the distance for carrying these articles is as short as possible
- avoiding situations where articles have to be carried from one level to another, eg from the back of a truck three feet high to the ground level, for example by providing mechanical devices
- making sure that the load is split into smaller portions, for example by using smaller sacks to transport goods in.

Equipment safety

Any equipment used in loading bays comes under the requirements of the **Provision and Use of Work Equipment Regulations 1998** (PUWER). Under PUWER, all equipment provided for use at work must be:
- suitable for its intended purpose
- maintained in good working order
- solely for the use of people who are adequately trained, if the equipment poses a specific risk.

Equipment, such as automatic gates, must be provided with stop controls and emergency stop controls where appropriate. These controls must be readily accessible and easily identifiable.

Hazardous substances

Under the **Control of Substances Hazardous to Health Regulations 1999** (COSHH), an assessment of risk must be carried out wherever there is a risk of exposure to hazardous substances, and suitable control measures put into place.

In the case of loading bays, potential exposure to hazardous substances would include exhaust fumes from vehicles. If exhaust fumes present a risk to the health of people working in loading bays, such as in relatively confined areas, vehicles should turn their engines off when they are not in motion, eg when loading and unloading. If this is not possible, other controls must be put into place, such as attaching a pipe to the point of emission and redirecting the fumes outdoors.

Questions and Answers

Q   What are the hazards associated with loading bays?
A   A risk assessment must be carried out for loading bays. The hazards found there are likely to include:
- injuries caused by unsafe manual handling methods
- slips and trips caused by obstructions, spillages, uneven floors, etc
- being crushed, trapped or hit by moving vehicles
- being hit by objects falling from the vehicle or items which have been stacked unsafely
- injuries to the feet if they are crushed by objects being dropped, or run over by vehicles or fork-lift trucks

- harmful effects of inhaling vehicle exhaust fumes
- effects of being subject to cold temperatures, both due the temperature itself and due to the cold making certain tasks more difficult to carry out
- being struck by automatic gates
- increased fire hazard caused by the storage of goods.

This list just gives some examples, and it is not exhaustive.

Q What personal protective equipment (PPE) should be provided for work in loading bays?

A Your risk assessment should have identified where PPE is needed. Remember it should be only used as a last resort where other control measures will not provide adequate control. The following PPE is likely to be needed in loading bays:

- safety footwear to prevent foot injury
- protective gloves to protect hands during loading and unloading, and to keep the hands warm in cold conditions
- head protection, where there is a risk of objects falling from a height
- warm clothing to protect against cold conditions
- high visibility clothing where necessary to make pedestrians more obvious to vehicle drivers.

Of course, all PPE should meet the requirements of the **Personal Protective Equipment at Work Regulations 1992**.

Q How high should loading bays be?

A The answer depends on the vehicles that use the loading bay. There must be adequate clearance for the tallest vehicle likely to use the bay. However, it should be remembered that the higher the ceiling, the more difficult it is to clean it or heat the area.

Local Exhaust Ventilation

Summary

Local exhaust ventilation (LEV) is the term used to describe a combination of ductwork, fans, enclosures or hoods and cleaning units that is used to control the emission of substances hazardous to health.

Practical Guidance

Introduction

Some substances encountered at work may cause significant damage to the worker's health, these include:

- dusts and particulates
- gases
- vapours
- fumes.

These substances can enter the body and cause harm in various ways. Health and safety legislation requires an employer to protect people at work by preventing exposure to hazardous substances or, where prevention is not reasonably practicable, by controlling exposure. Where control, rather than prevention, is to be used, there is a hierarchy of control measures as follows:

- total enclosure of the process to prevent the substance entering the workplace
- partial enclosure and use of LEV, to remove the substance before it can enter the workplace atmosphere
- general ventilation, where there is a flow of clean air into and out of the workplace, but no specific control of the contaminant
- using systems of work that minimise the chances of the escape of hazardous materials
- use of personal protective equipment.

LEV design

In practice, all the methods of control listed above should be considered when designing an LEV system, as a combination of measures may often be the most effective solution. The basic components of an LEV system are:

- a hood or other capture inlet to collect the contaminant close to its source
- ductwork to carry the contaminated air away from the source
- a filter or other air-cleaning device to remove the contaminant from the air in the ductwork
- an air mover such as a fan to provide the necessary air flow

- further ductwork to expel the cleaned air at an appropriate exhaust point (usually to the external atmosphere but in some cases back into the work area).

It is important that LEV design and installation are undertaken by a competent person; the specification of individual components, and the way in which they are used within the system, are complex issues, and small variations in design have a significant effect on the efficiency of the system as a whole. Similarly, any alterations to an existing LEV system should only be undertaken with competent assistance.

In order to design an efficient LEV system, consideration will need to be given to:
- the nature of the contaminant
- the way the contaminant is generated
- the size of the contaminant particles produced.

This often involves the need for sampling within the workplace, using both personal samplers and static samplers, to build up a picture of the concentrations of contaminants within the work area.

Below is a diagram of a basic LEV system.

Inlets to LEV systems

The inlet to the system is the hood or enclosure surrounding the source of contamination; the purpose of the inlet is to prevent the contaminant entering the work atmosphere. The size and design of the inlet will depend upon the nature of the contaminant and the work process itself. The effective design of the inlet is fundamental to the efficacy of the LEV system, as the system will be ineffective unless the contaminant is effectively captured. Inlets should be designed to enclose the source as far as possible, but restrictions will often be generated by the need for access to the work. There are two main types of inlet:

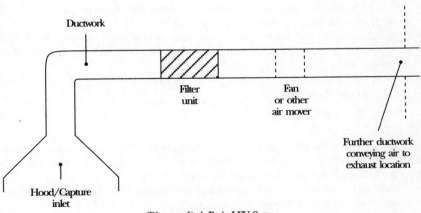

(Diagram 1) A Basic LEV System

- partial enclosures such as extraction booths and fume cupboards, where the source of contamination is located within the enclosure, and air flows from one area of the enclosure to another, taking the contaminant with it
- hoods which collect or capture the contaminant as close to the source as possible and direct it into the ensuing ductwork; hoods will vary greatly in shape and size, depending on the application, and because they do not completely enclose the source they cannot be relied upon to give complete control at all times.

Ductwork and air flows

The ductwork carries the contaminated air from the inlet, via the air cleaning device, to the exhaust point. For dusts and fumes, the design of the ductwork should be such that the air velocity is high enough to keep the particles suspended in the air until they reach the cleaning device. Ductwork should be made of material suitable for the particular application and should be sufficiently durable, eg resistant to chemical damage and mechanical wear and tear. Flexible ducting may be appropriate in specific situations but flow resistances tend to be higher and wear tends to be greater. Covered access holes should be provided at appropriate intervals to facilitate cleaning and testing.

Where a system has more than one inlet, it should be designed to ensure that the correct balance of air flows through each branch or inlet. The air flow in each branch will be a function of:

- the resistance of the inlet
- the length, diameter and resistance to flow within the branch
- the flow conditions at the junction between branches.

Air cleaners

There are three main types of air cleaners:

- air filters, which are designed to deal with large volumes of air, with low resistance to air flow, such as in an air-conditioning system
- particulate dust and fume collectors, such as cyclones, fabric filters and electrostatic precipitators, which are designed to handle higher dust concentrations
- devices to remove gases, mists and vapours by chemical absorption, condensation or combustion.

Air movers

In most LEV systems the air movement is provided by a fan; other options include turbo-exhausters and compressed-air driven air movers. Many types and sizes of fans are available, falling into two main categories:

- centrifugal — where air is thrown off at high velocity into the casing; these are used for all but the most basic LEV systems
- axial flow — which can only overcome lower flow resistances.

Selection of an appropriate air mover for an LEV system will depend upon several factors including:

- required air flow, both volume and speed
- the nature and properties of the contaminant
- the operating temperature
- noise levels
- space constraints.

Exhaust point
The point at which the cleaned air may be discharged will depend upon the nature of the contaminant and the residual levels within the discharged air. Further legislation may apply (eg the **Environmental Protection Act 1990**) to particular processes. In most cases the exhaust point should be such as to prevent the contaminated air re-entering the building. Any ductwork outside the building should be sufficiently robust as to withstand the necessary conditions.

Commissioning, maintenance and testing
Commissioning is the formal procedure used to bring an LEV system into use after installation. Initial testing should include similar sampling to that undertaken before the design of the system, to ensure its efficacy. Maintenance procedures should be designed to ensure the continuing efficiency of the system.

Questions and Answers

Q How often should LEV be examined and tested?

A The minimum requirements under the **Control of Substances Hazardous to Health Regulations 1999** (COSHH) for formal examination and testing of LEV stipulate an interval of not more than 14 months between tests. It is, however, important that managers and employees check the performance and correct use of LEV on a daily basis, and are aware of circumstances that might indicate unsatisfactory LEV performance (eg build-up of fumes within the work area). It is also important to have a regular planned maintenance schedule for LEV.

Q For how long should I keep records of examination and testing of LEV?

A Records maintained under COSHH must be kept for a minimum of five years; however, there is no stipulation as to the form these records should take.

Q We have a number of premises at which small amounts of welding are carried out, and we have identified hazards from exposure to the particular welding fumes. Do we need to install LEV equipment at all our premises?

A Where a COSHH assessment has identified a need for particular controls to exposure, this must be implemented. However, in this case it may be more cost-effective for you to consider installing the equipment at one central location for use by all operatives, or alternatively to employ a mobile fitter with the relevant equipment.

Lone Workers

Summary

People who work by themselves without close or direct supervision are lone workers. One person working in a fixed establishment, workers in remote locations, mobile workers, those working at other employers' premises or from home, and service workers are all examples.

Practical Guidance

When addressing the issue of lone working it is important to distinguish between employees finding themselves alone by chance, and work which is specifically intended to be carried out in isolation. The first instance may be addressed by simply implementing a procedure whereby employees alert fellow workers to the fact that they are leaving an area, and the remaining person will be on his or her own.

There is no general prohibition in health and safety law of working alone. However, when determining a safe system of work it is likely that there will be a need for additional controls to be put in place.

General duties

As far as the **Health and Safety at Work, etc Act 1974** is concerned, the responsibilities of the employer to ensure the safety of lone workers do not differ much from that of the responsibility to ensure the safety of employees working in a group or under close supervision. The responsibilities cannot be transferred to the employees because they are working alone or remotely.

The employer must ensure, so far as is reasonably practicable, the health, safety and welfare of employees whilst at work. When addressing this responsibility, the employer will need to consider in detail the hazards and risks involved in lone working and must take steps to minimise the hazards and so reduce the risk.

The employer must also provide and maintain safe plant and systems of work that are without risk to health. Special consideration should be given to establishing a system of work for lone workers. Plant includes any machinery, equipment or appliances in use.

Employees have a responsibility to take reasonable care of their own safety and that of anyone else who may be affected by their actions. They are also required to report any defects found with plant or equipment.

The employer must also provide adequate information, instruction and training. Lone workers need to fully understand the risks involved in the work and the necessary precautions to be taken, and they must be sufficiently experienced in the work. Training is particularly important to control, guide and help in situations of uncertainty where there is limited supervision. Lone workers should be sure of when to stop work and seek advice from a supervisor.

Although lone workers cannot be subject to constant supervision, it is still an employer's duty to provide appropriate control of the work. The extent of supervision required will depend on the risks involved and the proficiency and experience of the employee to identify and handle safety issues.

Prohibition of lone working

There is no general prohibition on working alone, but there is specific legislation where the hazards of a particular type of work have been identified as being too great for people to work unaccompanied. In these cases it is stipulated that at least two people must be involved in the work and it is specified that the safe systems of work are to be followed. Examples are contained in the following Regulations.

1. Under the **Diving at Work Regulations 1997**, a supervisor must be appointed to take control of an exercise.
2. Lone working is prohibited during certain fumigation work and other work with substances hazardous to health, under the **Control of Substances Hazardous to Health Regulations 1999**.
3. Except where an exemption has been issued, accompaniment is needed when unloading petrol at certain premises under the **Carriage of Dangerous Goods by Road Regulations 1996**, and for the supervision of vehicles carrying certain explosives (**Carriage of Explosives by Road Regulations 1996**).
4. The **Electricity at Work Regulations 1989** prohibit work on live electrical systems, except in certain circumstances. If live electrical work is necessary, suitable precautions must be taken, and these would include using a permit-to-work system. Anyone who is carrying out live work under a permit-to-work should be accompanied by someone who is familiar with the work and is capable of acting safely and effectively in an emergency.

Risk assessment

Even where work activities are not covered by the above legislation, there is a general duty to carry out a risk assessment of working alone. This requires the employer to identify the hazards of the work, assess the risks involved and devise and implement safe working arrangements to ensure that the risks are either eliminated or adequately controlled. The assessment should consider the following factors.

1. Foreseeable emergencies. It must be recognised that a lone worker is more vulnerable when the unexpected occurs, eg fire, equipment failure, illness and accidents, and violence.

2. The fitness and suitability of the person to work alone. Will working alone require additional physical or mental stamina? Is there a medical condition that makes the individual unsuitable for working alone? Is that person competent? Has he or she received appropriate training?
3. Whether the work can be done safely by a lone worker.

First aid

The employer is responsible for providing appropriate first aid facilities. In the case of lone workers, the employees should be provided with travelling first aid kits if they work in isolated locations, in places where access to emergency facilities is difficult or with dangerous tools or machinery.

Questions and Answers

Q What systems are available for monitoring lone workers?
A Some examples are:
  - the worker is visited
  - the worker telephones a permanently staffed point at specified, regular intervals
  - the worker carries an emergency call button that connects to a permanently manned point
  - the worker carries an automatic radio-signalling lone work device which is monitored at a central point.

Q Should lone workers be issued with first aid kits?
A If lone workers are required to work in isolated locations where access to emergency facilities is difficult or emergency facilities are a great distance away, or where the worker is required to operate dangerous tools or machinery, the provision of a travelling first aid kit would be a sensible precaution.

Q Is there any legislation which prohibits lone working?
A Although there is no general prohibition on working alone, there is specific legislation where the hazards of a particular type of work have been identified as being too great for people to work unaccompanied. In these cases it is stipulated that at least two people must be involved in the work and that a specified safe system of work must be followed. Examples of such Regulations include the **Diving at Work Regulations 1997**, the **Electricity at Work Regulations 1989** and certain fumigation work under the **Control of Substances Hazardous to Health Regulations 1999**.

Machinery Guarding/Controls

Summary

Employers must ensure that risk assessments have been carried out on all machinery used within the workplace, that necessary steps have been taken to prevent access to dangerous parts of machinery and that suitable controls have been installed.

Practical Guidance

Legislation requires an employer to carry out a risk assessment of all risks associated with the undertaking; this is particularly significant where dangerous machinery is in use.

In devising suitable control to combat risks associated with machinery there is a hierarchy of risk control principles.

1. Eliminate risks by:
   - avoiding processes altogether
   - substitution of dangerous substances or machinery with less dangerous options.
2. Control risks at source by using engineering controls such as:
   - suitable guards to protect the operator from dangerous parts
   - automatic machinery which is remotely controlled, removing the operator from the danger zone
   - enclosing the process so that exposure to a hazardous substance cannot take place.
3. Minimise risks by formulating and using suitable systems of work.
4. Minimise risks by the use of personal protective equipment.

Machinery hazards

Machinery hazards fall into two main classes:
- mechanical, from contact with machinery or material being machined
- non-mechanical, eg from chemicals, electricity or fire.

It is important to remember that minor hazards which pose little risk in isolation can become a major risk when combined with other hazards.

The selection of safeguards

Guards or safety devices suitable for the purpose should be used where there are hazards that cannot be eliminated or sufficiently controlled by design. Many of the accidents involving moving machinery are preventable by the use of reasonably practicable safeguards. About half of these preventable accidents occur because employers have failed to provide proper safeguards, and the other half are caused by employees removing the safeguards that have been provided.

The choice of guard or safety device must take into account the mechanical and other hazards involved. They must be compatible with the work environment and designed so they cannot be easily removed or evaded. They must cause the minimum interference with the operation of the machine in order to reduce the temptation to try to bypass them.

Guards and safety devices must:

- be strongly constructed
- present no additional hazards
- be difficult to bypass or make non-operational
- be positioned far enough away from the danger zone
- cause minimum obstruction to the operator's view of the production process
- enable routine maintenance such as lubrication or essential work to be carried out on the installation and/or replacement of tools; during maintenance, access should be restricted to the area where the work has to be done (if possible without the guard or safety device having to be removed).

Safeguards may have to perform one or more of the following functions:

- prevent access to the space enclosed by the guard
- contain or capture materials, workpieces, liquids, dusts, fumes
- reduce noise.

Additionally, they may need to have particular properties in relation to electricity, temperature, fire, vibration, visibility, etc.

Safeguards should be selected according to a hierarchy of reliability to give maximum protection.

1. Fixed enclosing guards (integral castings, permanently secured).
2. Other guards (perimeter fencing, moving guards) or protection devices (light curtains, pressure mats, proximity and displacement switches).
3. Protection appliances that distance parts of the body or clothing from the dangerous part (push-sticks, mechanical holding devices, jigs).
4. The provision of sufficient and proper information, instruction, training and supervision.

Controls

A control is the manual actuator that the operator touches to start a machine, change a function, such as speed or direction, and finally to stop the machine. It may operate directly but is more often a part of a control system incorporating sensors, limit devices, brakes, clutches and other components. A control may consist of nothing more than a simple on/off switch. New equipment will probably be supplied with appropriate controls; machines consisting of linked sub-assemblies may need a systematic risk assessment to determine the best positions for controls. The development of programmable electronic systems has brought into the workplace new and less obvious risks that cannot be easily assessed.

Controls must be positioned out of any danger zone, except those that perform a safety function, such as emergency stop controls. Emergency stop controls should be provided at every control position, and their operation should not increase the risk of injury from another source.

Operators should have a clear view from the control position so that no one is placed at risk when a machine is started up. On large or complex continuous production machinery this may not be possible, and procedures such as signalling will have to be devised to overcome the problem.

Standard layouts and markings complying with British Standards should be adopted to avoid confusion. Start controls and other functional controls should be constructed and positioned so that they cannot be operated by accident. It must not be possible for a machine to restart after a stoppage by the resetting of a protective device or by the restoration of power after a power failure. A stop control should be sited near every start control.

Controls must be clearly identifiable and easily distinguishable from each other by positioning, shape, colour, size, or labelling and their movement should be consistent with their effect (ie up for up, left for left, etc). Where a control is designed to perform several different actions, such as a programmable electronic system, then the action to be performed must be clearly displayed and subject to a confirmation command where necessary.

Components and systems must be reliable to avoid unforeseen and potentially hazardous machine behaviour. On certain installations, where the start control is in such a position in relation to the equipment that the operator cannot be certain that people are not in the vicinity, it may be appropriate for a warning signal to be given and the machine started through a predetermined time delay. Where a malfunction creates a hazard (such as uncontrolled temperature or pressure) sensors should be used to trigger an automatic or audible alarm. The manner and type of any audible or visual alarm signals should be known to all those likely to be affected.

Instrument displays and other information devices must be visible from the control position and their function known. The information displayed must be continuous, unambiguous and easily understood.

Questions and Answers

Q   If a machine, or parts of a machine, are at an extreme of temperature, but are not otherwise dangerous, would it be sufficient to post warning notices rather than installing guards?

A   The **Provision and Use of Work Equipment Regulations 1998** (PUWER) require that any work equipment that is at a very high or very low temperature must have protection where appropriate. It also accepts, however, that in some cases machinery must be accessible to operate, and in these cases the relevant risk assessments should determine the appropriate combination of controls (eg training, warning notices, personal protective equipment, safe systems of work, etc).

Q   What are the main mechanical hazards associated with machinery for which guards might be necessary?

A   There are five main mechanical hazards associated with machinery, as follows:
   • trapping, where moving parts draw in and trap an individual
   • impact, where moving parts hit an individual
   • contact, where moving or stationary parts that are hot, cold, sharp, abrasive or electrically live come into contact with an individual
   • entanglement of clothes, hair, jewellery, etc in any part of a machine
   • ejection of machine components or material being processed.

   More details are given in BS 5304: *Code of Practice for the Safety of Machinery.*

Q   What information and instructions should be available to employees and supervisors in respect of machinery?

A   Regulation 8 of the **Provision and Use of Work Equipment Regulations 1998** (PUWER) requires the following information to be available in a readily comprehensible form:
   • the methods by which and the conditions in which the machinery may be used
   • any forseeable abnormal situations and the action to be taken if they occur
   • any conclusions to be drawn from experience in using the machinery.

Management

Summary

Enforcing officers and insurance companies are increasingly looking for evidence of effective health and safety management in workplaces. Employers are required to identify and determine health and safety strategies which are tailored to their own workplaces — based on the findings of their risk assessments.

Practical Guidance

The management of health and safety can be considered in two distinct ways: legal obligations and practical management. Both of these are equally important and together form a sound basis for managing health and safety within a workplace.

Legal issues

The main legislative provisions covering the management of health and safety at work are the **Health and Safety at Work, etc Act 1974** (HSW Act) and the **Management of Health and Safety at Work Regulations 1999** (MHSWR). Together these provide the legal framework for managing occupational health and safety within workplaces.

Broad goal-setting objectives are defined in the HSW Act. Employers are obliged to apply these to their own specific workplaces. It is not a prescriptive Act, it does not list "Dos and Don'ts", but instead lays down duties on certain individuals to safeguard health and safety.

Within these general duties there is an implicit requirement to carry out a risk assessment — employers cannot ensure their employees' health and safety if they do not know the hazards associated with their work activities and the measures necessary to control those hazards. MHSWR adds more detail to the HSW Act and makes the requirement to carry out a risk assessment explicit.

The Regulations contain the following provisions.

1. Employers must undertake a risk assessment of all the risks associated with work activities and work processes, and ensure it is regularly reviewed and revised. Such assessments should specifically address fire risks and risks to new and expectant mothers and young persons. Where five or more employees are employed, the significant findings of the risk assessments must be recorded.
2. Employers must have arrangements for planning, organising, controlling, monitoring and reviewing the necessary control measures identified in the risk assessments and for complying with all relevant legal requirements. Again, where there are more than five employees, these must be recorded.

3. Competent persons must be nominated to assist employers with health and safety arrangements and for implementing emergency procedures. The competent person may be an employee or an external specialist — in either case adequate resources must be provided for them to fulfil their duties.
4. Health surveillance programmes must be provided where the risk assessment has identified risks to health.
5. Appropriate emergency procedures must be implemented by competent persons in cases of serious and imminent danger. Where certain areas are restricted on the grounds of health and safety, access may only be authorised if the employee has received adequate health and safety instructions.
6. Appropriate training, during work hours, must be given to employees when recruited and then be updated on a regular basis. Relevant and understandable information must be provided to employees on: the risks identified by the risk assessment, the necessary control measures, the emergency procedures, the identity of competent persons and the risks identified by other employers sharing the workplace.
7. Employers sharing a workplace must co-operate and co-ordinate in matters of health and safety, including informing each other of the risks associated with their work and the controls which have been put in place to manage them.
8. Temporary workers working on the premises, eg agency staff, must be provided with understandable information to enable them to work safely and without risks to their health, or anyone else's.
9. Employers have a duty to ensure that employees are capable of performing the intended tasks. A task must be fitted to the person, never the person to the task.
10. Employees must work in accordance with any training they have received and report any shortcomings in the health and safety arrangements.

Practical management stages
The five main stages of health and safety management are:
- setting policies
- organising staff
- planning and setting standards
- measuring performance
- auditing and reviewing these four stages.

In many cases, health and safety management is dealt with in isolation, as a separate entity of the business. In practice, the organisations which are most successful at managing health and safety are those that integrate and incorporate health and safety into their general management philosophy.

Setting policies
Where there are five or more employees in a company, there must be a written health and safety policy. This policy should give an undertaking to comply with all relevant legislation, define health and safety responsibilities throughout all levels

of the organisation and define relevant safe working practices for the various work activities. The policy should also tie in with other policies in the organisation, such as quality and personnel procedures, to recognise employees as the organisation's most valuable resource.

The commitment and involvement of senior management is very important and health and safety should be a constant item on all board meeting and senior executive meeting agendas. In this way a positive health and safety culture will develop and become established.

Organising staff

Staff need to know what their health and safety responsibilities are and where those responsibilities stop. In addition, it is important to clarify who has authority over whom and in what circumstances. Co-operation is vital.

Communication pathways for health and safety should be clearly defined through all levels of staff so information can be gathered, acted upon and disseminated.

Planning and setting standards

In order to manage health and safety there must be objectives — what the organisation is aiming to achieve, and how. The plan must include methods to measure all standards and objectives that have been defined. Risk assessments will provide important basic information on the current state of the organisation and highlight areas where more effort is required.

Measuring performance

Tangible and achievable performance standards and targets will allow the company objectives to be measured and monitored. It is vital that performances which do not meet the original standards are addressed. Measurement parameters may include active and reactive systems.

Active systems include:
• workplace inspections and audits
• comparisons of actual performances against projected performances
• the regular review and revision of management and organisational objectives.

Reactive systems include:
• accident figures
• sickness absences
• exit interview feedback
• damage to equipment or property
• the purchase of relevant new equipment.

Auditing and reviewing

The management of health and safety will only work if it is continually reviewed and revised to take account of changes and developments in the workplace, such as new staff or equipment and different work processes. It is vital that findings of audits or other monitoring systems are taken up and implemented, and that the health and safety plan is consistently checked to see whether it needs reviewing and revising.

Questions and Answers

Q Are there any figures for the costs of accidents to employers?

A Yes. A survey carried out by the Health and Safety Executive calculated that the annual costs associated with poor health and safety to all UK employers was between £4.5 billion and £9.5 billion for the year 1990. In many cases, these costs are accepted as normal business losses, even though the main causative factors were often preventable.

Q Who can be considered a competent person?

A As with most references to competent persons there is no comprehensive definition of what a competent person is. In general terms, it is usually taken to mean someone who has the experience, knowledge, training and skills to perform any intended duties. External specialists do not have to be used if the necessary competencies are available in-house.

Q What does the term "safety culture" mean?

A "Safety culture" is the positive involvement and commitment to the organisation's health and safety policy of employees at every level and may be considered to consist of four key functions:

- competence — skills, training, knowledge and experience for all work-related activities
- control — defined health and safety responsibilities throughout all levels of the organisation
- co-operation — throughout all levels of the organisation
- communication — consultation (verbal, written and visible), both up and down the relevant communication pathways.

Manual Handling

Summary

Manual handling activities, ie activities which require bodily effort to move, lift or support any load, are widespread throughout all work undertakings and account for the highest proportion of lost time injuries — especially back injuries. In many cases, the injuries sustained were preventable.

Practical Guidance

Under the **Manual Handling Operations Regulations 1992**, all manual handling activities which involve a risk of injury should be avoided where possible. If it is not possible to avoid the activity, then an assessment of the associated risks should be undertaken, and the risks reduced to the lowest level possible. The assessment should take into account the load (both animate, ie people and animals and inanimate, ie boxes, furniture), the task, the environment in which the activity is performed and the capabilities of the employees to perform the activity safely.

Anatomy and related health problems

Health problems associated with manual handling often, but not always, involve the back; the neck and shoulders may also sustain injury. Commonly, the injuries build up over a period of time as a result of a succession of poor manual handling techniques; it is less common for one single event to cause injury. The anatomy of the back makes it particularly vulnerable to the pressures and strains of poor manual handling techniques. The spine is divided into three distinct regions — the cervical, thoracic and lumbar regions. Of these the cervical and lumbar regions are most prone to injury because of their flexibility and rotational movements — this mobility can put pressure on the discs which sit between the vertebrae and eventually the discs become displaced and/or out of shape, resulting in stiffness and pain. The thoracic region is the least mobile because of the restraining effect of the rib cage.

Loads

The load is the person, animal or object being lifted, moved or supported, and mistakenly is often the only factor taken into account when manual handling activities are considered.

For inanimate loads, the following load factors should be considered:
• weight
• dimensions, ie whether it is bulky/unwieldy

- flexibility/rigidity
- shifting/moving weight
- stability
- available and effective grip, ie presence of handles or straps
- inherent harmful or awkward properties, ie hot or cold, splinters, sharp edges, slippery surfaces
- imposed work rates outside the control of the employees.

In addition to the relevant factors listed above, the following points should also be included when considering the lifting or moving of people and animals.

For animate loads:

- their level of dependence or ability and willingness to assist themselves
- their level of comprehension and communication
- the likelihood of unpredictable behaviour, fits or spasms, fear and uncertainty of what is happening
- existing medical conditions, ie proneness to dislocations, brittle bones
- the presence of medical or scientific/research aids, eg body or limb braces, feeding or sample tubes, etc.

While the weight of a load should not be the only point considered for manual handling, many employers find numerical guidelines useful. The guidelines given below represent values which would normally be expected to be safe and which may be used to indicate whether a more detailed assessment is required.

Body Reference Points	Load Held Close to Body	Load Held at Arm's Length
Full height (arms above head)	10kg (5kg)	5kg (3.5kg)
Shoulder height	20kg (10kg)	10kg (5kg)
Elbow height	25kg (12.5kg)	15kg (7.5kg)
Knuckle height (arms by side)	20kg (10kg)	10kg (5kg)
Mid-lower leg	10kg (5kg)	5kg (3.5kg)

Note: Female weight guidelines are written in brackets.

Task

This is the description of the actual manual handling activity, eg lifting boxes, pushing trolleys, etc and is probably the most important element of the risk assessment. Many of the body movements involved in a manual handling activity will significantly reduce the ability of a person to safely handle loads. For example, the weight guidelines shown above will be reduced by 20% for a task that involves a 90° twist of the body, or by 50% when someone has to bend or stoop through 90°.

The following task factors should be considered:

- whether loads are required to be held away from the body

- twisting
- reaching upwards, downwards or across, eg retrieving heavy files from high, low or wide shelves
- the distance the load has to be carried
- stooping
- strenuous pushing or pulling
- static supporting of a load
- repetitive activities, ie the frequency at which the activity is carried out
- the duration of each activity.

Environment

The environment in which a manual handling activity is carried out can also have a significant effect on the overall risk rating of that activity. For example, a hot humid environment will increase the likelihood of fatigue over a shift. Similarly, a small cramped working area may mean more bending or stooping, or adoption of a bad working posture. Stairs, steps and other changes in floor level are also important considerations.

The following environmental factors should be considered:
- restricted working space
- poor lighting
- noise
- changes in floor level, including steps and stairs
- poorly maintained floor surfaces and other trip or slip hazards
- very hot or cold temperatures
- high humidity
- limited furniture layout alternatives.

Individuals

The capability of an individual to perform a manual handling activity must also be established — this may be a delicate process requiring trust and tact — confidentiality must be maintained. The factors listed below give some important indications of key considerations. The culture of the organisation should encourage individuals to take responsibility for their own health and safety, and to inform their managers of any relevant problems. This does not absolve the employer from any related duties, ie to provide suitable and sufficient aids, but should assist in the management of manual handling. Employees should have the right, with independent adjudication, to refuse to carry out any manual handling activity that they cannot perform safely.

The following individual factors should be considered:
- level of fitness and strength required
- gender
- age
- existing health or other conditions, eg heart, respiratory or back problems

- pregnancy
- requirements for the use of protective clothing or equipment which could hinder the ability to manually handle a load
- height and weight
- training undertaken and any still required
- knowledge and familiarisation of, and adherence to, the correct techniques and procedures.

Control measures

The purpose of the risk assessment is to determine adequate and appropriate control measures to eliminate or at least reduce the risks evaluated in the risk assessment.

The following list details common manual handling control measures:
- splitting larger inanimate loads into smaller units
- getting assistance from colleagues
- knowing and accepting personal limitations
- mechanical aids, eg hoists for lifting and moving people or fork-lift trucks for lifting boxes, etc
- aids such as belts, turn-discs, glide sheets or transfer boards, height-adjustable beds, etc
- planning the activities and any associated movements and routes
- height-adjustable workstations
- adequate rest and recovery periods
- introducing the right for employees to refuse to carry out manual handling activities which they consider pose an unacceptable risk to them
- drafting and implementing a manual handling policy for the workplace
- comprehensive and comprehensible training, information, and instruction — with competent supervision where necessary.

Whatever control measures are introduced, they should be effective and regularly monitored, eg by looking at sickness absence accident figures or records of equipment purchase, to ensure their continued effectiveness.

Questions and Answers

Q Does every manual handling activity have to be assessed?

A No, only where there is a perceived risk of injury to the people carrying out those activities. In many cases, generic assessments can be undertaken, which means that any similar activities may be assessed as one, provided any differences, eg in the people performing the task, are identified and taken into account.

Q Can external manual handling experts be used to carry out the risk assessments?

A Yes, but make sure they are familiar with any special needs or circumstances in your workplace or associated with your work activities.

Q Do the **Manual Handling Operations Regulations 1992** apply to workplaces where people are not lifted or moved?

A Yes, they apply to all workplaces and are aimed at reducing the phenomenal number of work days lost through back injuries sustained from poor lifting, etc. In practice, inanimate manual handling is much more common than animate manual handling.

Q Do employees have the right to refuse to carry out manual handling tasks which pose a risk of injury?

A Yes. By law employers must ensure the health and safety of their employees so far as is reasonably practicable. The risks of injury associated with manual handling are well known and are often significant which means the employer has a greater duty to control those risks. Similarly, employees have a duty to ensure their own health and safety and performing a task which they know, or suspect, may cause injury is a breach of that duty.

In practice, it is more difficult as employees may be reluctant to refuse a task if they are afraid of repercussions from their employer. Likewise employers may be reluctant to introduce such a right in case employees take advantage and refuse to carry out any activities, although this is unlikely. Where such rights are introduced, they should be written into the manual handling section of the health and safety policy and supported by appropriate training and awareness sessions.

Night Work

Summary

Many organisations operate on a 24-hour basis, thus requiring employees to work shifts which include working at night. Traditionally, night work tended to be associated largely with the manufacturing sector, but in today's global marketplace there is potential for any job to operate at any time of the day or night. Where employees work on a changing shift pattern, they are more likely to suffer disruption to their body clock which may lead to sensations of tiredness and disorientation, similar to jet lag.

Practical Guidance

Medical aspects

The body experiences physiological changes which exhibit a rhythmic pattern of activity over 24 hours. This is called the *circadian rhythm*. This rhythm means that, for example, body temperature is at its maximum during the late afternoon and falls to a minimum during the early hours of the morning. Conversely, production of the antidiuretic hormone which reduces the production of urine is at a maximum during hours of sleep and a minimum in late morning.

The body clock that controls these rhythms is set by a combination of external factors such as exposure to sunlight, darkness, and noise variations between day and night.

Where a person undertakes night work, the circadian rhythm must be modified to ensure that the appropriate bodily functions are at their highest levels of activity during the hours of darkness. This process will begin after a few shifts, but is unlikely to show a complete reversal even after many weeks. Typically, an optimum adjustment will occur after about two weeks. It can be seen that a constantly changing shift pattern is never likely to allow the individual to completely adapt. From a physiological perspective it may seem that permanent night work is less demanding than frequent shift changes, but this is not necessarily the best solution from a psychological point of view. Current thinking is that short-term rotation of shifts is far better than prolonged periods of night work.

Until an individual becomes properly adapted to night work they will suffer, to a varying extent, sensations of tiredness and disorientation. This is commonly known to people who travel as "jet lag".

How quickly the individual adapts, and to what extent they adapt, depends largely on social factors. Particularly important is the extent to which the individual accepts the disruption to his or her domestic and social life, and whether circumstances at home allow adequate sleep during the day. Social factors are very important in determining whether a night worker is motivated to do night work.

It is difficult to demonstrate specific ill-health effects as a direct result of night work, and some studies have actually shown a negative correlation. What is known is that someone who does not adapt well to night work will experience tiredness that makes them prone to accidents and ill-health. In addition, certain diseases, such as diabetes or peptic ulcers, may be exacerbated if dietary habits and drug-taking routines are not suitably adjusted.

General legal duties

The employer has a general duty to ensure, so far as is reasonably practicable, the health, safety and welfare of all their employees. In particular they must provide and maintain:

- safe plant and systems of work
- safe use, handling storage and transport of articles and substances
- the provision of any necessary information, instruction, training and supervision
- a safe place of work with safe means of access and egress
- a safe working environment, and adequate welfare facilities.

The **Working Time Regulations 1998** (as amended) impose a maximum average night shift duration of eight hours. In addition, the employer must ensure that night shift workers have the opportunity of a health assessment before commencing the night shift work.

The employer should ensure that night workers are involved in all the usual activities that go to make up the organisation's health and safety management structure. This will require careful planning, as there may not be the same administrative infrastructure during night shifts.

Employees working at night need to be kept fully involved and informed. For example, fire drills should be carried out at night as well as during the daytime. Similarly, employees working at night should have the same rights to be trained, consulted and/or represented on matters of health and safety as those on day shifts.

Risk assessment

The **Management of Health and Safety at Work Regulations 1999** require the employer to make a suitable and sufficient assessment of risks to the health and safety of their employees whilst at work.

The risk assessment should:

- identify all hazards in the workplace
- eliminate hazards if possible
- evaluate the risks arising from the hazards, and decide whether existing precautions are adequate or whether more should be done (risk may vary with time of day; for example a poorly lit external walkway may be of great significance at night but little consequence during day time)
- devise and implement safe systems of work to ensure that the risks are either eliminated or adequately controlled
- be recorded and reviewed on a regular basis.

Risk assessments should take into account those employees who work nights and address the risk of harmful conditions being brought on by such work, eg additional training may be required if supervision levels are lower at night, and different emergency procedures may apply.

Young persons and women

There are no longer any general restrictions on the employment of young persons or women in terms of work periods. However, employers must carry out a specific risk assessment where women of child bearing age or new or expectant mothers may be at risk from a work process, working conditions or physical, chemical or biological agents. If it is not possible to control the risks identified, the employer must alter the working conditions or hours of work of the woman, or in extreme cases can suspend the woman from work in order to avoid the risk.

In addition, new or expectant mothers may be suspended from night work if a registered medical practitioner or midwife signs a certificate stating such work should be suspended on the grounds of the woman's health and safety.

Employers must also assess the risks to young persons (ie those under the age of 18) to ensure that risks are identified and addressed. The following factors should be taken into account:

- inexperience and immaturity of young persons
- lack of awareness of risks to their health and safety
- layout of their workstation and workplace
- the nature, degree and duration of any exposure to biological, chemical or physical agents
- the form, range, use and handling of work equipment
- the way in which processes and activities are organised
- any health and safety training.

The employer should take into account the young persons' physical and/or psychological capabilities when determining whether or not they should be allowed to do night work.

The employer must inform the young person's parents or guardians of any risks identified by the risk assessment, the necessary control measures and any other specified information, before the young person starts work.

First aid

When determining what is adequate and appropriate in terms of first aid facilities, consideration must be given to ensuring that there is access to first aid facilities during working hours, including during the night.

Questions and Answers

Q Are there any restrictions on whether people can be asked to work at night?

A The **Working Time Regulations 1998** (as amended) impose an average maximum night shift duration of eight hours.

Q Is there evidence to show whether accident rates are higher for those working at nights?

A There is nothing conclusive regarding accident rates and the way the body adapts to night work. However, it is certainly true that people are more prone to accidents when they are tired, and night workers are more likely to have disrupted sleep patterns than day shift workers.

Q Can young people be employed to undertake night work?

A Yes, there are no longer any general restrictions on the employment of young persons in terms of work periods. The employer should take into account the young person's physical and/or psychological capabilities when determining whether or not they should be allowed to do night work, as well as assessing other risks particular to young persons (ie those under the age of 18), eg inexperience, lack of awareness of risks to their health and safety, etc.

The employer must also inform the young person's parents or guardians of any risks identified by a risk assessment, the necessary control measures and any other specified information, before the young person starts work.

Noise

Summary

Noise is most simply defined as "unwanted sound", although it can have significant health effects if left uncontrolled. The adverse health effects of exposure to noise at work are now well recognised although its effects only become apparent over a long period. Careful pre-employment screening and monitoring are important controls.

Practical Guidance

The date when the adverse effects of noise were, or ought to have been, recognised by employers, is generally accepted as being in the early 1960s. Employers have to prove that they were not negligent or in breach of any statutory duty where exposure to damaging noise levels in their workplaces result in hearing damage among the employees.

Noise is generated in many ways, although in a work context it is usually associated with industrial work activities, such as heavy machinery, hammering and drilling. There are other noise sources which may not necessarily lead to hearing damage but which can nevertheless be extremely annoying or disturbing to people at work. Examples of these may include noisy computer printers or photocopiers operating in an office, and young children playing outside. Although there is no physiological damage, exposure to annoying sound can be very tiring and stressful. Irregular, intermittent sounds are probably more disturbing than continual background sounds which may eventually be ignored.

Assessment and noise reduction

As a general rule, if someone has to shout in order to be heard over a distance of two metres, a noise assessment is probably necessary (as required by the **Noise at Work Regulations 1989**).

The statutory action levels of exposure to noise are:

- first action level — daily personal exposure of 85dB(A)
- second action level — daily personal exposure of 90dB(A)
- peak action level — 200 pascals.

The first and second action levels are applicable to noise exposures throughout a normal working day. The peak action level is intended to provide an exposure limit for short, loud blasts of noise exposure, eg gunshots, in an otherwise quiet day. Exposure to noise at work must be assessed where the noise level is likely to be at the first action level or above. Where the noise levels reach the second action level, exposure should be reduced to the lowest level reasonably practicable.

Non-damaging noise levels

Noise levels which do not attract the provisions of the **Noise at Work Regulations 1989** (NAWR) may still need to be controlled under the risk assessment required by the **Management of Health and Safety at Work Regulations 1999** (MHSWR) if they pose a risk to workers. Consideration should be given to the type of work required to be carried out, as this will have some bearing on whether or not a certain noise level is acceptable. For example, employees required to concentrate extremely hard, eg proofreaders or air traffic controllers, may find any background noise levels disturbing and stressful, even though they do not represent levels of noise capable of causing any hearing damage.

Ear protection

Suitable ear protectors must be provided when the noise levels reach the first action level or above, if requested by employees. When noise levels reach the second action level suitable ear protectors *must* be provided and worn, regardless of whether such protection has been requested by the employees. In addition, ear protection zones must be designated in areas where noise levels are at or above the second action level. Such zones must be clearly demarcated and identifiable — ear protectors must be worn in ear protection zones.

Employee duties

Under the **Personal Protective Equipment at Work Regulations 1992** (PPE Regulations), employees have a duty to wear the ear protectors provided when noise exposure is at or above the second action level.

Maintenance and use of equipment

Any equipment, control measures or ear protection provided must be well-maintained and kept in efficient working order. Defective items must be removed and replaced.

Information

Adequate information, instruction and training must be provided on:
• the risks of hearing damage
• necessary control measures
• how to obtain and use suitable ear protectors
• employee duty to wear the protective equipment.
In the case of *Carragher v Singer Manufacturing Ltd*, taken under the now revoked s.29 of the **Factories Act 1961** which require employees to ensure that places of work are safe, it was held that noise from the use of drop hammers in this particular factory was so loud as to make the workplace unsafe.

The case of *Baxter v Harland and Wolff* confirmed that employers have a duty to take reasonable care to keep abreast of contemporary knowledge with regard to work-related hazards, eg noise. A fitter claimed damages for hearing loss from his employers after working for 25 years in a noisy work environment. Although he retired before the accepted date in 1963 of official recognition that excessive workplace noise could cause hearing damage, the Court held that there was sufficient medical, scientific and legal information available prior to 1963 to place a duty of care on the employer to control exposure to workplace noise.

Questions and Answers

Q Do equipment manufacturers and suppliers, etc have a duty to reduce noise emissions from their products?

A Yes. Section 6 of the **Health and Safety at Work, etc Act 1974** requires manufacturers, etc to ensure their articles are safe and without risk to health, and to provide all relevant health and safety information to employers, including information revised at a later date. This duty would apply to noise levels. The NAWR also require information to be provided where the noise emissions from machinery or equipment are at the first action or peak action levels or above.

Q What measures are available for reducing or controlling noise?

A The following measures form the hierarchy of effective noise control:
- reducing noise emissions at source, ie by design
- isolating the noise source
- ear protection, eg helmets, ear muffs, ear plugs
- reducing the duration of exposure, ie by offering rest breaks in a quiet area away from the noise.

Ear protection must be effective at reducing the noise exposure to safe levels, comfortable and safe to use, and must not cause adverse reactions in the wearer or impair speech communications.

Q Should the level of hearing ability be established for new employees joining an organisation?

A Given that the effects of hearing damage can take place over long periods of time, it may be prudent for employers to establish the hearing ability of all new employees. This has two advantages: first, it establishes the hearing level at the start of employment so any deterioration can be readily picked up. Second, it establishes the level of any previous hearing damage (if any), which should be the liability of previous employers if personal injury claims are subsequently made. This may be important if there is the possibility of non-occupational exposure such as regular attendance at discos and pop concerts, etc.

Q Can an employee who suffers hearing loss due to noise exposure at work claim industrial injuries disablement benefit?

A   Yes, under the **Social Security (Industrial Injuries) (Prescribed Diseases) Regulations 1985,** as amended, occupational deafness is a prescribed disease. However, the sufferer must have been in the corresponding prescribed occupation for at least 20 years, including the year prior to the claim, and must have at least 50 decibels hearing loss in both ears. The hearing loss in at least one ear must be due to occupational exposure.

Occupiers, Duties of

Summary

The term "occupier" is not defined under health and safety legislation. The courts have generally taken the view that an occupier is someone having control over premises, including control exercised through a third party, eg a manager. Occupiers of premises have responsibilities towards all invited visitors, including contractors. There are also duties towards unplanned visitors such as the emergency services, and uninvited persons such as trespassers.

Practical Guidance

The occupier is, in effect, the person who runs the premises in question. It is the occupier who regulates and controls the work that is carried out at the premises (and is, in most cases, the employer). That person may be a public sector employer, a limited company, an individual manager, a senior partner or the owner of the premises or the person who controls access to the premises.

Where premises are occupied by more than one tenant, there are responsibilities upon each party. Often the landlord, perhaps through the appointment of a managing agent, will be responsible for maintenance of the common part of the building. This would include communal reception areas, stairways, lifts, toilets and plant rooms. Each tenant must ensure the safety of visitors within those parts of the premises which they occupy and control, and the safety of others in the building who may be affected by the work activity.

Occupiers of premises have both a criminal liability under health and safety legislation, and a civil liability.

General obligations

Although occupiers are not specifically mentioned in the **Health and Safety at Work, etc Act 1974**, there are duties placed on controllers of premises. These duties include an obligation to provide means of access and egress, plant, substances in the premises or provided for use that are safe and without risks to the health of those who are not their employees.

Occupiers of premises have a duty to use the best practicable means to keep premises clean and safe, to prevent the emission of noxious or offensive substances, and to render harmless and inoffensive any substances that are emitted.

Insurance

Although employers are required by law to insure against civil liabilities for injury or disease sustained by employees in the course of their employment, they are under no similar legal obligation to insure against public liability. However, the failure to obtain public liability insurance would mean that any such claim would have to be met directly from the employer's own resources and may ultimately lead to insolvency of the business.

Occupiers' Liability Acts 1957 and 1984

Under the above Acts, an occupier owes a common duty of care to all visitors. This means that they must take reasonable care to see that visitors will be reasonably safe when using the premises for the purposes for which they are invited or permitted to be there. Where children are allowed in the premises, the occupier (or employer) must be prepared for the fact that children are less careful and often more inquisitive that adults.

The occupier also has a duty to non-authorised visitors, ie trespassers. Reasonable care must be taken to see that a trespasser does not suffer injury on the premises from dangers present, or from things done or omitted to be done at the premises. However, the occupier's liability extends only as far as:

- he or she is aware of the danger or has reasonable grounds to believe that it exists, and
- he or she knows or has reasonable grounds to believe that the trespasser is or may come into the vicinity of the danger
- the risk is one against which the occupier may reasonably be expected to offer some protection.

The occupier must take such steps as are reasonable in the circumstances of the case to see that the other person does not suffer injury. The duty may be discharged by:

- giving warning of the danger
- discouraging people from putting themselves at risk in the first place, eg making it difficult for trespassers to enter the premises by using an effective security system.

Occupiers cannot be prosecuted for a breach of their duties, but if a visitor is injured occupiers may be liable to pay compensation for the injury. Occupiers may not set traps to injure trespassers who enter or attempt to enter the premises.

Fire precautions

Under the **Fire Precautions Act 1971** and the **Fire Precautions (Workplace) Regulations 1997** occupiers of premises have a duty to:

- ensure that the existing means of escape can be safely and effectively used at all times
- train employees on the procedures to be followed in case of fire
- maintain any existing fire-fighting equipment in efficient working order.

The **Management of Health and Safety at Work Regulations 1999** require occupiers of premises to provide visitors and contractors with appropriate information and instructions regarding relevant risks to their health and safety. This should include information about foreseeable risks to which they may be exposed whilst under the care of the employer, the emergency procedures within the premises, and the identification of "appointed persons" to deal with specialist tasks or emergency arrangements.

Adequate supervision of visitors whilst on the employer's premises is also necessary to ensure that they do not endanger themselves or other personnel, eg by entering a hazardous area.

Risk assessments should consider any risks that may be created by a visitor to the site, as well as risks to which visitors may be exposed. The risk assessment should also take into account the likelihood that visitors will be unfamiliar with local organisational arrangements.

Questions and Answers

Q Who is responsible if a contractor has an accident whilst working on my premises?

A The occupier is not usually liable to an employee of a contractor who is injured whilst at work, unless the injury arose from the occupier's negligence. It is not reasonable to expect the occupier to be in a position to supervise every contractor.

Q If an intruder is hurt whilst breaking into the premises, how could the occupier be held liable?

A Injuries which arise during the course of obtaining entry, eg a cut from a broken window pane, would not be the occupier's responsibility. However, if a trespasser fell down an unguarded lift shaft, there is the potential for a claim for compensation.

Q Do we have to have public liability insurance?

A Although there is no legal obligation to have public liability insurance, failure to do so would mean that any claim would have to be met from the employer's own resources, which could put a financial burden (perhaps leading to insolvency) on the business.

Peripatetic Workers

Summary

Peripatetic workers are those who work away from their employers' premises, either on a part-time or full-time basis. The main problems of ensuring the safety of peripatetic workers include the constantly changing hazards and risks as they travel from site to site, and the lack of control that their employers have over their actions and the premises where they work.

Practical Guidance

Planning and risk assessment

The work of peripatetic employees should be carefully planned. Before sending a worker to an unknown site, a responsible person (acting for the employer) should contact the host employer to discuss the risks, safety arrangements, etc.

The **Management of Health and Safety at Work Regulations 1999** (MHSWR) require a risk assessment to be carried out for all work activities, including those performed by peripatetic workers. This is difficult to do for peripatetic workers, as a variety of different workplaces will normally be encountered, and it is likely that their employers will be relatively unfamiliar with them.

The average hours of work of peripatetic workers are regulated by the **Working Time Regulations 1998** (as amended). This would include the driving time between home or office and the intended working place.

However, host employers should have carried out a risk assessment for their own workplace and activities, and this should identify and consider risks to visiting peripatetic workers. If the work is hazardous, the responsible person should visit the site before work commences to check the risks and obtain a copy of the host employer's risk assessment.

Co-operation between employers

Under the MHSWR, where employees of two or more employers share a workplace the employers must co-operate and communicate with each other to ensure the health and safety of all employees on site.

The employer (or self-employed person) in control of the working premises must provide the visiting employees with comprehensible information on:

- the risks to their health and safety
- control measures that have been provided
- emergency procedures for the site.

The peripatetic worker must also inform the host organisation of any dangers, eg substances or equipment, which they are bringing on to the premises.

Supervision

Supervision of peripatetic workers is likely to be difficult. There should be strict procedures in place for the worker to follow, such as the following.

1. Upon arrival on site, peripatetic workers must report to the responsible person for the host employer. The worker's employer should identify who this person is before the worker is sent there for the first time.
2. The responsible person should instruct the peripatetic worker on the risks they should be aware of, such as:
   (a) site safety rules
   (b) the work that must be carried out
   (c) emergency procedures
   (d) information of any special hazards to which they may be exposed
   (e) the limits of their safe work area
   (f) any particular personal protective equipment needed while working in that area.
3. If the peripatetic worker cannot find the responsible person, they should contact their supervisor for further instructions. Work must not start unless the responsible person has given the appropriate instruction.
4. If the worker becomes aware of any risks to their health and safety, or encounters any other problems, they should stop work and contact their supervisor for further instructions.

Emergency procedures

If a peripatetic worker is visiting a site for the first time, they must be given appropriate instruction on emergency procedures. This may include telling them what action they should take if:

- they discover a fire
- they hear the fire alarm
- they are injured
- there is an accident or near miss incident
- there is a spillage, especially of hazardous chemicals
- they encounter verbal or physical abuse.

It is recommended that a written copy of the emergency procedures is given to the worker and to his or her employer.

Training

Under the MHSWR, employers must provide their employees with suitable information, instruction and training on the following:

- the risks to their health and safety, identified by the risk assessment
- the preventative and protective risk control measures in place
- emergency procedures.

Training is particularly important for peripatetic workers, due to the relatively low level of supervision they receive.

Accident reporting

Under the **Reporting of Injuries, Diseases and Dangerous Occurrences Regulations 1995** (RIDDOR), certain accidents and injuries must be reported to the enforcing authority. The person responsible for reporting injury to, or death of, a peripatetic worker would be that employee's employer. It is therefore important that any accidents involving peripatetic workers are reported immediately to their employer.

Violence

Many occupations that involve peripatetic work may present a risk of violence, eg working with the public or transporting money or valuable goods. The risk assessment should evaluate the risk of violence, both verbal and physical, to peripatetic workers, and control measures should be put into place. These may include:

- training workers in how to handle stressful and potentially violent situations
- an active method of communication, with workers reporting to their supervisor on a regular basis, perhaps with the use of mobile phones
- a personal panic alarm system (the situation may prevent the use of a telephone)
- employees working in pairs, if the risk of violence is high.

First aid

Under the **Health and Safety (First Aid) Regulations 1981**, employers must provide their employees, including peripatetic workers, with adequate provision for first aid, eg first aid equipment and trained first aid personnel. The contents of a first aid kit should be checked regularly and replenished as necessary. The Approved Code of Practice L74: *First Aid at Work* suggests that for peripatetic workers who work in urban areas and are engaged in low-risk activities, such as sales or delivery, the central provision of first aid at their employer's premises should be sufficient. However, peripatetic workers should be provided with a travelling first aid kit if they:

- work alone (or in small groups) in isolated locations where access to emergency facilities is difficult
- are engaged in hazardous activities, such as tree surgery, or are using hazardous equipment.

Questions and Answers

Q   What sort of jobs involve peripatetic work?

A   There are many types of work that involve the worker travelling away from an employer's premises, including sales, deliveries, maintenance engineers, estate agents, trainers, consultants, police and other enforcement officers, and so on.

Q   Should peripatetic workers be given mobile phones?

A   Mobile phones may prove a very useful method of communication between a worker and his or her supervisor. They are also a means of summoning help if the worker is alone or in a remote location. However, the worker should be given training in the use of the phone, including instruction not to use it while driving a vehicle.

Q   How often should peripatetic workers telephone their supervisors?

A   This very much depends on the nature of the work, and how hazardous it is. For low-risk work, such as sales to businesses in an urban area, workers may only need to contact their supervisor at the beginning of the day to give them details of which premises they intend to visit, and when. They should contact their supervisor when they leave each site, so that a responsible person knows where they are at all times. For more hazardous work, especially where employees are working alone, there should be an agreed frequency when the worker should telephone the supervisor, eg hourly. If a contact is missed, procedures should be in place so that the supervisor knows what action to take to check that the worker is safe.

Permits-to-work

Summary

A permit-to-work is a formal system which uses documentation and supervision to control hazardous activities. The permit sets down the conditions of the work and anyone involved in the activity must agree in writing to follow these conditions.

Practical Guidance

Risk assessment

The **Management of Health and Safety at Work Regulations 1999** (MHSWR) require employers to carry out a risk assessment for all work activities and introduce suitable arrangements protecting workers against the risks identified.

Safe working practices should be developed, in the form of written procedures and instructions. High-risk activities identified by the risk assessment should be changed to eliminate the risks. If this is not possible, a formal permit-to-work system may be needed to ensure the workers and their supervisors are aware of and follow the control measures required.

Permit-to-work situations

Permits-to-work are used for activities which are particularly hazardous, ie where a failure to implement the safety measures would have serious and immediate consequences. The following list is not exhaustive and the risk assessment for any individual undertaking should identify the activities subject to a permit-to-work.

Work equipment

Under the **Provision and Use of Work Equipment Regulations 1998** (PUWER), employers must provide work equipment which is properly maintained and in good working order. Maintenance operations on work equipment, particularly machinery, is often hazardous. PUWER requires work equipment to be designed, made or adapted to be shut down during maintenance operations. However, if this is not possible, maintenance must be carried out without presenting a health and safety risk, and appropriate measures must be taken. It is likely that an employer's arrangements would include a permit-to-work for these activities.

Radiation

Under the **Ionising Radiations Regulations 1999** (IRR), a detailed written scheme of work is required if non-classified people are to enter a controlled area. This written scheme is, in effect, a permit-to-work.

Offshore installations

The **Offshore Installations and Pipeline Works (Management and Administration) Regulations 1995** require a permit-to-work where it is necessary to control the risks to health and safety.

Electrical work

The **Electricity at Work Regulations 1989** (EAWR) require the provision and maintenance of electrical systems so that they are safe. Under EAWR, it is prohibited to work on live electrical systems, except in certain circumstances. If live electrical work is necessary, suitable precautions must be taken, including using a permit-to-work system. Anyone who is carrying out live work under a permit-to-work should be accompanied by someone who is familiar with the work and is capable of acting safely and effectively in an emergency. The permit-to-work should specify the many precautions which are necessary for live work, such as rubber mats, special tools, personal protective equipment, etc.

Confined spaces

The **Confined Spaces Regulations 1997** require employers to eliminate the need for working in a confined space. If this is not reasonably practicable, a risk assessment must be carried out and suitable health and safety precautions must be taken. Controls will include making sure that powered equipment and valves, etc are shut off and that appropriate rescue arrangements have been made in case of an emergency.

Elements of a permit-to-work

A permit-to-work system should contain the following:
- details of the work to be carried out
- details of the specific risk control measures, eg locking off, blanking, etc
- written authorisation allowing the work to be carried out
- acknowledgment by the worker that they have received and understood the instructions covered by the permit-to-work
- clearance stating that the work has, or has not, been completed
- cancellation of the permit, stating that it does not cover further work.

Permit-to-work document

The permit-to-work document should be given a serial number, and be under the control of a senior manager who is familiar with the work, safe working practices and health and safety precautions to be taken. It is divided into four parts, each of which must be signed, with the date and time of signature, by the person responsible.

- Part 1 should be completed by the senior manager and given to the job supervisor, once the necessary safety measures have been carried out. It should contain the following:
  - a statement declaring that all necessary safety measures have been implemented
  - information on the plant, system or equipment to be used
  - the job location
  - a description of the work involved
  - a detailed list of the safety measures, such as the location of warning notices, equipment and valves to be locked off, rescue arrangements, etc.
- Part 2 should be completed by the supervisor before the work begins. It should show that the supervisor accepts responsibility for the work, will ensure that it is carried out in accordance with the procedures and has checked the safety measures and found them satisfactory. The supervisor should sign Part 2 and give the date and time, his or her job title and the employer company name (if applicable).
- Part 3, to be used by the supervisor, should be completed if the work stops temporarily, and when the work is finished. It should state that the work has either been stopped or completed, and that the safety measures must not yet be removed or that they have already been removed.
- Part 4 should be used by the senior manager, to show that the permit-to-work is no longer in operation. It should state that the work has been completed, the safety measures removed, it is safe to resume normal operation and that the permit-to-work has been cancelled.

Training

Training and correct instruction is essential for a permit-to-work system to be effective. Training provision should ensure that employees are familiar with the following:
- the purpose of permit-to-work systems
- the types of permits-to-work
- the implementation, operation and cancellation of permits-to-work
- the limitations of permit-to-work systems
- correct use of any equipment and safety measures provided.

Questions and Answers

Q Is an oral agreement to follow the conditions specified in a permit-to-work enough to comply with it?

A No. The whole point of a permit-to-work is that it is a formalised system to keep track of each stage of a particularly hazardous activity. It is imperative that for the effectiveness of this supervision, it is shown in writing that each condition has been agreed to and understood by all of the people involved in completing the activity.

Q What action should be taken if someone breaches a permit-to-work?

A Breach of the safety measures specified in a permit-to-work, or carrying out the work without using a permit, is a serious offence, considering that the system is there because the risks are particularly high. If an employee of the company breaches the permit, it should be treated as gross misconduct, and the usual disciplinary action taken. If it is a contractor that breaches the permit, it is likely to be an infringement of the contract, which should be terminated. A contractor who can demonstrate a responsible attitude to health and safety should be hired for the work instead.

Q Does a permit-to-work make the work safe?

A No. The permit-to-work only communicates the safety measures to the workers, so they know how to carry out the work safely. The fact that the supervisor has certified that he or she is aware of the measures does not mean that they will be followed, so there should be a high level of supervision. The use of a permit-to-work should not lead to complacency: fatal accidents have occurred during work which was covered by a permit-to-work system.

Personal Protective Equipment

Summary

Personal protective equipment (PPE) includes any equipment or clothing intended to be held or worn by people at work to offer protection against identified risks. The use of PPE is widespread throughout many workplaces. It should be used, however, only as a "last resort" control measure, where risks cannot be controlled by other means.

Practical Guidance

Protective clothing includes aprons, gloves, safety footwear, safety helmets, adverse-weather clothing, high-visibility clothing and clothing designed to protect against temperature extremes, etc.

Protective equipment includes eye protectors, safety harnesses, respirators, life jackets, etc.

Provision and compatibility

Where risks cannot be controlled by other means, suitable PPE must be provided by the employer. Self-employed persons must provide their own PPE. In the case of *Ralston v Greater Glasgow Health Board* an employee contracted irritant dermatitis through the use of irritant chemicals, and the employer was found liable for failing to provide protective gloves for employees using such chemicals.

As a control measure PPE should be considered as a last resort. It offers individual protection only and does not protect the workforce as a whole. It can also be cumbersome and restrictive to wear, and may give a false sense of security.

There is no requirement to provide PPE for non-employees, although it may need to be considered in order to fulfil the duty to non-employees under s.3 of the **Health and Safety at Work, etc Act 1974** (HSW Act).

Risk assessment

An assessment must be carried out to ascertain the suitability of intended PPE — the selection of PPE should actively involve the employees required to use it. The selection of PPE should take into account:

- the risks to health and safety that cannot be controlled by other means, ie what risks the PPE is expected to offer protection against
- the performance and characteristics required for the PPE to be effective
- the comparison of the intended PPE against the performance and character criteria above.

In the case of *Daniels v Ford Motor Co Ltd* the court was asked to decide whether the term "suitable" implied that the protection offered had to be 100%. An employee was injured by a flying fragment while lifting his goggles to wipe away a build up of mist on the lenses. He claimed that because of the injury the goggles were not "suitable" despite being the preferred choice of his work colleagues. The court decided that the term "suitable" did not infer that the goggles had to offer 100% protection — it was sufficient that they were appropriate for the work process and the users.

An assessment carried out under the **Personal Protective Equipment at Work Regulations 1992** (PPE Regulations) does not have to be repeated under the **Management of Health and Safety at Work Regulations 1999** (MHSWR).

Maintenance and storage

PPE must be maintained (ie cleaned, repaired and replaced) in efficient working order — stocks of replacement parts, etc should be kept. Storage facilities should be provided to keep PPE which is not in use.

EU requirements

PPE must meet certain EU requirements and standards which confirm it meets specified safety and various test criteria. Generally PPE which carries the "CE mark" will meet these criteria. The relevant legislation is the **Personal Protective Equipment (EC Directive) Regulations 1992**, as variously amended.

Multi-use of PPE

Where more than one item of PPE is required to be used simultaneously, eg ear protectors and safety helmets, the items must be compatible and must not reduce the level of protection offered by those items individually. Many manufacturers and suppliers now offer integrated PPE systems, such as safety helmets which incorporate ear and eye/face protection.

Information, instruction and training

Employees must be informed of the:
- purpose of any PPE provided
- risks it is intended to protect against
- correct method of use and storage
- employer's duty to maintain PPE.

Employees' duties

Employees must use and store PPE properly in accordance with their training, and report any losses or defects.

PPE examples

Please see the following table.

PPE examples

Protection	PPE Examples	Work Examples
Head	Helmets	Construction, mining and other groundwork, work where there are risks of falling objects
Face	Visors, face shields	Welding, foundry work (molten metal splashes)
Eye	Goggles, glasses	Welding work with lasers or where there is a risk of flying fragments or chemical splashes
Ear	Plugs, muffs, helmets	Work in noisy environments, eg heavy duty drilling and/or hammering
Hand	Gloves (rubber, chain-mail)	Work involving the handling of hazardous substances, chain saws, knives, saws, hot/cold items, rough wood, etc
Respiratory system	Respiratory protective equipment (RPE) (breathing apparatus, respirators, nose/ mouth masks)	Work in unhealthy atmospheres and/or involving exposure to hazardous substances, work producing substantial quantities of dust
Body	Clothing (aprons, high visibility/thermal, life jackets, cut resistant, safety harnesses, etc)	Work involving risks of splashing or other contamination, work with chain-saws (arms and legs) or ionising radiations, etc, work where there is a risk of falling (fall arrest equipment)

Foot	Safety boots, gaiters (toe protectors, insulating)	Work where there is a risk of splashing or of falling objects, work with live electricity (insulating footwear)

Questions and Answers

Q Do employers have to provide PPE free of charge?

A Yes, s.9 of the HSW Act prohibits employers from charging for PPE required to be provided under any health and safety laws. This includes PPE identified as being necessary under the PPE Regulations as a result of the risk assessments carried out under MHSWR. Employers will also have better management of, and control over, any PPE they provide and can therefore ensure that it is maintained and replaced as required. However, in the case of *Associated Dairies Ltd v Hartley*, an enforcement inspector was found to have acted unreasonably by serving an improvement notice requiring the employer to provide safety boots free of charge to employees working in a certain area. The employer successfully argued that the existing system of providing the boots at cost price on a weekly repayment scheme (which was in line with trade practice at the time) was adequate and reasonable in relation to the risk.

Q What determines whether PPE is suitable?

A PPE is considered suitable if it is:
- appropriate for, and effective against, the risks it is intended to protect against
- suitable for the environment in which it is intended to be used
- adjustable to fit the user securely and comfortably.

Consideration should also be given to the need for communication, mobility and use in confined spaces.

Q Are any items of PPE excluded from the PPE Regulations?

A Yes. The following items are excluded:
- uniforms, eg for food hygiene purposes
- work clothing which does not offer protection against identified risks
- sports equipment
- crash helmets required under road traffic legislation.

Q What if an employee refuses to wear PPE which is identified as necessary and is provided by the employer?

A There are several factors to consider. Under regulation 10 of the PPE Regulations, every employee is required to use any PPE provided, and employers must take all reasonable steps to ensure that PPE provided is used. Employees also have a duty under s.7 of the HSW Act to ensure their own health and safety at work. Refusing to wear PPE identified as necessary in order to control exposure to certain workplace risks is a breach of that duty and of the

PPE Regulations. The employee could be liable for prosecution. Employers must establish the grounds on which the refusal has been made, and whether there is a sound reason why the employee will not wear the PPE by considering:

- is it uncomfortable to wear?
- does it restrict movement?
- does it create a greater risk from another hazard, compared to the one it is intended to protect against?
- has the employee been made aware of why the PPE is needed and how to use it correctly?

As a last resort employers may need to instigate disciplinary proceedings — these should be part of the organisation's health and safety policy statement and employment conditions. The bottom line is that where the PPE is necessary to protect against a significant workplace risk the employer must take all reasonable steps to ensure that employees use it — this is the criterion judges will probably base any prosecutions or civil claims on. Getting the employee to sign any form of disclaimer is unlikely to stand up under court scrutiny.

Portable Electrical Appliances

Summary

Approximately one quarter of all reportable electrical accidents involve portable appliances. The majority of these accidents are caused by electric shock, but others result in burns from arcing or fire. There are approximately five fatalities a year involving portable electrical appliances.

Practical Guidance

Definition

Portable electrical appliances can be defined as electrical equipment with a plug and a lead which is easily moved around, eg kettles, drills and vacuum cleaners. The definition extends to items such as computers, fax machines or photocopiers which are less easily moveable.

Accidents

The main causes of accidents involving portable electrical appliances are faulty flexible cables, extension leads, plugs and sockets. The injured person often touches a part of the appliance which has become "live" whilst in contact with an earthed conducting surface. The shock a person may receive can be potentially lethal.

Typically, accidents are caused by:

- appliances which are unsuitable for the conditions of use
- inadequate maintenance
- misuse
- the use of defective apparatus.

The electrical supply to portable appliances gives rise to three forms of danger:

- electric shock or electrical burns
- burns to anyone nearby from electrical arcing
- consequential injuries, such as a fall from a ladder, caused by the person's reaction to an electric shock.

Electrical safety in all workplaces is specifically legislated for in the **Electricity at Work Regulations 1989.** These Regulations are over and above the general duty of care owed by employers to their employees and members of the public under the **Health and Safety at Work Act, etc 1974.**

The Regulations put the onus on the employer to assess those work activities which utilise electricity or may be affected by it, and identify all foreseeable risks.

Construction and maintenance

All electrical appliances must be suitable for their intended use and maintained so as to prevent the risk of injury. Work activities such as the operation, use and maintenance of an appliance and any work near a appliance must be carried out in such a way as not to give rise to danger. Any protective equipment, eg special tools, must be suitable, well maintained and properly used.

Strength and capability of electrical equipment

The safe working limits of electrical equipment must not be exceeded. Consideration should be given to unusual conditions which may adversely affect the equipment, eg power fluctuations, surges, faults, heating, etc.

Adverse or hazardous environments

Electrical appliances must be constructed and protected against adverse or hazardous environments, eg mechanical damage, effects of weather, dirty or dusty conditions, and flammable or explosive substances.

Insulation, protection and placing of conductors

All conductors in a system must be either insulated or protected against mechanical damage with a suitable material, or sited so as to prevent any danger.

Earthing or other suitable precautions

Precautions must be taken, by earthing or other means, to prevent the risk of injury from a conductor which may become charged as a result of using the system or of a fault in the system.

A conductor in this context is everything capable of carrying an electrical current, eg metal casings, not just those conductors which are intended to carry current.

Integrity of referenced conductors

Measures should be taken to prevent an open circuit or high impedance in the so-called reference conductor, usually a circuit conductor connected to earth. An open circuit or high impedance (which would mimic an open circuit) in this conductor may lead to electric shock or burns from, for example, metal enclosures of switch gear.

Connections

Every joint and/or connector including plugs and sockets, whether temporary or permanent, must be mechanically and electrically suitable for the intended use.

Protection from excess current

There must be suitably located and efficient means for protecting all parts of a system against foreseeable excess currents, ie faults, overload, short circuiting, etc. The most common forms of protection are fuses or circuit breakers.

Cutting off the electrical supply and isolation

Suitable means for cutting off the electrical energy supply to appliances and for isolating any electrical equipment must be available. "Cutting off" may be achieved manually, or indirectly by using "stop" buttons.

Effective isolation ensures that the supply remains switched off and prevents inadvertent reconnection. When working on "dead" equipment, all conductors should be proved dead at the point of work.

Working space, access and lighting

Adequate working space, means of access and lighting must be provided at all electrical equipment when potentially dangerous work is being carried out.

Competent persons

No person may work on electrical apparatus unless they possess the necessary knowledge or experience or are under adequate supervision. Such knowledge or experience may include:

- adequate knowledge of electricity
- experience of electrical work
- knowledge of the system and practical experience of that class of system
- understanding of the hazards and their precautions
- the ability to recognise, at all times, whether or not it is safe to continue work.

The **Electrical Equipment (Safety) Regulations 1994** apply to electrical equipment operating in a voltage range of 50 to 1000 volts AC and 75 to 1500 volts DC. They require such electrical equipment to be safe including protection against risks of death or injury to humans or domestic animals and damage to property. Equipment must have the CE marking affixed. The Regulations also require second-hand and hired electrical equipment to be safe.

Guidance on the frequency of testing of portable electrical equipment in low-risk environments has been published by the Health and Safety Executive in leaflet INDG236L *Guidance on Frequency of Testing Portable Electrical Equipment in Offices and Other Low-risk Environments*. The table below gives examples of recommended inspections and testing of various types of equipment in offices and other low-risk environments.

Equipment	User checks	Formal visual inspection	Combined test and inspection
Battery operated (less than 20V)	No	No	No
Extra low voltage: (below 50V AC), eg telephones, low-voltage desk lamps	No	No	No
Desktop computers and VDU screens	No	Yes, 2–4 years	No if double insulated, otherwise up to 5 years
Fax machines, copiers and items not hand-held and rarely used	No	Yes, 2–4 years	No if double insulated, otherwise up to 5 years
Double-insulated items: not hand-held and only moved occasionally, eg slide projectors, desk lamps	No	Yes, 2–4 years	No
Double-insulated items: hand-held, eg some floor cleaners	Yes	Yes, 6–12 months	No
Earthed equipment (Class 1), eg kettles and some floor cleaners	Yes	Yes, 6–12 months	Yes, 1–2 years
Cables, leads and plugs connected to all of the above, and mains voltage extension leads	Yes	Yes, 6 months to 4 years depending on the type of equipment it is connected to	Yes, 1–5 years depending on the type of equipment it is connected to

Questions and Answers

Q Is a "competent" person required to be a qualified electrican?

A A competent person is defined as someone "having the necessary knowledge or experience". Such knowledge or experience may include adequate knowledge of electricity, adequate experience of electrical work, adequate knowledge of the system and practical experience of that class of system, understanding of the hazards and their precautions, and the ability to recognise at all times whether it is safe to continue work. The level of competency is dependent upon the type of equipment, its location and the work to be done, in some instances this may require the person to be a qualified electrician.

Q   Why must cable drums be completely unwound before use?

A   Cables wound on a drum act as a coil and must be de-rated to avoid overheating. Unless the manufacturer has indicated safe current/time-limits, the cable must be completed unwound from the drum when in use.

Q   Who is responsible for portable tools brought on site by contractors?

A   It is the client's responsibility to ensure that contractors are competent to carry out the work and that they have a safety policy, methods statement and systems in place to check their equipment. The provision and use of such equipment is the responsibility of the contractor. You may, however, wish to ensure that their equipment has been checked before use by inspecting "tested" labels or records.

Q   How often should we arrange to test our portable electrical appliances?

A   A myth has evolved to the effect that there is a legal duty to carry out annual testing of portable appliances. However, the word "portable" does not even appear in the legislation.

Nevertheless, the nature and use of some types of portable appliance means that there is an increased potential for problems to arise. The frequency and extent of tests and examinations of any electrical equipment (fixed and portable) must be determined by the employer, based upon factors such as:

- the type of use
- the likelihood of faults or damage arising
- the safety consequences of faults or damage

Consideration must be given to the frequency of use, the condition of the equipment and the method of storage. Suitable guidance is given in the Institution of Electrical Engineers *Code of Practice for In-service Inspection and Testing of Electrical Equipment*. To meet the Regulations there should be a combination of regular visual inspections and more detailed examination, including testing where appropriate. Suitable records should be kept.

Posters, Display of Health and Safety Notices

Summary

Communication is essential for providing a safe system of work, and the need for information, instruction and training is well established in health and safety law. One method of communicating information to employees is the posting of health and safety notices.

Practical Guidance

Health and safety law poster

The **Health and Safety Information for Employees Regulations 1989** require that employees must be made aware of the general requirements of health and safety law. This may be done by displaying the poster *Health and Safety Law: What You Should Know* (available from HSE Books) in a readily accessible and visible position in the workplace. The addresses of the local enforcing authority and the local HSE Employment Medical Advisory Service must be added to the bottom of the poster. Also the names and locations of safety representatives, and of competent persons appointed under the **Management of Health and Safety at Work Regulations 1999**.

Alternatively, this information may be disseminated to employees by giving them a leaflet designed for this purpose.

Dangerous equipment

Work with dangerous equipment must be assessed and safe systems of work set up. These systems should incorporate warning notices, where appropriate. However, there are also legal requirements for the display of posters for specific items of dangerous equipment. These include the following.

1. Under the **Kiers Regulations 1938**, the kier supervisor must put up a notice outside the kier (close to the entrance) which authorises entrance if someone has to go into the kier. This notice must remain in place as long as anyone is inside the kier.
2. Under the **Power Presses Regulations 1965**, a copy of the certificate of exemption, where granted, must be prominently displayed in the factory.

Insurance certificate

Under the **Employers' Liability (Compulsory Insurance) Regulations 1998**, employers must display a copy of their certificate of liability insurance at their place of business. It must be positioned so that it is easily seen and read by the employees.

Fire

An important aspect of fire safety is making sure that everyone on the premises is aware of what to do and how to escape in the event of a fire. The means of escape should be indicated by using suitable signs (which comply with the **Health and Safety (Safety Signs and Signals) Regulations 1996)** and notices should be posted which give instructions on "what to do in the event of a fire".

Under the **Fire Precautions (Special Premises) Regulations 1976**, the occupier of special premises (ie ones which are specified by the Regulations due to their high fire risk) must post a notice stating that a certificate has been obtained under the Regulations. This notice must also say where the fire certificate (or a copy of it) is available for inspection. The notice must be in a position which makes it easy for employees to see and read.

First aid

The **Health and Safety (First Aid) Regulations 1981** require employers to inform employees of the first aid arrangements that have been provided. This should include the posting of at least one notice which gives the location(s) of the first aid facilities and the name and location(s) of first aid personnel. The notice should be conspicuously located for easy reference.

Biological agents

The **Control of Substances Hazardous to Health Regulations 1999** contain specific requirements on biological agents. In order to comply with these requirements, notices should be displayed which give instructions on the procedures to be followed in the event of an accident or incident which leads to the release of any biological agent capable of causing severe disease in humans.

Asbestos

Under the **Control of Asbestos at Work Regulations 1987**, "asbestos areas" and "respirator zones" must be clearly marked by suitable notices.

Safety committees

Under the **Safety Representatives and Safety Committees Regulations 1977**, employers must post a notice in the workplace which gives the:

- composition of the safety committee
- workplace covered by the committee.

A programme of dates for safety committee meetings should also be posted, and a copy of the minutes from meetings either posted or copies given to employees.

Gas meters

Under the **Gas Safety (Installation and Use) Regulations 1998**, emergency notices must be displayed which detail the procedures to be followed in the event of a gas leak.

Radiation

Under the **Ionising Radiations Regulations 1999**, "controlled areas" must be clearly marked by suitable warning notices, and there should also be notices posted:
- at the entrance to radioactive substances stores
- indicating safety features and devices in place for compliance with the Regulations.

Under the **Radioactive Substances Act 1993**, all premises where radioactive waste is accumulated or deposited must have a certificate of authorisation. A copy of this certificate must be posted on the premises.

Questions and Answers

Q   We still have a poster displaying a summary of the **Factories Act 1961**. Is this necessary?

A   The requirements under the **Factories Act 1961** and the **Offices, Shops and Railway Premises Act 1963** to put up posters of abstracts of those Acts were revoked by the **Health and Safety Information for Employees Regulations 1989**. Instead, the Regulations require a poster of general health and safety law to be displayed, ie *Health and Safety Law: What You Should Know* (available from HSE Books). Alternatively, leaflets containing the same information may be given to each employee. The old posters on the 1961 and 1963 Acts should be taken down.

Q   Do we have to put a poster up on treatment of electric shock?

A   The **Electricity at Work Regulations 1989** replace earlier legislation on electrical safety. This earlier legislation required employers to display posters on how to treat electric shock. However, the 1989 Regulations do not require this, and so there is no longer a specific requirement for electric shock posters.

Remember though that you are responsible for providing a safe system of work with electricity. Consider what would happen if someone did receive an electric shock — would anyone in the area know what to do? If at any time when people are at work the answer may be no, a poster which is easy to see and follow, giving instructions on what to do, may save someone's life.

Q   What is the difference between a poster and a safety sign?

A A poster is a notice, which is usually large, rectangular and sometimes laminated, which gives instructions or conveys a message using pictures on how to do something safely, etc. There are no rules governing the content of posters, other than those specifically required by legislation and available from HSE Books.

Safety signs, on the other hand, are basic signboards, safety colours or illuminated signs which convey information or instructions by their shape, colour and an appropriate symbol or pictogram. The format of safety signs are strictly controlled by the **Health and Safety (Safety Signs and Signals) Regulations 1996**. They usually do not contain words, as the message should be clear without them, although sometimes they may be accompanied by key words underneath the sign, such as "No Smoking" or "Wear Your Hard Hat". The shape, colour, symbol and size, etc are all governed by the 1996 Regulations.

Power Presses

Summary

Power presses are a clearly defined group of machines used in industry. They are amongst the most dangerous of industrial machines, with trapping between the tools the most common type of accident. Such accidents frequently result in serious injury, including amputations to one or both upper limbs. Correct installation, guarding and inspection is vital to remove these risks.

Practical Guidance

The **Provision and Use of Work Equipment Regulations 1998** (PUWER), regulations 31 to 35, replace old regulations concerned specifically with power presses. Those people already familiar with the now revoked **Power Presses Regulations 1965** will find little change overall.

Power presses are clearly defined as a press, or press brakes, for the working of metal by means of tools, or die proving, which is power driven and which embodies a flywheel and clutch. Guarding of the moving parts of a power press, including the tools or dies, is covered by the other regulations contained in PUWER. Regulations 32 to 35 place duties on employers to carry out examinations and inspections, and to keep reports.

Regulation 31 removes the application of regulations 32 to 35 to power presses of a kind listed in schedule 2 to the Regulations. This includes those for working hot metal, compacting metal powder and others such as eyeletting, press-stud attaching and stapling machines.

General requirements of PUWER 1998

Although there are specific regulations concerned with power presses, most or all of the other duties in PUWER 1998 may apply. Some are specifically mentioned in the Approved Code of Practice. These include maintenance of the power press and all its guards and/or protection devices, which should be checked frequently. There are specific duties relating to examination, inspection and testing (see below).

Specific risks are dealt with by regulation 7, which requires that risks should be controlled by elimination, or by taking physical measures to reduce the risk, with residual risks being dealt with by safe systems of work and training. This is important in relation to the "setter", the person who carries out the setting of tools, changing of tools, die proving, etc. These setters must have been adequately trained, be competent to carry out their duties and have been specifically designated as setters for each power press, guard and protection device they intend to work on.

Thorough examination of power presses, guards and protection devices

Power presses, and any guard or protection device, must be thoroughly examined (by a competent person) before being put into service, to ensure it has been installed correctly, can be operated safely and that any defect has been remedied. Any closed tool which acts as a fixed guard must also be thoroughly examined when in position to ensure it is effective for its purpose. Power presses must then be thoroughly examined at intervals of 12 months where it has fixed guards, or 6 months in all other cases (including those fitted with closed tools). A thorough examination must also be carried out each time exceptional circumstances have occurred which may jeopardise the safety of the power press, its guards or protection devices. Where power presses were subject to the 1965 Regulations, then the first thorough examination (regarding installation) must be carried out before they were due under that previous legislation (regulations 32(1 to 32(7)).

The competent person who carries out the examination and tests should have sufficient practical and theoretical knowledge, experience in being able to detect defects or weaknesses, and the ability to assess their importance in relation to the safe use and operation of the power press. The competent person is usually an employee of an engineering insurance or service company that specialises in this type of work, rather than an employee of the company using the power press. There are no prohibitions in PUWER that prevent an employee of the power press operating company from carrying out thorough examinations, but in a small business with few power presses an employee is less likely to have the broad knowledge and experience of those working for an independent specialist. It is also possible that his or her independence in certain, legally required reporting matters could be also be questioned.

Closed tools do not need to be thoroughly examined due to an exclusion contained in regulation 32(40), but they must still be inspected and tested each work period as with any other guard or protection device. A closed tool (though this is not defined in the Regulations) is when the design is such that it is not possible to place any part of the body between the tools in a way that injury may result. This can be achieved by using a very short stroke with a minimum gap between the tools (less than 5 mm) or by enclosure.

Inspection of guards and protection devices

After setting, re-setting or adjusting the tools, a power press may not be used until every guard and protection device has been inspected and tested while in position by a person appointed in writing by the employer (regulation 33). That appointed person must be competent, or be undergoing training to become competent (in which case they should be under the direct supervision of a competent person). Note that the appointed person need not be the same person as the "competent person" who carries out the thorough examination and test, as outlined previously.

The appointed person is most often an employee of the power press operating company. It is vital they have the appropriate and adequate training for the class or classes of power press, guard or protection device they are to inspect, are competent to carry out their duties and are appointed in writing. Those undergoing training must have been appointed in writing first. The appointments should be recorded by making a signed and dated entry into a register

A certificate must be signed by the appointed person containing: specified particulars to identify the power press, guard, protection device, etc; date and time of inspection; and a statement to the effect that every guard and protection device is in place and effective for its purpose. A power press must be inspected in every work period that it is in use. A work period is the period in which the day's or night's work is done, or the shift, if a shift system is in place. No power press is allowed to be used after the expiration of the fourth hour of a working period unless this inspection and test has been satisfactorily carried out.

A power press must not be used after the tools on the press have been set, re-set or adjusted, unless every guard and/or protection device on the press has been inspected and tested by an appointed person and they have signed the daily log to show this.

Reports and keeping of information

Any person making a report of a thorough examination must notify the employer in writing, as soon as practicable, of any defect that could become a danger to individuals. The notification should contain specific details and must be signed. They must also send a copy of the report to the enforcing authority as soon as practicable (regulation 34), and in almost all cases the authority is the Health and Safety Executive. The report must be kept for two years after it was made, for the purposes of inspection. Records of inspections (the daily inspection or after re-setting, etc) must be kept at or near the power press and for six months after it is replaced by its subsequent report (regulation 35).

Questions and Answers

Q   We currently use an insurance company to carry out our thorough examination when we purchase new power presses, and for all our existing presses. Can we use one of our own employees instead?

A   There is no prohibition on you doing this. You must ensure the individual(s) is competent to do the thorough examination, and to test for each class of power press and the class of guards and protection devices. The person should have sufficient practical and theoretical knowledge and experience to be able to detect defects or weaknesses and assess their importance in relation to the safe use and operation of the power press.

Q We operate several hydraulic press brakes. Are these covered by the new requirements?

A No, they do not fall within the definition of a power press so do not attract those specific duties. They are, however, work equipment as defined in the **Provision and Use of Work Equipment Regulations 1998** and therefore you must comply, as appropriate, with the requirements contained in regulations 4 to 24 inclusive.

Q We have several employees under the age of 18. Can they operate power presses?

A The **Management of Health and Safety at Work Regulations 1999** require that a risk assessment is undertaken for work to be carried out by employees under the age of 18. Those under 18 years of age can be further split into those under minimum school leaving age (MSLA), and those above MSLA but under 18 years. You should not allow such people to operate power presses unless they have the necessary maturity and competence, including having successfully completed appropriate training. They may operate a press during the training period provided they are directly supervised. Adequate supervision must also be provided after training if they are not sufficiently mature. It is recommended that any person under MSLA is not allowed to operate a power press.

Pregnancy

Summary

Pregnancy puts certain strains on the body which may increase the risks to a worker's health and safety. The level of risk will vary between individuals and at different times during the pregnancy. The worker's welfare needs and her ability to carry out normal tasks may change. There may also be risks to the unborn baby from agents at work, such as radiation, chemical agents, micro-organisms, etc.

Practical Guidance

Risk assessment

The **Management of Health and Safety at Work Regulations 1999** require employers to carry out a risk assessment for all their work activities. Specific consideration must be made of pregnant workers in the risk assessment. The risk assessment must be made if any working condition, process, or biological, chemical or physical agent may adversely affect the health and safety of the pregnant woman or the baby. This may mean revising existing risk assessments if one of the workers involved in the work activity becomes pregnant.

Workplace facilities

Under the **Workplace (Health, Safety and Welfare) Regulations 1992**, employers must provide suitable rest facilities for pregnant workers. A similar requirement exists under the **Construction (Health, Safety and Welfare) Regulations 1996**.

Civil liability

The **Congenital Disabilities (Civil Liability) Act 1976** puts a civil liability on anyone who causes an occurrence affecting an expectant mother during her pregnancy which results in the baby being born disabled — or which affects anyone's ability to have a normal child. In terms of health and safety at work, this means that an employer is liable if it can be shown that his or her negligence of a pregnant employee lead to her baby being born disabled. However, if the occurrence happened before the child was conceived the employer will not be liable if it can be proved that the parent knew of the potential risk.

Working with lead

Lead has a harmful effect on the human body and can be particularly damaging to the human foetus. For this reason, under the **Control of Lead at Work Regulations 1998**, employers may not employ women of reproductive capacity in certain specified occupations in lead smelting and refining processes, and in lead-acid manufacturing processes.

Manual handling

Under the **Manual Handling Operations Regulations 1992**, employers must either eliminate hazardous manual handling tasks, or (where this is not reasonably practicable) assess the risks. Manual handling risk assessments must take a number of factors into consideration, including the individual capability of the person carrying out the task. Pregnant workers are likely to find manual handling tasks more difficult, especially later in pregnancy, and the assessment and control measures should take this into account. Manual handling should be avoided during the early months of pregnancy owing to the risk of miscarriage.

Chemicals and biological agents

Under the **Control of Substances Hazardous to Health Regulations 1999**, employers must carry out an assessment of the risk of exposure to hazardous substances in the workplace. Certain chemicals and biological agents have damaging effects on the unborn baby. The risk assessment should look at the possibility of pregnant women being exposed to such chemicals and agents, including women who are not aware that they are pregnant, and suitable control measures must be put into place to protect them and their baby.

Radiation

Ionising radiation is harmful to the unborn baby at lower doses than it is to adults. If the foetus is exposed to it during development deformations can occur. The **Ionising Radiations Regulations 1999** set a variety of dose limits, including a limit to control the dose to foetuses.

Suspension from work

The risk assessments carried out under the **Management of Health and Safety at Work Regulations 1999** should identify any activities which give rise to a significant risk to the health and safety of pregnant women. If the risk to a pregnant employee cannot be controlled, she should be removed from the harmful work activity.

Under the Employment Rights Act 1996, alternative work must be offered to a pregnant worker where that worker would otherwise have to be suspended on the grounds of health and safety. If alternative work is not available, the suspended worker must receive the salary she would have received if she had not been suspended.

The **Maternity (Compulsory Leave) Regulations 1994** require employers to make sure that no employee returns to work within two weeks of giving birth.

Questions and Answers

Q Is it safe for pregnant workers to use display screen equipment?

A Pregnant workers may be concerned that working with display screen equipment (DSE), eg computers, may damage their unborn baby, especially as there have been rumours of this for years. However, research has shown that there is no scientific evidence that DSE has any adverse effects on the developing foetus.

It may be useful to show pregnant women Health and Safety Executive (HSE) guidance note L26: *Display Screen Equipment Work. Health and Safety (Display Screen Equipment) Regulations 1992. Guidance on Regulations*, which gives official confirmation in writing that the risk of radiation from DSE is negligible.

Q Do workers have to tell their employer that they are pregnant?

A No. Health and safety law does not specifically require employees to tell their employer that they are pregnant. However, they *are* required by the **Health and Safety at Work, etc Act 1974** to co-operate with their employer to enable them to comply with their duties under health and safety law. If the employer does not know that an employee is pregnant, they cannot protect her from the additional health and safety risks that she may face. For this reason, and the fact that the pregnancy will become apparent sooner or later, employees should notify their employer in writing once they discover they are pregnant.

Q What constitutes a suitable rest facility for pregnant workers?

A Rest facilities for pregnant workers should be quiet and free of smoke or other fumes and strong smells. There should be somewhere for the worker to lie comfortably. The room should not be so isolated that the worker would not hear a fire alarm or safety messages given over the tannoy. It should be near enough to a toilet for the worker to reach it quickly. In many companies, the first aid room is used as the rest facility for pregnant workers, but this should not be allowed to compromise the provision of first aid to other staff.

Pressure Systems

Summary

Pressure systems are significant because of the considerable dangers associated with the release of stored energy resulting from system and/or component failure. The legislation covers the pressure system as a whole, ie it includes pipework, vessels and components, where the system contains steam or a "relevant fluid" at a pressure of 0.5 bar or above atmospheric pressure.

Practical Guidance

Information and marking

Manufacturers, designers, and suppliers must provide any information which may reasonably be required by the user or owner of the pressure system in order for them to fulfil their legal duties. The information should cover safe operating limits, design features, examinations and operation, or allow these to be readily determined. Relevant information on modifications and repairs should also be provided.

Pressure systems should be indelibly marked with the:

- manufacturer's name
- serial number (for identification)
- manufacture date
- construction standards
- maximum design pressure
- minimum design pressure
- design temperature.

It is an offence to remove these marks.

Installation

Installation must not give rise to danger or impair any safety or inspection devices.

Safe operating limits

Pressure systems must have an established safe operating limit before they can be used, and this should not be exceeded. The limit should be clearly marked on the system.

Written schemes of examination

A written scheme of examination which details the routine examination of the pressure system must be drawn up, implemented and regularly reviewed by a competent person. Such schemes should cover:

- protective devices
- systems where a fault or defect could give rise to danger (components may need to be specified)
- nature and frequency of examinations
- measures necessary to prepare the system for safe examination
- making provision for pressure systems to be examined prior to first use, where necessary.

Examinations

Competent people must examine pressure systems and/or components in accordance with the written schemes, and submit a signed and dated report.

The report should specify:

- the systems, components, etc examined, their condition and the examination results
- changes necessary to prevent danger and the time limit for repairs, etc
- the date after which the system may not be used without a further examination (subject to certain conditions, ie there must not be any danger arising from the postponement, only one postponement is made per examination and the enforcing authority is notified prior to the original date specified, the examinations may be postponed by written agreement)
- the suitability (or otherwise) of the written schemes of examination.

Imminent danger procedures

The competent person must make a report in situations where any modifications, repairs or changes in operating conditions to pressure systems are necessary to avoid imminent danger. A copy of this report must be given to the enforcing authority as well.

Operation

Pressure system operators must be given adequate and suitable instruction on the safe operation of the system and any emergency procedures. All pressure systems must be well maintained.

Preventing pressurisation

Where vessels are fitted with a means of preventing pressurisation, eg those fitted with a permanent outlet to the atmosphere or to a space where the pressure does not exceed atmospheric pressure, these fittings must be kept free from obstructions and kept open at all times when the vessels are in use.

Gas cylinders

Transportable pressure receptacles (gas cylinders) used to carry dangerous goods are covered by the **Carriage of Dangerous Goods (Classification, Packaging and Labelling) and Use of Transportable Pressure Receptacles Regulations 1996.**

Manufacturers, designers, importers and suppliers must ensure such pressure receptacles are safe, suitable, and conform to "approved requirements". Additional duties cover repairs, modifications, approval, certification, marking, filling and record keeping.

Case law

Although not a prosecution under the **Pressure Systems Safety Regulations 2000**, a case heard at Teeside Magistrates' Court in April 1997 illustrates the possible severity of an accident involving a system under pressure. In this case a pressure test technician was decapitated when a valve in a pipeline he was testing exploded — the valve smashed through a brick wall at 160 miles per hour. Neither of the two companies involved had checked to ensure that the valve could withstand the pressures necessary to carry out the tests.

Questions and Answers

Q What is a "relevant fluid"?

A A "relevant fluid" is steam at any pressure, or another fluid or mixture of fluids at a pressure of 0.5 bar above atmospheric pressure.

Q Are any other properties of the "relevant fluid" taken into account by the Regulations?

A No, other properties such as toxicity, flammability, etc are not taken into account and are covered by other legislation such as the **Management of Health and Safety at Work Regulations 1999** or the **Control of Substances Hazardous to Health Regulations 1999**.

Production Lines

Summary

Production lines are commonplace in many businesses, and range from those which involve a large number of people undertaking manual assembly tasks to those that are fully automated and require observation with infrequent human intervention. Many production lines run on a 24-hour basis, and consideration must therefore be given to the health and safety aspects of shift working/night working and statutory requirements regarding working hours.

Practical Guidance

The health and safety of those working on production lines has improved dramatically with improvements to general working conditions and equipment/machinery. However, there are still hazards involved in such activities which continue to result in employees having accidents or suffering ill-health effects.

General duties

Employers have a general duty of care to ensure the health, safety and welfare of their employees, and others who may be affected by work activities, eg contractors or members of the public.

In particular, they must provide and maintain:

- safe plant and systems of work
- safe use, handling, storage and transport of articles and substances
- the provision of any necessary information, instruction, training and supervision
- a safe place of work with safe means of access and egress
- a safe working environment, and adequate welfare facilities.

Risk assessment

The **Management of Health and Safety at Work Regulations 1999** (MHSWR) require employers to make a suitable and sufficient assessment of risks to the health and safety of their employees whilst at work.

The risk assessment should:

- identify all hazards associated with the production line, examples of which are given in the table below
- eliminate hazards if possible
- evaluate the risks arising from the hazards and decide whether existing precautions are adequate or whether more should be done

- devise and implement safe systems of work to ensure that the risks are either eliminated or adequately controlled.

These assessments should be recorded and reviewed on a regular basis.

The workplace

The **Workplace (Health, Safety and Welfare) Regulations 1992** expand upon the general duties shown above. They are intended to protect the health and safety of everyone in the workplace and to ensure that adequate welfare facilities are provided for everyone at work.

The specific duties relating to production lines are that the employer must ensure that:

- the workplace and the equipment and devices used in it are maintained in an efficient working order and in good repair
- any production lines in enclosed workplaces are effectively and suitably ventilated
- lighting is sufficient for people to work and move about safely
- the temperature during working hours is reasonable — a minimum of 16°C is considered acceptable
- all floors and traffic routes are of sound construction, and free from any holes or uneven surfaces, etc — they should be clearly marked and free of obstructions, particularly near corners or junctions, and there must be adequate drainage where necessary
- where possible, people and vehicles are segregated and sufficient and suitable traffic routes are provided
- adequate sanitary conveniences, washing facilities and drinking water are available
- there is suitable and sufficient accommodation for work and personal clothing and, where necessary, facilities to change clothing
- there is a separate area for employees to eat.

Rubbish should not be allowed to accumulate at the workplace, and access to production lines should be kept free from waste materials.

Every workroom must have sufficient floor area, height and unoccupied space to ensure the health, safety and welfare of workers. Workstations on the production line must be suitable for the people using them and the task being performed. The worker should be at a suitable height in relation to the work surface to assume the correct posture. Any work materials, equipment or controls which are used frequently should be within easy reach in order to avoid undue bending or stretching.

If the work, or a substantial part of it, can be done from a seated position, then suitable seating must be provided together with a foot-rest if necessary.

Work equipment

The employer must ensure that the work equipment provided is safe and appropriate for its intended use, that it is adequately maintained, and that employees are trained to use such equipment safely.

In particular, when considering production lines the employer should ensure that:

- access to dangerous parts of machinery or rotating stock bars is prevented, or the movement of such parts stopped before any person enters the danger zone
- any work equipment, component or articles/substances which are at high or low temperature are protected to prevent burning or scalding
- production lines are fitted with start controls and operating controls which require a deliberate action to activate them
- emergency stop buttons are readily accessible and have priority over all other controls
- all controls are clearly visible and identifiable
- there is a means of electrically isolating the production line or component parts of it, and bringing any moving machinery to a safe condition
- the production line has appropriate and clearly visible health and safety markings and/or warnings — these warnings may be visual (signs, lights, etc) or audible (horns, sirens, etc).

Electricity

Electrical safety in all workplaces is specifically legislated for in the **Electricity at Work Regulations 1989.**

Hazards arising from plant and equipment	
Machinery — moving parts, ejection/fall of materials, operating controls, stop buttons, emergency stop buttons, hot/cold parts	Provision and Use of Work Equipment Regulations 1998
Electricity — insulation, earthing connections, fuses, circuit breakers, isolation	Electricity at Work Regulations 1989
Stored energy	Pressure Systems Safety Regulations 2000
Mechanical failure	Provision and Use of Work Equipment Regulations 1998
Noise	Noise at Work Regulations 1989

Hazards arising from substances and materials	
Chemicals	Control of Substances Hazardous to Health Regulations 1999
Ignition sources	—
Glass	Workplace (Health, Safety and Welfare) Regulations 1992
Flammable solvents	—
Hazards due to place of work	
Segregation of vehicles and pedestrians	Workplace (Health, Safety and Welfare) Regulations 1992
Obstructions — access and egress	Workplace (Health, Safety and Welfare) Regulations 1992
Falling materials and objects	Workplace (Health, Safety and Welfare) Regulations 1992
Lighting	Workplace (Health, Safety and Welfare) Regulations 1992
Temperature	Workplace (Health, Safety and Welfare) Regulations 1992
Ventilation	Workplace (Health, Safety and Welfare) Regulations 1992
Waste materials	Workplace (Health, Safety and Welfare) Regulations 1992
Workstations	Workplace (Health, Safety and Welfare) Regulations 1992
Seating	Workplace (Health, Safety and Welfare) Regulations 1992
Hazards due to methods of work	
Manual handling — task, individual capacity, load, environment	Manual Handling Operations Regulations 1992
Repetitive movements	Manual Handling Operations Regulations 1992
Constrained position	Manual Handling Operations Regulations 1992
Lone working	Management of Health and Safety at Work Regulations 1999
Shift working	Management of Health and Safety at Work Regulations 1999

The employer must ensure that all electrical systems are constructed and maintained at all times to prevent danger, so far as is reasonably practicable.

Every work activity, including the operation, use and maintenance of and work near electrical systems, must be carried out without risk of danger. In particular:

- all conductors in a system must be insulated, protected or placed so as not to cause danger
- all conductors of electricity, eg metal conduits, must be earthed to prevent danger
- all connections in an electrical system must be both mechanically and electrically suitable
- electrical systems must be protected from any dangers arising from excess current, ie by using fuses or circuit breakers
- there must be an adequate means of switching off the electrical supply and an effective means of isolation to ensure that the electrical supply cannot inadvertently be switched back on
- those working with electricity must have the necessary knowledge and/or experience or be under appropriate supervision.

Manual handling

Where manual handling activities take place on a production line, employers must ensure that they are assessed taking into account the task, individual capability, load and environment. If possible, manual handling should be eliminated, but where this is not possible, the risk of injury should be minimised by one of the following means.

1. Automation.
2. Provision of suitable mechanical handling aids.
3. Redesign of the load, task or workplace, or a combination of these.
4. Job rotation.

Personal protective equipment

Personal protective equipment (PPE) should not be used as a substitute for other methods of risk control. Where required, employers must provide their employees with appropriate and suitable PPE and training in its usage.

Other legislation

Other Regulations which may be applicable in certain circumstances are as follows:

- **The Working Time Regulations 1998** (as amended)
- **Control of Substances Hazardous to Health Regulations 1999** (COSHH)
- **Noise at Work Regulations 1989.**

The list of hazards earlier in this section may be useful as a guide. Where appropriate, the specific or implied duty to carry out risk assessments under specific legislation has been identified.

Questions and Answers

Q What are the most common general risks associated with assembly lines, and how can they be overcome?

A The most common risks tend to be associated with manual handling hazards, particularly where there are repetitive actions involving strenuous effort. If the handling task cannot be designed out of the process, the production line should be configured in such a way as to reduce the need for reaching and twisting. Rotation of workers should also be considered.

Q Who should control the speed of a production line?

A In some cases, the flow of products may be determined by production rates further up the supply chain. For example, those employed to take packed cartons from a conveyor and stack them on a pallet will have a work pace determined by the speed of those packing the cartons. This means that it is important to have some mechanism whereby those "downstream" of the production process can control the speed of delivery to their section, eg to deal with a backlog. Methods can include the diversion of the conveyed goods to an overflow or holding area.

Public Safety

Summary

Employers are responsible not only for the health and safety of their employees (and the employees of other employers working on their premises), but also for the safety of members of the public who may be affected by their activities. This would include visitors to their site, local residents, their customers and even trespassers.

Practical Guidance

Duty of care

Section 3 of the **Health and Safety at Work, etc Act 1974** (HSW Act) requires employers to conduct their undertakings in such a way that non-employees, eg the public, who could be affected are not exposed to risks to their health and safety. Section 4 of the HSW Act puts a similar duty on the controller of the premises, which in many cases will be the employer.

The duty that employers owe to the public is not as onerous as that owed to their own employees, and in many cases if the situation is safe for employees, it is safe for the public, eg safe means of access. However, there are safety arrangements that must be made separately for members of the public, as they will not have the experience, training and familiarity with the workplace that the employees have. For example, as visitors to the site will not know the emergency procedures, they should be supervised at all times by a member of staff.

Premises safety

Under the **Occupiers' Liability Act 1957** and the **Occupiers' Liability Act 1984**, occupiers must take reasonable care of the safety of visitors to their premises. Children should be expected to be less careful than adults. This duty of care extends to unlawful visitors, such as trespassers, if the occupier:

- is aware of the danger
- knows (or should know) that a person may put themselves at risk
- might reasonably be expected to do something about the risk.

The Acts do not provide for criminal prosecution of an occupier who breaches them. However, they do provide for the injured person to sue the occupier for damages under civil law.

Product safety

The **Consumer Protection Act 1987** introduced strict product liability. This means that where damage is caused by a defect in a product, the producer or importer of the product may be liable for damages.

Major accidents

The **Control of Major Accident Hazards Regulations 1999** cover major industrial accidents resulting from the storage or handling of dangerous substances. The Regulations aim to protect both the employees on the premises and the public who are in the vicinity of the premises.

The requirements only apply to the industrial operations and the quantities of dangerous substances that are listed in the Regulations. If the Regulations apply to a workplace, the employer must:

- identify the major accident hazards associated with their activities
- have a Major Accident Prevention Policy (MAPP)
- carry out their operations safely
- report all major accidents on-site to the Health and Safety Executive (HSE).

Certain large-scale industrial operations have additional duties under the Regulations where:

- the HSE must be provided with a written safety report, which must be kept up-to-date
- the local authority must be provided with enough suitable information to allow them to draw up an off-site emergency plan
- the public must be provided with certain information.

Radiation

The **Public Information for Radiation Emergencies Regulations 1992** cover potential emergencies that would expose members of the public to certain levels of ionising radiation. The person in control of an activity which may result in a radiation emergency must provide members of the public who could be affected with:

- basic information on radioactivity, including its effects on people and the environment
- information on the type of radiation emergency that could occur, and what the consequences could be for them and the environment
- emergency measures that are planned to alert, protect and assist the public
- the action they should take in the event of a radiation emergency
- which authority is responsible for implementing the emergency measures and action.

Gas safety

The **Gas Safety (Installation and Use) Regulations 1998** aim to protect the public against the hazards of gas explosions and carbon monoxide poisoning from faulty gas heaters. The Regulations cover the safety of:

- gas fitters, eg all gas fitters must be a registered member of CORGI
- gas meters, eg gas meters must not be positioned so that they impede emergency escape from the premises
- installation pipework, eg marking of gas pipes
- gas appliances, eg an annual safety check must be carried out by a competent person.

Chemical safety

Under the **Chemicals (Hazard Information and Packaging for Supply) Regulations 1994** (as amended), containers of hazardous chemicals must be labelled with safety information in order to allow both employees and the public to use the product safely. Safety data sheets containing more extensive information must be supplied with any chemicals sold for use at work. However, chemicals sold in retail outlets for use by the public do not have to have safety data sheets, so long as there is sufficient information on the label.

Under the **Control of Substances Hazardous to Health Regulations 1999** (COSHH), employers must carry out an assessment of risk from hazardous substances, including micro-organisms, arising from work activities. The assessment must not only consider potential exposure of employees, but also of non-employees who may be affected. An example of where the public may suffer harmful effects which should be covered by the COSHH assessment is dispersal of *legionella* from air conditioning systems in the workplace to the surrounding area.

Insurance

Although the **Employers' Liability (Compulsory Insurance) Regulations 1998** requires employers to buy liability insurance to cover injuries and ill-health sustained by their employees, it does not require similar coverage for damage suffered by the public. However, many employers choose to also take out public liability insurance, which should cover them if they are faced with a successful claim for damages brought by a member of the public who has been injured by their work activity.

Questions and Answers

Q We regularly have members of the public visiting our premises. Do we have to provide first aid cover for them?

A The **Health and Safety (First Aid) Regulations 1981** only require employers to provide adequate first aid cover for their employees. It is, therefore, not a legal requirement to provide first aid for members of the public visiting your premises. However, many employers choose to use their first aid arrangements for visitors if they are injured on the premises. This not only shows a responsible attitude towards their moral duty, but a reduction in the extent of an injury which may be blamed on the employer, may reduce the level of compensation which could be claimed if the injured person were to sue them.

If first aid assistance is provided, the employer should bear in mind that if the first aider is negligent and causes the injury to be worse, the injured person may be able to claim damages against them. It is a good idea to have liability insurance to cover for the negligence of first aiders.

Q   There have been reports that children have been seen trespassing on our premises after working hours. What action should we take?

A   Under the **Occupiers' Liability Act 1957** and the **Occupiers' Liability Act 1984**, you have a duty of care to trespassers. If you have heard that children have been playing on your premises, you know that trespassers may be putting themselves at danger on your site. Therefore, if you are aware of any risks, and there is anything you can reasonably do to prevent these risks, you may be liable to pay damages if you are sued for injuries suffered by the children as a result.

If there are any dangers, you should take action to reduce the risks, such as fencing off deep holes and dangerous machinery. It may be best to prevent the children gaining access to the site in the first place, such as stepping up security and erecting fences around the perimeter. In some circumstances, warning signs are adequate means of trying to prevent injuries to trespassers, but in the case of children, who may not be able to read or understand the signs, the courts may determine that warning signs alone did not fulfil your duty of care.

Q   We rent our workplace, and share the premises with other tenants. Who is responsible for safety of visitors — the landlord or us?

A   Responsibility for the safety of your visitors will be divided between you and the landlord. The landlord will be responsible for common areas, such as access to the premises, stairways, toilets, etc, and you will be responsible for the areas and activities under your control. It is a good idea to consult with the landlord, preferably when the lease is drawn up, to identify who has responsibility for what. These responsibilities should be clearly defined and put down in writing, in case of any future dispute.

Radiation

Summary

The use of radiation, both ionising and non-ionising, is common in many types of work and domestic applications. Strict legislative and procedural controls are in place for ionising radiations given the serious health effects known to be associated with exposure, although non-ionising radiations are also capable of significant injuries if not adequately controlled.

Practical Guidance

Occupational control of ionising radiation

Legislative controls contained in the **Ionising Radiations Regulations 1999** require employers to assess any risks of exposure to ionising radiation and reduce such exposures as far as is reasonably practicable. Strict control measures are given along with detailed dose.

Notification and assessment

Before starting work with ionising radiation, employers must carry out a suitable and sufficient risk assessment. Additionally, the Health and Safety Executive (HSE) must be notified of work with ionising radiation at least 28 days before the work is to start.

Control measures

These include engineering and design controls such as shielding, ventilation, containment and minimising contamination, as well as safety features and warning devices. In addition, there must be detailed working arrangements for all work with ionising radiation and eating, drinking, smoking, taking snuff and applying cosmetics is prohibited in all "controlled areas". Personal protective equipment may only be used as a last resort where adequate control cannot be achieved by other means.

Dose limits

Dose limits specified in the Regulations are for both internal and external doses over a calendar year and include values for the whole body, individual organs and the eye lenses. Further dose limits are given for the foetuses of pregnant women. Workers who have received an overdose may not usually continue working with ionising radiation.

"Classified persons" and other specified persons must be provided with personal dosemeters. Workers who have received an overexposure of ionising radiation must undergo medical surveillance.

Record keeping

Certain records relating to ionising radiation must be maintained:
- dosemeter exposure records (must be maintained for 50 years)
- health records of medical surveillance (must be kept for 50 years)
- records of monitoring instrument performance tests (must be maintained for two years)
- accurate accounts of radioactive materials.

Radon

Radon is a naturally occurring radioactive gas which is prevalent in certain areas of the country. The **Ionising Radiations Regulations 1999** apply to any work with ionising radiation that takes place in areas where radon 222 may also be present.

Carriage

The carriage of radioactive materials is covered by the **Packaging, Labelling and Carriage of Radioactive Materials by Rail Regulations 1996** and the **Radioactive Material (Road Transport) (Great Britain) Regulations 1996**. The provisions of both Regulations are similar and cover safety, security, segregation of loads, filling of tanks and loading/unloading.

Radioactive substances

The **Radioactive Substances Act 1993** regulates the storage, use, accumulation and disposal of radioactive materials, and is administered by the Environment Agency.

Certificates of registration and authorisation are required for the storage/use and accumulation/disposal of radioactive materials.

Health effects

Ionising radiation is well known for its adverse effects on health, resulting in some cases in death. Exposure may damage the genetic material of people of reproductive age, causing stillbirths, birth defects in babies or other hereditary effects in their offspring.

Exposure may also precipitate the onset of cancerous growths in the body, and reddening of the skin, hair loss and skin burns are other common effects.

Non-ionising Radiation

There are no general legislative controls for non-ionising radiation so employers must ensure the health and safety of employees at work as required by the **Health and Safety at Work, etc Act 1974** (HSW Act), and carry out risk assessments, with appropriate control measures, as required under the **Management of Health and Safety at Work Regulations 1999**.

Ultraviolet radiation

Ultraviolet radiation covers the wavelength 100 nanometres to 400 nanometres (nm) (with 270nm being the most damaging), and is invisible to the human eye. Although easily stopped, it is powerful enough to excite atoms in materials it comes into contact with causing various chemical reactions. From a work point of view exposure to ultraviolet light is capable of causing damage to the skin and eyes. Skin effects include sunburn, while repeated long-term exposures have been implicated in premature skin ageing and skin cancer. Outdoor workers who expose their skin to the sun for long periods are at risk. Damage to the eyes includes keratoconjunctivitis and possibly the formation of cataracts in the long term.

Infrared radiation

Infrared radiation covers the wavelengths 700nm to 1mm, and is omitted by any hot entity. If infrared radiation is absorbed it causes burns, and as it is unable to penetrate deeply it tends to affect the skin and eyes. Thermal stress may occur if the core body temperature is raised by whole body irradiation.

Lasers

Laser is an acronym for Light Amplification by the Stimulated Emission of Radiation. Lasers are devices which emit small, high-intensity beams of light. Again the body areas most at risk are the eyes and skin. Damage is very localised, although permanent blindness may result from eye exposure to lasers. Manufacturers must classify any lasers they produce in accordance with British Standard BS EN 60825: *Safety of Laser Products*, which contains detailed safety information relevant to each laser class.

Radiofrequency radiation

Microwave radiation is contained in the radiofrequency region of the electromagnetic spectrum, ie where the wavelengths are greater than 1mm. Exposure to radiofrequency radiation causes a release of heat energy due to either the molecules in the exposed material, especially water, being induced to vibrate faster or the creation of electric currents in the body. Health effects are similar to those of infrared radiation although radiofrequency radiation is capable of much deeper penetration.

Questions and Answers

Q What is ionising radiation?

A Ionising radiation is a general term used to describe the radiation energy released by the decay of radioactive substances. These emissions will either be alpha or beta particles, or gamma or X-rays, all of which have sufficient energy to ionise atoms in matter they come into contact with, including atoms in human tissues and organs.

Q What are the common units of radiation measurement?

A The common units of radioactivity are:

- the Becquerel, which is a measurement of the activity (disintegration) of a radioactive substance — one Becquerel is equal to one disintegration per second

- the Gray, which is a measurement of absorbed dose — one Gray is the amount of energy deposited equivalent to one joule per kilogram

- the Sievert, which is the unit of dose equivalent, ie the absorbed dose weighted to take account of the ability of the particular form of radiation to cause damage to tissue.

Q What are common uses of ionising radiation?

A Ionising radiation is an extremely useful tool in medicine with both diagnostic applications, such as x-rays for clinical examinations and radioactive tracers to follow metabolic pathways, and therapeutic uses, such as treatment of cancer. In industry there are similar uses with ionising radiation being used to check the structural integrity of some plant components, baggage inspections and archaeological dating.

Q What is non-ionising radiation?

A Non-ionising radiation is radiation which does not release sufficient energy to ionise atoms and which consists entirely of electromagnetic waves. Although there is insufficient energy to ionise atoms in materials it comes into contact with, non-ionising radiation is still capable of causing significant adverse health effects. The energy contained in any particular wave is directly related to the frequency of the wave (its wavelength). Generally speaking, the shorter the wavelength the more easily it is stopped by the materials it comes into contact with. The skin and eyes are the body parts most at risk, although the somatic (sex) cells are also susceptible to damage.

Respiratory Protective Equipment

Summary

Respiratory protective equipment (RPE) is designed to provide the user with a supply of breathable air in a contaminated environment. The term RPE covers a wide range of equipment from a simple filtering respirator to highly sophisticated self-contained breathing apparatus.

Practical Guidance

Health and safety legislation requires employers to control exposure to hazardous substances encountered at work; these might include dusts, fumes, vapours, gases, mists and micro-organisms. The legislation requires that other more widespread measures of controlling exposure should be considered before the use of personal protective equipment (PPE), and that PPE, including RPE, should only be considered where it is not reasonably practicable to control exposure by other means.

Nature of the hazard

The nature of the substances involved must also be taken into account. There is always potential for leakage with RPE and, therefore, it cannot provide complete protection in all circumstances. For substances such as carcinogens or some micro-organisms, RPE alone is unlikely to provide an acceptable level of protection.

Dusts

Larger or heavier dust particles will tend to accumulate on surfaces and will then pose a further risk when disturbed (eg by sweeping). Lighter or smaller particles will tend to remain airborne for longer periods, and are thus more easily inhaled. The smaller particle size also means that they are inhaled deeper into the lungs, where the potential for damage is greater.

Dusts will often contain particles of potentially hazardous substances, for example asbestos or silica. Individual exposures to dusts containing hazardous materials can produce serious reactions in the body (such as shortage of breath and tightness of the chest), but repeated exposure may lead to long-term damage and lung disease.

Fume

Fume is most frequently generated by welding and soldering. Metal fume consists of very fine particles of metal, and is usually invisible. Symptoms of fume inhalation will vary according to the material in use, but all are potentially harmful.

Vapours and Gases

Vapours and gases are encountered in a wide variety of workplace activities, including painting and cleaning. Symptoms will vary depending on the substances involved, but vapours and gases are absorbed into the bloodstream after inhalation, enabling them to quickly affect other areas of the body. Some symptoms are irreversible, and the effect of repeated exposure will be cumulative.

Mists

Mists are created when tiny drops of liquid are suspended in the air as a result of mixing or spraying activities. As with vapours, mists can be quickly dispersed throughout the body via the bloodstream following inhalation.

Circumstances in which RPE may be appropriate

Circumstances where it might be appropriate to consider the use of RPE include:
- where periodic maintenance work is undertaken in areas which are not regularly accessed and where exposure levels are high
- where RPE is needed to protect employees only in the event of an equipment failure, ie for escape purposes
- where any exposure is very short-term in nature and there is no reasonably practicable alternative method for controlling exposure
- where other control measures are currently being installed and the use of RPE is a short-term measure until the installation is complete.

In some situations the most effective control of exposure will be obtained through a combination of types of control measure, including the use of RPE.

Types of RPE available

Many different types of RPE are available, but all fall into one of two categories, as follows:
- self-contained breathing apparatus and air-fed hoods that provide the wearer with breathable air from an independent source such as a cylinder; these must be used where there is any risk of asphyxiation or engulfment
- powered respirators, and face masks fitted with filters, which take contaminated air from the surrounding working environment and clean or filter it for the wearer to breathe.

Selecting RPE

A very wide range of RPE is available, much of which is designed for particular specialist applications; specialist advice should therefore be sought where necessary in order to select the most effective RPE for a particular working environment. In many cases, results of environmental monitoring will need to be taken into consideration in order to select appropriate equipment.

Other factors which may need to be considered include:

- fitness of the wearer (RPE may give additional weight to carry or provide some resistance to breathing)
- face size and shape and facial hair (efficacy of RPE depends on achieving a good seal where the skin meets the mask)
- wearing of spectacles
- the particular demands of the job to be done.

Questions and Answers

Q What should the regular testing of a fairly basic respirator involve and how often should it be carried out?

A A thorough examination should be made at least once per month, and if conditions are particularly severe this interval should be reduced as appropriate. The examination should comprise a thorough visual examination of all parts of the respirator, particularly the facepiece, straps, valves/filters, etc.

Q In what format should records of RPE issue and maintenance be kept?

A There is no prescribed format or type of storage system; records may be kept on a computer-based system or on paper. Whatever system is used it is important that records can be easily retrieved and understood, possibly some years hence.

Q How can we ensure that the RPE we select will be suitable for all of our employees?

A Where possible, choose RPE that is available in a range of sizes. In some cases it may be necessary to offer a selection of different models of RPE so that every employee can be provided with well-fitting RPE. A good fit and seal are essential for adequate protection — if this cannot be achieved for some reason it may be more appropriate to consider using types of RPE that do not rely on face seals for effectiveness (eg those incorporating hoods).

Rest Rooms

Summary

Many people spend at least eight hours a day at work. The work carried out during this period is usually demanding, either physically or mentally, and during the working day people will need periods of rest. Workers will therefore need somewhere they can rest relatively undisturbed.

Practical Guidance

Rest areas

Under the **Workplace (Health, Safety and Welfare) Regulations 1992** (Workplace Regulations), employers should provide suitable rest facilities for their workers. In the case of workplaces that existed before the Workplace Regulations came into force, ie those in use before 1.1.93, suitable rest facilities may be provided in the form of rest areas, rather than rest rooms.

Rest rooms

Under the Workplace Regulations, suitable rest facilities for new workplaces, ie those built or renovated after 1.1.93, must include one or more rest rooms.

Tobacco smoke

The rest rooms or rest areas provided to comply with the Workplace Regulations must include suitable arrangements for protecting non-smokers against the discomfort caused by tobacco smoke.

Eating facilities

Under the Workplace Regulations, if food eaten in the workplace is likely to become contaminated, the rest facilities must include suitable facilities for eating meals. Workplaces where food is likely to become contaminated may be identified by complying with other legislation, such as the **Control of Substances Hazardous to Health Regulations 1999**, **Ionising Radiations Regulations 1999** and **Control of Asbestos at Work Regulations 1987**.

New and expectant mothers

The Workplace Regulations require suitable rest facilities to be provided for pregnant women and new mothers. This is to allow for the increase in fatigue often experienced by new and expectant mothers due to the demands put on the body by pregnancy and breastfeeding.

Construction sites

The **Construction (Health, Safety and Welfare) Regulations 1996** apply to construction sites, and contain similar requirements as the Workplace Regulations in terms of rest facilities, ie:

- rest facilities must be provided at readily accessible locations
- there must be a sufficient number of rest rooms or rest areas
- rest facilities must include suitable arrangements for protecting non-smokers from the discomfort of tobacco smoke
- suitable rest facilities must be provided for new and expectant mothers
- there must be suitable arrangements for preparing and eating meals, and for boiling water.

Rest periods

Under the **Management of Health and Safety at Work Regulations 1999**, employers must carry out risk assessments for their work activities in order to identify and implement suitable arrangements to ensure the health and safety of their workers. The arrangements required to protect the health of their workers may include providing rest periods. This would particularly apply to those carrying out physically demanding work, such as manual handling tasks, or mentally demanding work, such as customer services involving constant telephone work.

Questions and Answers

Q I often work in remote, outdoor workplaces. Does my employer have to provide suitable rest facilities?

A Remote outdoor workplaces are exempt from the Workplace Regulations, apart from the requirements which relate to toilets, washing facilities and drinking water, which must be provided so far as is reasonably practicable. This means that your employer does not have to provide you with rest facilities while you are working in these areas. However, if your work is physically demanding, your employer should have identified the need for rest breaks when they carried out the risk assessment. During these rest breaks, you should find somewhere suitable to sit down and rest, preferably protected from the weather. It may be possible to sit in your vehicle, but if not, your employer should consider providing you with a portable folding chair or stool and some means of protection from the rain and cold.

Rest Rooms

Q I run a small stall in the food hall of a shopping centre. I do not have enough space to provide a rest area for my staff. What should I do?

A It is likely that the food hall has plenty of seats and tables where your staff can take their rest breaks. As it is unlikely that their breaks will be taken during the busy part of the day when all the tables are taken, the food hall facilities should be suitable as rest facilities. However, you should make sure that they are not disturbed during their breaks, eg by having to return to the food stall whenever a customer arrives.

Q How many chairs and tables do we need to provide in our rest room?

A There should be enough chairs and tables to seat the number of people who are likely to use the rest room at any one time. Find out what time of day the most people use the room, eg lunchtime, and count the number of people who usually use the rest room at that time. Provide a basic number of chairs and tables to begin with, and time and experience will show how many you need, bearing in mind that many people may habitually leave the workplace for lunch. If there appears to be a shortage of chairs and tables, you will need to supply more, so allow for this in your budget. Remember that the level of usage will probably vary depending on the time of year — more people will stay indoors during the winter.

Risk Assessment

Summary

One of the most important tools in managing health and safety is risk assessment, the purpose of which is to determine and implement the control measures necessary to eliminate or reduce the risks associated with identified hazards. There are four stages to risk assessment: hazard identification, risk evaluation, the determination of control measures and monitoring the effectiveness of the assessment.

Practical Guidance

The Regulations below contain a risk assessment requirement:
- **Manual Handling Operations Regulations 1992**
- **Noise at Work Regulations 1989**
- **Control of Asbestos at Work Regulations 1987**
- **Control of Lead at Work Regulations 1998**.

However, many Regulations imply the need to carry out a risk assessment in order to be able to determine what measures are adequate, appropriate and suitable. Some of those Regulations are listed below:
- **Health and Safety (First Aid) Regulations 1981**
- **Provision and Use of Work Equipment Regulations 1998**
- **Workplace (Health, Safety and Welfare) Regulations 1992**
- **Personal Protective Equipment at Work Regulations 1992**.

Hazard identification

Risk assessments must start with the identification of every hazard in the workplace associated with the work activities. A 10 minute walk around should indicate main areas of concern and this can be supported by using recorded accidents in the accident book to highlight problem areas. Where work activities are the same "generic assessments" may be used, ie one assessment which is applicable to several similar work activities, although any differences must be identified and evaluated in each case. It may be useful to draw up a list of hazards for each area. The identification stage should also identify the people at risk from each hazard.

Evaluating risks

Once all the hazards have been identified the risks associated with them must be evaluated. In the simplest form this means designating "high", "medium" or "low" ratings to each hazard, taking into account the likelihood of harm occurring and the severity of the outcome if it did, and any existing control measures which are in place.

The method of undertaking risk assessments is arbitrary and the level of complexity assigned to the risk ratings is a matter of personal preference. For example, some systems are more complicated and assign numerical values to the likelihood and severity factors to give a numerical risk value.

The parameters used to categorise likelihood and severity are also arbitrary, although a simple breakdown could be as follows.

Likelihood	Very Likely Likely Unlikely Extremely Unlikely
Severity	Death Major Injuries Minor Injuries No Injuries

Determining and monitoring control measures

The risk evaluation stage should identify the high, medium and low risk activities in the workplace so a hierarchy of priorities is established. High risks are the highest priority, ie most likely to happen and/or cause greatest injury, and should be addressed first, followed by medium risks and finally low risks. The purpose of risk assessment is to determine the control measures necessary to prevent or at least reduce the risks associated with identified hazards at work.

The risk assessment should help to determine when the control measures should be monitored, as without the monitoring of control measures the whole process may be compromised.

Information, instruction, training and supervision are common control measures which are applicable to every hazard identified in a workplace. For a list of specific hazards see table below.

Common hazards and control measures

Hazards	Controls
Manual handling	Mechanical aids, hoists, getting assistance, breaking loads into smaller units
Hazardous substances	Substitution for less hazardous alternatives, extraction ventilation, personal protective equipment

Work equipment (ladders, machinery, tools, etc)	Substitution for less hazardous alternatives, extraction ventilation, personal protective equipment
Work equipment (ladders, machinery, tools, etc)	Guarding, demarcation of danger zones, restricted operation/use, planned preventative maintenance
Electricity	Insulated tools, residual circuit breakers, fuses, earthing, planned preventative maintenance
Stairs, etc	Good lighting, handrails, non-slip surfaces, slightly raised front edges
Fire	Detection/warning systems, suitable storage facilities for substances and goods, fire-retardant furniture and fittings
Shift work	Individual suitability to shift work, adequate rest periods, standard shift patterns (night shifts or day shifts but not mixtures of the two), controlling hours worked
Noise	Reduction at source, isolation, ear protection, demarcation of danger zones
Stress	Reduce/increase workload, more control over work, work suitable for individual, avoidance of monotonous repetitive work
Work environments (temperature, space, lighting, ventilation, etc)	Good lighting, ventilation, redesign layout of area, heaters/coolers

Case law

There are many statutory and common law cases based on risk assessments. For example, in *Jenkinson v Brook Motors Ltd*, the court held that even an experienced employee was still owed a duty to have risks associated with his work assessed and a safe system of working defined.

Specific assessments

Details of risk assessments required under specific legislation are given in the relevant sections of this publication. However, a comprehensive risk assessment, as required by the **Management of Health and Safety at Work Regulations 1999** (Management Regulations), would cover all other requirements.

Questions and Answers

Q Is there a difference between the terms "hazard" and "risk"?

A There *is* a difference between these two terms although they are often used interchangeably. "Hazard" is the potential something has to cause harm, while "risk" is the actual realisation of that harm, ie the likelihood and severity of the harm if the hazard did occur. The following example should clarify the meanings. A sealed bottle of bleach in a cupboard is a "hazard", ie it has the potential to cause harm when the bottle is opened, but not when it is closed. The bleach becomes a "risk" when the bottle is opened, ie when there is exposure to the hazardous contents. However, the degree of risk depends on whether any control measures have been taken, such as use by designated people only, wearing gloves and goggles and ensuring appropriate training has been given.

Q   Do risk assessments have to be repeated for all the different sets of Regulations?

A   No. Where a risk assessment has been carried out under, and complies with, the more specific Regulations, such as COSHH, it does not have to be repeated under the Management Regulations, provided it remains valid.

Q   When should risk assessment be reviewed?

A   The legislation requires risk assessments to be reviewed regularly or when there have been any changes in the workplace, work equipment and/or work procedures which make the original, or previous, assessment invalid. There is no predetermined or standard time period for reviews to take place and it will depend on individual circumstances, eg pregnant women will need the risk assessments of their work reviewed frequently throughout their term of pregnancy as their abilities, etc will alter during this time. In a recent case heard at Hartlepool Magistrates' Court, a construction company was fined for failing to review its risk assessments, in respect to public safety, when it became apparent that children were playing with some of the materials being stored on the construction site and one child was killed as a result of an accident involving those materials.

Q   Who should carry out the risk assessments?

A   The only real criterion is that the person should be competent to assess the particular risks in any risk assessment. Competent is not legally defined but is generally accepted as someone who has the necessary experience, training, qualifications and/or skills to do whatever task is required competently. In practice, the employees carrying out the work being assessed should be actively involved in the risk assessment process as they will have first-hand knowledge of what actually goes on (this may be different to what the managers assume goes on). A nominated person, ie the manager, should co-ordinate all the assessment findings and calculate the various risk ratings in order to provide some continuity to the process.

Q   Do external health and safety experts have to be employed as the competent people to do risk assessments?

A   No, the Health and Safety Executive (HSE) encourages employers to undertake their own assessments utilising in-house knowledge and experience where possible. An external consultant will only provide a "snapshot" picture of what was going on at the actual time of the consultation visits and may miss important points which are not obvious or being carried out, etc at that time. However, there may be very specialised risks where an external expert is necessary, eg ionising radiations, asbestos, etc and in-house expertise is not sufficient. Even in these cases the employees involved in the work should be included.

Roof Working

Summary

Accidents associated with people falling through or from roofs are all too common in the construction industry, and during maintenance activities. Health and Safety Executive (HSE) figures show that almost one in every five accidents in the construction industry occur during roof work, and many of these involve people who are simply involved in cleaning and maintaining roofs, rather than building them.

Practical Guidance

Many of the accidents which occur when working on roofs could have been prevented by the provision and proper use of readily available equipment. A safe system of work will address this issue by careful planning prior to the activity; in particular, close attention should be paid to the means of access to the roof and the system of work adopted once on the roof.

Those involved in the design of new roofs have a duty to take ease of access into account and consider how maintenance work can be carried out in safety.

The consequences of falling from heights are serious and therefore a high standard of protection is required.

General duties

All employers must ensure, so far as is reasonably practicable, the health and safety of employees at work, and of any other person who may be affected by the work activity. In particular they must provide and maintain a safe working environment and a safe means of access and egress to the place of work.

The employer also has a duty to ensure that all employees are provided with adequate information, instruction, training and supervision on risks to health and safety.

Risk assessment

An employer must make a suitable and sufficient assessment of risks to the health and safety of their employees whilst at work. The purpose of the risk assessment is to enable an employer to identify the action necessary to comply with the requirements of any relevant legislation and to identify the preventative or protective control measures necessary to control the risks highlighted.

The main hazards associated with roof work are:
• worker falls

314

- falls of materials
- exposure to radiation from transmitter antennae.

Falls or falling objects

Employers have a duty to ensure that in workplaces which are under their control, suitable and sufficient measures are taken to prevent any person falling a distance likely to cause personal injury or any person being struck by a falling object likely to cause personal injury. Any area where these events are likely to happen must be clearly indicated.

A similar duty applies to work on construction sites, which are covered by specific legislation, whereby employers must take measures to prevent persons falling through fragile roof materials.

Where regular access is needed to roofs, suitable permanent access equipment should be provided. There should also be fixed physical safeguards to prevent falls from edges and through fragile roofs.

If fixed ladders are used to access roofs, they should be of sound construction, properly maintained and securely fixed. If they are at an angle of less than 15° to the vertical, and are more than 2.5m high, they should be fitted with suitable safety hoops or permanently fixed fall-arrest systems.

Secure fencing should be provided wherever possible at any place where a person might fall a distance of two metres or more.

Fencing should be sufficiently high, with any gaps filled in sufficiently, to prevents falls of people or objects over or through the fencing. The minimum requirement is that fencing should consist of two guard-rails, the top one being at a height at least 1100mm above the roof.

The fencing should be of adequate strength and stability to prevent any person or object falling through it. It should be designed to prevent objects falling from the edge. Where necessary a toe-board should be provided.

Where only occasional access is required, other less permanent safeguards may be acceptable. Access should be limited to specified authorised people, and in high-risk situations a formal written permit-to-work system should be adopted. A safe system of work should be operated, which may include the provision and use of a fall-arrest system, or safety lines and harnesses and secure anchorage points. Safety lines should be short enough to prevent injury if a fall occurs, and if possible should prevent the worker from reaching the edge of the roof.

All fragile roofs should be clearly identified with prominent warning signs (eg Caution — Fragile Roof). The signs must meet the requirements of the **Health and Safety (Safety Signs and Signals) Regulations 1996**. A fragile roof is defined as one which would be liable to fracture if a person were to walk or fall on to it. All glazing and asbestos cement or similar sheeting should be treated as fragile, unless there is clear evidence to the contrary.

When working on fragile roofs, roof ladders or crawling boards must be used. Where a valley or parapet gutter is used as a means of access, and if the adjacent roof is covered by fragile materials, suitable covers which extend a minimum of one metre up the roof or other means should be provided to prevent a fall through the fragile material.

Flat roofs

When working on flat roofs, the main hazard is falling from the edge of the roof. Guard-rails and toe-boards should be provided in these circumstances and around any openings or roof lights; alternatively these could be covered over.

Sloping roofs over 10° pitch

Three main hazards exist when working on such roofs:
- working close to the edge
- working at the edge itself
- working on the roof which may result in sliding down and falling from the edge.

The degree of danger of slipping on the roof will depend upon the pitch of the roof, the possibility of the surface being made slippery by weather conditions (eg ice, snow or rain) other natural phenomena (eg moss, bird droppings) and the type of footwear worn by the individual.

During extensive work on a roof, barriers or guard-rails will usually be required to prevent falls. These should be high enough and strong enough to stop a person who is rolling or sliding down the roof slope. Purpose-built roof ladders and/or crawling boards should be used.

Construction work

There is specific legislation relating to construction work, although the duty of the employer to employees carrying out construction work is the same as above, ie to take suitable and sufficient steps to prevent persons falling.

Where the distance of a potential fall is two metres or more, sufficient guard-rails, toe-boards, barriers or other means of protection must be provided. Where it is not practical to provide such protection, suitable personal suspension equipment must be provided, and must be securely attached to a structure and capable of supporting the person.

Where it is not practical to provide either of the above, fall-arrest equipment must be used. This includes safety nets and harnesses designed to arrest a fall from height.

Materials and objects may not be thrown or tipped from a height where there is a danger of injury to those below.

Access consideration

Authority to access a roof, for any purpose, must first be obtained from the person responsible for the premises. There may be a "permit to work" system operating.

Care should be taken when climbing ladders. Always maintain three point contact whilst climbing. Vertical ladders over two metres in height should be protected by hoops to prevent falls.

Where access is via a trap door avoid "billowing" clothing, which may get caught up. Do not stand on trap doors and ensure any stays are firmly secured. Be extra careful when closing traps, they can swing unexpectedly.

Clothing

Wear safety footwear with a well defined heel; trainers and flat-bottomed shoes are not suitable. Women should avoid high heels.

Helmets must be worn where there are overhead structures or people working above.

Other protective clothing may be needed, including waterproofs. Gloves and warm clothing may be needed in winter. Protecting the head from cold is very important.

Weather

The weather can cause great danger on a roof. A mild breeze at ground level can be a gale 10 floors up. Try to avoid going out when there is heavy rain. Apart from slipping, you are likely to work in haste and lose concentration.

Snow and ice will be slippery. The edge of the roof may be hard to see and you could even experience a whiteout in a blizzard. Snow can make fragile roof-lights difficult to see. Beware of icicles falling as a result of your actions, or due to a slight rise in temperature. Beware of "black" ice. Avoid going on roofs in fog, changes in visibility can be abrupt.

Do not go on a roof when the windspeed is over 25 mph, (listen to weather forecasts if you are unsure), or during a storm when there is lightning. Baggy clothing or large items being carried can act like a "sail".

Pathways

Keep to defined pathways where possible. There are numerous tripping hazards on a roof including gulleys, lightning conductors, drain covers etc. Also be aware of algae or chemical spillage on paths. Algae can make any surface very slippery. Bird droppings are slippery as well as a health hazard. Birds may also swoop without warning, causing you to lose your footing.

Aerials

Do not approach aerials with any of the following: heart pacemakers, pagers, cell phones, walkie talkies, etc. Keep clear of all aerials/antennae on roofs. All aerials should be assumed to be live and transmitting. Some may have a caged area around them and a radiation warning.

Beware of carrying/using objects around aerials. Extended metal tape-measures and aluminium ladders, amongst others, can act as conductors.

317

The effects of radio frequency (RE) and microwave radiation can be serious where high power outputs are concerned. Electronic equipment can be affected, but of greater concern are the possible health effects. For example, high power microwave transmissions can cause heating of the gonads, very quickly resulting in sterilisation.

Chimneys, exhaust flues and vents

Fumes exhausted at roof level many well be harmful. Where exhaust stacks are present it may be necessary to restrict access to when a permit-to-work ensures safety by taking those stacks out of use. Some steel chimneys may have guy ropes and wires which cross the walkways. They are not always easy to see and may form tripping hazards.

Roof located plant

A large variety of plant can be found on roofs of buildings. Condensers and other fans may start without warning. Fans or drives may have loose or missing covers or guards. There may be hot parts of chiller units and pipework exposed to the touch. Certain types of cooling towers may be flush with the roof floor level — do not walk across the vents, or cover them. Avoid inhaling the vapour from cooling towers. All wet cooling towers can provide a breeding environment unless regularly treated to prevent bacteria forming, typically in large drums, these chemicals are highly toxic and corrosive.

Never walk on pipes or ductwork. They may collapse or fracture and spray chemicals. Always use the bridges provided.

For access onto a roof at night, ensure there is adequate lighting. Temporary lighting must be safe and fit for the purpose. If a torch is used, always take a working spare.

Personal protective equipment

The employer must provide suitable personal protective equipment for the risks involved. All fall-arrest personal protective equipment should carry the CE mark.

Checklist for Safe Roof Access

- Do I have permission for access to this roof?
- Is there a permit-to-work I need to follow?
- Are there any local rules I must follow?
- Is the weather suitable for roof acces?
- Have I suitable clothing for the conditions and not baggy or unsuitable clothing that may be a hazard?
- Do I need a safety helmet?
- Is access to the work area safe and protected by adequate edge protection?
- Is there adequate lighting at night or do I need a torch?
- Are there any aerials or other transmitters in use which could be a risk?

- Are there any stacks or other discharges at roof level which could be a risk?
- Are there any overhead power lines or other electrical hazards?
- Are there any trip hazards to note?
- Are there any areas specifically prohibited from access?
- Do I really need to go on the roof?

Questions and Answers

Q What should I look for when checking the safety of a ladder?

A Split uprights, broken feet, loose or distorted rungs. Ladders should not be painted as these types of defaults may be hidden.

Q Do I always have to provide guard-rails on the roof edge?

A No, it depends on the nature of the work, eg whether it is carried out regularly, and the duration of the work. Where it is not practical to provide guard-rails, a safety harness must be worn.

Q If a mobile access tower is used as the means of access to a roof, can my own employees erect it?

A Yes, providing they are trained and competent in the erection, modification and dismantling of scaffolds.

Room Dimensions and Space

Summary

Employers must ensure that every room in which their employees work has sufficient floor area, height, and space to enable them to carry out their work in safety and without risk to health. In making the calculation, allowances must be made for space used by fixtures and fittings, and the volume of work equipment or materials.

Practical Guidance

Employers have a general duty to provide a safe place of work without risk to health to their employees. With regard to the dimensions of rooms in which employees work, they must be of sufficient size to enable work activities to be carried out without the risk of anyone being injured or suffering ill-health.

The main hazards of working in an area which is small, is that the employees may injure themselves by bumping into furniture or equipment. Equally, if they have insufficient room to maintain a comfortable posture, the employee may suffer musculo-skeletal problems. Inadequate space may hamper evacuation in the event of an emergency. There may be inadequate ventilation in small or crowded workplaces, and this will be of particular significance if hazardous fumes or dusts are generated.

Specific legislation

Employers have a responsibility under the **Workplace (Health, Safety and Welfare) Regulations 1992** to ensure that every room in which people work has enough free space to allow people to get to and from workstations, and move within the workroom, with ease.

The number of people who are permitted to work in a room at any one time will depend not only on the size of the room, but on the space which is occupied by furniture, fittings, equipment, materials and the layout of the room.

Each work room should be of sufficient height to enable persons safe access to workstations. If there are any obstructions such as low beams, these should be clearly marked. The exception to this is if the room is only used for short periods of time.

The total volume of the room when empty divided by the number of people normally working in it should be at least $11m^3$. Where a room has a very high ceiling, ie above 3m high, the calculation should ignore the height in excess of 3 metres.

The figure of 11m^3 per person is the minimum suggested in L24, the Approved Code of Practice to the **Workplace (Health, Safety and Welfare) Regulations 1992**. Even if this is achieved, there may still be insufficient space if much of the workplace is taken up by furniture or machinery.

The figure of 11m^3 does not apply to:

- retail sales kiosks, attendants' shelters, machine control cabs or similar small structures where space is necessarily limited
- rooms being used for lectures, meetings or other similar purposes
- workplaces of a very temporary nature, eg plant rooms.

Examples of room sizes

In a typical room that has a ceiling that is 2.4 metres high, a floor area of 4.6 m^2 would be needed to achieve a space of 11m^3. This means that the floor area would have to be 2.0 x 2.3m (about the size of a large desk and return unit). Where the ceiling is three metres high (or more), the minimum floor area will need to be 3.7m^2. This means that the floor area would need to be 2.0 x 1.85m. The above figures are based upon single person occupancy, and the floor areas and volumes to be achieved must be multiplied by the actual number of occupants.

It must be remembered that the Regulations require there to be sufficient unoccupied space. Rooms will therefore tend to need larger dimensions (or have fewer people working in them), according to the purpose of the room. Factors will include the type of machinery in use, work equipment, siting of fixtures and fittings, and the general layout of the room. Where space is limited, it is important to carefully plan the workplace.

Although the regulation about space applied to existing workplaces from 1 January 1996, it does not apply to rooms in factories existing before 1993. This is because the equivalent part of the **Factories Act 1961** required employers to ensure that each person employed in the workplace should have 11m^3 of space not taking into account the space which is more than 4.2m above floor level has been replaced by Schedule 1 to the Workplace Regulations. The difference between the current Regulations and the 1961 Act as maintained in Schedule 1 is the height. In factory premises which pre-date the present legislation, it is acceptable to meet the requirements of Schedule 1 to the Workplace Regulations. However, any new premises, conversions or extensions must comply with the **Workplace (Health, Safety and Welfare) Regulations 1992**.

Although no specific work area is mentioned, the **Electricity at Work Regulations 1989** require the employer to ensure that there is sufficient working space provided for work on or near expected live conductors.

Questions and Answers

Q   Do plant rooms have to meet a minimum space requirement?

A   No, providing the work carried out in them is of a short duration. Note that there must be enough free space to enable electrical work to be carried out safely.

Q Does each individual employee have to be given a personal allocation of $3.7m^2$ floor space, or is it acceptable for this to be an average figure over the whole office?

A You should work to an average figure, but must also take into account the needs of each worker. On balance it will almost certainly be found that an average floor area in excess of the minimum is required, once you have allowed for furniture, etc.

Q If there is a lot of furniture does the employee need more space?

A Yes, you should undertake a risk assessment, and if the employee does not have enough space to move around furniture safely, they will need more space.

Safety Committees

Summary

Communication between managers and workers is the key to an effective occupational health and safety management system. One way of providing a communication link, especially for employers who have a large workforce, is to set up safety committees, which meet on a regular basis to discuss health and safety issues and provide feedback.

Practical Guidance

Union committees

Section 2(7) of the **Health and Safety at Work, etc Act 1974** (HSW Act) requires employers to establish a safety committee if they receive a request in writing from two or more safety representatives appointed by one or more recognised trade unions. The committee must be set up within three months of the employer receiving the written request.

In setting up a safety committee following a request by safety representatives, the employer must:

- enter into consultation with the safety representatives
- post a notice in the workplace which states the composition of the safety committee and the workplaces covered by it.

Non-union committees

Section 2(7) of the HSW Act only applies where the request for a safety committee comes from safety representatives officially appointed by a recognised trade union. If this is not the case, employers are not under any specific legal requirement to set up a safety committee.

Employers are required, however, to have effective arrangements in place to plan, organise, control, monitor and review health and safety systems and procedures, under the **Management of Health and Safety at Work Regulations 1999** (MHSWR). Employers may choose to set up a safety committee as a means of communication between the workforce and managers, as part of the arrangements for planning, organising and monitoring health and safety in the workplace.

MHSWR also requires employees to notify their employers of any perceived shortcomings in their health and safety arrangements. Safety committees provide a useful and structured opportunity for employees, or their representatives, to do this.

Functions

The basic aim of a safety committee should be to facilitate communication and co-operation between managers and workers, in order to provide a safe workplace. When the committee is first set up, the functions should be defined and preferably put into writing. These functions are likely to include:

- examining reports of accidents and diseases resulting from work activities, in order to identify problem areas and ways of improving health and safety
- discussing safety audits carried out, in order to review the results and decide what action needs to be taken
- reporting by the safety representatives of employees' concerns and requests in relation to health, safety and welfare
- co-operating on planning, implementing and monitoring safe systems of work and safety procedures, for example, if a manager wants to introduce new procedures for a particular activity, the plans should be given to the safety representative who will consult with the workers affected to provide feedback
- examining health and safety training provided, and checking whether it is proving effective
- discussing what health and safety information needs to be communicated to the workers, and how it should be done, eg poster campaigns, regular departmental meetings, memos, etc
- providing a point of contact with health and safety enforcement inspectors, and examining reports from these inspectors and Health and Safety Executive (HSE) guidance which is relevant to the workplace
- comparing the commitments given in the health and safety policy to the actual situation in the workplace
- occasionally carrying out inspections of the workplace, eg to check up on the operation of health and safety measures and to increase familiarity of committee members with the workplace and work activities.

Membership

Membership of safety committees should be determined by consultation between managers and safety representatives. If the committee is being set up following the official request of union safety representatives, it is likely that the representatives that put in the request will want to be members of the committee.

Each committee should have a chairperson, who will be in control of the discussions, make sure the agenda is followed and keep order. There should also be a secretary, who will take minutes and provide administrative support, such as providing copies of the written programme of meetings and agendas, distributing reports and minutes, and chasing up people who are late for the meetings.

Meetings

A programme of meetings should be drawn up at the first committee meeting, and should be planned well in advance. The programme should be displayed on notice boards, so that workers can raise issues with their representatives before the next meeting.

Meetings should be given an allocated time period, eg an hour, which should be followed as closely as possible, with the chairperson taking control when necessary. An agenda should be drawn up and followed, giving time for "any other business" at the end of the meeting.

The frequency of meetings depends on:

- volume of business
- size of the workplace
- the number of employees
- level of risk in the workplace
- the type of work carried out.

Once the programme has been set, meetings should not be cancelled or postponed, except in extreme circumstances, as this will reduce the credibility of the committee. On some occasions, it may be necessary to hold *ad hoc* meetings at short notice, eg following a serious accident or incident.

Members should be discouraged from missing meetings. The chairperson should keep a record of who was present, and should take issue with those members who are frequently absent. If their attendance record fails to improve, they should be replaced with an equivalent representative.

Minutes

The secretary should take minutes during the meeting. After each meeting, the minutes should be typed up as soon as possible (at least within a week) and a copy given to each committee member and a member of the senior management, preferably the top person who has ultimate responsibility for health and safety, eg the managing director. Copies of the minutes should also be distributed to the workforce, or pinned to notice-boards so that anyone who is interested has easy access to them.

Questions and Answers

Q How often should the committee meet?

A For a medium-sized office, a meeting held every month or two is likely to be enough. However, in a large, hazardous industrial workplace, meetings will should be held more frequently, eg fortnightly.

Q Do you need special training to be on a committee?

A Once a member of a safety committee, in practice, you need specific health and safety training to enable you to perform your functions effectively.

Q Do employees on a safety committee qualify for paid time off work?

A   Yes, when they are undergoing training, etc to enable them to perform their functions properly, they qualify for paid time off work.

Safety Policies

Summary

In order to be effective, management of health and safety in the workplace needs to be structured and tangible. This involves drawing up documents which define the company's commitment to health and safety, outline its objectives, set out the organisational structure and responsibilities of specific job holders, and give detailed health and safety rules and procedures. This document, or set of documents, is the safety policy.

Practical Guidance

Policy statement

Under s.2(3) of the **Health and Safety at Work, etc Act 1974** (HSW Act), employers of five or more employees must prepare a written statement of their health and safety policy. The policy must be brought to the attention of their employees, eg by giving each employee a copy.

Review

Section 2(3) of the HSW Act requires that the policy must be reviewed where appropriate and any necessary revisions must be made following the review.

The reasons for reviewing the policy include:
- the introduction of new equipment, processes or activities
- changes in the company's organisational structure
- results of new research on subjects which are relevant to the company's activities
- the need to change safety practices and procedures identified by a risk assessment
- serious incident.

Exemption

Employers who employ less than five people "for the time being" are exempt from the requirement to have a written safety policy by the **Employers' Health and Safety Policy Statement (Exception) Regulations 1975**. "For the time being" has been interpreted by the courts in *Osborne v Bill Taylor of Huyton Ltd* as meaning "at any one time". This means, for example, that a company which employs a staff of eight, only four of whom are ever at work at any one time, is exempt.

Safety arrangements

The **Management of Health and Safety at Work Regulations 1999** require employers to set up appropriate arrangements for planning, controlling, monitoring and reviewing health and safety measures. Where there are five or more employees, these arrangements must be documented and disseminated to employees. An effective method of doing this is to incorporate them into the health and safety policy.

Consultation

Section 2(6) of the HSW Act, accompanied by the **Safety Representatives and Safety Committees Regulations 1977**, and the **Health and Safety (Consultation with Employees) Regulations 1992** require employers to consult with safety representatives with a view to making and maintaining arrangements to enable them and their employees to co-operate in providing and monitoring effective health and safety measures. The policy is the foundation on which health and safety arrangements are built, so the safety representatives should be consulted when it is formulated, implemented and monitored.

BS 8800

BS 8800: *Guide to Occupational Health and Safety Management Systems* gives a system of structuring health and safety management in the workplace. One of the requirements under the standard is for an occupational health and safety policy, which commits the company to providing adequate resources to implement the policy.

Recording and keeping the policy

If there are five or more employees, the safety policy must be made in writing. In many cases, this will by done using a word processor, which makes it easy to add to and update the policy. An original copy of the policy should be kept in a safe place in the control of a responsible person, usually the health and safety manager. There should be a hard copy, and back-up files should be made and stored with other back-ups for valuable business information, eg on another premises in a fireproof safe.

Each page in the policy document should be numbered and dated, so that it is possible to check whether individual copies are up to date. It is usual to provide each employee with a copy of the safety policy, and give a copy to new recruits on their first day at work. Updates should be circulated to everyone who has a copy of the policy when it is revised, so the person co-ordinating the policy should keep an up-to-date list of the names and locations of each employee.

Questions and Answers

Q What is the maximum penalty for not having a safety policy?

A If the offence is punished by a Magistrates' Court (Sheriffs' Court in Scotland), a fine of up to £20,000 may be imposed. This penalty also applies if you have a policy, but you have not brought it to the attention of your employees.

Q How do I know whether our policy statement is adequate?

A Make sure it contains the three main elements, ie statement of commitment, description of organisation of health and safety within your company, and details of health and safety arrangements and procedures under relevant subject headings. It may be worth checking your policy against the Health and Safety Executive (HSE) guidance as this will show you what the enforcing authorities are looking for in a safety policy.

Q I am the health and safety manager for a company. Does our managing director have to sign our safety policy, or can I do it on his behalf?

A The ultimate responsibility for health and safety, and therefore the authority to commit your company to meeting its duties, cannot be delegated to you from the senior management. Commitment to, and a responsible attitude towards, health and safety must be initiated at the top, and communicated down throughout the company. If the senior managers do not take safety seriously, how can workers be expected to?

As a competent person working on behalf of the company, you are probably the person best placed to draft, write, formulate, distribute, monitor and revise the safety policy. However, the statement of commitment must be signed by the most senior person in your company, ie the managing director.

Safety Representatives

Summary

Employees in recognised trade union workplaces are represented by union safety representatives who have certain rights and duties. In non-unionised workplaces employers must consult on health and safety matters with the employees, either directly or through elected representatives of employee safety.

Practical Guidance

Union safety representatives

Union safety representatives, in addition to representing their colleagues in consultations with the employer and carrying out inspections of their workplace, may also request a safety committee to be established and attend suitable and appropriate training courses. Reasonable time off (without detriment in terms and conditions) and facilities provided to allow safety representatives to perform their duties.

Union safety representatives must be members of the recognised union for their workplace, and have been employed by the employer or have been in similar employment for at least two years. They must also be able to keep up with any legislative and technological developments applicable to their workplace, and understand hazards and control measures associated with the work activities of the employees they represent.

Information and documents

Safety representatives, upon request, are entitled to see and receive copies of any relevant health and safety documents relating to their workplace, including plans of proposed changes. Such documents may include accident statistics, reportable accidents, cases of ill-health, dangerous occurrences and monitoring procedures. Information which breaches national security, is involved in legal proceedings or breaks personal confidentiality, etc need not be made available.

Consultation, facilities and assistance

Employers must consult with safety representatives on matters affecting health and safety at work. They must also provide reasonable facilities and assistance for the representatives to perform their duties; this could include providing office space, secretarial support and time away from their normal work activities.

Time off

Safety representatives are legally entitled to time off for performing their safety duties and attending any appropriate training associated with those duties. There is useful case law supporting time off for safety representatives to attend training courses and to perform their other duties. The following cases are significant.

In *White v Pressed Steel Fisher* it was held that an employer may legitimately refuse time off for a safety representative to attend an approved union training courses if the employer provides an acceptable alternative which meets the requirements of the Approved Code of Practice. However, any gaps in the employer's course may have to be filled by attendance at an approved union course and time off would have to be granted for this.

The attendance at specialist union-approved training over and above the basic course is addressed by the case of *Howard v Volex Accessories Division,* where the employer refused a union safety representative paid time off to attend a specialist training course in chemical hazards on the basis that the control measures in place were such that there were no health risks from the chemicals in the workplace. The tribunal held that the employer was wrong to make such an assumption and that the safety representative was entitled to attend the additional training in this circumstance.

The case of *Scarth v East Herefordshire District Council* held that an employer was wrong to refuse paid time off for a safety representative to attend an approved union training course without first looking at the syllabus or making alternative training available.

In the case of *Howard & Peet v Volex plc* the employer was held to be correct in refusing to allow two safety representatives to carry out an inspection of their work section as changes in internal union procedures had resulted in an excess of safety representatives within the organisation for the number of work sections in existence. The work section concerned was adequately represented by other safety representatives.

Liability

Safety representatives do not incur criminal or civil liability for any act or omission whilst performing their representative duties, although they may still be personally liable for breaches of ss.7 and 8 of the **Health and Safety at Work, etc Act 1974**, ie duties to ensure their own health and safety and that of others, and intentionally misusing equipment, etc provided in the interests of health and safety.

Safety committees

Establishing a safety committee

A safety committee must be established by the employer if requested by two or more trade union safety representatives. The committee must be set up within three months of the request, and details of membership and work areas covered must be posted around the workplace. The committee should be independent of both management and safety representatives.

Membership

There are no definite rules on committee membership, although it should be compact and representative of the whole workforce (both employees and management). The number of management members should not exceed the number of safety representatives, but should include line managers and supervisors. Managers should ensure full and proper authority and consider any points raised.

Specialists, eg works managers, personnel managers, etc may be invited to join the committee as ex officio members, or may attend individual meetings as necessary. Attendance at meetings should be considered part of the members' normal work. Meetings should be held as often as necessary, planned well in advance and made known to the workforce. The meetings should be minuted, with copies given to each member and distributed around the workplace.

Non-union representatives of employee safety

In non-unionised workplaces employers must still consult with their employees on certain health and safety matters — these matters are exactly the same as those on which employers must consult union safety representatives, and are listed in *Key Facts"* below.

Employee representatives

Employers may consult with their employees either directly or through elected "representatives of employee safety". In very small workplaces direct consultation with the employees may be more beneficial.

Self-employed people and non-employees, eg agency staff, volunteers, etc do not have to be consulted, although including them in such consultations is good practice, particularly if they are working long term at the employer's workplace. Trainees on work experience are covered by the **Health and Safety (Consultation with Employees) Regulations 1996** and must therefore be consulted.

Provision of information

Employers must provide any information necessary for employees or their representatives to effectively participate in the consultations.

This information includes:

- likely hazards and risks associated with the work, or with proposed changes to the work
- details of reportable injuries, diseases and dangerous occurrences
- implemented and proposed control measures, and safe working practices.

In addition, representatives of employee safety must be provided with relevant information from reportable accident records so far as that information relates to the group of employees they represent or their workplace.

Functions of representatives of employee safety
Employee representatives may advise their employers on potential hazards and on general health and safety matters which affect the employees, or the workplace, they represent. They may also participate in consultations with enforcement inspectors. The employee representatives may make such representations at any time; they are not restricted to the occasions when the employer consults with them.

Training, time off and facilities
In order to fulfil their duties and responsibilities, representatives of employee safety must:
- be appropriately trained, ie able to understand the hazards, risks and appropriate control measures associated with the work of the employees they represent, keep up-to-date with legislative changes and technological developments
- be allowed time away from their work
- be provided with any reasonable facilities
- be paid for any time and other expenses, eg travelling, etc spent on these duties, including training and canvassing in representative elections.

Elections
The representatives of employee safety must be employed within the group of employees they represent. There is no guidance on the length of office for representatives of employee safety, although where there is a rapidly changing workforce a representative may need to be elected more frequently in order to continue to remain the choice of those workers. There is no limit on the number of representatives elected although they should take into account the size of the workforce, the different activities and/or shift work undertaken and the nature of the work. All of the above points should be clarified and made known before an election is held.

Questions and Answers

Q Are "union safety representatives" and "representatives of employee safety" the same?

A No. Union safety representatives are appointed to represent the members of their union if it is recognised by the employer, while representatives of employee safety are elected to consult with employers in non-unionised workplaces. Under the **Safety Representatives and Safety Committees Regulations 1977**, safety representatives have a greater number of duties than representatives of employee safety elected under the **Health and Safety (Consultation with Employees) Regulations 1996**.

Q Do union safety representatives have to attend union training courses?

A   No, provided that the alternative training covers essentially the same syllabus, ie follows the recommendations in the Approved Code of Practice (L87) and is relevant.

Q   Can representatives of employee safety take on a wider role in health and safety than just consultation?

A   The **Health and Safety (Consultation with Employees) Regulations 1996** only require representatives of employee safety to consult with their employers on health and safety matters. However, there is no reason why individual employers cannot extend the consultation duties, eg to include workplace inspections, accident investigations and attendance at safety committees, etc by mutual consent with the representatives of employee safety involved. Appropriate training should be provided to support any duties undertaken.

Q   Do employers have to make all information available to representatives of employee safety?

A   No, the following information need not be disclosed:

- information which could affect national security or substantially harm the employer's undertaking
- information which contravenes any legally imposed prohibition
- information which would breach individual confidentiality (unless with their consent)
- information the employer is using, or intending to use, for their defence in any legal proceedings
- any information not related to health and safety matters.

Safety Signs

Summary

Safety signs are defined as signboards (signs which convey information or instructions by their shape, colour and appropriate symbols or pictograms), safety colours, illuminated signs, acoustic or hand signals or oral communications which provide information or instructions about specific objects, activities or situations relevant to health and safety at work.

Practical Guidance

Risk assessment

The **Management of Health and Safety at Work Regulations 1999** require employers to carry out risk assessments of their work activities. These assessments should identify what control measures are needed, including where safety signs should be displayed (see the diagram below).

Provision

Under the **Health and Safety (Safety Signs and Signals) Regulations 1996** (Safety Signs Regulations), safety signs must be provided for identified risks if other measures cannot adequately control them. Employers must ensure that:

- safety signs are provided to warn people of the risks and instruct them on any necessary control measures
- arrangements for hand or oral signals are in place where relevant to the particular risks
- employees are given appropriate information, instruction and training in the meaning of the signs and what action needs to be taken
- safety signs are properly designed
- enough safety signs are provided
- safety signs are correctly positioned
- powered signs are provided with an emergency power source in the event of power failure
- illuminated signs and/or acoustic signals operate to start a predetermined action, eg evacuation of a building, and continue for as long as that action is necessary
- the needs of partially sighted and hearing-impaired people are taken into account, including temporary impairment, eg due to wearing hearing protection.

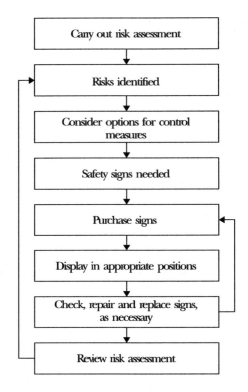

Maintenance

Under the Safety Signs Regulations, employers must ensure that safety signs are maintained, including:

- regular cleaning
- making repairs and replacements where necessary
- frequent testing of illuminated signs and acoustic signals to ensure they remain effective.

Permanent signs

The Safety Signs Regulations require that permanent signs must be used:

- for prohibition, mandatory and warning signs
- to indicate the location and identity of fire-fighting equipment
- on pipes and containers
- for traffic routes
- in places where there is a risk of falling objects
- in places where there is a risk of collision with obstacles.

Occasional signs

The Safety Signs Regulations designate illuminated signs, acoustic and hand signals, and oral communications as occasional signs. They should be used to:

- signal danger
- prompt people to take a particular course of action, eg evacuation
- help with hazardous manoeuvres.

Combined signs

The Safety Signs Regulations allow interchanging or combinations of different types of signs and signals, so long as there is no reduction in the overall effect, for example:

- safety colours and signboards where they identify obstacles or drops
- illuminated signs, acoustic signals and verbal communications
- hand signals and verbal communications.

Safety colours

The Safety Signs Regulations specify the following safety colours:

- red signifies dangerous behaviour and identifies stop, shut down and emergency cut devices and fire-fighting equipment
- yellow indicates possible dangers
- blue shows mandatory behaviour or actions
- green indicates safety, ie the direction of emergency escape routes, emergency exits, first aid equipment and a return to normality.

Interference

The Safety Signs Regulations require that the effectiveness of safety signs are not reduced by:

- too many signs placed together
- the use of similar but different illuminated signs, causing confusion
- visual interference from another illuminated source
- the use of two or more acoustic signals at once
- the use of acoustic signals where there is interference from significant background noise.

Signboards

The Safety Signs Regulations set out minimum requirements for signboards. They must be:

- shockproof
- weather resistant
- suitable for the location where they are used
- easy to see and understand.

Any pictograms used on signboards must be as simple as possible and should only contain the essential details. The Safety Signs Regulations designate shapes and colours for the main types of signboard:

- prohibition signs indicate that something must not be done. They must:
  - be round
  - have a white background with a red border and red diagonal cross bar
  - have pictograms, where applicable, which are black, central and do not obliterate the cross bar
- warning signs indicate a particular hazard or danger. They must:
  - be triangular
  - have a yellow background with a black border
  - have a black, central pictogram
- mandatory signs indicate specific actions or behaviour that is required. They must:
  - be round
  - have a blue background
  - have a white pictogram
- emergency escape and first aid signs must:
  - be square or rectangular
  - have a green background
  - have a white pictogram
- fire-fighting equipment signs indicate the location and identity of this equipment. They must:
  - be square or rectangular
  - have a red background
  - have a white pictogram.

Containers and pipes

The Safety Signs Regulations require containers and visible pipes which contain dangerous substances to be labelled. The labels must be:

- positioned near dangerous points, eg valves, on pipes, and at suitable intervals in between
- clearly visible.

If containers are only used for a short period of time or the contents change regularly, they may be exempt from the requirement to be labelled, provided that the same level of safety is achieved by using other measures, such as training. Appropriate warning signs:

- may be used instead of labels
- must be displayed in areas where dangerous substances are stored, unless the labels on the containers provided a satisfactory level of safety.

Fire-fighting equipment

The Safety Signs Regulations require that signboards or the red safety colour must be used to indicate the identity and location (or access point) of fire-fighting equipment.

Traffic routes, dangerous locations and obstacles

Under the Safety Signs Regulations, yellow and black or red and white strips must be used to indicate a risk of:

- colliding with obstacles
- falling
- being hit by falling objects.

The stripes must be an even size and be placed at an angle of around 45°. Their size should be appropriate to the scale of the area.

Traffic routes, including external ones, must be indicated with continuous white or yellow stripes. They should allow enough space for traffic to move at a safe distance.

Illuminated signs

The Safety Signs Regulations require that illuminated signs are in contrast to the surrounding environment. Some illuminated signs are intermittent, and these must:

- use the intermittent signal to indicate a higher level of danger (which must be kept under greater surveillance), where the sign is capable of intermittent and continuous display
- not obscure the meaning or cause confusion with continuous signs by the frequency of flashing
- use identical codes where they are used with, or instead of, acoustic signals.

Acoustic signals

The Safety Signs Regulations require that acoustic signals must:

- be easy to recognise
- be easy to hear over foreseeable background noise
- use the intermittent signal to indicate a higher level of danger, where it is capable of sounding both continuously and intermittently
- use a continuous sound to indicate the need for evacuation.

Oral communications

The Safety Signs Regulations set the following requirements for oral communications:

- they must be short, simple and as clear as possible
- account must be taken of people with impaired hearing
- account must be taken of people who do not understand English

- the person making the communications must have a good command of the language and be easy to understand
- if they are used with, or instead of, gestures, a standard system of code words should be used.

Hand signals

Under the Safety Signs Regulations, hand signals must:
- be simple, precise, and easy to carry out and understand
- be distinct from other signals
- use symmetrical movement and indicate only one signal, where both arms are required to carry out the signal.

The person giving the signals must be able to see all manoeuvres to ensure the health and safety of the people in the area. More than one signalperson may be needed to ensure health and safety. The signalperson must be easily recognisable, and must wear distinctive clothing or use suitable equipment. The Safety Signs Regulations depict acceptable hand signals.

The person following hand signals must stop his or her manoeuvre if the signals are unclear or if new instructions are required.

Traffic signs

Road traffic signs are covered by the **Road Traffic Act 1984**. If the movement of traffic gives rise to risks covered by a sign designated under the Act, that sign must be used, regardless of whether the Act applies to the workplace.

Dangerous substances

The Safety Signs Regulations require storage rooms and areas for substantial quantities of dangerous substances to be marked with appropriate safety signs.

Under the **Dangerous Substances (Notification and Marking of Sites) Regulations 1990**, if 25 tonnes or more of dangerous substances are present on a site the entrances must be marked with a warning sign depicting an exclamation mark.

Radiation

The **Ionising Radiations Regulations 1999** require warning signs (which must comply with the Safety Signs Regulations) to be displayed to protect persons during the handling, storage and use of all forms of radioactive substances and electrical machine sources of ionising radiations, eg X-rays.

Questions and Answers

Q In some safety product catalogues there seem to be different styles of green and white emergency signs — can we use a combination of these different styles?

A   It is good practice to ensure that there is a consistency in the type of signs used (ie the pictogram style) across the whole of any single work site.

Q   Where can I get safety signs from?

A   There are a number of suppliers of safety signs, who produce catalogues of a huge variety of signs available from them. Safety signs purchased from a reputable supplier should comply with the Safety Signs Regulations and relevant British Standards.

Q   What is meant by oral communications?

A   Oral communications are defined in the Safety Signs Regulations as "predetermined messages spoken by a human or artificial voice". Oral communications will often contain codes, which both the giver and receiver of instructions must understand before they are used to deal with a hazardous situation. In many cases, the code will be relatively basic, eg using words like "start", "stop", "higher" or "lower".

Q   We have a dangerous machine in our workplace. Is providing a safety sign enough to fulfil our legal duties?

A   No. Safety signs are very limited. They rely on people understanding them, noticing them and complying with them. They are only effective if used in conjunction with a range of other safety measures, to protect your employees against the dangers of the machine. This means that not only should you put up a safety sign, but you must guard dangerous parts of the machine, train anyone who uses it, provide adequate supervision to ensure the machine is used safely, have procedures for the safe use of the machine, such as tying back hair and removing loose clothes and jewellery where there is a risk of entanglement, regularly check and maintain the machine, provide appropriate personal protective equipment, and so on.

Scaffolding

Summary

Scaffolding is often used to provide a working platform from which people can work safely, eg during construction work or for painting operations. The common causes of accidents involving scaffolding are falls of persons or materials, and collapse of part of the scaffolding.

Practical Guidance

The most common type of fatal accident in the construction industry is falling from height. The main causes of accidents include the use of unfenced or inadequately fenced working platforms, insufficient or inadequate boarding and instability of the scaffold itself.

Employers have a general duty to ensure, so far as reasonably practicable, the health, safety and welfare of all their employees. When using scaffolding, the duty to provide and maintain a safe place of work with safe means of access and egress must be considered.

Any work which involves the use of scaffolding should be assessed to:
- identify all hazards involved in the activity and the scaffold itself
- eliminate all hazards if possible
- evaluate the risks arising from the hazards and decide whether existing precautions are adequate or whether more should be done
- devise and implement safe systems of work to ensure that the risks are either eliminated or adequately controlled.

Specific legislation

The **Workplace (Health, Safety and Welfare) Regulations 1992**, which apply to employers whose workplaces are under their control and the **Construction (Health, Safety and Welfare) Regulations 1996** which apply to construction activities both lay down requirements with respect to falls or falling objects.

In relation to scaffolding, employers have the responsibility to take reasonable steps to avoid any person falling a distance which is likely to cause personal injury, or any person being struck by a falling object likely to cause personal injury.

The basic requirements for safe working on scaffolds are:
- the correct erection of the scaffold
- a suitable system for inspection and maintenance of the scaffold.

Erection of scaffolds

The erection, alteration or dismantling of scaffolding must be undertaken in a safe manner under the supervision of a competent person. A competent person must inspect scaffolding materials before each occasion on which they are used. All parts must be constructed of suitable and sound materials, and must be of adequate strength.

Every part of a scaffold should be fixed, secured or placed to prevent it accidentally being displaced. All scaffolds should be rigidly connected to the building or other structure, unless the scaffold is designed to be independent. The building or structure to which the scaffold is connected must be of sound material, and sufficiently strong and stable for the purpose. Gutters must not be used for supports, unless they are suitable for the purpose and of adequate strength. Bricks and small blocks should not be used as supports, except for certain low platforms.

Scaffold platforms from which a person may fall more than 2m should have guard-rails and toe-boards. Guard-rails must be at least 920mm above the edge where someone may fall. Toe-boards must be at least 150mm high. There should be no unprotected gaps between any guard rails, toe-boards or barriers unless the gap is below 470mm. Where there is a risk of materials falling from the scaffold, vertical guards or scaffold fans, netting or sheeting should be provided.

Working platforms should be at least 600mm wide.

Inspection and maintenance of scaffolds

All scaffolds in use must be inspected every seven days by a competent person. They should also be inspected after exposure to any adverse weather conditions likely to affect their strength and stability or displace any part of the scaffold. The inspections must be recorded.

The exceptions to this are ladder scaffolds, trestle scaffolds and those scaffolds from which a person cannot fall more than 2m. Employers whose employees use scaffolding must satisfy themselves that the scaffold complies with the Regulations, whether or not their employees erected it themselves. All scaffolds must be properly maintained.

Personal protective equipment

Employers must provide suitable personal protective equipment (PPE) for the risks involved. Head protection should be provided to employees working on, beneath or near to scaffolding. All fall-arrest PPE should carry the CE mark. It should also be checked before each use and regularly tested by a competent person.

Reporting of dangerous occurrences

Any incident that involves the collapse or partial collapse of scaffolding that was more than 5m high and which results in a substantial part of the scaffolding falling or overturning must be reported to the local enforcing authority by the quickest practicable means (ie the telephone), and followed by a written report (on form F2508) within 10 days.

Scaffolding

The following checklist will help employers to identify whether scaffolding has been erected correctly and is safe to be used, and any hazards that could result in a person being injured by falling from the scaffold or materials falling on to people below.

Checklist for the safe use of scaffolding

General points to consider	*Tick points* (√)
Was the scaffold erected by competent persons?	
Is there proper access to the scaffold platform?	
Are access ladders incorporated into the scaffold?	
Is the scaffold secured to the building in enough places to prevent collapse?	
Are the ties strong enough?	
Is the scaffold adequately braced to ensure its stability?	
Are load bearing fittings used where required?	
Have any uprights, ledgers, braces or struts (items of scaffolding structure) been removed?	
If the scaffold has been designed and constructed for loading with materials, are these evenly distributed?	
Is there a suitable means of transferring materials and equipment down from the scaffold, eg hoist or chute?	
Has the scaffolding, or any covering, been designed with the prevailing wind loading in mind?	
Working platforms	
Are working platforms fully boarded?	
Are the boards free from obvious defects?	
Are the boards arranged to avoid tipping or tripping?	
Are there adequate guard-rails and toe-boards at every side from which a person could fall two metres or more?	
If not, has suitable personal suspension equipment, eg bosun's chairs, abseiling equipment, been provided?	
Have the users been trained in the use of such equipment?	
Is the equipment checked on a regular basis?	
Where it is not possible to provide personal suspension equipment, is fall-arrest equipment, eg safety nets and harnesses provided?	
Are safety nets suspended at a distance not greater than 1m below the working place?	

Are safety nets strong enough to catch the heaviest object which could fall?	
Are safety nets provided to prevent people below being hit by falling objects or materials?	
Are safety harnesses thoroughly examined by a competent person at least every three months and a record kept of the examination?	
Has the user been trained in the correct use of a safety harness?	
Does the user make a visual inspection at least daily before use?	
Warning notices and barriers	
Are there effective barriers or warning notices to stop people using an incomplete scaffold?	
Are barriers and warning notices in place to prevent people walking beneath the scaffold?	
Inspections	
Does a competent person inspect the scaffold at least once a week?	
Does a competent person inspect the scaffold after bad weather, eg high winds?	
Are the results of the inspections recorded by the person carrying out the inspection?	
Employees	
Have all employees working on scaffolding been provided with the correct personal protective equipment?	
Do they use the personal protective equipment?	
Do all personnel required to work at height have the appropriate medical and physical fitness?	
Are they all adequately trained?	

Questions and Answers

Q How do I know if an organisation is competent to erect scaffolding?

A You should check training records, ask for references, inspect copies of the orgnisation's safety policy, method statement and any other relevant documentation.

Q Where can I get my employees trained in scaffolding?

A Various training courses are available; in particular the Construction Industry Training Board (CITB) runs training schemes for scaffolders of all abilities.

Q How can I ensure that no one uses the scaffold when the site is unoccupied?

A By removing the access to it, eg taking the ladder away or effectively blocking it off.

Self-employed Persons

Summary

The **Health and Safety at Work, etc Act 1974** defines a self-employed person as "An individual who works for gain or reward otherwise than under a contract of employment, whether or not he himself employs others". Most employers use self-employed people at some point, whether only for a few hours, as with window cleaners, or on a long-term basis, as with catering contractors.

Practical Guidance

Employee or self-employed?

An employee is employed by an employer under a "contract of employment", whereas a self-employed person is employed otherwise than under a "contract of employment". In many cases, it is obvious whether a person is an employee or a self-employed person, but sometimes the distinction is much less clear. When determining whether a person comes under the category of employee or self-employed, the following should be considered:

- employers have no obligation to provide work for self-employed people, who have no obligation to accept it when they do
- self-employed people generally work for an employer intermittently, rather than continuously
- self-employed people are generally free to take on work from other employers
- self-employed people usually have to issue an invoice to get paid and no deductions are made from their fee, while employees are usually paid regularly and have tax, national insurance, etc deducted by the employer
- self-employed people do not usually get holiday or sickness pay
- self-employed people generally supply their own equipment and materials.

Duty of care

Under s.3(2) of the **Health and Safety at Work, etc Act 1974** (HSW Act), self-employed people must carry out their activities in such way that they do not expose themselves and others to health and safety risks. If the self-employed person employs others, he or she is an employer under health and safety law, and must therefore comply with all relevant statutory provisions.

347

Management

Under the **Management of Health and Safety at Work Regulations 1999** (MHSWR), self-employed people must make an assessment of the risks to themselves from their work activities. They must then put into place suitable health and safety arrangements to protect themselves and others. The significant findings of the assessment and health and safety arrangements only have to be recorded where an employer has five or more employees.

MHSWR also requires a competent person to be employed to help self-employed people comply with their duties under health and safety law. However, self-employed people do not need to hire a competent person where they are able to adequately meet the requirements themselves.

Under the MHSWR, if two or more employers share a workplace, they must co-operate and co-ordinate with each other to take appropriate measures for health and safety. The presence of a self-employed person on an employer's premises would come under this requirement, even if it were only for a very short time. The self-employed person must inform the employer of any health and safety risks to others on site that may arise from their work activities.

Reporting accidents and diseases

Under the **Reporting of Injuries, Diseases and Dangerous Occurrences Regulations 1995** (RIDDOR), if an accident arising from a work activity injures someone, the responsible person must make a report to the relevant enforcing authority. An accident is reportable if the injuries are fatal, major, or result in more than three days' incapacity for work. Fatal and major accidents (and dangerous occurrences) must be reported immediately, ie by telephone, and followed by a written report (on form F2508) within 10 days. Injuries which result in more than three days' incapacity for work must be reported on F2508 within 10 days.

For injured employees, the responsible person is their employer. However, for injured non-employees, such as the self-employed, the responsible person is the person in control of the premises.

Where self-employed persons are injured on premises which they own or occupy, they are exempt from the requirement to report the accident immediately. However, they must still send in a written report on F2508 within 10 days of the accident, or make arrangements for someone to report the accident on their behalf. They are also responsible for reporting any reportable diseases that they contract, on form F2508A.

Hazardous substances

The requirements of the **Control of Substances Hazardous to Health Regulations 1999** (COSHH) apply to self-employed people as if they were both employer and employee, except that they do not have to monitor exposure or carry out health surveillance.

First aid

Under the **Health and Safety (First Aid) Regulations 1981**, self-employed people must provide suitable first aid equipment, where appropriate, to allow them to administer first aid to themselves if they are injured at work. The equipment needed will depend on the hazards and level of risk. For example, for a low-risk activity in a situation where medical help is quickly and easily obtained, eg a management consultant in an urban area, a small travelling first aid kit should be sufficient. However, in more remote areas or where the work is more hazardous, the self-employed person is likely to require a wider range of first aid equipment, and preferably a means of summoning help, eg a mobile phone.

Application of safety law

The extent to which health and safety law applies to self-employed people varies. The self-employed (assuming they are not also an employer) are exempt from a number of statutory requirements:

- the requirement to have a written health and safety policy under s.6 of the HSW Act does not apply
- the requirement to apply the provisions of the **Health and Safety (Display Screen Equipment) Regulations 1992** to their own activities.

In other cases, self-employed people must apply health and safety legislation to their own activities, in so far as to protect their own health and safety; for example, they must comply with the:

- **Personal Protective Equipment Regulations 1992** in relation to selecting, using and maintaining any personal protective equipment they need for their work activities
- **Manual Handling Operations Regulations 1992** in relation to any manual handling tasks they carry out
- **Provision and Use of Work Equipment Regulations 1998** (PUWER) in relation to any equipment they provide for themselves to use at work.

On the other hand, employers do have a duty to ensure the health and safety of self-employed people working for them, for example:

- work equipment they provide for self-employed people to use must comply with PUWER
- they must comply with the **Noise at Work Regulations 1989**, eg providing hearing protection and training, in relation to self-employed people who may be affected by noise arising from the host employer's undertaking.

Some health and safety legislation applies equally to the self-employed and employers, including the:

- **Electricity at Work Regulations 1989**
- **Control of Asbestos at Work Regulations 1987**
- **Control of Lead at Work Regulations 1998**
- **Construction (Health, Safety and Welfare) Regulations 1996**.

Questions and Answers

Q As a health and safety officer for a large employer, what self-employed people am I likely to work with?

A Certain occupations are commonly carried out by small, self-employed businesses. These include window cleaners, caterers, management consultants (including health and safety consultants), couriers, builders, carpenters, decorators, electricians, plumbers and so on. They may only be on your premises for a matter of minutes, or could be under a long-term contract, eg up to a year. You must have arrangements in place for controlling them and ensuring their health and safety while they are on your premises.

Q I have noticed that our self-employed window cleaner does not wear a safety harness when working at height. Are we responsible for making sure he wears one?

A Self-employed people are responsible for identifying risks to themselves from their activities, and providing themselves with, and using, appropriate personal protective equipment (PPE). The window cleaner should know that there is a high risk of falling when working at height, and should either find a safe way of cleaning upper storey windows or, if this is not possible, wear a safety harness.

Having said that, you are responsible for the health and safety of non-employees on your site. As you are paying for his services, you have a degree of control over him. Your premises should have anchor points for window cleaners if it is not possible to clean windows from the inside without being at risk of falling. Consider the effects on the workforce if the window cleaner fell from his ladder and was killed. Your contract with him should require him to follow site safety rules, and using PPE where necessary should be one of these rules. If the window cleaner persistently fails to wear his safety harness this would breach such a contract, and you should find someone who takes a responsible attitude to health and safety.

Q I work as a casual kitchen hand for a temporary agency. Who is my employer?

A Many temporary agencies are set up so they act as a job finder on behalf of self-employed people. It is likely that your agency considers you to be self-employed, with all the health and safety responsibilities that entails, unless you have signed a contract of employment with them. Whether or not you would be classified as an employee of the agency or as a self-employed person in the event of a breach of health and safety law depends on individual circumstances, and can only really be determined by a court.

Sick Building Syndrome

Summary

Sick building syndrome is a generic term used when a particular workforce appear to suffer from certain symptoms (eg runny nose, sore eyes, etc) more frequently than a general cross-section of the population might do, and where these symptoms become worse when more time is spent in the workplace.

Practical Guidance

Sick building syndrome is not a medically recognised illness as such and its precise cause is not known. Different individuals may be affected in different ways, making the problem hard to define and difficult to address. It is important not to confuse sick building syndrome with specific illnesses — such as Legionnaires' disease or humidifier fever — that may also be related to the workplace. Most cases of sick building syndrome occur in large office buildings, although cases have also been reported in many other types of workplace.

Recognising the symptoms

Any of the following may suggest a problem with sick building syndrome, particularly if they occur in combination:

- poor staff morale
- reduced efficiency
- increase in sickness absence and/or staff turnover
- members of staff complaining about persistent symptoms such as stuffy or runny nose, dry or itchy nose, eyes, throat or skin, headaches, skin rashes, lethargy or inability to concentrate.

Not all staff are equally at risk. Evidence shows that employees most at risk are those doing routine clerical work, often spending a significant amount of time using display screen equipment, while having little control over environmental factors (such as temperature, lighting levels, etc) or their own workload.

It may be prudent to compile information to try and get a wider picture. Questions to ask staff might include:

- what are the specific symptoms?
- for how long has the problem been apparent?
- what time of day do the symptoms appear and how long do they last for?

Causes of sick building syndrome

Sick building syndrome is thought to be caused by a combination of various factors, most of which are environmental, but job-related factors may also have a bearing:
- the fabric of the building
- the fixtures, furnishings and general work environment
- the organisation of the work.

In a building which has been in use for some time without significant problems, the sudden appearance of symptoms related to sick building syndrome is likely to be attributable to something fairly obvious such as new furniture or equipment, or a fault in the air conditioning system.

Environmental factors

Examples of factors that may, individually or in combination, give rise to sick building syndrome are given below:
- large open-plan areas or large areas of open filing/shelving
- new furniture, paint work or flooring
- large areas of soft furnishings
- air conditioning or other limitations on user control of the working environment
- inadequate cleaning, giving rise to high levels of dust/fibres in the air
- inadequate or inappropriate lighting
- poor standards of maintenance/repair
- chemical pollutants, eg ozone from printers/photocopiers and tobacco smoke
- dust particles or fibres in the air
- very high or low humidity.

Job-related factors

Examples of job-related factors include:
- routine work with little task variation/rotation
- significant amounts of work with display screen equipment.

Preventing sick building syndrome

Since many of the factors listed above are linked to building and building services design, the best way to minimise problems is to design them out before building and fitting work is carried out. Reputable architects and office interior design organisations will be able to help minimise the risk of sick building syndrome.

Curing the problem

If the problem arises in a building that has been occupied for some time it is important to involve the staff or staff representatives at an early stage in any discussions. It may also be necessary or prudent to involve trades union representatives and medical staff or consultants. Staff themselves will be able to give the most insight into the problems, but it is also important to realise that different individuals will have their own preferences when it comes to working temperatures and other environmental controls. Staff will be able to tell you about their symptoms and the times of day when these are worst.

As a guideline, the following steps should be taken if sick building syndrome is suspected.

1. Ensure that all the requirements of the **Workplace (Health, Safety and Welfare) Regulations 1992** and the Approved Code of Practice have been complied with.
2. Consult with employees and their representatives in order to determine the precise nature of the problem and consider possible courses of action.
3. Review cleaning and ventilation arrangements.

The most cost-effective solution is likely to be to tackle the obvious problem areas or potential problem areas first, and then consider other issues as they arise. More expensive and sophisticated solutions should only be considered once the more straightforward options have been exhausted. Management issues may arise from the nature of individual employee's workloads, as well as the obvious physical issues. Consideration may need to be given to increasing job rotation or variety within particular jobs.

Seeking advice

If the problem is not alleviated by action resulting from any staff consultation process it may be necessary to look more closely at the maintenance and cleaning arrangements for the building, and at the building services themselves — at this stage the use of specialist contractors may be appropriate. Where necessary the following professionals may be able to help:

- building services engineers
- occupational hygienists
- occupational health doctors and nurses
- ergonomists
- management consultants.

Specialist engineers will be able to advise on the building services and whether they are adequate and appropriate, and occupational hygienists will be able to advise on sources of pollutants, conducting measurements where necessary, although pollutants are usually present at very low levels and there is no guidance available on what levels are reasonable.

Questions and Answers

Q I have been told that new furniture within an office may cause sick building syndrome — is this correct?

A New furniture and office equipment may give off chemicals called volatile organic compounds and it is thought that these may be associated with sick building syndrome. The problem should diminish quite significantly after the immediate introduction, so it may be advisable to introduce equipment gradually, or allow it to "stand" in a less frequented area of the premises for a few weeks prior to use.

Q How can we test for substances in the air that may be causing sick building syndrome?

A Because any such pollutants in the air are likely to be present at levels where detection is very difficult, and well below prescribed occupational exposure limits, testing can be difficult, expensive and inaccurate. It is, however, worth considering emission characteristics when purchasing building and furnishing materials and ensuring that low-emission products are specified where possible.

Q How can cleaning methods within an office be improved, in order to minimise the risk of sick building syndrome?

A It may be worth drawing up procedures for cleaning, specifying intervals at which particular parts of the building and its furnishings should be cleaned. This might include the following:
- annually — ventilation systems, deep cleaning of upholstery and soft furnishings
- quarterly — light fittings and windows
- daily — internal surfaces, carpets, furniture.

Evening cleaning allows for stale odours within the workplace (eg from tobacco) to be promptly dealt with and gives time for the dusts created by the cleaning activities to settle before the start of the day. Cleaning products with strong odours should be avoided, as should cleaning methods which disturb dusts, etc, making particles airborne again.

Smoking

Summary

Tobacco smoking in the workplace may result in health and safety hazards for your workforce through the presence of environmental tobacco smoke (ETS) and fire hazards.

Practical Guidance

Preventing fire hazards

Smoking should be prohibited in any areas where discarded smoker's materials are likely to act as a source of ignition. Prominent signs should be displayed.

Examples of where fires could develop are:

- areas where flammable liquids or gases are present
- areas where there is combustible storage, waste or packing materials
- storage areas and loading bays
- plant rooms
- infrequently visited areas
- computer rooms and rooms housing sensitive electronic equipment.

Smoking banned

Smoking is banned in certain circumstances under the following legislation:

- **Explosives Act 1875**
- **Manufacture of Cinematograph Film Regulations 1928**
- **Cinematograph Film Stripping Regulations 1939**
- **Magnesium (Grinding of Castings and Other Articles) Special Regulations 1946**
- **Highly Flammable Liquids and Liquified Petroleum Gases Regulations 1972**
- **Control of Lead at Work Regulations 1998**
- **Ionising Radiations Regulations 1999**
- **Control of Asbestos at Work Regulations 1987**
- **Gas Safety (Installation and Use) Regulations 1994**
- **Food Safety (General Food Hygiene) Regulations 1995.**

Rest rooms

Under the **Management of Health and Safety at Work Regulations 1999** suitable arrangements must be made to protect non-smokers from discomfort caused by tobacco smoke. This may mean the provision of a separate room for smokers.

Health risks

There is a duty of care under the **Health and Safety at Work, etc Act 1974** for employers to protect the health of their workforce. If, after a risk assessment, a smoky atmosphere is seen to cause possible health risks, action should be taken.

The main processes that are necessary in drawing up a smoking policy are shown in the following flowchart.

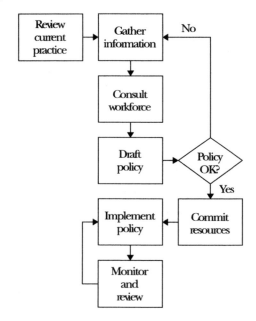

Questions and Answers

Q   Can I just ban smoking in all areas immediately?

A   No, you should consult the workforce and introduce a policy (see diagram below). As seen in recent case law simply banning smoking could constitute constructive dismissal for some smokers (*Dryden v Greater Glasgow Health Board* 1992).

Q   How can I make sure that the smoking room doesn't become a fire hazard?

A   Ensure that it is regularly cleaned, and that there are adequate ashtrays, etc. The relevant fire extinguishing equipment should be readily available.

Q   Do I have to provide an area for smokers?

A   No, you don't — you do have to provide an area for non-smokers though. However, it is useful to provide a smoking area when you are introducing a ban on smoking — this must be properly ventilated to the outside.

Stress

Summary

Work-related stress is the second most common form of occupational ill-health, behind musculo-skeletal disorders. Managing stress at work is difficult as staff are often reluctant to admit that they are suffering from work-related stress and managers do not always recognise the symptoms. There are also problems with isolating work-related stress from stress associated with external social or other factors.

Practical Guidance

Legal issues

There is no specific legislation on stress at work, although the general duty on employers to ensure the health and safety of employees at work, so far as is reasonably practicable under s.2 of the **Health and Safety at Work, etc Act 1974** will apply. In addition, where work-related stress is identified in a workplace, the **Management of Health and Safety at Work Regulations 1999** require employers to assess the associated risks and take any necessary preventive or protective measures. This includes ensuring that employees are not subject to excessive levels of stress at work.

The case of *Walker v Northumberland County Council* demonstrated that employers have a duty to provide a "safe place" of work which includes taking steps to relieve the pressures which result in stress. In this particular case, Walker had an initial nervous breakdown due to overwork. On return to work he informed his employers that his workload must be reduced; this was not carried out and Walker suffered a second breakdown which led to retirement on the grounds of ill-health.

The case succeeded because the employers were fully aware of the pressure Walker had been under but had not taken any preventive measures.

In contrast, the case of *Petch v Commissioners of Customs and Excise* demonstrated that the employers were not held liable for negligence when Petch suffered a mental breakdown due to overwork, as they had taken measures to persuade him to take sick leave and had moved him to a less stressful job.

Practical issues

Work-related stress is associated with pressures at work. It is difficult to determine when positive, constructive pressure, which provides challenge and job satisfaction, becomes negative, destructive pressure resulting in stress. The difficulty is increased by the fact that everyone has different levels of tolerable pressure — what is constructive pressure for one employee may be destructive for another.

It is important for employers to recognise when the critical point has been reached. It is also important for employers to be aware of any external factors which may make employees more susceptible to work pressures, even though those factors are outside the responsibility and control of the employer.

Causative factors

Factors which may be associated with work-related stress are:
• lack of control over the work
• conflicting demands
• overwork
• underwork
• monotonous, repetitive work
• uncertainty about job security
• unrealistic targets or performance standards
• peer pressure, including harassment
• poor management
• lack of support, both from peers and managers
• the work environment: excessive noise, temperature, humidity, poor decor, etc.

Control and monitoring stress

Directly addressing the known causes of work-related stress, eg allowing employees more control over their work, providing consistent management and demands, etc will all have an effect in reducing the incidence of stress in the workplace. In addition, staff should be encouraged to report stress at work, and managers should be trained to recognise the symptoms and causes of stress and not regard it as an inconvenience, nuisance or personal weakness.

Any control measures implemented should be monitored to ensure their effectiveness. Monitoring may include scrutinising sickness absences, distributing and assessing confidential health questionnaires, exit interviews, measuring work performance levels and work relationships, etc.

Employers may also consider providing support facilities such as counselling and stress management training, although these will only relieve the symptoms, without addressing the actual causes.

Questions and Answers

Q What is meant by the term "work-related stress"?

A Stress is basically an inability to cope and can be caused by a wide range of factors; bereavement, divorce and moving house are well-recognised stress factors in society. However, many people also lose or suffer a reduction in their ability to cope due to pressures at work, eg unrealistic targets, long hours, overwork, too much or too little control over work, etc — this is work-related stress.

Q Are some occupations more susceptible to work-related stress than others?

A The 1990 Labour Force survey on self-reported ill-health suggested that teachers and other educational and welfare workers had greater than average rates of stress (however the figures were coincidental to the report questions and have not yet been substantiated by detailed research). It is likely that jobs involving work performance criteria, strict deadlines, potentially violent situations, bereavement and contact with horrific accidents/injuries will almost certainly have associated work-related stress factors.

Q Are the symptoms of stress reversible?

A Generally yes, in most cases the symptoms are short-lived and do not cause permanent harm. However, if the causative factors are allowed to continue the effects will be more sustained and may cause long-term psychological and physical problems. The range of symptoms displayed is highly individual and will vary between employees.

Sunlight and Sunburn

Summary

Strong sunlight can be hard on the skin because of the ultraviolet (UV) rays it contains. People with outdoor jobs, or those with a significant amount of time outdoors, may have more exposure of their skin to UV rays than is good for them.

Practical Guidance

What is the risk?

In the short term sunburn can cause blisters to the skin and make it peel. In summer enough UV rays can still penetrate cloud to cause burning — direct sunlight is not necessary. In the long term, the most serious effect is an increased risk of skin cancer later in life. Excessive exposure to sunlight can also speed up the ageing process of the skin making it wrinkled, mottled and leathery. Sometimes, taking certain drugs or working with chemicals at work can make the skin more sensitive to sunlight and therefore more at risk. Those chemicals include wood preservatives, coal tar and pitch products.

Who is at risk?

People of Asian or Afro-Caribbean origin are at virtually no risk. Not everyone has the same susceptibility to sunlight and people with white skin are more at risk. Those most at risk are people with fair or freckled skin which does not tan, or burns before tanning, red or fair hair and light coloured eyes, or have a large number of moles — over 100 in young people or over 50 in older people.

Skin types can be broken down into four categories:

Type 1 — skin always burns and never tans. Light skin and blue eyes, red or blond hair or freckles (of Celtic origin).

Type 2 — skin burns easily but eventually tans. Fair skin and fair hair.

Type 3 — skin burns sometimes, tans, but slowly. Light brown hair, blue, green or brown eyes, medium skin tone.

Type 4 — skin burns occasionally but mostly tans well. Dark hair and eyes.

Workers most at risk are those spending prolonged periods outside or fully/partly exposed to sunlight. Most at risk might include farm workers, gardeners or others connected to similar activities, construction, demolition or similar manual workers, some public service workers, those whose leisure activities keep them outside for long periods of time.

What is it that goes wrong?

The skin consists of two layers, the epidermis (or cuticle) and the dermis (or corium). The visible, outermost part of the epidermis is known as the horny layers and is made up of flat, thin, scale like cells which are constantly being cast off and replaced by newer cells from below. The deepest part is made of basal cells where this new cell production begins. When skin is exposed to ultraviolet light, those rays can penetrate to the pigment producing layers, down to the basal cell layer. As these layers are exposed to UV they produce increased amounts of a substance known as melanin. How much melanin is produced depends on the skin type. The melanin is actually produced by pigment producing cells called melanocytes, then dispersing towards the skin surface to act as a protection.

If skin is exposed to too much sunlight before adequate amounts of melanin have been produced, the epidermal cells can become damaged — sunburn. The medical term for this erythema, or redness of the skin, unfortunately most people have experienced this painful burning which in extreme cases can result in dizziness and sickness. The treatment for this is to cool the skin by immersion in cool water and applying a suitable emollient cream to allow rehydration of the outer skin layers and reduce the tenderness. Blistering should suggest medical attention is necessary. Ideally one should never allow exposure to reach the point of burning.

How do we recognise the problem?

Skin cancer can take several forms and the first warning signs can often be a small, scabby, persistent spot. People can develop moles until adulthood, but any developing in later life should be taken special note of. Any appearing on the backs of the hands, face and especially the nose or around the eyes are of particular concern, but any new moles, or moles which change shape or colour, or any discolouration of the skin needs investigation.

Employees should see a doctor if they have or develop moles which:

- itch
- grow
- change shape
- change colour
- become inflamed
- bleed.

There are about 400,000 reported cases of skin cancer every year in the UK. When caught early enough, treatment can be highly effective with about a 90% success rate.

How to stay safe in the sun

The first principle of risk assessment and management applies — avoid the hazard — avoid exposure to direct sunlight. Where exposure is likely take care to avoid reddening of the skin which is the first indication of burning, which means damage to the skin. Getting burnt increases the risk of developing skin cancer in later years. A tan provides some protection against burning, but depending on skin type, does not prevent the longer term cancer risk.

Cover the skin and use close woven fabrics to protect the body. This may need to include a hat, with a wide brim, which will help shade the face and head. If the work includes much forward leaning, a loose fabric flap will protect the neck. Keep your top on and use a sunscreen where parts of the body are still exposed. This will need to be an adequate protection factor, taking into account skin type and amount of existing exposure and tanning. Use a sun protection factor (SPF) of at the very least 10. It is important to repeat the application at the intervals specified in the product instructions and if it is likely that the protection has washed off, re-apply.

Make regular checks of the skin condition. If any new moles appear, existing ones change, or there is skin discolouration, seek medical advice. The earlier the problem is found, the easier it is to cure completely.

Questions and Answers

Q I have had a small mole on my arm for a number of years, should I have this checked by a doctor?

A Having a mole is not in itself an indication that you may be developing skin cancer. If the mole changes in size, shape or colour, itches, becomes inflamed or bleed then seek medical help.

Q I work in a road gang outside all the time. When summer starts I always work with my shirt off and get very red (sometimes it is painful) for a week or two but then I go brown and do not have any problems. Am I OK?

A Burning of the skin is the way to increase the risk of permanent damage and of a cancer developing. Outdoor workers should always use physical protection such as clothing plus the chemical protection of creams, etc until a natural protection has built up slowly without any burning.

Q Is exposure to sunlight a matter that has to be assessed under the **Control of Substances Hazardous to Health Regulations 1999**?

A No, COSHH does not apply to exposure to sunlight, but the general requirements of the **Management of Health and Safety at Work Regulations 1999** to carry out assessments of risks do. Employers who have employees who may be at risk from exposure to sunlight should assess the level of risk and decide if any protective measures are needed.

Temperature

Summary

The temperature of the workplace affects the comfort, the efficiency and the health and safety of people at work. Extremes of temperature may put workers at risk, for instance from heat exhaustion in hot environments and hypothermia in cold environments. It is therefore important for employers to control the temperature of the workplace or, where this is not possible, protect workers against the temperature.

Practical Guidance

Workplace temperature

Under the **Workplace (Health, Safety and Welfare) Regulations 1992** (Workplace Regulations), the temperature in internal workplaces must be reasonable during working hours. The Approved Code of Practice (ACOP) accompanying the Workplace Regulations advises that the minimum acceptable temperature is 16°C, or 13°C where heavy physical work is carried out.

The Workplace Regulations state that methods of heating or cooling used to maintain an acceptable temperature must not give off adverse fumes, gases, etc.

In areas of the workplace that are not normally used for work, eg corridors, washing facilities and meeting rooms, the temperature should be reasonable taking into account:

- the length of time people are likely to use them
- the activities likely to take place.

Construction sites

Under the **Construction (Health, Safety and Welfare) Regulations 1996**, the temperature of internal workplaces should be reasonable during working hours, taking the nature of the work into account. For external workplaces, arrangements must be in place to protect workers against adverse weather conditions, including the provision of suitable personal protective equipment where necessary.

Work equipment

The **Provision and Use of Work Equipment Regulations 1998** require work equipment which operates at very high or low temperatures to be protected to prevent burns, scalds and sear injuries through contact with their surface. A number of engineering controls may be used to do this.

Risk assessment

Under the **Management of Health and Safety at Work Regulations 1999**, employers must carry out assessments of risk for their work activities. These assessments should include consideration of the risks from temperatures, and should identify the control measures necessary to protect workers against these risks.

Electrical equipment

Under the **Electricity at Work Regulations 1989**, electrical equipment must be constructed and protected against natural hazards, such as temperature extremes. This means that electrical equipment used in hot or cold environments must be suitable for such work, and safe to use in the temperatures likely to be encountered.

Protective equipment

If other health and safety measures fail to provide adequate protection against the risks from temperatures, suitable personal protective equipment (PPE) should be provided. Where PPE is needed, employers must comply with the requirements of the **Personal Protective Equipment at Work Regulations 1992**.

In terms of temperature, suitable PPE may include:

- warm gloves, boots and clothing to protect people working outside in the winter
- protective clothing and other equipment used for protection against extremely hot temperatures up to 100°C, eg molten metal, emergency rescue in fires
- protective clothing and other equipment for use in extremely cold temperatures, eg emergency protection for people trapped in walk-in chill rooms
- protective gloves in laboratories for working with cryogenic liquids, such as liquid nitrogen
- heat and burn-resistant foot, leg, hand, arm and body protection for work involving exposure to sparks, eg welding
- gloves with extra grip for manual handling tasks in warm temperatures, which may increase the risk of loads slipping from workers' hands.

Manual handling

Under the **Manual Handling Operations Regulations 1992**, employers must carry out assessments of risk for any manual handling operations that cannot be eliminated. The assessments must consider a number of factors, including the working environment such as the temperature. High temperatures may cause rapid fatigue and increased sweating, making the load more slippery to carry. Low temperatures may also make manual handling tasks more difficult.

Hot work

For hot work that cannot be avoided, such as work with furnaces, precautions may include:

- providing cooling fans
- wearing reflective and heat-resistant clothing
- wearing cooling clothing, such as air cooled suits
- wearing respiratory protective equipment where there is a risk of burns to the respiratory system
- only allowing workers who have suitable physical qualities to enter the hot area, eg depending on age, obesity, history of heart or kidney disease, recent dehydration due to vomiting, diahorrea or excess alcohol intake
- entering the hot area for as short a time as possible
- monitoring of the worker by a competent person
- self-monitoring of the pulse while in the hot area.

Cold work

Where work in extremely low temperatures cannot be avoided, eg in food chillers, precautions may include:

- wearing warm protective clothing
- entering the cold area for as short a time as possible
- monitoring of the worker by a competent person.

Questions and Answers

Q Is there a maximum temperature for workplaces under health and safety law?

A Although the ACOP accompanying the Workplace Regulations states a minimum temperature for workplaces, it does not recommend a maximum temperature. The Regulations do, however, require a sufficient number of thermometers to be located around the workplace, so that it is possible to tell what the temperature is. There are many occasions when workers will experience discomfort due to high temperatures, such as during warm summers, in kitchens and in areas where equipment and machinery generate heat. Employers have a duty of care for the welfare of their employers under s.2 of the **Health and Safety at Work Act, etc 1974**. This means that, so far as is reasonably practicable, they should reduce the workplace temperature, or set up other measures to protect workers against the discomfort of heat.

Q What can we do in the summer, when our office becomes excessively warm at times?

A Ventilation is the key to reducing discomfort in hot offices. An air-conditioning system is the most effective method of cooling an office, and may be permanently installed in the premises. Portable air-conditioning systems are also available to buy or hire. They can either be installed into the premises, or portable air-conditioning systems are available to buy or hire.

If air conditioning is not a reasonably practicable option, ventilation can be improved by using electric fans and opening windows. Make sure that open windows do not cause additional risks of falling from a height, or protruding into a narrow passageway where people may accidentally collide with them. Make sure that all electrical equipment such as printers, photocopiers, etc which is not being used is turned off, as it can generate a significant amount of heat.

Q How can manual handling tasks outdoors in cold weather be made safe?

A It may be necessary to provide the worker with warm gloves. Make sure these are also waterproof where they may be used in wet conditions, as wet gloves will draw heat away from the hands. Bear in mind that wearing gloves may reduce dexterity, and make the task more difficult.

Workers will become tired faster in cold weather, so allow for breaks to be taken along the way if the load has to be carried over a significant distance. Trolleys or other non-manual methods of carrying may be needed.

Provide workers with hot drinks at regular intervals to help keep them warm. If the load itself is cold, put it in an insulated container for manual handling.

Temporary Workers

Summary

Most temporary workers do not have a contract of employment with the employer — either their employers are a different organisation, or they are self-employed. They are likely to be unfamiliar with the premises and company safety rules and procedures, which increases the level of risk that they face.

Practical Guidance

Duty of care

Under s.3 of the **Health and Safety at Work, etc Act 1974** (HSW Act), employers must carry out their undertaking in such a way that it does not give rise to health and safety risks to non-employees, eg temporary workers. Unlike the duty of care for employees in s.2 of the Act, the HSW Act does not expand on what this duty may entail.

Section 4 of the HSW Act extends the duty of care for non-employees to include anyone in control of premises where people are at work.

Risk assessment

Under the **Management of Health and Safety at Work Regulations 1999** (MHSWR), employers must carry out assessments of the risks posed by their work activities. These assessments should include the risks to temporary workers on-site who may be affected by the employers' work activities.

Provision of information

Under MHSWR, employers must give comprehensible information to the employees of others who are working on their premises, eg temporary workers, on:
- any relevant risks
- the control measures in place to safeguard their health and safety
- emergency procedures
- the qualifications or skills they need to carry out their job safely
- any health surveillance required.

MHSWR also requires the host employer to provide the temporary worker's employer or employment agency with information on:
- the qualifications or skills they need to carry out the job safely
- any health surveillance required.

Shared workplaces

MHSWR requires that if a workplace is shared by employees of more than one employer, the employers must co-operate and co-ordinate with each other with regard to the arrangements for health and safety. This would include workplaces where temporary workers are present.

Host employer: legal duties

The duties of the host employer to temporary workers under health and safety legislation include the following:

- reporting dangerous occurrences involving temporary workers under the **Reporting of Injuries, Diseases and Dangerous Occurrences Regulations 1995 (RIDDOR)**
- informing the worker and his or her employer of any personal protective equipment required for the job
- providing and maintaining suitable work equipment, and providing training and instruction for the worker on how to use it under the **Provision and Use of Work Equipment Regulations 1998**
- assessing any display screen equipment workstations used by temporary workers and ensuring the workstations meet the requirements of the **Health and Safety (Display Screen Equipment) Regulations 1992**
- assessing any manual handling tasks carried out by the worker, making arrangements to reduce the risks and providing the worker with information on the load
- assessing the risks to the worker's health from hazardous substances, controlling these risks, training the casual worker on the safe use of relevant chemicals, and informing the agency of any health surveillance which it should provide, as required by the **Control of Substances Hazardous to Health Regulations 1999 (COSHH)**
- providing and maintaining safe electrical systems under the **Electricity at Work Regulations 1989**
- assessing exposure of temporary workers to noise and providing hearing protection where required by the **Noise at Work Regulations 1989**
- protecting temporary workers from ionising radiations under the **Ionising Radiations Regulations 1999**.

Workers' employer: legal duties

Employers of temporary workers also have duties under health and safety law, including the following:

- providing the host employer with information about the health of the worker, what training the worker has received and whether the worker is experienced in the type of work he or she will be doing for the host employer
- reporting injuries to, death of, or occupational diseases contracted by the temporary worker under RIDDOR

- providing adequate first aid arrangements for the worker under the **Health and Safety (First Aid) Regulations 1981**
- providing suitable personal protective equipment for the worker under the **Personal Protective Equipment at Work Regulations 1992**
- providing eyesight tests and glasses, where necessary, under the **Health and Safety (Display Screen Equipment) Regulations 1992**
- providing any health surveillance identified as necessary by the host employer under COSHH
- considering whether workers will be exposed to noise in excess of the levels set in the **Noise at Work Regulations 1989** and deciding how to restrict this exposure
- providing personal dosimetry, medical surveillance and dose records as required under the **Ionising Radiations Regulations 1999**.

Temporary workers are often self-employed, in which case the person may have to act as both employer and employee.

Questions and Answers

Q   What information should we give temporary workers on our site with regard to fire safety?

A   Fire safety is an important issue with regard to the employment of temporary workers. Such workers will be unfamiliar with the fire precautions and means of escape, etc when they start work at each new site. Therefore, it is important that a responsible person gives them relevant training when they arrive. Such training should include:
- the action they should take if they discover a fire
- how to raise the alarm
- the procedure for evacuation
- how to use the fire extinguishers and where they are located
- the location of the fire escape routes.

If a temporary worker is working on-site for a long time, eg more than a year, refresher training in fire safety may be appropriate.

Q   Who is responsible for reporting an injury to, or fatality of, a temporary worker to the enforcing authority?

A   In most types of workplace, the person responsible for reporting accidents is the employer of the injured person. Therefore if a temporary worker is injured on your premises, his or her employer must report the accident, though of course you should inform his or her employer as soon as possible after he or she is injured. However, if the temporary worker is a self-employed person, the person in control of the premises, ie the host employer, is responsible for reporting the accident. It is important to know the status of *all* individual temporary workers (whether they are employed or self-employed) on the premises *before* an accident happens. Contact information for the worker's employer should be easy to obtain.

Q   Do we have to provide first aid arrangements for temporary workers on our site?

Temporary Workers

A Under the **Health and Safety (First Aid) Regulations 1981**, it is the responsibility of the worker's employer to provide adequate first aid. In the case of self-employed people, they must make adequate provisions for themselves.

In practice, it may be more straightforward for the host employer and worker's employer to enter into an agreement that the first aid personnel and equipment on the host premises will be made available for the temporary worker. In the event of an accident, it is likely that a qualified first aider for the premises will be summoned. It would be difficult for the first aider to stand back and not help an injured person just because the injured person is a temporary worker, especially if the worker is having difficulty administering first aid to him or herself. Arrangements for sharing first aid provisions should be agreed before the temporary worker starts working on the premises.

Time Off Work

Summary

Employees are entitled to time off work in relation to health and safety for a number of reasons, such as to fulfil their functions as safety representatives. Time off work in this context means time off from normal work activities while still receiving normal salary.

Practical Guidance

Safety representatives

The **Safety Representatives and Safety Committees Regulations 1977** provide for recognised trade unions to appoint official safety representatives in the workplace. These representatives have a number of functions, and will usually require specific training in health and safety on appointment, plus occasional refresher training to keep them up-to-date with changes in legislation and practice.

The 1977 Regulations entitle safety representatives to reasonable time off with pay during normal working hours in order to:

- carry out their functions as a safety representative, eg undertaking workplace inspections, attending safety committee meetings, investigating accidents, etc
- attend training on their functions as safety representatives, so that they may carry out those functions more efficiently.

Disputes on time off for safety representatives may be resolved through the industrial tribunal system.

Employee representatives

In workplaces where employees are not represented by a trade union, the **Health and Safety (Consultation with Employees) Regulations 1996** require employers to consult with their employees on health and safety matters. This consultation may take place either directly with the employees, or through an employee representative (a "representative of employee safety") elected by them.

Under the 1996 Regulations, employers must allow employee representatives paid time off to:

- perform their functions as employee representatives
- attend training courses which are relevant to these functions
- perform their functions as candidates, in the case of potential employee representatives who are standing for election.

The employer must also pay for all reasonable costs associated with training as an employee representative, including travel and subsistence.

Pregnant workers

The **Trade Union Reform and Employment Rights Act 1993** requires employers to find alternative work for pregnant workers who cannot continue with their normal work for reasons of health and safety. If no suitable alternative work is available, the employer must suspend the pregnant worker until it is safe for her to return to work. During this time off, the worker must be paid the salary that she would have received if she had not been suspended.

First aiders

Under the **Health and Safety (First Aid) Regulations 1981**, many employers need to provide their workers with qualified first aiders. These first aiders are usually drawn from the workforce, in order to ensure that they are on the premises should an accident occur. The Approved Code of Practice for these Regulations contains details of adequate training for first aiders.

Although not explicit in the 1981 Regulations, first aiders should be given training during normal working hours, and be allowed time off with pay in order to attend training courses. Training is required initially to those new to first aid, and qualified first aiders should attend a refresher course at least once every three years.

Questions and Answers

Q How much time off work are safety representatives entitled to?
A There is no set amount of time off work for safety representatives. Basically, they must be allowed enough time off to perform their functions properly, and to attend training courses which will give them enough knowledge and experience to carry out these functions. The amount of time this takes will depend on:
- the individual's capacity for learning
- the individual's speed at carrying out his or her functions as a safety representative
- the number of employees he or she is representing
- the number of other safety representatives from the same trade union
- the size of the workplace
- the complexity of the work activities
- the level of risk associated with the work
- the frequency of changes in practice, eg legislation, new machinery, new processes, etc
- the frequency of accidents
- the frequency of, and time taken by, safety committee meetings
- the frequency of visits by enforcement authority inspectors.

It should be possible for the safety representative and his or her manager to consult with each other and determine the length of time off that is reasonable, and the best times of the day, week, month and year for the employee to be absent from his or her normal work. The safety representative is also entitled to the same time off for holidays and sickness as anyone else who holds the same job within the company, and the manager should not try to discourage safety representatives from using this entitlement.

Q How much time off work should first aiders be given?

A First aid courses are generally four days long, either all in one week or spread out over a number of weeks. Refresher training courses, which qualified first aiders should attend every three years, are usually two days long. Some first aiders will be given special training for particular hazards, eg in workplaces where oxygen may need to be administered. This will increase the time taken for training and refresher training.

   First aiders should be selected from job holders who can leave their work at short notice to attend a casualty. Of course, they should be allowed time off with pay while they administer first aid, and as long as is necessary for them to stay with the injured person afterwards, eg until the emergency services arrive.

Q One of our night workers has informed us in writing that she is pregnant. We are unable to offer her alternative daytime work, as there is none that is suitable for her. What is her entitlement to time off?

A Under the **Management of Health and Safety at Work Regulations 1999**, employers must suspend pregnant workers from night work if their doctor or midwife informs them in writing that it is necessary to do so for their health and safety. If suitable alternative day time work is not available suspension should be granted, and under employment law the worker is entitled to receive the salary she would normally receive if she had not been suspended. If the worker has not provided a letter from her doctor or midwife saying she should not continue with night work, there is no reason to suspend her. However, it may be a good idea to ask her to check with her doctor or midwife about the suitability of night work, if she has not already done this.

Traffic Routes

Summary

A traffic route is a route for pedestrian traffic, vehicles or both and includes any stairs, staircase, fixed ladder, doorway, gateway, loading bay or ramp. Many work activities involve the use of vehicles as well as people. Where the two integrate there is a high potential for an accident to occur unless steps are taken to minimise the risk of injuries occurring.

Practical Guidance

Many industrial accidents involve vehicles, which may be fork-lift trucks, lorries, tractors, delivery vans or cars. In most undertakings there is a need, therefore, for an efficient traffic control system. This will reduce internal traffic accidents.

There may also be risks on traffic routes frequented only by pedestrians; obvious examples would include a staircase without an adequate handhold, or a corridor with trip hazards caused by accumulated empty cartons.

General duties

It is the duty of employers to ensure the health, safety and welfare of all their employees whilst at work. The duty to provide safe systems of work, the safe transportation of articles and substances, a safe place of work, and safe access and egress, would apply to traffic routes. Drivers of workplace transport should be adequately trained and provided with refresher training at suitable intervals.

Condition of floors and traffic routes

The **Workplace (Health, Safety and Welfare) Regulations 1992** place responsibilities on the employer with regard to the condition of floors and traffic routes. They should be of sound construction and suitable for the purpose for which they are used. A surface for pedestrian traffic in an office environment may not be suitable for the passage of vehicles, mechanical aids such as trolleys or workers carrying certain loads.

Routes should be free from any hole, slope or uneven or slippery surface that would be likely to cause a person to trip, slip or fall, or cause instability or loss of control of a vehicle or its load. The surface of any floor or traffic route which is likely to get wet should be of a type which does not become unduly slippery.

Where possible, processes and plant which may discharge or leak liquids should be enclosed by suitable bunding, and leaks from taps or discharge points on pipes, drums and tanks should be caught in drip trays or drained away. Where the work involves carrying or handling liquids, the likelihood of spillage should be minimised. There should also be a procedure for ensuring that spillages are attended to. It may be necessary to provide slip-resistant footwear in work areas where slipping hazards arise.

Arrangements should be made to minimise risks from environmentally variable conditions, such as snow and ice.

Floors and traffic routes should be kept free of obstructions which may present a hazard or impede access. In particular, areas on and around stairs, doors, corners or junctions should be kept clear.

Vehicles should not be parked where they are likely to be a hazard to other vehicles or pedestrians.

Effective drainage should be provided where the floor is liable to get wet. Drains and channels should have covers which should be as near flush as possible with the floor surface, to avoid creating a trip hazard.

Every open side of a staircase should be securely fenced. A handrail should be provided on at least one side of every staircase, except where it may obstruct egress or access. If there is a particular risk of falling, or the staircase is very wide, there should be two handrails.

Organisation of traffic routes

There should be sufficient routes with sufficient width and headroom to allow people on foot or in vehicles to circulate safely and without difficulty. Special consideration should be given to those people in wheelchairs, or with other special needs.

Access between floors should normally be by means of a conventional staircase. If this is not possible, fixed ladders or steep stairs may be used, providing they can be used safely. Spiral staircases present particular risks and should be avoided.

Vehicles must not use routes which are inadequate or unsuitable. Any necessary restrictions should be clearly indicated. Potentially dangerous obstructions such as overhead electrical cables should be shielded.

Screens should be provided where necessary to protect people who have to work in the close vicinity of vehicles, to guard against exhaust fumes or materials which are likely to fall from vehicles.

Sensible speed limits should be set, clearly displayed on vehicle routes, and then enforced. Where necessary, speed humps should be provided but these are not suitable in areas where lift trucks are used.

Vehicle routes should be wide enough to allow vehicles to pass oncoming or parked vehicles without deviating from the route. Vehicles should not have to pass close to the edge of any drop, nor anything which is likely to collapse if hit, unless there is adequate fencing or protection.

Where possible, the need for vehicles to reverse should be eliminated. If large vehicles have to reverse, measures should be taken to reduce the risks to pedestrians and any people in wheelchairs. The use of banksmen is advisable.

If crowds of people are likely to overflow on to roadways, for example, at the end of a shift, consideration should be given to stopping vehicles from using the routes at such times. Any traffic route which is used by both pedestrians and vehicles must be wide enough to enable them to pass each other safely, and ideally there should be a means of segregation, eg a handrail and/or clearly demarcated areas highlighted by signs and painted hatching on the floor.

Where automatic, driverless, vehicles are used, steps should be taken to ensure that pedestrians cannot be trapped by these vehicles. In doorways, gateways, and other restricted routes, vehicles should be separated from pedestrians by a kerb or barrier. Where pedestrian and vehicle routes cross, appropriate crossing points should be provided and used. Pedestrians should be prevented from crossing at particularly dangerous points.

Loading bays should be provided with at least one exit point from the lower level, or if this is not practicable a refuge should be provided to avoid the potential for a pedestrian to be hit or trapped. All potential hazards and restrictions should be indicated by suitable signs. Road markings and signs should comply with the traffic signs regulations and the Highway Code.

Questions and Answers

Q What should the speed limit be for vehicles on site?

A The standard speed limit would not normally be in excess of 10 or 15 miles per hour. Whatever speed limit is set, it must be enforceable.

Q Can I introduce speed humps if the roads are used by fork-lift trucks as well as cars?

A Where possible they should be avoided, unless the truck is of a type that can pass over them safely, or gaps can be provided for the trucks to pass through.

Q Do I have to repair holes or uneven areas immediately?

A No, although adequate provisions must be taken to prevent accidents, eg barriers should be erected around them.

Trainees

Summary

A trainee is someone who is receiving training as part of their employment. Many trainees are young school leavers, with practically no experience of working and the associated hazards. Trainees, by definition, are unfamiliar with the workplace or work activities and are therefore likely to be exposed to a higher level of risk.

Practical Guidance

Trainees as employees

Section 2 of the **Health and Safety at Work, etc Act 1974** (HSW Act) puts a duty of care on employers to ensure the health, safety and welfare of their employees. Originally, the HSW Act did not include trainees under the definition of employees. However, the **Health and Safety (Training for Employment) Regulations 1990** changed that by extending the requirements of health and safety law relating to the HSW Act to include people who are being provided with relevant training. This means that the following must be treated as employees in terms of health and safety at work:

- those receiving training from the employer in the workplace, eg apprentices
- trainees on Government training schemes
- school children on work experience
- college students on placement schemes.

However, employers are no longer responsible for trainees attending courses at an educational establishment, eg college students studying at their university or school children at school. Section 3 of the HSW Act would apply in these circumstances.

Increased risks

The risk assessments carried out under the **Management of Health and Safety at Work Regulations 1999** (MHSWR) should consider the increased risks to trainees. Although the hazards are likely to be the same with an experienced worker as with a trainee, the level of risk will be higher where trainees are involved. This is due to their lack of experience and, in the case of younger trainees, possible personal qualities, such as immaturity, inability to comprehend foreseeable risks and inclination towards horseplay. Obviously, these qualities depend very much on the individual.

Young people

Specific provisions within the **Management of Health and Safety at Work Regulations 1999** require employers to:
- carry out assessments of risk to young persons before they start work
- control any aspects of the work which put the young person at risk
- inform the parent or guardian of anyone under school leaving age of the risks identified and the control measures in place to protect their health and safety.

People under the age of 18 must not be involved in the following:
- any activity beyond their physical or psychological capability
- exposure to substances or agents which are toxic, carcinogenic, toxic for reproduction, or which have other long-term effects
- exposure to harmful levels of ionising radiation
- work activities involving risks which they are unlikely to be able to recognise or avoid, due to their inexperience, lack of training or attention to safety
- exposure to noise, vibration or extreme temperatures.

Safe systems of work

Safe systems of work for trainees are likely to require additional control measures to the ones already in place. Control measures suitable for reducing the risks to trainees include the following:
- ensure that trainees are supervised by a competent person
- employ them in less hazardous areas and work activities, where possible, unless they are being specifically trained in such processes
- restrict the activities that they are allowed to be involved in
- make sure they receive adequate training
- make sure that all work equipment they use is safe
- ensure that all dangerous parts of machinery are guarded.

Supervision and training

Section 2 of the HSW Act specifies certain requirements of the duty of care. Of particular relevance to trainees, given their inexperience, are the requirements for the provision of adequate information, instruction, training and supervision.

Under MHSWR, employers must provide their employees — trainees are therefore included in these Regulations — with comprehensible information on:
- risks to their health and safety
- arrangements in place to control these risks
- emergency procedures
- the competent people in charge in the event of an emergency.

Trainees will require a higher level of supervision than experienced employees. Supervisors should:
- provide trainees with the company's instructions for young people
- ensure they understand the instructions and the importance of following the rules

- provide trainees with training on how to carry out their job safely
- make sure the trainee is under constant observation if they are not confident that the trainee is mature, able or responsible enough to carry out his or her work safely.

Reporting accidents

Under the **Reporting of Injuries, Diseases and Dangerous Occurrences Regulations 1995** (RIDDOR), certain injuries must be reported to the enforcing authority. The person responsible for reporting injuries sustained by a trainee, is the employer who is providing him or her with the training. In the case of trainees exempt from employee status under the **Health and Safety (Training for Employment) Regulations 1990**, eg school children at school, the responsible person is whoever is in control of the premises. As an example, if a school child is injured during work experience, the employer must report the accident. If a school child is injured at school, the school must report the accident.

Display screen equipment

Trainees may be expected to work with display screen equipment (DSE). Young trainees may be unable to relate working with computers with long-term effects they may suffer, eg work related upper limb disorders. They should be given comprehensible training in the risks from DSE and shown how to avoid these risks, eg how to adjust their screens and chairs, the correct posture they should adopt and the necessity to take frequent breaks. Additional supervision is likely to be required.

Manual handling

Trainees may be at risk of injury caused by manual handling operations. As with DSE, they may be unable to relate lifting and carrying with the long-term effects they may suffer, eg back problems in later life. If they are physically immature, ie smaller and weaker than an adult, they may be unable to perform certain manual handling tasks safely and should be prohibited from carrying out such tasks.

Questions and Answers

Q Are all trainees young people?

A No. A trainee is someone who is receiving training as part of their employment, an apprenticeship, student placement, work experience, etc. In many cases, trainees will be new to working, as with school leavers. However, many people require training throughout their career if the way they carry out their work changes, they relocate to a different job or different company, take on extra tasks or responsibilities, etc. Young people who are totally new to the work are likely to be at greater risk than those who are used to workplace hazards but have taken on another job. However, managers sometimes overlook the fact that experienced workers need training in new tasks. While a hazardous task is being learnt, an increase in supervision will be needed.

Q What factors increase the risks to trainees?

A The lack of experience in the work, the hazards and how to avoid them are the major factors increasing the risks to trainees. For example, a person who has been operating a dangerous machine for many years will have the skills to use it safely. A trainee who is using the machine for the first time may be unaware of the dangers and make mistakes. If the machine becomes jammed, they may guess at how to deal with the problem, and come into contact with dangerous parts or become entangled. The other factors relate to the person's attitude to the workplace. Some young people may act irresponsibly, and this will increase the risk significantly. Many health and safety measures rely on workers behaving in a mature and responsible manner, remembering safety rules and procedures, and sticking to them.

Q When does a trainee become a competent person?

A The crucial period for the trainee will be the first few weeks on the job. This is when their learning curve will be the steepest. However, learning is likely to continue for months, even years, depending on the complexity of the task and the ability of the trainee. Supervisors should not leave trainees to work alone unless they are confident that they are competent enough to carry out the work safely, and to stop work and seek help if they encounter problems. This is a subjective judgment that can only be made on an individual basis. However, it is usual for the supervisor to leave the trainee to carry out straightforward tasks alone, and then check on their performance, gradually increasing the level of responsibility and freedom they have.

Training

Summary

Training involves giving someone information, instruction and practice in order to bring him or her to a desired standard of efficiency. Training is an essential element in providing safe systems of work — control measures will not work unless employees know how to use them properly.

Practical Guidance

Duty of care

Section 2 of the **Health and Safety at Work, etc Act 1974** (HSW Act), puts a duty of care on employers to ensure the health and safety of their employees while at work. The HSW Act covers the main elements of this duty of care, including a requirement to provide employees with suitable and sufficient information, instruction, training and supervision.

Management of health and safety

Under the **Management of Health and Safety at Work Regulations 1999** (MHSWR), training must take place during normal working hours. If this is not possible, the time taken for training must be regarded as an extension to the employee's time at work. This means that if the employee normally gets paid overtime, the time they spend after hours on training courses for health and safety should be remunerated in the same way as if they were working.

Competence

Competence is a combination of the following:
- training
- knowledge
- experience
- skill.

Employers must make sure employees are competent to carry out their jobs safely, particularly in relation to providing health and safety assistance (required by MHSWR), and for anyone working on electrical systems (required by the **Electricity at Work Regulations 1989**).

Training needs

Before adequate training can be provided, it is necessary to identify individual training needs. General induction training must be given to all employees, but in addition to this each new and existing worker is likely to require more detailed training to meet specific needs.

Training needs should be identified when a person first begins a job, and should be reviewed regularly, the annual appraisal between the employee and manager is a good time to do this. In between reviews, training needs may become apparent, for example if the supervisor notices an employee using work equipment incorrectly. Training needs may be influenced by:

- previous experience and training
- the individual's capability and capacity for learning
- the level of expertise and competence required for the job.

The training requirements of each particular job should be identified using a task analysis, and should be included as part of the job specification. Under the MHSWR employers must provide employees with adequate safety training if they change jobs or responsibilities and if new equipment or technology is introduced, or if existing equipment is modified significantly.

Methods of training

There are a variety of different training methods, including:

- lectures, eg for short briefings, technical training, large audiences
- lessons, eg for covering new subject areas and general principles
- demonstrations, eg for showing how to carry out specific activities or methods
- tool-box talks, eg for passing on information on working procedures to groups of employees
- on the job, eg for teaching an individual how to carry out the tasks he or she is responsible for
- workshops, eg for encouraging participation during training sessions.

Training may be given by:

- in-house personnel, eg line managers, safety officers, fire wardens
- external trainers coming to the workplace
- external trainers at an external venue.

Induction training

All employees should receive induction training on joining the company. Induction training should cover:

- the company's health and safety policy
- workplace safety rules and procedures
- their duties under health and safety law, eg reporting problems, using control measures
- identification of the individuals with special health and safety functions, eg safety managers, first aiders, fire wardens and safety representatives

- first aid arrangements
- fire safety and emergency evacuation procedures.

It is helpful for any individuals with health and safety responsibilities to be present during induction training.

Refresher training

Refresher training is necessary to help refresh employees' memories on a particular subject area, and to update them on changes in legislation, practice and policy. Refresher training is usually specific to a policy or procedure, and would be expected by the following workers:

- those working with asbestos
- crane drivers
- those handling flammable substances
- those working with ionising radiation
- operators of fork-lift trucks
- drivers of vehicles carrying dangerous substances by road
- safety representatives
- qualified first aiders
- safety officers.

The frequency of refresher training will depend on the complexity of the subject, how rapidly it changes and the ability of the individual to retain the information. In order to remember when the individual is due for fixed frequency refresher training, eg every three years for qualified first aiders, a written reminder should be included in the individual's training records.

If there is a significant change in legislation or practice, refresher training may have to be provided *ad hoc*, as well as on a regular basis. For example, fire safety officers would have required training when it became illegal to manufacture halons for use in fire extinguishers, and when changes were made to the colour schemes for portable fire-fighting equipment.

Managers

Line managers should be trained in:

- the requirements of health and safety law, in relation to their areas of responsibility
- the company's health and safety policy
- safety rules, procedures, control measures, etc relevant to their areas of responsibility
- communication with their staff and their managers
- how to supervise staff in relation to safety procedures, etc
- identification of problems or improvements in health and safety arrangements
- how and when to take disciplinary action against staff breaching safety rules, etc
- effective recruitment
- recognition of personal limitations in relation to health and safety knowledge

- how, where and when to find specialist advice.

Questions and Answers

Q When should we use an external trainer to give in-company training?

A It is likely that many of your company's training needs can be met by your own staff giving on-the-job training, or by one member of staff, eg the safety officer, attending an external course and passing the information on to other managers. However, if a particular training need is beyond the expertise of in-house staff, you should look at employing an external trainer to come to your workplace and give a tailor-made training programme. This is likely to be the most effective and cost-efficient method of training when:

- several employees require training
- the training needs to be specific to your company's activities and procedures
- new equipment or methods of work are being introduced.

Q What fire safety training is required?

A All staff should be trained in the following when they start work with the company.

- Background of fire safety, including:
  - legal obligations of employers and employees
  - the main causes of fire, how it develops and spreads
  - fire precautions, such as fire doors
  - losses and damage caused by fire.
- What to do if they discover a fire, including:
  - how to raise the alarm
  - where to find alarm call points
  - procedures for calling the fire brigade
  - location of fire extinguishers
  - situations in which they should attempt to tackle the fire
  - how to use fire extinguishers.
- What to do if they hear the fire alarm, including:
  - locations of means of escape
  - the key elements of a rapid escape, eg using the nearest escape route and not stopping to collect anything
  - how to use exits, eg panic bars
  - arrangements for visitors
  - arrangements for evacuating disabled people
  - location of fire assembly points and the procedures when they get there
  - identity of those with special responsibilities, such as managers checking their area is empty, fire wardens, etc.

Q What are the advantages and disadvantages of using computer-based training?

A   Computer-based training has the advantages of being reusable and interactive, it allows individuals to go at their own pace, usually gives feedback on their performance, often has colourful and imaginative displays which encourage the users' interest, and requires little or no supervision.

However, it may be very expensive, only one person may be able to use the package at a time, it cannot recognise why an individual is having problems understanding, and it does not support the trainee by answering questions.

Transport

Summary

Every year an average of around 70 people are killed in transport-related accidents in the workplace. In addition, there are more than 1000 major injuries, eg broken bones and amputations. The cost of a major accident has been estimated to be around £16,000, most of which is borne by the owner, employer or haulier.

Practical Guidance

The term "workplace transport" refers to any vehicle or piece of mobile equipment which is used by employers, employees, the self-employed or visitors in any work setting. It covers a wide range of vehicles, eg cars, vans, HGVs and industrial trucks. Use of vehicles on the public highway is covered by the Road Traffic Act, and is outside the scope of this section.

Most accidents involving workplace transport involve people being struck or run over by moving vehicles, being struck by objects falling from vehicles or being injured due to vehicles overturning. The underlying causes of most of these accidents are normally poor management control in terms of failure to provide a safe system of work, or failure to ensure that it is followed.

General duties

Employers have a general duty of care to ensure the health, safety and welfare of their employees and others who may be affected by work activities, eg contractors or members of the public.

In particular they must provide and maintain:

- safe plant and systems of work
- safe use, handling, storage and transport of articles and substances
- the provision of any necessary information, instruction, training and supervision
- safe place of work with safe means of access and egress
- safe working environment, and adequate welfare facilities.

Risk assessment

Employers and those who are self-employed have a responsibility to carry out suitable and sufficient assessments of all work activities to identify hazards and assess the risks to workers and anyone else, eg contractors and members of the public. They must decide whether existing precautions are adequate or whether more should be done to either eliminate the risks or minimise them.

This requirement applies to all work activities including those involving transport, eg driving, loading/unloading, sheeting, arrival and departure of vehicles.

Legislation applying to specific sectors of industry

Factories Act 1961
Docks Regulations 1988
Agriculture (Tractor Cabs) Regulations 1974 (as amended)
Agriculture (Avoidance of Accidents to Children) Regulations 1958

The workplace
Employers have a duty to ensure that workplaces under their control are organised in such a way that pedestrians and vehicles can circulate in a safe manner.

Traffic routes in each work place must be suitable for the persons or vehicles using them, sufficient in number, in suitable positions and of adequate size.

Employers must take measures to ensure that:
- vehicles can use a traffic route without causing danger to the health or safety of persons who work near it
- there is sufficient separation of any traffic route for vehicles from doors or gates or from traffic routes for pedestrians which lead on to it
- there must be sufficient separation between vehicles and pedestrians using the same routes
- all traffic routes must be suitably indicated.

Vehicle safety
The employer has a responsibility to ensure that vehicles must be suitable, by design, construction or adaptation, for the work being done.

The design of transport used at work should take into account the following factors:
- high degree of stability under working conditions
- safe means of access to and exit from the cab and other parts of the vehicle
- provision of windscreen wipers and mirrors
- provision of safety features such as horn, lights, reflectors, reversing lights and other warning devices
- paintwork and markings to make the vehicle conspicuous
- provision of seats and seat belts
- guards on any dangerous parts, eg power take-offs
- provision of protection against bad weather conditions
- provision of protection for the driver from falling objects or overturning of the vehicle.

Maintenance

The workplace

The employer has a responsibility to ensure that:

- materials or objects which fall on to the road from vehicles are removed as soon as possible
- roadways are adequately maintained to provide a good surface and good grip, particularly in ice or snow
- pot holes or uneven surfaces should be repaired as soon as possible
- vehicles are kept away from maintenance work where possible
- signs and lighting are kept clean and maintained to ensure visibility at all times.

Vehicles

All vehicles must be maintained so that they are mechanically sound.

Drivers should be trained to carry out basic appropriate checks on a daily basis.

Planned preventative maintenance should be carried out, paying particular attention to braking systems, tyres, steering, mirrors, windscreen washers and wipers, warning signals and specific safety systems, eg control interlocks.

Precautions during maintenance work on vehicles

Employers must ensure that where maintenance work on vehicles is carried out by their own employees, safe working practices are in place and used, which take into account the particular risks associated with this work.

Selection and training of drivers

The employer must ensure that all employees required to drive receive adequate health and safety training, training in the operation of the vehicle and any risks involved, and precautions to be taken. They must ensure that:

- employees are capable of safely operating the vehicle and any associated equipment
- employees receive instruction and training as appropriate
- employees are mature and have a reliable attitude in order to perform their duties responsibly and carefully
- employees are not allowed to drive if unfit through drink or drugs.

The training needed will depend on the individual's previous experience and type of work to be done. It should cover general information about the job, traffic routes, associated risks, reporting of faults, accidents, etc, particular hazards, speed limits and appropriate parking.

The employer should always check out previous training and any certification, and test all new employees in the operation of the vehicle.

There should be a programme of planned refresher training, and records should be kept of training.

The employer may wish to introduce a licensing or authorisation system.

The employer/site operator should check the competence of any contractors driving within the workplace, and visitors should be made aware of the layout of the workplace, the route to take and relevant safe working practices for parking, unloading/loading, etc.

Questions and Answers

Q What maintenance should be carried out on workplace transport, and how often?

A This will depend on the vehicles in question; advice should be sought from the vehicle manufacturer.

Q How old must employees be before they can drive vehicles in the workplace?

A It is recommended that the same or even higher standards are applied than on the public highway, ie 17 or over for cars, etc and 21 or over for large vehicles or HGVs.

Q What control do I have over privately owned cars which come on to the site?

A The amount of control is limited, but use on site can be regulated by restricting the routes they may use, clearly signposting parking areas, enforcing speeds limits, and making it clear that driving in the workplace calls for the same or an even higher standard than on public roads.

Upper Limb Disorders

Summary

The term "upper limb disorder (ULD)" is generally used to cover a variety of different conditions affecting the soft tissues of the hands, wrists, arms and shoulders. In the past few years the term "repetitive strain injury (RSI)" has been increasingly used to describe this type of condition, but it is an imprecise term which is not medically accurate enough to encompass these conditions.

A work-related upper limb disorder (WRULD) is an ULD which is caused or exacerbated by features of an individual's employment.

Practical Guidance

The musculo-skeletal system of the human body is capable of withstanding much wear and tear but obviously it has its limitations. Evolution has not yet modified the body to cope with the stresses placed on it by modern working conditions. ULDs involve damage to the soft tissues (muscles, tendons, nerves and ligaments) and are the result of cumulative over-use of particular parts of the hands, arms or shoulders. ULDs may not be permanent, if the body is given time to repair itself, but where damage is irreparable, long-term pain, and in many cases restricted use of the affected area, are likely to result.

The following chart may help to identify particular problems.

QUESTION	ANSWER (Y/N)	IF YES, WHAT CAN BE DONE?
TASK-RELATED FACTORS		
Are frequent repetitions of movement required?		
Are quick movements required?		
Do the actions involve movements of the wrist?		
Do the actions involve flexing of the hands or fingers?		

Are the actions carried out for long periods without a break?		
Are individuals expected to undertake repetitive tasks for long periods of time?		
Are parts of the body static for long periods?		
Do individuals work without adequate rest breaks?		
Is work rate dictated to the (individual) employees?		
Are the upper arms away from the vertical for periods of time?		
Are the forearms raised above the horizontal?		
Do the shape or size of the equipment or accessories in the work area result in poor posture?		
Are individuals using tools or working with processes that are not appropriate for their size, strength or other capabilities?		
Do the tools used generate stress or vibration that is transmitted to the individual's body, or do they need to be held excessively firmly?		
Do the tools used have handles that are the best shape size and texture to ensure comfortable operation for the individual?		
Have the tools been modified in any way? (This may indicate problems with the original design.)		
If operators have to wear gloves or other protective equipment, does this affect the use of the tools?		
Do the tools have controls that are awkward to reach?		
Are there incentive schemes that encourage individuals to work faster or for longer?		
Are individuals consulted when alterations are made to work processes?		
WORKING ENVIRONMENT		
Are the working temperatures uncomfortable throughout the year?		
Do noise levels affect concentration, disrupt communication or cause stress? (Rhythmic noises including music may cause particular problems.)		

QUESTION	ANSWER (Y/N)	IF YES, WHAT CAN BE DONE?
Does the lighting flicker, or is it otherwise unsuitable?		
Do any other environmental factors cause problems or stress to individuals?		
TRAINING		
Has the individual missed out on training appropriate to his/her capabilities/experience		
Do individuals miss out on review/refresher training?		
Are trainees made to work at the rate dictated to them?		
Are individuals unaware of out-of-work activities which may exacerbate WRULD problems?		
OTHER FACTORS		
Has the individual had previous upper limb or back problems?		
Is the individual pregnant (pregnancy causes a degree of softening and stretching of body tissues that makes the body more vulnerable to injury)?		
Are any other factors (whether work-related or otherwise) affecting the individual's performance or motivation?		

Potential problem areas

The factors in a task which are likely to increase the risk of ULDs are repetition, force, static or awkward posture and inadequate rest. Typically, those suffering from WRULDs are those using keyboards, those in production line employment and those involved with other repetitive tasks such as meat processing, telephony, fabric cutting and mail sorting.

Poor job design and use of inappropriate work equipment will increase the risk of WRULDs. ULDs are not necessarily work related; they may be caused by hobbies or other activities. Where an individual's out-of-work activities cause similar physical stresses to those encountered at work, any problem is likely to be exacerbated.

The human musculo-skeletal system is very capable of repetitive movements where small forces are involved, but particular stresses may be placed on the body by work tasks which involve greater forces and/or awkward movements such as twisting and awkward postures, or by long periods of static posture. Awkward postures or working positions cause stress to the upper limbs and are likely to contribute to the development of WRULDs. Particular problems are likely to be caused by holding the limbs in one position for long periods of time and by any twisting, weight-bearing or application of force that loads the joints unevenly.

In some cases, a WRULD will be caused by just one of these factors, but more frequently a combination of factors is involved. In many cases, provided adequate breaks from the task are scheduled, the body will be able to recover from these stresses, but ideally the job design should be such that the problem is removed altogether.

Work equipment that is suitable for an average user is unlikely to be suitable for all the working population, and care must be taken when selecting such equipment. Similarly, all employees have different capabilities and this should be considered when designing work tasks and training programmes.

"Piece work" and machine-controlled rates of activity are likely to increase the risk of WRULDs because of the requirement or incentive to work uncomfortably fast. These factors should be considered when planning methods of work, particularly in a production line situation where an employee may perform the same movements many times each day. Adequate work breaks should be programmed into all work schedules where these types of problem may occur.

The use of hand tools may also present problems, particularly where a large force is concentrated over a small area of the body, eg when cutting something stiff with scissors or shears — particularly when the hand is at an angle to the wrist. The use of power tools, where the vibration necessitates a firmer grip, may also be a contributory factor in the development of ULDs as may extremes of temperature which make the use of equipment difficult.

How the damage is done

Various part of the upper limbs may be affected by these conditions, but the connective tissues, such as tendons, etc and the muscles and related nerves are most commonly damaged. Contraction of the muscles in the forearms provides the motive force to enable the hands and fingers to work. This force is transmitted to the bones in the fingers by a network of tendons; in order to move a finger, a tendon can travel as much as five centimetres. Each tendon is surrounded by synovial fluid, contained within a synovial sheath, which protects it from the effects of friction. Tendons and nerves leading to the hands have to pass through the carpal tunnel, which consists of cartilage and bones and is therefore relatively inflexible. When the synovial sheath swells the flow of blood into the hands is restricted, which causes the symptoms of carpal tunnel syndrome.

Because the onset of ULDs is usually gradual, an individual's perception of a problem may be affected; compensation may be subconsciously made in the method of work to overcome one problem, which may eventually give rise to other problems. Repeated strains and sprains, resulting in swelling of tissues, should indicate a serious problem that is not likely to get better without intervention.

Questions and Answers

Q If an employee already has a history of ULDs, what particular action should we take to minimise any risks to that individual?

A Where the individual might be employed in any work that might give rise to ULDs particular attention should be given in the risk assessment to any greater levels of risk to that individual. Whilst the results of the risk assessment should guide your actions in each particular case, it may be that it would not be appropriate to employ the individual on that particular task.

Q A number of our employees are involved in assembly tasks where small components are picked out of crates or boxes for use. Some employees have complained of upper limb pains and find that stretching to retrieve the last few parts from the crates causes particular problems. Can you suggest any improvements that we could make, bearing in mind that there is no reasonably practicable way to avoid the task?

A The following ideas might be considered:
- keep the crates or boxes at waist height to prevent excessive bending/stretching
- put the crates or boxes on a sloping surface so that the components slide to a more accessible area
- ensure that job rotation or suitable breaks in the work mean that individual employees' time spent on the task is kept to a minimum.

Q If an employee working almost full-time on display screen equipment has complained of shooting pains in the forearms, would some physiotherapy and a couple of weeks' break from work be sufficient to cure the problem?

A In this situation it is likely that some long-term damage has already been done, in which case this solution is unlikely to be adequate. The job itself should be reassessed, and the requirement for periods of intensive keyboard work reduced as far as possible. Job rotation and sensible work schedules with varied work tasks will help to minimise future problems. It may be that the particular individual will need to be moved to a job with little or no keyboard work, either in the short term or long term; advice on this should be sought from a specialist medical practitioner.

Ventilation

Summary

Ventilation is basically the movement of air to remove contaminated or stale air and replace it with fresh, clean air. It is necessary not only to provide comfort for workers, but also to remove harmful, airborne substances. It may be as simple as opening windows in warm weather, or may involve the installation of complex and expensive ventilation equipment.

Practical Guidance

Workplaces

The **Workplace (Health, Safety and Welfare) Regulations 1992** (Workplace Regulations) require enclosed workplaces to be effectively and suitably ventilated with a supply of fresh or purified air. Mechanical ventilation systems must be fitted with a failure warning alarm, if failure of the equipment would give rise to a health and safety risk.

The Approved Code of Practice recommends that the fresh air rate should be at least five to eight litres per second per occupant. Ventilation should not create uncomfortable draughts.

If work in humid, close atmospheres is unavoidable, workers should be allowed regular breaks in well-ventilated areas.

Maintenance

Under the Workplace Regulations, ventilation systems must be maintained in an efficient state, in efficient working order and in good repair. Maintenance of ventilation systems will include:

- regular cleaning
- regular checks and tests at suitable intervals
- repair or replacement, where necessary
- regular replacement of filters, where applicable, at suitable intervals
- a system of record keeping.

The frequency of cleaning, tests, replacements, etc will depend on:

- the manufacturer's instructions

- the level of use of the system
- the type of contaminant
- the age and condition of the system.

Hazardous substances

The **Control of Substances Hazardous to Health Regulations 1999** (COSHH) requires exposure to hazardous substances to be assessed. Where exposure creates a risk to health and cannot be avoided, control measures must be put into place. Control measures that may be required include engineering controls, such as ventilation, which removes hazardous substances from the air breathed by the operators.

COSHH requires regular maintenance of engineering controls for hazardous substances. It specifies that local exhaust ventilation must generally be thoroughly examined and tested at least once every 14 months, or more frequently for certain processes specified by the Regulations.

Confined spaces

Under the **Confined Spaces Regulations 1997**, if work in a confined space cannot be avoided, a safe system of work must be provided. In some cases, forced ventilation into the confined space is part of this safe system of work.

Flammable substances

Under the **Highly Flammable Liquids and Liquefied Petroleum Gases Regulations 1972**, closed vessels containing flammable liquids must be stored in the open air, where possible. This is for reasons of ventilation, so that flammable vapours do not build up in the storage area.

Manual handling

The **Manual Handling Operations Regulations 1992** require employers to assess unavoidable manual handling operations. One of the factors affecting the level of risk in manual handling tasks is whether there is sufficient ventilation. A lack of ventilation may lead to excessive temperatures and humidity, which results in rapid fatigue during manual handling of loads and slipperiness of the load caused by increased perspiration.

Radiation

The **Ionising Radiations Regulations 1999** set out a hierarchy for control of exposure to ionising radiations. The first priority (if the exposure cannot be eliminated altogether) is to use engineering controls where possible, including ventilation.

Industrial processes

Certain health and safety legislation for specific industrial processes cover provision and maintenance of ventilation, including:

- **Control of Asbestos at Work Regulations 1987**
- **Magnesium (Grinding of Castings and Other Articles) Special Regulations 1946**
- **Manufacture of Cinematograph Film Regulations 1928**.

Questions and Answers

Q What is the recommended level of relative humidity?

A Relative humidity in the workplace should be between 40% and 70%. The factors affecting relative humidity include the local environment, weather conditions, geographical location and the amount of air movement. If the air is too dry, people will experience discomfort, ie dry eyes, respiratory system and skin. If the air is too humid, people will experience discomfort, excessive perspiration, rapid fatigue, etc.

Q What records should we keep in terms of ventilation?

A Whenever you have mechanical ventilation equipment supplied, keep the manufacturer's instructions in a safe, easy to locate place (after you have read them). Under COSHH, maintenance records must be kept for engineering controls. To ensure an efficient system, you should keep maintenance records of all ventilation systems, not just local exhaust ventilation. This will include the results of tests, eg relative humidity readings and air velocity measurements. You should also keep records of any controls you take in relation to preventing the growth of *legionellae* in air conditioning.

Q What information, instruction and training should we provide in relation to ventilation?

A You should set procedures for ventilation in the workplace, which could be disseminated to employees as part of your health and safety policy. Supervisors should check that these procedures are being followed, and take action if they are not.

Anyone carrying out maintenance of ventilation systems, such as local exhaust ventilation (LEV) or air conditioning, should be suitably trained and experienced to carry out their job effectively and safely.

Vibration

Summary

Exposure to vibration, ie contact with a "shaking" object, is a common occupational hazard which, if left uncontrolled, can cause physical discomfort, a reduction in productivity and adverse health effects. The two transmission routes for vibration exposure are whole-body vibration and hand–arm vibration. It can also occur through airborne "vibration", ie high-level sound.

Practical Guidance

There is no specific legislation covering vibration so employers must apply the provisions of the **Management of Health and Safety at Work Regulations 1999**, particularly the requirement to carry out a risk assessment, to any work which involves exposure to vibration, whether whole-body or hand–arm. The duties to ensure the health and safety of employees at work, so far as is reasonably practicable, under the **Health and Safety at Work, etc Act 1974** (HSW Act) also apply.

Vibration exposure

The adverse health effects caused by exposure to whole-body and hand–arm vibration have been known for some time. The case of *Armstrong and Others v British Coal Corporation* confirms the date of knowledge as 1973, ie from this date employers should have been aware that there are adverse health effects associated with work-related exposure to vibration.

Susceptible employees

Both pregnant women and young persons are recognised as being at particular risk from exposure to vibration, especially whole-body vibration. In pregnant women such exposures may increase the chance of miscarriage and possibly premature births and low birth weights.

Young people are at risk because of their physical immaturity — common problems include back pain and spinal disorders as their back muscles and bones have not fully developed and strengthened. They may also be unable to perceive the risks associated with vibrating tools, etc.

Vibrating machinery and tools

The **Supply of Machinery (Safety) Regulations 1992** require the suppliers of hand-held or hand-guided machinery to provide instructions on the correct installation of that machinery in order to control any associated vibration. Suppliers must also provide information on the vibration levels that operators are likely to be exposed to.

In addition, the **Provision and Use of Work Equipment Regulations 1998** require equipment used at work to be suitable for its intended task — part of this includes taking into account any inherent risks to the operator.

Effective planned preventive maintenance programmes will help prevent machinery and tools vibrating through wear and tear.

Health surveillance

Given the progressive nature of many ill-health conditions associated with exposure to vibration, employers should consider pre-employment medical examinations for all new employees who will be exposed to vibration. This will establish the exact state of any pre-existing conditions and if necessary may form a basis for the defence in claims made by employees for personal injury. It will also help to establish employees who may be at special risk when exposed to vibration, eg smokers and pregnant women. Generally speaking, where a relevant condition already exists it will be advisable to avoid offering such work in situations where the vibration cannot be dampened. Initial health checks should be repeated after six months and then annually unless a valid reason becomes apparent for more frequent checks.

The provision of information, instruction and training to employees in the use of tools, damping measures and reporting relevant health concerns are important.

Reporting vibration injuries and compensation

Under the **Reporting of Injuries, Diseases and Dangerous Occurrences Regulations 1995** (RIDDOR) both carpal tunnel syndrome and hand-arm vibration syndrome must be reported to the enforcing authority where the causative work was one of the specified occupations. The **Social Security (Industrial Injuries) (Prescribed Diseases) Regulations 1985**, as variously amended, define similar conditions associated with the same occupations as acceptable for claiming industrial injuries disablement benefit. In cases where vibration-induced ill-health has arisen through an employee's work, but his or her work is not in the specified list, a claim may still be made, provided it is possible to prove that the work caused the condition.

Questions and Answers

Q   What is whole-body vibration?

A   This is vibration which is transmitted to the whole-body of a person who is in direct contact with a vibrating surface and consequently affects all the body organs. Associated symptoms include dizziness, headaches, nausea, weight loss, varicose veins, blurred vision, spinal damage, rectal bleeding, lung damage and in some cases heart failure. The effects are often reversible once exposure ceases. The most dangerous frequencies from a work point of view are between 60 and 70Hz, which affects the eyeball, causing blurred vision, and 10 and 20Hz, which affects the brain and induces sleep.

Q   What is hand–arm vibration?

A   This is vibration which is transmitted to the hands and arms through direct contact with a vibrating tool; it is generally more serious than whole-body vibration. The main effect is a thickening of the arteries carrying blood to the fingers thus impeding the flow of blood which results in blanching (whitening) of the fingers and eventually the hands. In extreme cases, the blood vessels become completely blocked and tissue death (gangrene) occurs, possibly leading to amputation. The effects are made worse by secondary factors such as smoking. The most damaging frequencies are between 5 and 20Hz.

Q   Are any parts of the body particularly susceptible to vibration?

A   The parts of the body affected by the vibration will depend on the type of vibration, its frequency and the duration. However, all parts of the human body have different natural resonances which means that they will amplify any vibration which is at the same frequency as their natural resonance, ie the overall effects of the vibration will be increased — in some cases the amplification can be up to four times that of the original vibration. The frequency ranges for some of the most susceptible body parts, where harm on exposure to vibration is likely to occur, are:

- upper torso 4–8Hz
- head 25Hz
- eyeball 30–60Hz
- hand 50–150Hz.

Violence

Summary

Violence at work, ie both verbal and physical abuse, is an increasingly significant problem in many workplaces. The violence may be deliberate, eg confrontations between employees and the public in public service industries or services, or unintentional, eg when working with people with mental illnesses or behavioural problems.

Practical Guidance

There are no specific pieces of legislation covering the control of violence at work. Statutory duties therefore fall under the general duty of care provided by s.2 of the **Health and Safety at Work, etc Act 1974** to ensure the health and safety of employees at work, and the **Management of Health and Safety at Work Regulations 1999**. Where the risk assessment identifies violence as a work-related hazard, employers should draw up and implement a violence policy for their workplace.

Developing a violence policy

Where violence is identified as a work-related risk to employees, employers should draw up and implement a violence policy. As with all health and safety associated policies there should be clear definitions of responsibility throughout the organisation, along with procedures for dealing with violent or potentially violent situations, and means of monitoring and measuring the effectiveness of the policy.

Full consultation with, and involvement of, staff is very important.

Violent employees

Although cases of violence at work tend to be considered with the employee as the victim, employers may find it useful to develop and implement a behavioural standards policy for dealing with any employees who are the perpetrators of violence. The case of *Whitbread Beer Company v Williams* demonstrates the seriousness with which tribunals deal with violent employees. Three employees were dismissed after they had become drunk and violent at a training seminar. Their claim for unfair dismissal failed as the Employment Appeal Tribunal (EAT) found that their behaviour was in fundamental breach of their contract of employment. Having a behaviour standards policy will help employers to defend such cases.

In another case, *Vasey v Surrey Free Inns*, two nightclub doormen and their manager assaulted Mr Vasey who had become violent and caused damage to the property after being refused admission. Mr Vasey claimed compensation from the club's owners on the basis that they were vicariously liable for their employees actions. The claim succeeded as the Court of Appeal found that the nightclub employees were at work and not pursuing a private quarrel, therefore the club owners were liable for their actions.

Preventing violence

Employers have a duty to protect their employees from violence, so far as is reasonably practicable. In the case of *Keys v Shoefayre Ltd*, Miss Keys left her job as a shop assistant and claimed unfair dismissal after the manager had failed to take any precautionary measures following two armed robberies at the shop. The claim succeeded as the employer's failure to protect the employees amounted to constructive dismissal.

Reporting violence

Under the **Reporting of Injuries, Diseases and Dangerous Occurrences Regulations 1995** (RIDDOR), acts of physical violence suffered by employees at work have to be reported to the enforcing authority by the organisation if they result in death, a specified major injury or more than three consecutive days off normal work duties.

Dealing with post-violence trauma

Depending on the actual incident and individual involved, violence may cause considerable trauma to the victim. In addition to any personal suffering, there will also be an economic loss to the business through extra advertising and training if the employee is away recuperating or even leaves the organisation. It is therefore very important that any violence policy also includes post-trauma support procedures for the affected employees. This may mean reassurance, particularly in relation to any new control measures implemented, counselling and, if necessary, re-training or provision of suitable alternative work. Associated risks after a violent attack should also be addressed, ie dealing with an employee's fear of being recognised or followed by the assailant.

Questions and Answers

Q   Is there a standard definition of violence at work?

A   The final interpretation of what is meant by the term violence will be up to individual employers with regard to their own workplaces. However, it may be useful to use the following definition as a starting point: *violence to staff at work is any form of abuse, threat or assault which arises as a direct consequence of the employee's work activities.* Individual employers may wish to include bullying and harassment at work within their definition. Where violence occurs as a result of a person's mental illness or disability it may be useful to consider intentional and unintentional assaults.

Q What occupations are at greatest risk from exposure to violence?

A Violence can arise in any workplace at any time, although there are some jobs where there is a greater likelihood of violence. In particular, workers who regularly make contact with members of the public, eg nurses, local authority clerks, teachers, etc — especially in situations where members of the public are likely to be uptight, angry, upset or otherwise highly emotional — may be considered to be at high risk. Similarly, workers involved in handling money are also at high risk, eg shop workers, bank cashiers, charity fundraisers, security guards, etc. Care staff and nurses looking after people with mental illnesses, mental disabilities or behavioural problems may also be exposed to violence, although in these cases there may not be a deliberate or rational intention to cause harm.

Q Should the police be involved in dealing with violence at work?

A The answer to this is very dependent on the individual circumstances of any particular incident. Although the police are unlikely to want to be involved in minor internal situations, where personal injury and/or theft has occurred there may be cases of assault and/or robbery to be answered and the police may need to be informed. The police can also provide a useful preventive service by making available local crime statistics for the area in which the workplace is located and advising on security measures, etc. They will also know of any local neighbourhood watch or similar schemes which are in place. The police will also want to be made aware of any high-risk personnel in the workforce who may be targets for kidnapping and ransom demands, or for bomb threats, etc.

Visitors

Summary

Workplace hazards not only put employees at risk, but also put visitors to the premises at risk. A risk factor associated with visitors is that they are likely to be unfamiliar with the workplace, its hazards, the activities that take place there and the company's safety procedures. Arrangements should be in place to ensure the safety of visitors. There is a duty of care to all visitors, even those that are uninvited (see Illegal visitors below).

Practical Guidance

Duty of care

Section 3 of the **Health and Safety at Work, etc Act 1974** (HSW Act) requires employers to conduct their undertakings in such a way that non-employees, eg the visitors, who could be affected, are not exposed to risks to their health and safety. Section 4 of the HSW Act puts a similar duty on the controller of non-domestic premises, which in many cases will be the employer. In other cases, it may be the landlord who must make sure the premises are safe for people who work there and for visitors. In particular, s.4 relates to the safety of the access to, and egress from, the premises, and to ensuring that any equipment or plant, such as furnaces or air conditioning, or substances provided are safe.

The duty that employers owe to visitors is not as onerous as that owed to their own employees, and in many cases if the situation is safe for employees, it is safe for visitors, eg safe means of access. However, there are safety arrangements that must be made separately for visitors, as they will not have the experience, training and familiarity with the workplace that the employees have. For example, as visitors to the site will not know the emergency procedures, they should be supervised at all times by a member of staff who is familiar with the procedures.

Occupiers' liability

The **Occupiers' Liability Act 1957** puts a duty on occupiers, in terms of civil liability, to take reasonable care of visitors invited to or permitted on their premises. The 1957 Act:
- points out that occupiers should expect children to be less careful than adults
- allows that the occupier should expect visitors exercising their calling, eg electricians, to take measures to protect against the risks associated with that calling

406

- imposes civil liability for occupiers to pay compensation to someone injured on their premises (if liability can be proven), although breach of the Act cannot lead to a criminal prosecution.

Illegal visitors

The **Occupiers' Liability Act 1984** puts a duty on occupiers to take reasonable care (depending on the circumstances) to protect illegal visitors, eg trespassers, against injury on their premises, so long as:

- the occupier is aware of the danger
- the occupier knows (or should know) that an illegal visitor may put themselves at risk
- the occupier may reasonably do something about the risk.

This duty of care to trespassers, etc may be carried out by:

- giving warning of the dangers
- discouraging illegal visitors from putting themselves at risk, eg by making it difficult for them to enter the premises.

Risk assessment

Under the **Management of Health and Safety at Work Regulations 1999** (MHSWR), employers must carry out risk assessments for their activities. These assessments must include risks to both employees and non-employees, such as visitors. Arrangements to control the risks identified must be implemented.

Providing information

Under the MHSWR, employers must provide employees of others who are working on, or visiting, their premises with:

- comprehensible information on health and safety risks
- control measures in place to protect them against these risks
- emergency procedures.

Accident reporting

The **Reporting of Injuries, Diseases and Dangerous Occurrences Regulations 1995** (RIDDOR) require the responsible person to report any of the following that result from their work activities:

- fatalities
- major injuries to employees
- injuries to non-employees which require immediate hospital treatment
- major injuries to non-employees resulting from hospital work (accidents caused by medical or dental treatment are excluded).

RIDDOR specifies who the responsible person is for a number of specialised industries, such as mines, quarries, transport of dangerous goods, etc. In most other cases, the responsible person for reporting injuries, etc to visitors is the injured person's employer. If the person does not have an employer, the responsible person is whoever is in control of the premises where the accident occurred.

Hazardous substances

Under the **Control of Substances Hazardous to Health Regulations 1999** (COSHH), employers are required to assess and control the risks of exposure to hazardous substances. This applies to protection of both their employees and to non-employees who may be affected by their work activities, eg visitors. However, employers do not have to provide visitors with health surveillance, and they only have to provide them with monitoring and information, instruction and training if the non-employee is carrying out work on their premises.

Noise

The **Noise at Work Regulations 1989** put duties on employers to protect both employees and non-employees from excessive exposure to noise at work. This would include, for example, providing visitors with hearing protection if they enter areas where noise exposure exceeds the second action level.

Questions and Answers

Q Do we have to provide visitors with personal protective equipment?

A The **Personal Protective Equipment at Work Regulations 1992** only apply to personal protective equipment (PPE) provided for use by the employer's employees. However, employers do have a duty to ensure the safety of visitors. If their risk assessment identifies a risk to visitors that can only be controlled by the provision of PPE, this PPE should be provided and maintained.

If PPE is provided for visitors, for example head protection for visitors to construction sites, it may be necessary to have a variety of sizes available. If, for example, school children visit, all necessary PPE should be available in a size that will fit them, as well as sizes large enough to fit the adults accompanying them.

Q It is impossible to have a visitors' book in a shop, and to have someone accompanying visitors at all times. What arrangements should we make in terms of emergency procedures and supervision of visitors?

A In shops, there is usually a rapid turnover of visitors, and it is impossible to keep track of who is on the premises when. The solution may be to put up notices that tell visitors what to do in the event of an emergency, and escape routes should be well marked. Also, staff should be trained in evacuating the public, bearing in mind that the behaviour of these visitors will be unpredictable in a panic situation. Staff training should include regular evacuation practices, with role playing to give them experience in evacuating disabled people, the elderly and children, and in dealing with people who are acting illogically due to panic. It may also help to use a tannoy to give visitors directions in case of emergency.

In terms of supervision, staff should be instructed to keep a close eye on visitors to the shop, which is likely to be the case anyway to reduce shoplifting. They should know what to do if visitors try to enter restricted areas. Any dangerous equipment or hazardous areas of the shop premises should be locked off from visitors.

Q What should premises occupiers do to take reasonable care to prevent injury to trespassers?

A Measures to fulfil the duty of care to unlawful visitors include:

- deterring entry by the use of warning signs
- preventing entry by erecting suitable fences
- detecting entry by employing security guards, burglar alarms and closed circuit TV
- preventing access to particular hazards, hazardous areas or dangerous machinery, eg fencing holes, locking off areas where there are live electrical conductors, and keeping dangerous machinery in locked enclosures.

Warehouses

Summary

Many companies have warehouses as part of their business. Some undertake limited processes, such as the breaking down of bulk quantities into smaller units, while others may be far more complex, involving hazardous samples or the use of fully automated systems. The potential for accidents and incidents to occur in such areas may be high, and safe systems of work must be put in place to minimise the risk of injury to those working in such areas.

Practical Guidance

General duties

As with any other workplace, it is the duty of employers to ensure the health, safety and welfare of all their employees working in warehouses. In particular, they must provide and maintain:

- safe plant and systems of work
- safe use, handling storage and transport of articles and substances
- the provision of any necessary information, instruction, training and supervision
- safe place of work with safe means of access and egress
- safe working environment, and adequate welfare facilities.

In order to achieve the above, employers have a duty to carry out suitable and sufficient risk assessments of their workplaces (these risks will vary depending on the type of operation and the material/substances being handled). The risk assessment should:

- identify all hazards in the warehouse
- eliminate the hazards if possible
- evaluate the risks arising from the residual hazards, and decide whether existing precautions are adequate or whether more should be done
- devise and implement safe systems of work to ensure that the risks are either eliminated or adequately controlled.

The findings from these assessments should be recorded and reviewed on a regular basis.

The workplace

The **Workplace (Health, Safety and Welfare) Regulations 1992** expand upon the general duties above and are intended to protect the health and safety of everyone in the workplace and to ensure that adequate welfare facilities are provided for everyone at work.

With reference to warehouses, the employer must ensure that the workplace, and the equipment and devices used in it, are maintained in an efficient working order and in good repair.

There must be adequate ventilation — generally this is not a problem in warehouses, although it must be remembered that certain lift trucks emit toxic exhaust gases and airborne particulates. Similarly, delivery vehicles may emit hazardous exhaust fumes.

Lighting should be sufficient for people to work in safety. In warehouses there may be obstructions to lighting, such as items upon racking, and it is therefore important to configure the lighting to avoid shadows.

The floor and traffic routes should be of sound construction, and free from any holes or uneven surfaces, etc. This is particularly important in warehouses where lift trucks are used, as defective surfaces may make a truck become unstable. Traffic routes should be clearly marked and free of obstructions, particularly near corners and junctions. Signs must be used to indicate potential hazards, eg sharp bends.

Where possible, people and vehicles should be segregated with sufficient and suitable traffic routes provided. On routes used by automatic, driverless vehicles and pedestrians, the vehicles should be fitted with safety devices, eg whiskers, to prevent collision and sufficient clearance to avoid a person being trapped, for example against a wall.

Sufficient and suitable crossing points should be provided for pedestrians to cross vehicle routes. Emergency exits must be kept clear at all times.

Materials and objects should be stored and stacked so that they are not likely to fall and cause injury. Racking must be of adequate strength and stability, and may require protection to prevent damage from collision by lift trucks.

The need to climb on top of vehicles or their goods when loading or unloading vehicles should be avoided if possible. Where it is not possible, effective measures should be taken to prevent falls, eg sheeting a lorry from a gantry, use of safety lines and harnesses.

Loading bays should be provided with at least one exit point from the lower level, or a refuge provided, which can be used to avoid being struck or crushed by a vehicle.

Adequate sanitary conveniences, washing facilities and drinking water must be available. There should be suitable and sufficient accommodation for work and personal clothing and where necessary facilities to change clothing. There should be a separate area for employees to eat.

Work equipment

The employer must ensure that work equipment provided is safe and appropriate for its intended use, that it is adequately maintained, and that employees are trained to use such equipment safely. The equipment must be so designed to eliminate hazards or for controls to be put in place, eg protection against dangerous parts of machinery.

Manual handling

Where manual handling activities take place in a warehouse, the employers must ensure that these are assessed. It is necessary to take into account the task, individual capability, load and environment. If possible, hazardous manual handling should be eliminated. Where this is not possible, the risk of injury should be minimised.

Personal protective equipment

Where required, employers must provide suitable personal protective equipment (PPE) and appropriate training in its usage. PPE in warehouses may include safety footwear, hard hats and gloves. Where it is not reasonable to heat the warehouse to a comfortable temperature, eg due to perishable goods or doors that are open to the outside, warm clothing should be supplied.

PPE should not be used as a substitute for other methods of risk control.

Accidents and first aid

The employer must ensure that all accidents are recorded and investigated, and where necessary, eg a major injury or absence from normal work for over three days, reported to the enforcing authority.

Warehouses should have first aid provision. The form it takes will depend on the nature and degree of hazards present, what medical services are available and the number of employees involved.

Electricity

The employer must ensure that all electrical equipment and systems should be suitable for the purpose, in good repair, and installed and maintained by a competent person, including portable equipment.

Other regulations which may be applicable in certain circumstances

Control of Substances Hazardous to Health Regulations 1999
Noise at Work Regulations 1989
Highly Flammable Liquids and Liquefied Petroleum Gases Regulations 1972.

Questions and Answers

Q How should I control access to an automated storage and retrieval system for maintenance purposes?

A This is best achieved by introducing a permit-to-work system which should set out a clear hand over procedure, what work is to be done, who is to carry it out and the equipment necessary for the task, what safety precautions are to be taken, and a clear hand-back procedure.

Q How often should my fork-lift truck drivers undergo refresher training?

A Although the time period is not defined, many companies adopt the practice of refresher training every three years.

Q Do fork-lift trucks have to be inspected daily?

A Yes, the operator should carry out basic checks before commencing work. A log book should be kept of these checks.

Washroom and Toilet Facilities

Summary

For reasons of employee personal hygiene and welfare, it is necessary to provide an adequate number of clean washing and toilet facilities. These must meet certain standards, in terms of what is provided, which will depend on the number of employees, whether both men and women are employed, the type of work and nature of the workplace.

Practical Guidance

Washing facilities — general

The **Workplace (Health, Safety and Welfare) Regulations 1992** (Workplace Regulations) require the provision of readily accessible, suitable and sufficient washing facilities. These facilities should:

- include showers, where necessary for health and safety
- be located near to toilets
- be located near to changing rooms, where provided
- have a supply of hot and cold (or warm) water
- be provided with a supply of soap, or other method of cleaning
- have a means of drying, eg towels or hand dryers
- be well ventilated
- be well lit
- be cleaned and maintained regularly
- be separate for men and women, unless they are in a room used by one person at a time which is lockable from the inside
- be provided for agricultural workers and others in remote, outdoor workplaces, so far as is reasonably practicable.

The Approved Code of Practice (ACOP) for the Workplace Regulations sets out how many washing facilities should be provided. These are as follows.

Number of employees	Number of washstations
1–5	1
6–25	2
26–50	3
51–75	4
76–100	5
Over 100	5 plus 1 basin per 25 employees, or part of 25

If work causes heavy soiling of the hands, arms or face, the number of washing facilities should be increased to 1 per 10 employees (or part of 10), up to 50 employees, and then 1 per 20 employees (or part of 20).

It may also be necessary to increase the number of washing facilities if the quantities outlined in the table are insufficient to allow employees to use them without delay, for example where they share them with members of the public.

Toilet facilities — general

The Workplace Regulations require the provision of readily accessible, suitable and sufficient sanitary conveniences. These facilities should:

- be well ventilated
- be well lit
- be connected to a suitable drainage system
- have flushing water
- take into account access for disabled people
- be regularly cleaned and maintained
- be separate for men and women, unless the toilet is in a separate room which is lockable from the inside
- have toilet paper in an appropriate dispenser
- have a coat hook
- have a means of disposing of sanitary dressings, where women are employed
- be provided for agricultural workers and others in remote, outdoor workplaces, so far as is reasonably practicable.

The ACOP for the Workplace Regulations sets out how many toilets should be provided. However, these numbers should be increased, if necessary to avoid employees experiencing undue delay, eg where they share them with the public.

Where both men and women use them, the numbers are as follows.

Number of employees	Number of waterclosets
1–5	1
6–25	2
26–50	3
51–75	4
76–100	5
Over 100	plus 1 per 25 employees, or part of 25

If the toilets are only used by men, the numbers required are as follows.

Number of male employees	Number of water-closets	Number of urinals
1–15	1	1
16–30	2	1

31–45	2	2
46–60	3	2
61–75	3	3
76–90	4	3
91–100	4	4
Over 100	4 plus 1 per 50 (or part of 50)	4 plus 1 per 50 (or part of 50)

Urinals means one stall. If stalls are not provided, then one is 60cm of urinal space.

Construction

The **Construction (Health, Safety and Welfare) Regulations 1996** require the provision of readily accessible, suitable and sufficient:
• washing facilities, including showers where necessary
• sanitary conveniences.
The requirements, in terms of what is suitable and sufficient, are similar to those of the Workplace Regulations, outlined above.

Food premises

Under the **Food Safety (General Food Hygiene) Regulations 1995**, food proprietors must:
• provide adequate and stocked hand-washing facilities
• provide adequate, ventilated, flushing toilets (which do not lead directly into a food area)
• ensure that food handlers maintain a high standard of personal hygiene
• provide facilities for cleaning and disinfecting equipment
• provide facilities for washing food.

Asbestos

Under the **Control of Asbestos at Work Regulations 1987**, employers must provide adequate and suitable washing and changing facilities where employees are exposed to asbestos at work. These facilities should include somewhere to store:
• protective clothing and personal clothing, when not in use
• respiratory protective equipment.

Lead

The **Control of Lead at Work Regulations 1998** require the provision of adequate washing facilities. These facilities must enable workers who are exposed to lead to maintain a high standard of personal hygiene, so that they do not ingest lead. Washing facilities should:
• have a constant supply of hot and cold (or warm) running water
• have soap and nail-brushes

- have individual towels, or other means of drying
- be sufficient in number, so that the maximum number of people expected to use them at one time can do so without undue delay.

Radiation

Under the **Ionising Radiations Regulations 1999**, if a supervised or controlled area may become contaminated by radiation, it must be provided with adequate washing facilities for people entering or leaving the area. These facilities must be well maintained.

Other hazardous substances and agents

Most hazardous substances and agents other than asbestos, lead and radiation, are covered by the **Control of Substances Hazardous to Health Regulations 1999** (COSHH). COSHH puts a general duty on employers to assess the risks of exposure to hazardous substances, including chemicals and biological agents. They must implement control measures to prevent the risks, or reduce them to an acceptable level. In many cases, the control measures will include the provision, maintenance and use of adequate washing facilities. These facilities are necessary for exposed workers to maintain a high standard of personal hygiene, and avoid contaminating themselves and others with hazardous substances they come into contact with.

Compressed air

Under the **Work in Compressed Air Special Regulations 1958**, employees who work in compressed air must be provided with adequate and suitable washing facilities. These must include soap and clean towels.

Questions and Answers

Q Do we have to provide showers for our employees?

A Showers only have to be provided where they are needed for health and safety because of the nature of the work, eg if hazardous substances are likely to contaminate more than the face, hands and forearms. They may also be needed for health reasons, eg where the work is particularly strenuous.

Where showers are available, they should allow the user privacy, and there should be somewhere suitable to hang clothes and to dry wet towels. Ventilation of shower areas is essential. Showers should have hot and cold, or warm, running water. Those fed by hot and cold water should have a device, such as a thermostatic mixer, to allow adequate mixing of the water to avoid scalding. Spray heads should be cleaned regularly to prevent the growth of *legionellae*.

Q What is a suitable disposal method for sanitary dressings?

A If you only have a few women using each toilet and you are confident that blockages will not occur, it is possible for them to be flushed. However, many plumbing systems combined with frequent use of the toilets cannot cope with the amount of sanitary dressings produced. In this case, separate bins should be provided. These bins must be suitable for disposal of clinical waste, reduce odour to the lowest possible level and be emptied regularly by a specially trained person. It is not suitable to dispose of sanitary dressings as part of your normal waste disposal system, eg that used for office waste.

There is a choice of specialist disposal contractors who provide bins and emptying services. Bear in mind that sanitary dressings are clinical waste, which is classified under environmental legislation as special waste. Clinical waste should be incinerated at a licensed facility.

Q   What washing and toilet facilities should we provide for remote workplaces?

A   The Workplace Regulations require remote, outdoor workplaces to be provided with suitable and sufficient washing and toilet facilities. This is qualified by the term "so far as is reasonably practicable". The standard of facilities required will depend on a number of factors, including:

- how feasible it is to provide facilities
- how long the area will be used as a workplace
- the nature of the work, eg the level of contamination likely and how strenuous the work is.

Portable toilets and washrooms are available, and these are often used on construction sites in operation for more than a few days.

Waste Disposal

Summary

The safe disposal of waste is an important part of any work activity. Where possible, recycling initiatives should be taken in order to help protect the environment and make better use of resources. The incorrect handling of waste products may lead to accidents, ill-health, damage to the environment and subsequent prosecution.

Practical Guidance

The management of waste is as important as the management of raw materials and finished products. The benefits are two-fold.

1. The minimisation of the amount of waste that is generated will prove cost effective to the business.
2. Less waste will reduce the risk of injury or ill-health from waste accumulations. In addition to direct savings, reducing the effect of waste upon the environment has a cumulative benefit which extends to the concept of environmentally sustainable consumption of resources.

Definition

The definition of "waste" is determined by the test of usefulness of the material to the producer of the waste. The fact that a material may have a residual value and be sold on, eg to a scrap metal merchant, does not mean that it avoids the definition of "waste". Therefore the relevant environmental protection legislation will apply.

General duties

Health and safety
The employer has a general duty under the **Health and Safety at Work, etc Act 1974** to ensure, so far as is reasonably practicable, the health and safety of employees and other persons who may be affected by the storage, handling or disposal of waste products.

It is also their responsibility to provide and maintain safe systems of work for dealing with the disposal of waste.

The employer must also provide adequate instruction, information, training and supervision, which extends to the safe handling and collection of waste materials. Such training should include:

- the recognition of different categories of waste, and appropriate collection, storage and disposal arrangements for each category
- the ability to give an accurate and relevant description of wastes and be aware of any special arrangements for segregation, collection, storage and disposal of wastes
- information about what to do when waste containers are unavailable or have become full
- understanding the restrictions regarding disposal of liquid waste into the drainage system
- knowing how to safely use equipment provided for preparation of waste, eg bailers, crushers, etc.

The employer is also required to carry out a suitable and sufficient risk assessment of all work activities to identify hazards, evaluate the risks arising from the hazards and decide whether existing precautions are adequate or whether more should be done. Such risk assessments should take into account the safe disposal of waste.

Employers who have control of their premises have a responsibility to ensure that, where refuse accumulates in workplaces, it is removed at least daily unless there are suitable receptacles available for it. Spillages and leaks, etc should be cleared as soon as possible.

Environmental Protection Act 1990
This Act states that employers must not dispose of controlled waste in a manner which is likely to cause harm to the environment or to human health. Controlled waste is defined as household, commercial and industrial waste.

Legal duties
Anyone who produces waste has a duty to:
- prevent anyone from dealing with their waste illegally
- prevent the escape of waste
- ensure waste is only transferred to an authorised person
- ensure an accurate description of waste is provided when waste is transferred and a transfer note is completed.

Description of waste
The written description of the waste may be included as part of the transfer note. The length and detail given in the description will depend on the nature of the waste. For example, in the case of mixed commercial waste with no special handling or disposal requirements, a statement of the type of premises or business or origin may be sufficient. If the waste consists of a few non-hazardous substances or a single substance or material, the name of the substances should be given.

For most industrial wastes, the process producing the waste should be described, eg:
- details of materials and equipment used

- changes which produced the waste
- relevant information from the suppliers of the materials and equipment, eg waste disposal guidelines from hazard data sheets.

Liquid waste

It is an offence to discharge trade effluent either into controlled waters (eg most watercourses in the UK) or into a sewer, without formal consent. Consent must be obtained from the relevant authority, eg the relevant office of the Environment Agency, the appropriate water company or the regional council.

Transfer note

Employers must ensure that records of waste transfer and disposal arrangements are kept. A transfer note must be completed and handed to the carrier or authorised waste disposal body. Copies of transfer notes for controlled waste must be kept for a minimum of two years. Where regular collections of non-hazardous commercial waste occur, a single transfer note (a "season ticket") would be valid for up to one year.

The transfer note should contain the following information:

- the identify and quantity of the waste
- the type of container, if applicable
- the time and place of transfer
- the name and address of the transferor and transferee
- whether the transferor is the producer or importer of the waste
- which (if any) authorised transport purpose applies
- the categories into which the transferor and transferee fall, eg waste producer, registered carrier, etc
- for a waste management licence holder, the licence number or name of the licensing authority
- for a registered carrier, the name of the Waste Regulation Authority where the carrier is registered and the registration number.

Waste containers should be in good condition, and be covered or secured, as generally the waste producer is responsible for the security of the waste during carriage.

Registration

It is an offence for a carrier who is not registered with the Environment Agency to transport waste. There are limited exemptions, eg in the case of a charity collecting materials for recycling. It is important, therefore, that the employer producing the waste checks the carrier's registration certificate.

Special waste

There are specific regulations which apply to the transport, handling and disposal of wastes that are deemed to be hazardous to the environment. Movements of special waste must be pre-notified to the Environment Agency and a five-part *special waste consignment note* must be completed by those in the waste chain, ie producers, carriers, disposers, etc. A few examples of special wastes are those that have a flash point of less than 21°C, used engine oils, and substances that are dangerous to life. There is a comprehensive list of special waste categories given in the **Special Waste Regulations 1996**.

Waste management licence

It is an offence for anyone to dispose of, treat or store waste without a waste management licence. The employer who produces the waste must ensure that it is disposed of by someone who is the holder of a waste management licence.

Asbestos

The **Control of Asbestos at Work Regulations 1987** requires that waste which contains asbestos is transported in a suitable and sealed container that is clearly marked to show that it contains asbestos. These containers should be designed, constructed and maintained to prevent any of the contents escaping during normal handling.

Questions and Answers

Q Am I responsible for the waste after it has left my company?

A Yes, in so far as that waste must be transferred only to an authorised person and that all consignments of waste must be accurately described.

Q How should I dispose of clinical waste?

A All clinical waste should be bagged in yellow bags, and "sharps" should be in a suitable container which is clearly labelled. Disposal should be arranged with the local authority for special collection, or via an independent contractor for incineration.

Q Am I allowed to store waste prior to its removal for disposal?

A Yes, although long-term storage is undesirable. It should be stored in designated locations protected from the effects of weather, and precautions taken to prevent incompatible materials being mixed together.

Welding

Summary

Welding may be necessary for repairs to vehicle components, chassis sections, trainers, doors, etc. Welding may occur using mixed gas, usually oxy-acetylene, or oxy-propane, or electric. Electrical welding includes electric arc, MIG (metal inert gas) and TIG (tungsten inert gas). Cutting may be carried out using a mixed gas system and use of electric plasma cutting equipment is now frequently found. Many of the comments below also apply to spot welding and gas or carbon arc brazing.

Practical Guidance

Hazards

These vary depending on the particular equipment in use, the type of welding being carried out and the material being welded or cut. Common hazards include: flying sparks, hots surfaces, hot parts of the welding equipment, fumes, intense light emission, manual handling of equipment and noise.

Gas welding and cutting can engender the following: leaking cylinder valves, hoses or torches, gas build-up in confined or badly ventilated areas, open, very high temperature flames, trailing hoses, flash-back into hoses and cylinders. Misuse of oxygen for "sweetening" air.

Electic arc, MIG and TIG welding and plasma cutting have the following hazards: electricity, leaking cylinder valve/hose/torch, trailing hose/cable, intense ultraviolet and infrared light emission.

Harmful effects

The hazards outlined above can result in many varied harmful effects to those using the equipment and persons nearby are also at risk from almost all of them. Persons at a distance can still be exposed to ultraviolet and infrared emissions and also noise from plasma cutting operations. The following is not an exhaustive list of possible problems:

- fire, damage to clothing or skin burns from flying sparks
- eye injury from flying sparks and flying slag during chipping
- fire, skin burns from contact with hot surfaces and equipment
- respiratory irritation from inhalation of fumes. Some fumes can be highly toxic (eg from welding zinc plated steel)

- eye irritation (arc eye) from exposure to welding arc or flash, or from gas flames. Any significant exposure could lead to permanent damage due to effects of ultraviolet and infrared light
- manual handling injuries when moving gas cylinders incorrectly, moving all types of welding equipment
- leaking acetylene of propane (all LPGs) may result in an explosive mixture
- leaking inerting gases result in oxygen exclusion from confined space and unconsciousness or death
- leaking oxygen will cause oxygen enrichment which results in enhanced combustion of materials and increased fire risk
- flash-back into hoses or cylinders can result in gas cylinder overheating, failure and explosion
- faulty electric welding equipment or wrong use can result in electric shock causing burns, unconsciousness or death
- gas cutting and plasma cutting both create large amounts of high temperature sparks with a substantial fire risk
- plasma cutting produces high noise levels which may exceed statutory limits in some circumstances.

Most of the above hazards can be adequately controlled and if any of the activities are carried out correctly the overall risk can be reduced to low to moderate. Some activities will always remain high risk such as gas cutting:

- fire risk when cutting is high, when welding may still be high depending on actual activity
- risk of electric shock is high if there are any faults in the equipment or if the operator is inadequately trained in its use
- risk of eye injury from UV or IR exposure, or flying particles, is high and unfortunately common. With correct precautions this should reduce to low risk.

Controls
- the specific controls will vary depending on the equipment in use and the circumstances of use
- only equipment to recognised standards should be used and must be properly maintained by a person competent to carry out such maintenance and repair. Most manufacturers and major suppliers run training courses for those persons maintaining, repairing and using equipment
- only properly trained and authorised persons should use welding and cutting equipment
- refer to the HSE guidance note CS15 for a description of the hazards and correct working methods for welding or brazing repairs to fuel tanks or tankers
- use fixed or portable exhaust ventilation to control the release of welding or cutting fumes into the workshop atmosphere
- where short-term welding or cutting is carried out, personal respiratory protection may still be necessary

Welding

- beware of lead loading in bodies, galvanised steel, lead paint or foam in body cavities. All can form toxic fumes on heating causing respiratory irritation or more serious injury. There can also be acute effects causing unconsciousness or death in extreme cases
- never use old oil, paint or solvent drums as temporary supports for any item being welded or cut. Residues in apparently empty drums can explode on heating
- use of correct personal protective clothing is essential
- any person not familiar with welding and cutting activities who may pass through or nearby the area must be warned about flying hot particles, UV and IR light emissions and training hoses and cables.

Electric arc, TIG, MIG welding, brazing and plasma cutting
- severe shocks and death can result from use of single or three-phase electrical welding equipment
- electrode holders, MIG torches, earth return cables, clamps and power supply earth must all be maintained in good condition
- only use a properly insulated MIG torch, insulated spool in an insulated wire feed chamber, insulated wire feed rollers, and feed tube to prevent heavy welding currents flowing back through the earth continuity conductor and destroying it
- earth the workpiece with a robust cable from a clamp on the workpiece to the earth terminal of the power source to protect the operator in the event of a fault between the primary and secondary windings and the transformer
- provide fixed and/or movable screens to protect those not involved from UV and IR radiation.

Gas welding and cutting equipment
- store full and empty gas cylinders upright, in a well-ventilated, secure area, preferably outside, and secured to prevent them falling over. Acetylene cylinders in particular must always be stored and used upright to prevent possible liquid loss
- never keep gas cylinders below ground level next to drains, basements or vehicle pits. Gases that are heavier than air can accumulate in low lying areas and a flammable or explosive mixture develop
- ensure that every workshop has effective high and low level ventilation to minimise the risk of flammable gas build-up
- always use the correct trolley for cylinder support and movement, correct valves, regulators, hoses and torches
- minimise possible flash-back in to hoses or cylinders by fitting non-return valves, flame arrestors and training of users in correct lighting and working procedures
- never simply rely on torch valves or regulators for gas shut-off; always shut off cylinder valves at the end of the working day.

Emergency procedures

Minor burns are likely during welding and associated work. First aiders should be familiar with treatment of burns and a selection of suitable burns dressings should be included in the appropriate first aid box.

As eye injuries may result from flying sparks or hot slag, it is important to ensure that quick and easy access to eye-wash facilities are available. As a minimum, there should be sterile eye-wash bottles immediately to hand.

PPE

- full overalls that are flame retardant are advised, failing that a cotton mixture
- safety footwear with high ankle protection particularly when carrying out cutting, to prevent sparks entering footwear
- flameproof apron for use when cutting
- heavy duty gloves to protect against sharp edges, hot components and flying sparks
- goggles or full face visor for use when chipping slag, to BS EN 166 impact standard
- full face shield or goggles as appropriate fitted with suitable grades of welding filter, or automatic electronic filter system
- where welding or cutting is carried out overhead, wear a flame retardant balaclava which protects the top of the head and neck.

Questions and Answers

Q   We have to carry out electric arc welding inside a steel vessel which has been cleaned and contains no harmful substances. Do we have to treat this as a confined space?

A   The **Confined Spaces Regulations 1997** will probably apply to this situation. Before welding beings the vessel is safe to enter, however electric arc welding creates large amounts of toxic fumes which, in a restricted area with limited ventilation, would quickly accumulate to dangerous levels. A proper assessment should be carried out resulting in correct ventilation equipment and respiratory protection being used.

Q   Why is it dangerous to use oxygen from a welding set to "sweeten" the air in a restricted area and make it better to breathe?

A   Doing this increases the percentage of oxygen in the atmosphere which greatly increases the fire risk for many materials and also the explosion risk where there is a potentially flammable gas present. Secondly, the oxygen supplied for welding is not of the appropriate quality for breathing, although this is a minor consideration. Never release oxygen deliberately into the atmosphere except when purging hoses and mixing torches.

Q   Can wearing contact lenses be dangerous when welding?

Welding

A   There have been stories of almost folk-loric status about what happens when welding whilst wearing contact lenses. If a normal eye is exposed to severe ultraviolet or infrared radiation it can become inflamed and very sore. Arc-eye can be rapidly acquired whilst arc welding through short-term exposure due to bad arc striking technique or use of the wrong grade of protective filters. If the same happens to an eye wearing a contact lens, the irritation will be aggravated even more. The lense does not become "welded" to the eye surface. With proper protection and welding technique there is no reason why a contact lens wearer should not carry out welding.

Window Cleaners

Summary

Windows and skylights usually need to be cleaned periodically, and systems must be in place to ensure that this work can be done safely and without risk to health. The major hazard of window cleaning is falling from height, which can be fatal.

Practical Guidance

A common fatal accident for window cleaners is falling from an external window-sill or ledge. This can be due to a loss of balance or a slip, the breakage of part of a sill or the breakage of part of a building being used as a foothold or handhold.

Other accidents have occurred where cleaners have fallen through fragile roofs, fallen from suspended scaffold or boatswain's chairs due to failure of the equipment, or fallen from ladders due to unexpected movement or breakage.

General requirements for safe window cleaning

When a window cleaner, either as an employee, an employee of a contractor or a self-employed person cleans windows, there are duties placed on everyone involved to ensure that the job is done safely:

- an employer must provide and maintain safe plant and systems of work, and provide information, instruction, training and supervision to ensure that window cleaning is carried out safely
- employed window cleaners must co-operate with their employer and take reasonable care of themselves and others who may be affected by their actions
- self-employed window cleaners are responsible for conducting their work in such a way that they do not endanger themselves or anyone else who may be affected by their work
- the employer, person in control of the workplace or the occupier must ensure that all windows and skylights in a workplace are designed or constructed to be cleaned safely.

Risk assessment

The **Management of Health and Safety at Work Regulations 1999** place a duty on employers and self-employed persons to carry out a suitable and sufficient risk assessment of their work.

429

Where the window cleaner has contracts with several companies, a risk assessment should be carried out on each specific location/building and in co-operation with the occupier of the premises in order to take account of any circumstances or problems relating specifically to it.

Where, for instance, a self-employed person is cleaning windows on similar types of domestic premises, it would be sufficient to carry out a model risk assessment concentrating on the broad range of risks encountered.

Safe system of work

The window cleaning employer or self-employed person should establish a safe system of work taking into account the hazards identified and risk as established by the risk assessment. This will help to reduce the likelihood of an accident occurring. All employees should be trained in the safe system and be competent to carry out the work.

Personal protective equipment

The employer of window cleaners must provide them with suitable personal protective equipment and train them in its use, for example:
- sill pads or special slippers when working from polished or slippery interior sills or ledges
- safety belt/harness, ropes and clips.

The employee should check their equipment before use and report any defects.

The workplace

It is the responsibility of the employer, person in control of the workplace or occupier to ensure that all windows and skylights are designed or constructed to be cleaned safely.

For example:
- fitting windows that can be cleaned safely from inside, eg windows which pivot
- fitting access equipment, eg suspended cradles, or travelling ladders with an attachment for a safety harness
- providing adequate access and a firm, level and safe surface for mobile access equipment, eg ladders and tower scaffolds
- providing suitable points to tie or fix ladders over 6m long
- suitable and suitably placed anchorage points for safety harnesses.

Employers and others who use the services of independent window cleaners should take some measures to check that the window cleaners are operating in a safe manner, and should not use those who do not operate safely.

Access to windows

The equipment used by a window cleaner must comply with the **Provision and Use of Work Equipment Regulations 1998**, in that:
- the equipment provided must be suitable and safe for use

- it must be maintained in an efficient state
- the employees must have adequate information, instructions and training in its use.

The range of equipment used to clean windows from the outside includes: suspended scaffolds, mobile tower scaffolds, power operated work platforms, roof ladders, travelling ladders, boatswain's chairs and safety harnesses. Guidance on the correct use of these and other equipment is given in HSE Guidance Note GS25: *Prevention of Falls to Window Cleaners.*

There may be circumstances when it is not reasonably practicable to use the access equipment described above. In such instances the use of a safety harness or belt attached to an anchorage may be used provided all other methods have been considered first. The disadvantages of this method is that the window cleaner must accept the discipline involved with using the equipment, and if the window cleaner falls there is still a chance of injury before the fall is arrested. Suitable anchorage points which are capable of sustaining the anticipated shock must be provided.

Where windows can be cleaned from the inside, the window cleaner should ensure that there is no risk of falling through the open window. This will depend on the window cleaner's height, the length of arm reach, the depth of the sill, and the arrangement of furniture in close proximity. The window cleaner should not step on to the outside sill.

Specialist cleaning operations

There may be situations where window cleaning requires the use of specialist chemicals. Where hazardous chemicals are used, the employer must carry out a separate risk assessment as required by the **Control of Substances Hazardous to Health Regulations 1999** (COSHH).

Questions and Answers

Q Can I insist that contracted window cleaners use their own equipment?

A Yes, providing it is feasible to clean with windows using mobile access equipment, eg ladders and tower scaffolds.

Q How many anchorage points for safety harnesses do I need to provide?

A The anchorage points must be suitably placed to ensure that they can be used correctly. The number will depend on the work being done. The risk assessment should identify the need for any additional points.

Q As a self-employed window cleaner, must I carry out risk assessments?

A Yes, the **Management of Health and Safety at Work Regulations 1999** require you to carry out risk assessments. You do not, however, have to record them, although it would make sense to do so.

Woodworking Machinery

Summary

Woodworking machines are commonly found in all different types of businesses. They include circular saws, routers, vertical spindle moulding machines, tenoning machines and many others. Each different type has its own characteristics and risks of injury. Accidents resulting from incorrect installation, maintenance and use are common where the correct procedures and standards are not adhered to, often leading to serious amputation injuries.

Practical Guidance

The **Woodworking Machines Regulations 1974,** which placed specific duties on employers, have been completely revoked and replaced by the **Provision and Use of Work Equipment Regulations 1998** (PUWER) and a specific Approved Code of Practice (ACOP) on safe use of woodworking machines. The requirements of PUWER 1998 apply in full to woodworking machines, and there are additional matters contained in the ACOP which must be attended to in ensuring compliance with the full range of legal duties.

Suitability of woodworking machines

The general requirement for suitability of work equipment in PUWER is made specific by the ACOP (as with much of the following). The risk of accidents can be influenced considerably by the design of the machine or the cutters and tools used with it. For example, the use of a router to cut a channel in board represents the correct selection, whereas the use of a table circular saw without a top guard does not. Limiting the projection of cutters reduces the risk of accidental contact and should be achieved to the greatest extent possible, and tools speeds should also be looked at to reduce the possibility of chatter, kick-back (see *Protection against specified hazards* below), etc. A prohibition in the old Regulations on use of square cutter blocks on planing machines with manual timber feed is carried over to the ACOP.

Maintenance

Correct maintenance of woodworking machines will ensure faster and better quality work with less risk of kick-back and other incidents, and also help to reduce noise emissions. Suppliers can often advise on the required frequency of maintenance, but this should be reviewed regularly to ensure a preventive approach, rather than reactive maintenance, is achieved. Those employees involved in maintenance should be competent, having had appropriate training for each type of machine, and be specifically designated as such.

Specific risks

As with many types of dangerous machinery, there is a fundamental need to restrict usage to those individuals considered suitable and competent to undertake the work. If there is easy access to the area containing the woodworking machines, then a system of individual lock-off for each machine or, more commonly, a ring circuit lock-off system, should be used. Only those persons authorised to use the machines should be able to unlock and switch power to them.

Information, instruction and training

All those who use woodworking machines must have been provided with adequate health and safety information, including written instructions where appropriate. Information and training can be carried out in-house or externally by a suitable training provider. The training must be adequate for the purposes of health and safety, rather than just teaching methods of using the machines, and should include information on risks and precautions. Refresher training should be provided at appropriate intervals.

In addition to users of woodworking machines, those who supervise or manage the users must also receive adequate information and training. For example, a supervisor who does not know the correct maximum clearance specified for a particular machine between a work piece and guard where the guard is adjustable, would not be able to properly supervise the safe use of the machine. The information and training provided must include matters such as suitability for particular machining tasks, maintenance requirements, risks, methods of guarding and use of other protective devices such as push sticks, jigs and power feed devices.

Dangerous parts of machines

Under PUWER, access to parts of machines which may be regarded as dangerous should be prevented and dangerous movement should be stopped before any part of an individual enters a danger zone. Both of these requirements are applicable to woodworking machinery. For larger machines, there may be the possibility of providing access inside perimeter guarding instead of using individual guards to separate dangerous parts.

Protection against specified hazards

As with many machines, hazards may be created by ejection of the material being worked on — a common problem for some types of woodworking machines such as circular saws, planing machines and vertical spindle moulding machines. To minimise these risks, those tools least likely to result in ejection and which are in good condition should be selected. Kick-back is the condition where, for example, timber being fed through a circular saw is suddenly projected forward due to the cut edges of the timber binding on the rear edge of the circular saw blade. To prevent this a riving knife of suitable dimensions must be used to keep the cut in the timber closing up and binding. Other methods of preventing kick-back, and also keeping parts of the body away from dangerous blades, tools and cutters, include power feeds and jigs or workpiece holders.

Stop controls

Stop controls must be fitted in a readily accessible position. Where unauthorised use has to be prevented, they may be of a design capable of being locked. A continuing problem with woodworking machines is the long run-down time for many once power is removed. Leaving a running-down machine unattended, or carrying out adjustments in this condition, can result in unintentional contact with dangerous parts. With the intention of reducing this problem, the ACOP introduces certain dates by which different categories of machine must be fitted with braking devices. The specific requirements are complex and may not apply to certain machines. Generally, the following dates apply: 5 December 2003 for circular saws, cross-cut saws and tenoning machines; 5 December 2005 for narrow band saws, re-saws and vertical spindle moulders; and 5 December 2008 for all others, following risk assessment.

Stability, markings and warnings

All machines should be stable which usually requires fixture to a worktable or floor unless they are intended for handheld use. They must not be able to topple or move. Markings of safe working speeds can be vital to prevent overspeeding of blades and cutters. For circular saws, the smallest permissible blade size should be marked. For planer/thicknessers not fitted with power feed, a notice should be clearly visible prohibiting feeding more than one workpiece at a time (to limit the possibility of kick-back).

Noise

Many types of woodworking machinery create high levels of noise. Correct maintenance and selection of blades and cutters can reduce emitted levels. For larger production line machines, noise enclosures are commonly used to control the exposure of employees to noise to an acceptable level.

Dust

Most types of wood dust are considered to be a potential health risk and dust from hardwood is recognised as a carcinogenic material. Wood dust can also increase the overall fire risk and, when mixed in air as a dust cloud, is highly explosive. For all of these reasons, capture of dust at source is usually desirable, except where small volume work is being carried out. In this case suitable respiratory protection should be worn and good housekeeping measures applied to the workplace. Respiratory protection should also be worn whilst carrying out cleaning. Blowing a machine clean with compressed air must not be done as this will raise dust into the general atmosphere, increasing both the risk of inhalation and ignition.

Questions and Answers

Q We still have a copy of the Woodworking Machines Regulations poster in the workshop. Do we still need this?

A No. There are several free posters regarding specific machines available from HSE Books.

Q We have several managers who run local workshops which include woodworking machines. The staff who work in each workshop have ready access to all the machines there. What are the training requirements?

A All those who use woodworking machines must have been provided with adequate health and safety information, including written instructions where appropriate.Training can be carried out in-house or externally by a suitable training provider and must be adequate for the purposes of health and safety and include information on risks and precautions. Refresher training should be provided at appropriate intervals. The managers must also have received adequate information and training to allow them to carry out satisfactory supervision.

Q We have several employees under the age of 18. Can they operate woodworking machines?

A The **Management of Health and Safety at Work Regulations 1999** require that assessment of risks are undertaken for work to be carried out by employees under the age of 18. Those under 18 years of age can be further split into those under minimum school leaving age (MSLA) and those above MSLA but under 18 years. You should not allow such people to operate woodworking machines unless they have the necessary maturity and competence, including having successfully completed appropriate training. They may operate a machine during training provided they are directly supervised. Adequate supervision must also be provided after training if they are not sufficiently mature. It is recommended that any person under MSLA is NOT allowed to operate a woodworking machine.

Workstations

Summary

Inadequately adjusted and inappropriately designed workstations may lead to health problems such as upper limb pains and discomfort, as well as fatigue and stress. Over 8.5 million display screen equipment (DSE) workstations are in regular use in the UK. It is impossible to put a figure on the number of other workstations that employees use, for example in a production environment or in offices where DSE is not present. However, they should all be designed with ergonomic principles in mind, ie fitting the task and the equipment to the needs of the person.

Practical Guidance

The main hazards associated with workstations are those which relate to the design and layout of the area, and which may lead to musculo-skeletal problems for the worker. A range of conditions of the arm, hand and shoulder areas are linked to work activities. In some instances, such a condition may arise from use of workstations, in which case it is described as a work-related upper limb disorder (WRULD). WRULDs range from temporary fatigue or soreness in the limb, to chronic soft tissue disorders, eg carpel tunnel syndrome.

The exact cause of this type of injury is unclear, although it is likely that a combination of factors is concerned. Prolonged static posture is known to cause musculo-skeletal problems of the back, neck and head. Awkward positioning of the hands and wrists as a result of poor working technique, or inappropriate work height, are further likely factors, as is the high repetition rate required by some work tasks.

Therefore, it is essential that workstations are designed with the worker and the task to be performed in mind.

Employers have a general duty to provide and maintain plant and equipment which is safe and without risks to health.

Requirements for workstations

Under the **Workplace (Health, Safety and Welfare) Regulations 1992**, employers have a duty to ensure that every workstation is arranged so that each task can be carried out safely and in comfort.

The worker should be at a suitable height in relation to the worksurface in order to assume a correct posture. Any work materials and equipment, or controls which are used frequently should be within easy reach in order to avoid undue bending or stretching.

Workstations, including seating and access to workstations, should be suitable for any special needs of the individual worker, including workers with disabilities.

There should be sufficient space at the workstation to allow freedom of movement and the ability to stand upright. Where cramped conditions are unavoidable, spells of work should be kept as short as possible and there should be room nearby to enable the worker to stand upright and relieve discomfort.

There should be sufficient clear and unobstructed space at each workstation to enable the work to be done safely. This should allow for the manoeuvering and positioning of materials used. Safe routes to and from the workstation, eg to fire exits, must also be considered.

If it is possible to do the work activity, or part of it, from a seated position, a seat should be provided. Where possible, the seat should provide support for the lower back. A footrest should be provided for those workers who cannot comfortably place their feet flat on the floor.

DSE Workstations

Definition

DSE means any alphanumeric or graphic display screen, regardless of the display screen involved. The term is applied to conventional visual display units (VDUs), as well as non-electronic systems such as microfiche viewers and production process control panels.

Employers are required to carry out an analysis of DSE workstations to assess and reduce risks. The main risks being physical (musculo-skeletal) problems, visual fatigue and mental stress.

"Workstation" in this context is defined as an assembly comprising:
- DSE
- any optional accessories to the DSE
- any disk drive, telephone, modem, printer, document holder, work chair, work desk, worksurface or other item peripheral to the DSE
- the immediate work environment around the DSE.

The employer must assess the workstations of all users employed by them, users employed by others, eg agency employed "temps" and self-employed contractors.

Assessments

A suitable and sufficient analysis of the workstation should be:
- systematic — including investigation of non-obvious causes of problems, eg poor posture may be due to screen reflections or glare, rather than the furniture
- appropriate to the likely degree of risk — this will depend on the duration, intensity or difficulty of the work undertaken
- comprehensive — covering organisation, job, workplace and individual factors
- thorough — incorporating information provided by both employer and worker.

Workstations

Information provided by the user of the workstation is an essential part of the assessment. This may be obtained by using an ergonomic checklist.

The employer should ensure that assessments are recorded and are kept readily accessible.

Assessments should be reviewed when users change, individual capability changes or there is a significant change to the workstation.

Reducing risks

The employer must reduce the risks identified by the assessment to the lowest extent reasonably practicable.

Requirements for workstations

Employers must ensure that workstations meet the minimum requirements of the Regulations which cover:

- equipment — display screen, keyboard, work desk or worksurface and work chair
- environment — space requirements, lighting, reflection and glare, noise, heat radiation and humidity
- interface between computer and operator/user — software and systems.

Questions and Answers

Q Who should carry out assessments of workstations?

A Assessments may be carried out by health and safety professionals (this may be a consultant employed especially to undertake this function) or line managers who are conversant with the Regulations and their requirements.

Q Do I need to carry out DSE assessments for temps?

A Yes, it is your responsibility to assess the workstation.

Q Where can I get help and information on the preferred height, size, etc of workstations?

A Either from the appropriate British Standard, guidance from HSE Books, or by using the services of a qualified health and safety consultant in difficult situations.

Work Equipment

Summary

Work equipment is found in every workplace and is anything that a person at work has to use in order to do their job, eg machinery, tools, ladders, etc. The health and safety of particularly vulnerable groups of employees, such as disabled people and young persons, should also be considered.

Practical Guidance

The **Health and Safety at Work, etc Act 1974** (HSW Act) places a duty on employers to ensure the health and safety of employees at work, so far as is reasonably practicable. Providing machinery and equipment for use at work which is safe and without risks to health is part of the overall duty. Furthermore, the HSW Act requires extra consideration to be given to employees, or others, who are particularly vulnerable to work-related risks — the use of dangerous machinery by young people who may not perceive inherent or associated dangers is an example of this.

Provision and Use of Work Equipment Regulations 1998

The **Provision and Use of Work Equipment Regulations 1998** (PUWER) replace the **Provision and Use of Work Equipment Regulations 1992**. The Regulations expand the general rule set out in s.2 of the HSW Act, requiring employers to provide and maintain safe equipment, plant and work systems. PUWER applies to all work equipment, including any that is leased, hired or second-hand. The Regulations apply in most working environments and working relationships where the HSW Act applies, including all industrial, offshore and service operations. PUWER applies to all activities involving work equipment, including:

- starting
- stopping
- regular use
- transport
- repair
- modification
- servicing
- cleaning.

Work Equipment

Work equipment includes any machinery, appliance, apparatus or tool, and any assembly of components which, in order to achieve a common end, are arranged and controlled so that they function as a whole, for use in non-domestic premises. Examples include dumper trucks, angle grinders, overhead projectors and scalpels. Items specified as falling outside this definition include substances, private cars and structural items.

The main legislation is divided into three sections as follows:

- general
- mobile work equipment
- power presses.

The requirements of the Regulations apply to employers, but also to:

- the self-employed, in respect of equipment used by them for their work
- those who have control of work equipment or the way in which it is used
- anyone who supervises or manages the use of work equipment.

The general duties require:

- equipment to be suitable for its intended purpose and only to be used in conditions where it is suitable
- equipment to be maintained in an efficient state, with maintenance records where appropriate
- any equipment that depends on the installation conditions to be inspected before first use, and after any re-location, to ensure that it is safe to use, and that suitable records of such inspection are maintained
- any work equipment that may be subject to deterioration to be subject to regular checks at suitable intervals, and that records of such inspection are maintained
- work equipment that poses a particular risk to be only used, repaired and maintained by suitably trained personnel
- all those who use, supervise or manage work equipment to have suitable information and instruction for the purposes of health and safety, including written instructions where appropriate
- all those who use, supervise or manage work equipment to have received appropriate training for the purposes of health and safety
- access to any dangerous parts of machinery to be prevented or controlled by an appropriate method
- exposure to risks to health and safety of users to be prevented wherever reasonably practicable, and otherwise adequately controlled
- injury to be prevented from any work equipment or components, or any substance in use, having a very high or low temperature
- suitable controls to be provided for starting and controlling work equipment
- suitable stopping devices to be fitted to work equipment to bring the equipment to a safe condition in a safe manner, as appropriate
- suitable emergency stopping devices to be fitted to work equipment (regulation 16)
- controls for work equipment to be clearly visible and easily identified

- control systems for work equipment to be safe, and realistic in relation to the work being carried out
- work equipment to be able to be isolated from all its sources of energy, where appropriate
- work equipment to be stabilised where necessary
- suitable and sufficient lighting to be provided for the use of work equipment
- work equipment to be constructed or adapted such that maintenance work can be carried out without risks to health and safety
- work equipment is clearly marked where necessary with any marking appropriate for reasons of health and safety
- work equipment incorporates warnings or warning devices as appropriate

The specific regulations governing the use of mobile work equipment (regulations 25-30) stipulate that:

- no employee should be carried by mobile work equipment unless it is suitable for carrying persons and incorporates features that reduce the risks to their safety as far as reasonably practicable
- suitable roll-over protection should be provided where there is any risk of overturning, except for situations where this would increase the risks to safety, or where, on equipment first provided for use before 5 December 1998, it is not reasonably practicable; it also does not apply to certain types of fork lift truck
- fork lift trucks should be adapted or equipped to reduce the risk of overturning so far as is reasonably practicable
- self-propelled equipment, and remote controlled self-propelled equipment, is fitted with appropriate safety features
- any risk of seizure of a drive shaft between work equipment and its accessories or any towed item is adequately controlled, where it might involve a risk to safety.

Regulation 37 gives the transitional arrangements for the measures required in regulations 25-30 (those concerning mobile work equipment) whereby equipment first provided for use in the undertaking before 5 December 1998 does not have to comply with the specific regulations 25-30 until 5 December 2002.

The specific regulations governing the use of power presses stipulate the requirements for:

- the thorough examination and testing of power presses, guards and protection devices before first use in a new location, and every 12 months where there are fixed guards only, and every six months in other cases, with all defects being remedied before further use
- further inspection and testing during regular use
- records of examinations to be kept and maintained.

Supply of Machinery (Safety) Regulations 1992 (as amended)

Machinery imported into the UK must comply with these Regulations and meet the essential health and safety requirements. These requirements cover machinery construction, moving parts, lighting, controls, fire, noise, vibration, radiations, various emissions, maintenance, instructions, stability and other dangers to operators or anyone else in a danger zone. Such machinery must also have a declaration of conformity (machines) or incorporation (machine components), carry the CE marking and be safe, ie pose a minimal risk of injury or damage when properly installed, used and maintained for the intended purpose.

Electromagnetic Compatibility Regulations 1992 (as amended)

These Regulations require most electrical and electronic equipment made or sold in the UK to be constructed so that it does not create excessive electromagnetic disturbance, and is not affected by such disturbance from other equipment.

Questions and Answers

Q   What does the term "use of work equipment" actually include?

A   Work equipment is taken to include all machinery, appliances, apparatus, tools and/or any plant made from assembled components, while "use" is defined as any activity associated with work equipment, eg starting, stopping, programming, setting, transporting, repairing, modifying, maintaining, servicing and cleaning.

Q   What is the relationship between the PUWER and Safety of Machinery Regulations?

A   Both sets of Regulations must be complied with, although machinery which complies with the **Supply of Machinery (Safety) Regulations 1992** (as amended) is recognised as complying with the specific requirements of PUWER, ie the provisions relating to dangerous parts, controls, extreme temperatures, isolation, stability, etc. The **Supply of Machinery (Safety) Regulations 1992** (as amended) are not retrospective and therefore only apply to machinery supplied to the UK since the Regulations were brought into force on 1 January 1993.

Q   What is the situation regarding second-hand work equipment?

A   Second-hand equipment is deemed to be new equipment and the purchasing organisation must ensure it meets the requirements of the PUWER Regulations. The same applies to leased or hired equipment.

Workplace Environment

Summary

Employers must provide a safe and healthy workplace and working environments for their employees. Factors such as workspace, lighting, ventilation, temperature, cleanliness, traffic routes, falls, building structures (ie drainage, windows and doors, etc) and welfare facilities (ie toilets, wash-hand basins, changing accommodation) should all be taken into account.

Practical Guidance

The **Health and Safety at Work, etc Act 1974** and the **Workplace (Health, Safety and Welfare) Regulations 1992** both require employers to provide a safe and healthy place of work — this also includes any means of entry to and exit from the work premises. The two cases of *Allen v Avon Rubber Co Ltd* and *Sloan v Almond Fabrication Ltd* were both successful prosecutions where the employers had failed to provide a safe means of access to and egress from their workplaces. In the former case an unguarded loading bay ramp resulted in a fork-lift truck falling backwards over the edge; the employer argued that that particular activity only occurred twice a year and therefore it was unreasonable to fence off the bay. The court held that the frequency of a task did not make it less dangerous and the employers should have addressed the problem. In the second case the employer failed to provide safety hoops around a vertical ladder. When an employee fell from the ladder and was injured the employer was held to be in breach of a statutory duty and, therefore, liable for damages.

Maintenance

The workplace, equipment and devices must be well-maintained, including cleaning, through a routine maintenance programme.

Ventilation

Enclosed workplaces must be well ventilated, where possible by fresh air. If mechanical ventilation is necessary it must be fitted with appropriate alarms to warn of failure. The case of *Nicholson v Atlas Steel Foundry and Engineering Co. Ltd* demonstrates that failure to provide adequate ventilation can give rise to damages claims for personal injury when that injury results from that failure. The court found that failure to provide adequate ventilation to remove silica dust was a significant contributory factor in the death of Mr Nicholson and his employer was therefore liable to damages to the widow and family.

Temperature

A reasonable temperature must be maintained — 16°C is considered reasonable for sedentary work; 13°C for strenuous physical work. A thermometer should be provided in all workplaces, and any means of heating or cooling provided must not give off any noxious fumes.

Lighting

Adequate lighting must be provided in all workplaces, where possible by means of natural light. Emergency lighting must be provided in situations where failure of the main lighting systems creates a danger. Failure of an employer to provide adequate lighting which leads to an injury makes the employer liable for damages. In *Thornton v Fisher & Ludlow*, an employee was injured when she fell over an obstacle on an unlit road on the work premises. Although the lighting was installed it was switched off. The court held that in order to be effective, lighting must be switched on.

Cleaniness and waste materials

All workplaces and furniture must be cleanable and kept clean. Rubbish must be kept in suitable containers and must not be allowed to accumulate.

Workspace

All workplaces should have sufficient unoccupied space to ensure the health and safety of occupants and allow them to move around safely. The recommended space per person is $11m^3$.

Workstations and seating

Workstations must be suitable for the user and the tasks intended to be performed, and should allow rapid evacuation in emergencies. Where work can be carried out sitting down, seating, and if necessary a footrest, must be provided.

Floors and traffic routes

Floors and traffic route surfaces must not create slipping, tripping or falling risks, through obstructions, worn carpet, holes, uneven surfaces, snow/ice, etc. Traffic routes including stairways, fixed ladders, doorways, gateways, loading bays, etc cover both pedestrian and vehicular traffic which should be able to move around safely. Open sides of stairways should be fenced if there is a risk of falling through.

Falls and falling objects

Measures must be taken to prevent people falling from height, and objects falling on to people below.

Glazed structures

Where there is a risk of contact and subsequent breakage of the glazed areas, the glazing should be made of a safety material or otherwise protected against breakage and be clearly marked to show its presence.

Windows and skylights

Windows and skylights should be able to be opened, closed and adjusted safely, and must not create any risks when open. Windows must also be easy to clean safely.

Doors, gates and escalators

These must be fitted with appropriate safety devices.

Welfare facilities

Minimum recommended toilet facilities

Numbers Regularly Employed at any One Time	Number of Toilets to be Provided
1–5	1
6–25	2
26–50	3
51–75	4
76–100	5
Over 100	5 + 1 for every 25 people (or fraction of 25) in excess of 100

The following table may be used where the toilets are only used by male employees

Number of Males Reuglarly Employed at any One Time	Number of Toilets	Number of Urinals
1–15	1	1
16–30	2	1
31–45	2	2
46–60	3	2
61–75	3	3
76–90	4	3
91–100	4	4
Over 100	4	4
	with 1 toilet for every 50 men (or fraction of 50) exceeding 100, provided an equal number of urinals are also included	

Minimum recommended washing facilities

Numbers Regularly Employed at any One Time	Number of Washstations to be Provided
1–5	1
6–25	2
26–50	3
51–75	4
76–100	5
Over 100	5+1 basin for every 25 people (or fraction of 25) in excess of 100

Additional facilities should be provided where the work results in heavy soiling.

Questions and Answers

Q Do toilets have to be provided for non-employees?

A No, although in some situations, eg shops, the comfort of customers may be an important consideration. If toilets are provided for public use they should be separate from any facilities provided for employees.

Q Is there a maximum recommended temperature limit?

A No. In workplaces where hot temperatures cause adverse health effects then the general duty under s.2 of the **Health and Safety at Work, etc Act 1974** for employers to ensure the health and safety of employees would apply and necessary control measures would have to be taken. Controls could include insulating hot pipes, etc to reduce heat transmission, increasing air movement and extraction of hot air, and air coolers. Workers in hot environments should have free access to drinks and sufficient rest breaks to overcome loss of body fluids through sweating and fatigue.

Q What is sick building syndrome?

A This is a non-specific condition which generally causes mild symptoms of discomfort such as running noses, itchy eyes, headaches, dry throats, etc when an affected person is in the workplace. The symptoms reduce or disappear when the sufferer is away from the workplace. The precise causes are not known, although physical and environmental factors such as ventilation, air conditioning, lighting, temperature, humidity, cleanliness, work area design and layout and building maintenance, and work factors such as monotonous, repetitive work and a lack of control over the work are often implicated.

Young Persons

Summary

Modern legislation is based on achieving a satisfactory standard of protection for all employees regardless of their age, although where young people are perceived as being at greater risk then additional control measures, including prohibitions, should be considered. Factors known to contribute to the vulnerability of young people are their inexperience, lack of knowledge, training, perception of danger, and their immaturity — both physically and mentally.

Practical Guidance

Employers who employ young people in factory premises must notify the local careers office within seven days. The details which have to be notified are: name; date of birth; address; name and address of last school.

This enables a check to be kept on young people who have a medical problem or who require medical supervision. The Employment Medical Advisory Service (EMAS) of the Health and Safety Executive (HSE) provide advice on the medical aspects of employing young people. EMAS are located in the HSE area offices around the country.

The main requirements of the **Management of Health and Safety at Work Regulations 1999** in respect of young people are given below.

Definitions

A "young person" is someone who has not reached 18 years of age. A "child" is someone who has not reached compulsory school leaving age.

The European Directive on the Protection of Young People places certain obligations on an employer employing children under the minimum school leaving age. Within the UK these requirements have been implemented by the **Children (Protection at Work) Regulations 1998**.

The Regulations provide for the following.

1. In principle, children under 14 should not be employed. However, an exception is made for 13–year-old children who may be employed to do "light work" (see below) that is specifically permitted by local authority byelaws.

447

2. Children may only carry out "light work". This is defined as work which, on account of the inherent nature of tasks which it involves and the particular conditions under which they are performed, is not likely to be harmful to the safety, health or development of children.
3. No child under 15 may be employed for more than 5 hours on a non-school day which is not a Sunday. No child of 15 or over may be employed for more than 8 hours on a non-school day.
4. During school holidays, a limit of 25 working hours per week is placed on under 15s with a limit of 35 hours for the over 15s.
5. Children working more than four hours must have a rest break of one hour.
6. During school holidays, two consecutive weeks must be kept free from employment.

Risk assessments

Young people may not be employed unless a risk assessment of the risks to their health and safety has be carried out, or reviewed, as appropriate.

The following factors (below and in the table) should be taken into account when assessing the risks to young people.

Factors for Consideration	Related Work
Beyond physical capacity	work involving: repetitive or forceful movements, awkward postures, insufficient rest periods, imposed work rates
Beyond psychological capacity	work involving: violence, aggression, stressful decisions
Physical agents	work in high-pressure atmospheres, ie in compressed air, diving
Biological agents	work involving exposure to bacteria, viruses and other sources of infection
Chemical agents	work involving exposure to substances which are: • toxic/very toxic • harmful • irritant • corrosive • carcinogenic • lead • asbestos or which cause heritable genetic damage, harm to unborn children or any other chronic health effects

Radiation	work involving ionising radiations, eg radioactive materials or non-ionising electromagnetic radiations, eg ultraviolet light, infrared radiation, electromagnetic fields
Insufficient experience, training, maturity or perception of danger	work involving: fireworks or other explosive devices; fierce/poisonous animals; animal slaughtering; handling, storing or using compressed, liquefied or dissolved gases; vats, tanks, reservoirs or carboys containing chemical agents; risk of structural collapse; high-voltage electrical hazards
Temperature extremes	work involving very hot or very cold temperatures
Noise	work involving loud and/or prolonged exposures to noise
Vibration	work involving exposures to whole body and/or hand–arm vibration

Information

Young people should be provided with comprehensible and relevant health and safety information. In addition the parents or guardians of children must be given information on any identified risks and necessary control measures, including any arrangements, etc between employers in shared premises.

Protection and prohibitions

Young people must be protected against risks to their health and safety arising form their immaturity, inexperience or lack of awareness.

They may not be employed where the work:

- is beyond their physical and/or mental capacities
- involves exposure to toxic or carcinogenic substances, or substances which cause heritable genetic damage, harm to unborn children or cause any other chronic health effect
- involves harmful exposure to radiation
- involves a risk of accident which a young person may not reasonably recognise
- involves harmful exposure to extreme temperatures, noise or vibration.

These prohibitions do not apply to young people where the work is part of their training, is under the supervision of a competent person, and any risks are reduced to the lowest level reasonably possible.

Children

There are various legal restrictions on the employment of children and local authorities may, by the use of by-laws, prohibit the employment of children in any way which is prejudicial to their health or education. There are proposals for drawing up a list of acceptable jobs for children who are aged 13 years or over, and for licensing children who participate in cultural, artistic, sporting and advertising activities.

In a case heard at Leicester Crown Court in December 1995, a director of a food company was fined £7500 under the **Women, Young Persons and Children Act 1920** for illegally employing two children in a dangerous environment. The children worked 12-hour shifts over a weekend period and operated dangerous machinery.

Questions and Answers

Q Do any of the older legal restrictions and prohibitions on the employment of young people still exist?

A Yes, some existing older legislation which restricts or prohibits the employment of young people in certain industries and/or activities is still in force. The restrictions and/or prohibitions apply to work in agriculture, specified lead processes, radiation and woodworking machinery. There are also some prohibitions on the employment of children as follows:
- where the child is under the age of 13 years
- before the close of school on any school day
- for more than two hours on any school day
- before 7.00am or after 7.00pm on any day
- for more than two hours on Sundays.

Q Do young people still need to be certified "fit to work"?

A Yes, there is an implicit duty under the **Health and Safety at Work, etc Act 1974** to ensure the health and safety of employees at work, and this would include ensuring employees are fit and capable to carry out the intended tasks — this is also an explicit requirement under the **Management of Health and Safety at Work Regulations 1999**. In addition, the Regulations prohibit the employment of young people in work which is beyond their physical and/or mental capabilities. Under s.119 of the **Factories Act 1961** factory employers may have to find suitable alternative work for young people where an enforcing officer is of the opinion that a certain factory or work process is prejudicial to the health of the young person. A certification of fitness to work from an appointed doctor or employment medical advisor is required before the young person can return to the prohibited work.

Q What is the situation regarding trainees who are not necessarily employees?

A The **Health and Safety (Training for Employment) Regulations 1990** include the following people as employees for the purposes of health and safety law:
- those on work experience associated with a training course/programme
- those training for employment
- those undertaking both the above
- school pupils on work experience
- college students on sandwich courses
- participants on Government training schemes.

This means people on any of the above training programmes, which could well involve young persons, are entitled to the same level of health and safety protection as employees at work.

Appendices

Glossary

Access
The means of entry into a building/work area, etc.

Accident
An unexpected event which causes damage to plant or machinery or causes injury.

Act
Acts lay down general principles and allow for subordinate legislation, such as Regulations, to be passed, eg the **Health and Safety at Work, etc Act 1974**.

Appeals
An appeal is a proceeding by which the decision of an inspector, a lower court or a tribunal is challenged in a higher court by one or any of the parties.

Appointed person
An appointed person is regarded as competent, in respect of his or her qualifications and experience, to carry out the duty for which they are appointed — eg an appointed doctor would be a fully registered medical practitioner appointed by written certificate of the chief employment medical advisor.

Approved Code of Practice
A Code of Practice which has been "approved" by the Health and Safety Commission, as provided under s.16 of the **Health and Safety at Work, etc Act 1974**. An Approved Code of Practice may be used in criminal proceedings.

Audit
A safety audit subjects each area of a company's activity to a systematic critical examination, with the object of minimising loss. Every component of the total system is included.

Best practicable means
The best measures possible in the light of current knowledge and according to means and resources — not an absolute requirement, but cost may not be taken into account and so it is stricter than "reasonably practicable".

Breach
The infringement of a legal duty or right.

Child
A child is someone not over the compulsory school leaving age.

Code of Practice
A Code of Practice is a standard which gives specification and a documentary form of practical guidance.

Common law
The body of law created by judicial decision rather than by Parliament.

Compensation
A payment to make amends for loss or injury to a person or propery.

Competent person	A person who has sufficient training, experience, knowledge or other qualities to enable them to undertake a task/job.
Contractor	A person or company which agrees to undertake an operation for another person or company, not under a contract of employment but as an independent business.
COSHH	An acronym for the **Control of Substances Hazardous to Health Regulations 1999**. The Regulations outline the duties of employers and employees who work with (handle, manufacture or use) hazardous substances. See Hazardous substance.
Crown Court	A court of criminal jurisdiction dealing with indictable offences, and appeals for summary offences from Magistrates' Courts.
Delegated legislation	See Subordinate legislation.
Display screen equipment	Any alphanumeric or graphic display screen, eg a VDU.
Domestic premises	Premises occupied as a private dwelling — this may include a garden, yard or outhouse, etc.
Egress	Means of exit.
EHO	See Environmental Health Officer.
Employee	A person who works under a contract of employment or apprenticeship, whether express or implied, oral or in writing.
Employer	A person, business, organisation, firm, etc which employs workers.
Employment Medical Advisor (EMA)	EMAs advise and take steps on all medical aspects of employment.
Employment Medical Advisory Service (EMAS)	A body set up in 1972 under the **Employment Medical Advisory Service Act 1972** to advise and take practical steps on all aspects of employment.
Employment tribunal	Originally established under the **Industrial Training Act 1964**, tribunals are usually associated with employment provisions, eg unfair dismissal, redundancy, etc but s.24 of the HSW Act provides that appeals against improvement and prohibition notices.
Enforcing authority	The HSE or any other authority (eg local authority).
Environmental Health Officer	Local authority enforcement officer.
Expectant mother	See New or expectant mother.
Fire certificate	A certificate issued under the **Fire Precautions Act 1971** by the fire authority.
First aid	Help given to an injured person until proper medical treatment is available.

Good practice	The provisions of any Code of Practice, or practice which is reasonable in the circumstances.
Guidance notes	Published by the relevant enforcing authorities, these give advice on the safe performance of the activities to which they relate — they have no binding authority.
Hazard	Something with the potential to cause harm.
Hazardous substance	A substance with the potential to cause harm.
Health and Safety at Work, etc Act 1974 (HSW Act)	The primary piece of health and safety legislation which was passed in 1974 and is an umbrella Act.
Health and Safety Commission (HSC)	The supervisory and advisory body established by the HSW Act. The HSC is responsible for seeing that the purposes of the Act are fulfilled.
Health and Safety Executive (HSE)	The operational and enforcement arm of the HSC.
Health and safety policy	A document or collection of documents outlining a company's commitment to health and safety, its objectives, the organisational structure and the health and safety rules.
Improvement notice	A notice under s.21 of the HSW Act served by inspectors when in their opinion a person is contravening or has contravened and is likely to continue contravening one or more of the relevant statutory provisions.
Indictable offence	An offence which is triable before a judge and jury in the Crown Court. These are more serious than summary offences and include the illegal use of explosives and contavention of the terms of a prohibition or improvement notice.
Inspection	A formal, routine scheduled inspection of the workplace or department carried out by safety representatives, with the aim of assessing standards of maintenance, systems of work, etc.
Inspector	A person appointed under s.19 of the HSW Act and employed by the HSE, local authority or some other enforcement body.
Legislation	The process of making laws, and the term given to that collection of laws — including Acts and Regulations.
Liability	Legal obligation or duty.
Local authority	In relation to England and Wales, a metropolitan or county council, a district council or a London borough council; in relation to Scotland, a regional, islands or district council.
Machinery	Apparatus of fixed or moving parts used for the purpose of applying power.

Magistrates' Court	A court of summary jurisdiction in which most health and safety prosecutions are conducted.
Manual handling operations	The transportation or carrying of any load — including lifting, setting down, pushing, pulling and moving.
Medical suspension	Suspension from doing a particular job in prescribed circumstances when a medical examiner is of the opinion that such work could damage the employee's health.
Negligence	A technical legal concept, generally meaning careless conduct, but subject to strict and complex legal rules.
New or expectant mother	An employee who is pregnant, who has given birth in the last six months or who is breast-feeding
Non-domestic premises	Defined as the opposite of Domestic premises (see above). Section 4 of the HSW Act applies to non-domestic premises.
Occupier	Someone who has control of premises.
Operator	The **Health and Safety (Display Screen Equipment) Regulations 1992** defines an operator as a self-employed person who habitually uses display screen equipment as significant part of his or her normal work.
Penalty	The sanction imposed for breach of a legal provision.
Personal protective equipment (PPE)	Any equipment or clothing provided as a "last resort" measure to protect an employee against one or more risks to his or her health and safety.
Place of work	The place where the employee is required to be at any time in the course of employment.
Portable electrical appliances	Although not specifically defined in the **Electricity at Work Regulations 1989**, portable electrical appliance is taken to mean any apparatus with a plug and lead which is easily moveable or could be moved, eg a kettle or a photocopier.
Prohibition notice	A notice under s.22 of the HSW Act served by inspectors when they are of the opinion that a person is carrying on or is likely to carry on activities that involve a risk of serious personal injury. The notice requires that the activity or activities be stopped.
Reasonably practicable	This is less strict than "practicable" and means that a risk/sacrifice computation has to be made to see what is reasonable under the circumstances.
Regulations	Legislation delegated from an Act by the relevant Secretary of State. Sometimes known as subordinate or delegated legislation.

Relevant statutory provisions	The provisions of Part 1 of the **Health and Safety at Work, etc Act 1974** (HSW Act) and any health and safety Regulations made under it and the existing statutory provisions.
Repeal	Annulment of an Act.
Representatives of employee safety	The term given to non-unionised safety representatives under the **Health and Safety (Consultation with Employees) Regulations 1996**.
Revocations	Annulment of a regulation or set of Regulations.
Risk	The probability of a hazard actually causing harm.
Risk assessment	An assessment of the likelihood of the occurrence of accidents/illnesses in the workplace.
Safe system of work	A formal procedure designed after a formal examination of the risks of a task. It defines safe methods to ensure that all hazards are eliminated or minimised.
Safety committee	A committee established by the employer to monitor safety matters at a place of work.
Safety representative	A person appointed by a trade union from employees of an employer recognising that trade union in accordance with the **Safety Representatives and Safety Committees Regulations 1977**.
Sanction	A measure of punishment.
Sentence	The penalty imposed upon a convicted person, normally subject to a statutory maximum.
SI number	A statutory instrument number (usually of a set of Regulations) number.
Statute	An Act of Parliament, passed by the House of Commons and House of Lords and signed by the Sovereign.
Subordinate legislation	Legislation made under an Act by the relevant Secretary of State, eg Regulations.
Summary offence	An offence tried in a Magistrates' Court, appeals are heard in a Crown Court.
Suspension	A debarment from carrying out certain work (see Medical suspension).
Tort	The branch of law dealing with liability for civil wrongs.
Traffic route	A route for pedestrian or vehicular traffic including stairways, fixed ladders, doorways, gateways, loading bays or ramps.
Trainee	A person undergoing training.
Unfair dismissal	The termination by the employer of the employee's contract of employment in circumstances which are deemed to be unfair.
User	An employee who habitually uses display screen equipment for a significant part of his or her job.

Vicarious liability   Liability arising through one person's relationship with another. An employer may be liable for wrongful acts committed by an employee during the course of employment.

Visitor   Someone who is lawfully on the premises, ie not a trespasser. Section 3 of the HSW Act requires that lawful visitors be protected from the effects of an employer's undertaking.

Work equipment   Any machinery, appliance, apparatus or tool, assembly or components which work together to function as a whole. This would include machinery, scaffolding, hand-held tools, etc.

Workplace   The normal premises or part of premises, which are not domestic premises and available to a person as a place of work.

Workplace environment   The workplace environment includes all factors (such as heating, lighting, ventilation, toilets, washing facilities, seating, overall design, etc) which are relevant to the physical conditions in which the employee is required to work.

Workstation   An assembly comprising display screen equipment (DSE) and any optional accessories to the DSE, any disk drive, telephone, modem, printer, chair, desk, surface, etc and the immediate environment around the DSE.

Young person   A person who has ceased to be a child (over school leaving age) but has not attained the age of 18.

Government Agencies

Health and Safety Executive

Public Enquiries (written)

HSE Information Services
Broad Lane
Sheffield S3 7HQ
Fax: 0114 289 2333

HSE Infoline

Tel: 0541 545500

Field Operations Directorate (FOD)

This Directorate, incorporates the factory, agricultural and quarries inspectorates, as well as the Employment Medical Advisory Service (EMAS). Communications should be addressed to the nearest office.

Head Office

Daniel House
Trinity Road
Bootle L20 7HE
Tel: 0151 951 4000

Regional Office — Home Counties

39 Baddow Road
Chelmsford CM2 0HL
Tel: 01245 706 200
Fax: 01245 706 222
Covering: Essex (except parts covered by London and the South East Regional office), Norfolk, Suffolk

Government Agencies

Main Offices

Northern Home Counties

14 Cardiff Road
Luton LU1 1PP
Tel: 01582 444 200
Fax: 01582 444 320
Covering: Bedfordshire, Buckinghamshire, Cambridgeshire, Hertfordshire

South

Priestley House
Priestley Road
Basingstoke RG24 9NW
Tel: 01256 404 000
Fax: 01256 404 100
Covering: Berkshire, Dorset, Hampshire, Isle of Wight, Wiltshire

Regional Offices — London and the South East

St Dunstan's House
201-211 Borough High Street
London SE1 1GZ
Tel: 020 7556 2100
Fax: 020 7556 2200
Covering: Metropolitan Boroughs — Barking and Dagenham, Barnet, Bexley, Brent, Bromley, Camden, City of London, Croydon, Ealing, Enfield, Greenwich, Hackney, Hammersmith and Fulham, Haringey, Harrow, Havering, Hillingdon, Hounslow, Islington, Kensington and Chelsea, Kingston-upon-Thames, Lambeth, Lewisham, Merton, Newham, Redbridge, Richmond-upon-Thames,Tower Hamlets, Newham, Redbridge, Southwark, Sutton, Tower Hamlets, Wandsworth, Waltham Fores

Main Office

South East

3 East Grinstead House
London Road
East Grinstead RH19 1RR
Tel: 01342 334 200
Fax: 01342 334 222
Covering: Kent, Surrey, East Sussex, West Sussex

Regional Office — Midlands

McLaren Building
35 Dale End
Birmingham B4 7NP
Tel: 0121 602 6200
Fax: 0121 607 6349
Covering: West Midlands

Main Offices

East Midlands

5th Floor
Belgrave House
1 Greyfriars
Northampton NN1 2BS
Tel: 01604 738 300
Fax: 01604 738 333
Covering: Leicestershire, Northamptonshire, Oxfordshire, Warwickshire

North Midlands

The Pearson Building
55 Upper Parliament Street
Nottingham NG1 6AU
Tel: 0115 971 2800
Fax: 0115 971 2802
Covering: Derbyshire, Lincolnshire, Nottinghamshire

Regional Office — North West

Quay House
Quay Street
Manchester M3 3JB
Tel: 0161 952 8200
Fax: 0161 952 8222
Covering: Greater Manchester

Government Agencies

Main Offices

Merseyside

The Triad
Stanley Road
Bootle L20 3PG
Tel: 0161 952 8200
Fax: 0151 479 2201
Local authorities within each area: Cheshire, Merseyside

North West

Victoria House
Ormskirk Road
Preston PR1 1HH
Tel: 0161 952 8200
Fax: 01772 836 222
Covering: Cumbria, Lancashire

Regional Office — Wales and West

Government Buildings
Ty Glas
Cardiff CF14 5SH
Llanishen
Tel: 029 2026 3000
Fax: 029 2026 3120
Covering: Clwyd, Dyfed, Gwent, Gwynedd, Mid Glamorgan, Powys, South Glamorgan, West Glamorgan

Main Offices

Marches

Marches House
Midway
Newcastle-under-Lyme ST5 1DT
Tel: 01782 602 300
Fax: 01782 602 400
Covering: Hereford and Worcester, Shropshire, Staffordshire

South West

Inter City House
Victoria Street
Mitchell Lane
Bristol BS1 6AN
Tel: 0117 988 6000
Fax: 0117 926 2998
Covering: Avon, Cornwall, Devon, Gloucestershire, Somerset, Isles of Scilly

Regional Office — Yorkshire and North East

Woodside House
261 Low Lane
Horsforth
Leeds LS18 5TW
Tel: 0113 283 4200
Fax: 0113 283 4344

Main Offices

South Yorkshire

Sovereign House
110 Queens Street
Sheffield S1 2ES
Tel: 0114 291 2300
Fax: 0114 291 2379
Covering: Humberside, South Yorkshire

West & North Yorkshire

8 St Paul's Street
Leeds LS1 2LE
Tel: 0113 283 4200
Fax: 0113 283 4296
Covering: North Yorkshire, West Yorkshire

Government Agencies

North East

Arden House
Regent Centre
Regent Farm Road
Gosforth
Newcastle-upon-Tyne
NE3 3JN
Tel: 0191 202 6200
Fax: 0191 202 6300
Covering: Cleveland, Durham, Northumberland, Tyne & Wear

Head Office — Scotland

Belford House
59 Belford Road
Edinburgh EH4 3UE
Tel: 0131 247 2000
Fax: 0131 247 2121
Covering: Borders, Central, Fife, Grampian, Highland, Lothian, Tayside and the island areas of Orkney & Shetland

Area Office

Scotland West

375 West George Street
Glasgow G2 4LW
Tel: 0141 275 3000
Fax: 0141 275 3100
Covering: Dumfries and Galloway, Strathclyde and the Western Isles

Local Offices

FOD
Room 303
Lord Cullen House
Fraser Place
Aberdeen AB25 3UB
Tel: 01224 252500
Fax: 01224 252525

HM Inspectorate of Mines

Headquarters

Daniel House
Room 611
Trinity Road
Bootle L20 7HE
Tel: 0151 951 4133
Fax: 0151 951 3896

District Offices

Scotland and East England

Silver House
32 Silver Street
Doncaster DN1 1HR
Tel: 01302 368165
Fax: 01302 326521

Wales and West England

Daniel House
Room 611
Trinity Road
Bootle L20 7HE
Tel: 0151 951 3991
Fax: 0151 951 3896

HM Nuclear Safety Division

Rose Court
2 Southwark Bridge
London SE1 9HS
Tel: 020 7717 6000
Fax: 020 7717 6681

HM Railway Inspectorate

Rose Court
2 Southwark Bridge
London SE1 9HS
Tel: 020 7717 6000
Fax: 020 7717 6717

The Environment Agency

Head Office

Rio House
Waterside Drive
Aztec West
Almondsbury
Bristol BS32 4UD
Tel: 01454 624400
Fax: 01454 624409

Head Office also located at:
Millbank Tower
25th Floor
21–24 Millbank
London SW1P 4XL
Tel: 020 7863 8600
Fax: 020 7863 8650

Regional Offices

Anglian Region

Kingfisher House
Goldhay Way
Orton Goldhay
Peterborough PE2 5ZR
Tel: 01733 371811
Fax: 01733 231840

Midlands Region

Sapphire East
550 Streetsbrook Road
Solihull
West Midlands B91 1QT
Tel: 0121 711 2324
Fax: 0121 711 5824

North East Region

Rivers House
21 Park Square South
Leeds LS1 2QG
Tel: 0113 244 0191
Fax: 0113 246 1889

North West Region

Richard Fairclough House
Knutsford Road
Warrington WA4 1HG
Tel: 01925 653999
Fax: 01925 415961

South West Region

Manley House
Kestrel Way
Exeter EX2 7LQ
Tel: 01392 442074
Fax: 01392 444238

Southern Region

Guildbourne House
Chatsworth Road
Worthing
West Sussex BN11 1LD
Tel: 01903 832000
Fax: 01903 821832

Government Agencies

Thames Region

Kings Meadow House
Kings Meadow Road
Reading RG1 8DQ
Tel: 0118 953 5000
Fax: 0118 950 0388

Wales

Rivers House/Plas-yr-Afon
St Mellons Business Park
St Mellons
Cardiff CF3 0EY
Tel: 029 2077 0088
Fax: 029 2079 8555

Scottish Environment Protection Agency

Head Office

Erskine Court
The Castle Business Park
Stirling FK9 4TR
Tel: 01786 457700
Fax: 01786 446885

Regional Offices

East Region

Clearwater House
Heriot Watt Research Park
Avenue North
Riccarton
Edinburgh EH14 4AP
Tel: 0131 449 7296
Fax: 0131 449 7277

North Region

Graesser House
Fodderty Way
Dingwall Business Park
Dingwall IV15 9XB
Tel: 01349 862021
Fax: 01349 863987

West Region

5 Redwood Crescent
Peel Park
East Kilbride G74 5PP
Tel: 01355 574200
Fax: 01355 574688

Employment Tribunals Service (Employment Tribunals)

Employment Tribunals Service Head Office

19–29 Woburn Place
London WC1H 0LU
Tel: 020 7273 8666
Fax: 020 7273 8670

Employment Tribunals Offices — England and Wales

Ashford

Tufton House
Tufton Street
Ashford
Kent TN23 1RJ
Tel: 01233 621346
Fax: 01233 624423

Bedford

8–10 Howard Street
Bedford MK40 3HS
Tel: 01234 351306
Fax: 01234 352315

Government Agencies

Birmingham

Phoenix House
1–3 Newhall Street
Birmingham B3 3NH
Tel: 0121 236 6051
Fax: 0121 236 6029

Bristol

1st Floor
The Crescent Centre
Temple Back
Bristol BS1 6EZ
Tel: 0117 929 8261
Fax: 0117 925 3452

Bury St Edmunds

Registrations Unit:
100 Southgate Street
Bury St Edmunds IP33 2AQ
Tel: 01284 762171
Fax: 01284 706064

Cardiff

Caradog House
1–6 St Andrews Place
Cardiff CF1 3BE
Tel: 029 2037 2693
Fax: 029 2037 2693

Exeter

10th Floor
Renslade House
Bonhay Road
Exeter EX4 3BX
Tel: 01392 279665
Fax: 01392 430063

Leeds

3rd Floor
11 Albion Street
Leeds LS1 5ES
Tel: 0113 245 9741
Fax: 0113 242 8843

Leicester

Kings Court
5a New Walk
Leicester LE1 6TE
Tel: 0116 255 0099
Fax: 0116 255 6099

Liverpool

Cunard Building
Pier Head
Liverpool L3 1TS
Tel: 0151 236 9397
Fax: 0151 231 1484

London East

Stratford
44 The Broadway
Stratford
London EH15 1XH
Tel: 020 8221 0921.
Fax: 020 8221 0398

London North

19–21 Woburn Place
London WC1H 0LU
Tel: 020 7273 3000
Fax: 020 7273 8686

Government Agencies

London South

Montagu Court
101 London Road
Croydon CR0 2RF
Tel: 020 8253 5769
Fax: 020 8667 9131

Manchester

Alexandra House
14-22 The Parsonage
Manchester M3 2JA
Tel: 0161 833 6145
Fax: 0161 832 0249

Newcastle-upon-Tyne

Quayside House
110 Quayside
Newcastle-upon-Tyne NE1 3DX
Tel: 0191 260 6900
Fax: 0191 222 1680

Nottingham

3rd Floor
Byron House
2A Maid Marion Way
Nottingham NG1 6HS
Tel: 0115 947 5701
Fax: 0115 947 7612

Reading

5th Floor
30/31 Friar Street
Reading RG1 1DY
Tel: 0118 959 4917
Fax: 0118 956 9168

Sheffield

14 East Parade
Sheffield S1 2ET
Tel: 0114 276 0348
Fax: 0114 276 2551

Shrewsbury

Prospect House
Belle Vue Road
Shrewsbury SY3 7NR
Tel: 01743 358341
Fax: 01743 244186

Southampton

3rd Floor
Dukes Keep
Marsh Lane
Southampton SO1 1EX
Tel: 023 8063 9555
Fax: 023 8063 5506

Employment Tribunals Offices — Scotland

Aberdeen

Mezzanine Floor
Atholl House
86-88 Guild Street
Aberdeen AB11 6LT
Tel: 01224 593137
Fax: 01224 593138

Dundee

13 Albert Square
Dundee
DD1 1DD
Tel: 01382 221578
Fax: 01382 227136

Government Agencies

Edinburgh

54–56 Melville Street
Edinburgh EH3 7HF
Tel: 0131 226 5584
Fax: 0131 220 6847

Glasgow

3rd Floor
The Eagle Building
215 Bothwell Street
Glasgow G2 7TS
Tel: 0141 204 0730
Fax: 0141 204 0732

Employment Appeals Tribunals

England & Wales

Audit House
58 Victoria Embankment
London EC4Y 0DS
Tel: 020 7273 1040
Fax: 020 7273 1045

Scotland

52 Melville Street
Edinburgh EH3 7HF
Tel: 0131 225 3963
Fax: 0131 220 6694

HSE Books

PO Box 1999
Sudbury
Suffolk CO10 6FS
Tel: 01787 881165
Fax: 01787 313995

The Stationery Office

The Stationery Office Publications Centre

(Mail and telephone orders only)
PO Box 276
London SW8 5DT
Telephone orders and enquiries: 0870 600 5522
Fax orders: 0870 600 5533

The Stationery Office Bookshops

Belfast

16 Arthur Street
Belfast BT1 4GD
Tel: 028 9023 8451
Fax: 028 9023 6394

Birmingham

68/69 Bull Street
Birmingham B4 6AD
Tel: 0121 236 9696
Fax: 0121 236 9699

Bristol

33 Wine Street
Bristol BS1 2BQ
Tel: 0117 926 4306
Fax: 0117 928 4515

Cardiff

18-19 High Street
Cardiff CF10 1PT
Tel: 029 2039 5548
Fax: 029 2038 4347

Government Agencies

Edinburgh

71 Lothian Road
Edinburgh EH3 9AZ
Tel: 0870 606 5566
Fax: 0870 606 5588

London

123 Kingsway
London WC2B 6PQ
Tel: 020 7242 6393
Fax: 020 7242 6394

Useful Addresses

Action on Smoking and Health (ASH)
102 Clifton Street
London EC2A 4HW
Tel: 020 7739 5902
Fax: 020 7613 0531
Website: www.ash.org.uk

Agricultural Engineers Association
Samuelson House
Paxton Road
Orton Centre
Peterborough PE2 5LT
Tel: 01733 371381
Fax: 01733 370664

Alcohol Concern
Waterbridge House
32–36 Loman Street
London SE1 0EE
Tel: 020 7928 7377
Fax: 020 7928 4644
Website: www.alcoholconcern.org.uk

Alcoholics Anonymous
PO Box 1
Stonebow House
Stonebow
York YO1 2NJ
Tel: 01904 644026
Fax: 01904 629091

Association of British Insurers
51 Gresham Street
London EC2V 7HQ
Tel: 020 7600 3333
Fax: 020 7696 8999
Website: www.abi.org.uk

Useful Addresses

Association of Noise Consultants
6 Trap Road
Guilden Morden
Nr Royston
Herts SG8 OJE
Tel: 01763 852958
Fax: 01763 853252
Website:www.isvr.soton.ac.uk\ANC\

British Industrial Truck Association
Scammell House
High Street
Ascot
Berks SL5 7JF
Tel: 01344 623800
Fax: 01344 291197

British Institute of Radiology
36 Portland Place
London W1N 4AT
Tel: 020 7580 4085
Fax: 020 7255 3209
Website: www.bir.org.uk

British Medical Association
BMA House
Tavistock Square
London WC1H 9JP
Tel: 020 7387 4499
Fax: 020 7383 6400
Website:www.bma.org.uk

The British Occupational Hygiene Society
Suite 2, Georgian House
Great Northern Road
Derby DE1 1LT
Tel: 01332 298101
Fax: 01332 298099
Website: www.ed.ac.uk/~robin/bohs.html

The British Psychological Society
St. Andrews House
48 Princess Road East
Leicester LE1 7DR
Tel: 0116 254 9568
Fax: 0116 247 0787
Website: www.bps.org.uk

British Standards Institute
389 Chiswick High Road
London W4 4AL
Tel: 020 8996 9000
Fax: 020 8996 7400
Website: www.bsi.org.uk

Chartered Institute of Environmental Health
Chadwick Court
15 Hatfields
London SE1 8DJ
Tel: 020 7928 6006
Fax: 020 7827 5865

Chartered Institution of Building Services Engineers (CIBSE)
Delta House
222 Balham High Road
London SW12 9BS
Tel: 020 8675 5211
Fax: 020 8675 5449

Chartered Society of Physiotherapy
14 Bedford Row
London WC1R 4ED
Tel: 020 7306 6666
Fax: 020 7306 6611

Chemical Industries Association Ltd
Kings Buildings
Smith Square
London SW1P 3JJ
Tel: 020 7834 3399
Fax: 020 7834 4470

Construction Industry Training Board (CITB)
Walker House
London Road
Riverhead
Sevenoaks
Kent TN13 2DN
Tel: 01732 467300
Fax: 01732 460561
Website:/www.citb.org.uk

Useful Addresses

Department of Health
Richmond House
79 Whitehall
London SW1A 2NL
Tel: 020 7210 4850
Fax: 020 7210 5661
Website: www.open.gov.uk/doh/dhhome.htm

Drinkline
Weddel House
13–14 West Smithfield
London EC1A 9DL
Tel: 0345 320202

Employers' Advisory Service on AIDS and HIV
PO Box HP 346
Leeds LS6 1UC
Tel: 0113 2941212
Fax: 0113 2427782
Website: www.healthworks.co.uk

Environment Agency
Head Office
Rio House
Waterside Drive
Aztec West
Almondsbury
Bristol BS12 4UD
Tel: 0645 333111
Fax: 01454 624409
Website:www.environment-agency.gov.uk/gui/index.html

The Ergonomics Society
Devonshire House
Devonshire Square
Loughborough
Leicestershire LE11 3DU
Tel: 01509 234904
Fax: 01509 235666

Forestry Commission
231 Corstorphine Road
Edinburgh EH12 7AT
Tel: 0131 334 0303
Fax: 0131 334 4473
Website: www.forestry.gov.uk

The Health Development Agency
Trevelyan House
30 Great Peter Street
London SW1P 2HW
Tel: 020 7222 5300
Fax: 020 7413 8900
Website: www.hda-online.org.uk

HSE Books
PO Box 1999
Sudbury
Suffolk CO10 6FS
Tel: 01787 881165
Fax: 01787 313995
Website: www.open.gov.uk/hse/publicat.htm

Institution of Occupational Safety and Health (IOSH)
The Grange
Highfield Drive
Wigston
Leicester LE18 1NN
Tel: 01162 573100
Fax: 01162 573101
Website: www.iosh.co.uk

Loss Prevention Council
Melrose Avenue
Borehamwood
Hertfordshire WD6 2BJ
Tel: 020 8207 2345
Fax: 020 8207 6305
Website: www.lpc.co.uk

National Asthma Campaign
Providence House
Providence Place
London N1 0NT
Tel: 020 7226 2260
Fax: 020 7704 0740
Website: www.asthma.org.uk

Useful Addresses

National Back Pain Association
16 Elmtree Rd
Teddington
Middlesex TW11 8ST
Tel: 020 8977 5474
Fax: 020 8943 5318
Website: www.backpain.org.uk

National Radiological Protection Board (NRPB)
Chilton
Didcot
Oxon OX11 0RQ
Tel: 01235 831600
Fax: 01235 833891
Website: www.nrpb.org.uk

Royal Society of Chemistry
Burlington House
Piccadilly
London W1J 0BA
Tel: 020 7437 8656
Fax: 020 7437 8883
Website: www.rsc.org.uk

Royal Society for the Prevention of Accidents (RoSPA)
Edgbaston Park
353 Bristol Road
Edgbaston
Birmingham B5 7ST
Tel: 0121 248 2000
Fax: 0121 248 2001

The Suzy Lamplugh Trust
14 East Sheen Avenue
London SW14 8AS
Tel: 020 8392 1839
Fax: 020 8392 1830

Trades Union Congress
Congress House
Great Russell Street
London WC1B 3LS
Tel: 020 7636 4030
Fax: 020 7636 0632
Website: www.tuc.org.uk

The World Health Organisation (WHO)
Regional Office for Europe
Scherfigsvej 8
DK-2100 Copenhagen
Denmark
Tel: 00 45 39 17 17 17
Website: www.who.ch

Index

Introduction. Please note the following points.

1. Index entries are to page numbers.

2. Alphabetical arrangement is word-by-word, where a group of letters followed by a space is filed before the same group of letters followed by a letter, eg "hand tools" will appear before "handrails". In determining alphabetical arrangement, initial articles and prepositions are ignored.

D

R

S

U

V

Registration/Enquiry Card — A-Z Essentials of Health and Safety

1.   Customer details — this box must be completed
Name:
Job title:
Company:
Address:
Postcode:
Telephone number: **Date:**

- - - - - - - - - - - - - - Fold in half and seal outside edges - - - - - - - - - - - - - - -

2.   Details of purchase

Please tell us where you purchased this book
- ❑ Bookshop
- ❑ Croner.CCH
- ❑ Other please state:

_____

If applicable, please tick box(es) below:

❑ Do you wish to automatically receive the next edition of A-Z Essentials of Health and Safety in Autumn 2001?
NB: This will be despatched with an invoice.

❑ Would you like us to contact you about additional copies of this book for your colleagues at a discounted price?

3.   Your signature: _____

4.	**Further information**

Would you like to receive further information about other books in this series on, please tick:

❏ Education   ❏ Employment/Personnel
❏ Environmental Management   ❏ Facilities
❏ Health and Safety   ❏ Hospitality
❏ Manufacturing, Trade & Transport ❏ Tax and Accountancy

5.	**How to order**

■ Telephone Customer Services on 020 8247 1175, or
■ Fill in your details, fold in half, seal outside edges and post this reply paid device.

RQSVF

BUSINESS REPLY SERVICE
Licence No. KT 1332

Salvatore Callari
Croner.CCH Group Limited
145 London Road
Kingston upon Thames
Surrey
KT2 6BR